S0-AHE-335

Beyond Same-Sex Marriage

Beyond Same-Sex Marriage

Perspectives on Marital Possibilities

Edited by Ronald C. Den Otter
Foreword by Elisabeth Sheff

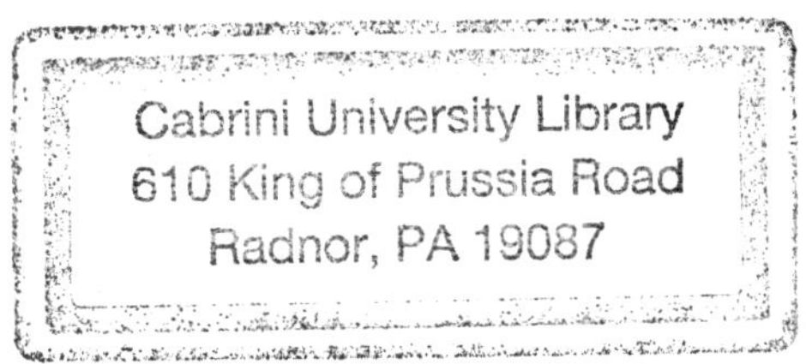

LEXINGTON BOOKS
Lanham • Boulder • New York • London

Published by Lexington Books
An imprint of The Rowman & Littlefield Publishing Group, Inc.
4501 Forbes Boulevard, Suite 200, Lanham, Maryland 20706
www.rowman.com

Unit A, Whitacre Mews, 26-34 Stannary Street, London SE11 4AB

A version of chapter 4 originally appeared as an article entitled "Robotic Marriage and the Law" in the Journal of Law and Social Deviance, Vol. 10. (Fall 2015).
A version of chapter 9 originally appeared as an article in the 64 Emory Law Journal 1815 (2015).

British Library Cataloguing in Publication Information Available

Library of Congress Cataloging-in-Publication Data
The hardback edition of this book was previously catalogued by the Library of Congress as follows:

Names: Den Otter, Ronald C., editor.
Title: Beyond same-sex marriage : perspectives on marital status possibilities / edited by Ronald C. Den Otter ; foreword by Elisabeth Sheff.
Description: Lanham : Lexington Books, 2016. | Includes bibliographical references and index.
Identifiers: LCCN 2016029342| ISBN 9781498512015 (cloth : alk. paper) | ISBN 9781498512022 (electronic)
Subjects: LCSH: Marriage--United States. | Same-sex marriage--United States. | Marriage law--United States. | Polygamy--United States.
Classification: LCC HQ519 .B489 2016 | DDC 306.810973--dc23 LC record available at https://lccn.loc.gov/2016029342

∞™ The paper used in this publication meets the minimum requirements of American National Standard for Information Sciences Permanence of Paper for Printed Library Materials, ANSI/NISO Z39.48-1992.

Printed in the United States of America

This book is dedicated to my wife, Grace, who always has been there for me for better or worse, and to my father, Clifford R. Den Otter, the first college graduate in his family, a member of the graduating class of 1959 at the U.S. Naval Academy, and now a retired civil engineer. His efforts made my professional success possible.

Contents

Foreword ix
Dr. Elisabeth Sheff

Introduction 1
Ronald C. Den Otter

1 *Obergefell* and the Liberal Case Against Civil Marriage 7
Sonu Bedi

2 Progressive Polygamy in Western United States 25
Janet Bennion

3 Plural Marriage, Exemptions, and the Redundancy of the Free Exercise Clause 41
Ronald C. Den Otter

4 Robotic Marriage and the Law 63
Mark Goldfelder and Yosef Razin

5 A Friendship Model of Sex, Polyamory, and Plural Marriage 83
Diane Klein

6 Public Reason, Liberal Neutrality, and Marriage 103
Andrew Lister

7 The Dialectic of Islam and Polygyny 129
Ameneh Maghzi and Mark Gruchy

8 The Need for a Sociological Perspective on Polyamory 147
Kristin McCarty

9 Scrutinizing Polygamy: Utah's *Brown v. Buhman* and British Columbia's *Reference Re: Section 293* 167
Maura Strassberg

10 The Paradox of Big Love in the Liberal State: Treating Adults like Children and Children like Adults 205
Olivia Newman

Index 235

About the Contributors 245

Foreword

Dr. Elisabeth Sheff

Families are changing in numerous ways, which is perhaps one of the few things upon which all of us can agree these days. Longer life-spans, separating sexuality from procreation, greater personal freedom of self-determination, paid work for women becoming the norm instead of the exception, divorce, cohabitation, and more people than ever choosing to remain single have influenced the evolution of the family in the last century. Whether these changes are deemed good or bad often depends on the political or personal orientation of the person asked to evaluate them. Some persons see these changes as decline and fear that society is crumbling around them, with divorce, tolerance of homosexuality, and single parenting as evidence that "the" family is under attack. For others, shifting gender roles, increased freedom, and greater tolerance for diversity are part of social progress towards equity that has not yet gone far enough.

Although the pace of family change has never before been quite as fast as it was in the second half of the twentieth century, it is abundantly clear that families have always been in a state of flux. Shifting definitions and expectations of family members are a permanent feature of the human social landscape.[1] Contrary to popular belief that has fossilized the male-breadwinner family as "the" traditional family, there has never been a singular form of family in the United States or worldwide. Even in the 1950s—a time that many Americans memorialize as the height of the mythical traditional family—American families experienced divorce, single-parenthood, spousal abandonment, incest, alcoholism, substance abuse, and intimate partner violence. Perhaps more importantly, people of color and working class people were excluded from idyllic visions of the male-breadwinner family, and even now, too often remain invisible in nostalgic discussions of the good old days when the family wasn't under attack. The subtext in many of those conversations is rooted in a longing for a time when women, people of color, and sexual minorities knew their respective places, without white heterosexual male power being challenged.

A comparatively young nation amalgamated from many different cultural and religious traditions, the United States has a history of accommodating the shifting gender roles and economic circumstances that influence family structures. Legal recognition of same-sex marriage is simply the most recent and visible sign of these ongoing changes. Progressives hailed the U.S. Supreme Court's recent decision in *Obergefell v. Hodges* recognizing same-sex marriage nationwide as "marriage equality."[2] Certainly the *Obergefell* decision legitimized marriage for an entire category of people who had been denied their fundamental human rights to form their own intimate relationships and families, guaranteed by the United Nations Human Rights Declaration.[3] The advent of same-sex marriage *is* marriage equality, but only for those whose relationships adhere to what Elizabeth Emens labels "compulsory monogamy."[4] Others, however, whose relationships do not conform to a dyadic (two-person) model still have not achieved marriage "equality." In a stroke *Obergefell* decoupled marriage from heterosexuality, but it remains firmly attached to monogamy.

Or does it? *Beyond Same-Sex Marriage: Perspectives on Marital Possibilities* explores the social terrain outside of same-sex, dyadic marriage, to examine the implications of the legal recognition (and growing social acceptance) of same-sex marriage for the future of civil marriage and other marriage-like relationships. Ronald C. Den Otter has edited eight new works for this delightfully innovative volume that significantly expands knowledge of polygyny, polyandry, and polyamory, examines their intersections with race, technology, and religion, and theorizes how thinking outside of the box of monogamy might impact social institutions. Rich with engaging and even provocative ideas, readers of this book are in for a very thoughtful treat.

NOTES

Dr. Elisabeth "Eli" Sheff is the Director of Legal Services at Sheff Consulting Group where she serves as an expert witness and diversity consultant. In addition to numerous articles, Sheff is the author of *The Polyamorists Next Door* and *Stories from the Polycule*. Her third and shortest book, *When Someone You Love Is Polyamorous*, comes out Spring 2016.

1. Stephanie Coontz, *Marriage, A History: How Love Conquered Marriage* (New York: Penguin Books, 2006).
2. *Obergefell v. Hodges*, 135 S. Ct. 2071 (2015).
3. Article 16 of the United Nations Declaration of Human Rights guarantees the right to marriage and divorce, and freedom to establish a family, provided that each spouse is old enough to consent to the marital arrangement, accessed November 16, 2015, http://www.claiminghumanrights.org/udhr_article_16.html#at17
4. Elizabeth F. Emens, "Monogamy's Law: Compulsory Monogamy and Polyamorous Existence," *New York University Review of Law and Social Change* 29 (2004): 277–376.

Introduction

Ronald C. Den Otter

Although Mae West may not have been ready for an institution like civil marriage, the vast majority of Americans are. The trouble is that they do not seem to know what they are ready for. Many of them sincerely and reasonably disagree about the purpose(s) of marriage, its meaning, its eligibility requirements, its effects, its structure, its dynamics, the appropriateness of state involvement, what should happen if it ends, and the forms that it could (and should) take in the future. At present, for the most part, competent adults are allowed to exercise their own judgment in deciding whom to marry, even when their reasoning is flawed or their marriage is at high risk of violence, dysfunction, or divorce. As long as they are not marrying solely for immigration purposes, and meet the other minimal eligibility requirements put into place by the state where they reside, they can marry another consenting adult for whatever personal reasons that happen to strike their fancy. As far as the state is concerned, the quality of their respective reasons is no more legally relevant than the alignment of the planets.

The same-sex marriage drama in the United States finally has come to an end, despite pockets of resistance here and there, and it has a happy ending for those who care about gays and lesbians being treated equally with respect to their right to marry. The end of one conversation—about whether a man should be allowed to marry another man or a woman should be allowed to marry another woman—could turn out to be the beginning of another conversation about how marriage could be legally defined in the future. After all, it is far from self-evident that marriage has to be predicated upon romantic love, as opposed to, say, other kinds of love, care, or friendship, that the legal status of marriage should continue to exclude plural marriage enthusiasts like polygynists or polyamorists, or that the state should remain in the marriage business. Nor is the empirical case on behalf of marriage, which underscores its benefits, open and shut. As Cass Sunstein and Richard Thaler put it, "The most that can be said is that official marriage *might* [their italics] contribute to a kind of commitment that benefits most couples and children."[1]

Skepticism about a more traditional understanding of marriage, which the marriage equality movement helped to bring about, is here to stay, and its existence makes radical ideas about reform more plausible than they ever have been. True, many of the slope slippery fears put forth by conservative opponents of same-sex marriage as part of their rhetorical strategy to discredit it fail to be credible. The implication of constitutional right to same-sex marriage (or its equivalent on equal protection grounds) is not that someday I may marry my favorite golf club (my driver). As of now, we do not know what exactly may lie at the bottom of the slope, even though we can rule out some possibilities as incoherent. Indeed, it stands to reason that a new and perhaps more morally attractive understanding of marriage could emerge. The possibility that marriage could occupy a different normative space is no longer confined to the musings of academics. In his dissent in *Obergefell*, Chief Justice Roberts linked the constitutionally-mandated legal recognition of same-sex marriage to the view that states may also have to recognize multi-person intimate relationships as well to avoid discriminating against plural marriage enthusiasts. Roberts may not be right and his citation was designed to cut against nationwide legal recognition of same-sex marriage. At the same time, it is not obvious that he is wrong either, inasmuch as some of the arguments, which opponents of same-sex marriage formulated in defense of their position, resemble those that now are being put in the service of limiting marriage to couples, same-sex or opposite-sex.

The purpose of this book is not to try to settle, once and for all, whether states ought to abolish marriage, make it more inclusive, make it more contractual, call it something else, regulate it differently, or filter different benefits through it. Instead, its overarching aim is to expose readers to some of the legal, normative, and empirical issues that need to be addressed before Americans can deliberate thoughtfully about the merits of departing from a marital status quo that not only privileges monogamy but also a certain kind, namely one that takes for granted that romantic thoughts, feelings, and actions are the essence of marriage. These days, only those who do not follow politics would be optimistic about the quality of the public discourse that could result. If the debate over same-sex marriage provides any insight into what defenders of the marital status quo will do when popular discourse moves beyond couples' right to marriage, then Americans ought to expect appeals to emotion, religion, vicious stereotypes, questionable data, and anything else that might help them to put some points on the board. In any real democracy, one has to be realistic about the extent to which the better argument will compel anyone to change her mind and produce reasonable policies and laws. Still, over time, it is possible that what scholars dedicate their lives to doing may trickle down and influence how ordinary Americans, their elected representatives, and judges ultimately decide the most important questions of political morality.

This edited volume deliberately and unapologetically takes an interdisciplinary approach to comprehending the historical, empirical, normative, and legal dimensions of marriage. In the last few years, some of the best books on marriage ever written have appeared, like Tamara Metz's *Untying the Knot*, Elizabeth Brake's *Minimizing Marriage*, Janet Bennion's *Polygamy in Primetime*, Elisabeth Sheff's *The Polyamorists Next Door*, Mark Goldfeder's *Legalizing Plural Marriage*, Sonu Bedi's *Beyond Race, Sex, and Sexual Orientation* (the final chapter), Stephen Macedo's *Just Married, After Marriage* (a collection of philosophical essays edited by Elizabeth Brake), and John Witte's *The Western Case for Monogamy Over Polygamy*. Surely, more are on the way. Eight of the following contributions are original. Some of the contributors are well-known and others are less so, at least for the time being. All of the chapters add something important to the growing scholarship about the institution of marriage in this nation: what marriage has been, what it is, what it does, and what it could be like someday. No volume, including this one, could come close to being comprehensive. As such, this book is supposed to demonstrate just how important an interdisciplinary perspective is. The best evidence must inform the normative discourse that Americans engage in, especially when an issue, such as marriage, provokes such strong emotional reactions in so many of us. That is something that all of us, hopefully, can agree on.

In "*Obergefell* and the Liberal Case Against Civil Marriage," Sonu Bedi reflects on the implications of *Obergefell v. Hodges*, where the United States Supreme Court affirms a constitutional right to marry the person of one's choice. Justice Anthony Kennedy, writing for the majority, grounds his constitutional argument, in part, on the importance of marriage for gays and lesbians, providing a powerful objection to bans on same-sex marriage. Bedi argues that in making this positive and indeed strong case for gay marriage, Kennedy unintentionally underwrites the core liberal case against marriage itself. By affirming the status of civil marriage as a crucial lynchpin of society, *Obergefell* problematically treats marriage as both superior to other types of intimate relationships and as a significant component of an essentialized and troubling view of gay identity.

In "Progressive Polygamy in the Western United States," Janet Bennion examines a new marital phenomenon—progressive polygamy—a politically and socially liberal version of polygynous family life, emerging in the last twenty years along the Wasatch Front of Utah. Based on twenty years of ethnographic fieldwork and analysis of a purposive sample of five cases of polygamist families associated with Mormon fundamentalism in the Intermountain Western United States, she makes the case that this poly form emerged in response to the large influx of female converts from mainstream orthodox Mormon society as well as several key factors related to the Allred Group and the adoption of a new age/feminist paradigm. These unique polygynous families contain women who are both highly educated and career-oriented, who adhere to a loosely-based faith in the Mormon doctrine of celestial marriage (along with other Eastern ideologies), along with an absence of male supremacy and an emphasis on female autonomy. Bennion predicts that these progressive forms will increase as fewer familial models become available for disenfranchised mainstream Mormon women who have experienced divorce, widowhood, un-marriageability, and/or lack of female networking.

In "Plural Marriage, Exemptions, and the Redundancy of the Free Exercise Clause," I connect two legal debates that normally run parallel to each other: whether religion is special and whether states must treat multi-personal intimate relationships as marriages. If religion is not special, then the religious nature of the personal reason of, say, a Fundamentalist Mormon for seeking a plural marriage does not differ from the nonreligious personal reason of a polyamorist for wanting the same marital arrangement. In the absence of justification for the contrary, fairness requires the same treatment. States must allow all plural marriage enthusiasts to marry, regardless of their personal reasons for wanting to do so, or they must deny all of them such a right. As it turns out, no independent free exercise of religion argument for a constitutional right to marry more than one person at the same time exists.

In "Robotic Marriage and the Law," Mark Goldfeder and Yosef Razin point out that Americans are living in the midst of fundamental changes not only in family law but in technology. The remarkable advances in robotics over the last few decades have closed the gap between science fiction and science. Robots already spend time with the elderly and the young, work in factories and mines, and can do many things that human workers traditionally have done. Humans are already forming social relationships with robots, ranging from platonic love to prostitution. It may only be a matter of time before humans want to marry robots. Their chapter addresses whether a human and a robot ever could legally wed and elaborates on how this kind of marriage could occur in the future.

In *A Friendship Model of Sex, Polyamory, and Plural Marriage,* Diane Klein reflects on what might follow if, instead of treating sexual intimacy as conferring a unique status on relationships, we understood sexual relationships in a way more closely resembling non-sexual friendships. In presenting her "friendship model of sex," Klein sets out the underlying structural similarity, morally speaking, between friendships and sexually intimate relationships, and uses this similarity to undermine sexual exclusivity as the sole presumptive psychosexual ethical norm. In the absence of the usually unstated and unquestioned assumption of radical discontinuity between friendships and relationships of sexual intimacy, the claim that it is both psychologically possible and morally acceptable to be a part of multiple simultaneous relationships that include sexual intimacy becomes more plausible.

In "Public Reason, Liberal Neutrality, and Marriage," Andrew Lister addresses the question of whether one can criticize arguments against same-sex marriage for appealing to controversial religious doctrines while at the same time defending marriage on suitably public or neutral grounds. Answering this question requires spelling out the different forms neutrality can take and their relationship with the idea of public reason. There is a plausible public case for civil marriage, Lister contends, but it depends upon generalizations. Marriage is threatened not by the exclusion of non-public reasons but by a strongly individualist interpretation of a particular type of public reason, equal treatment, when it is understood to require individualized treatment, and any reasonable objection to differential treatment based on group characteristics is taken to be decisive.

In "Polygamy in Islam: Origins, Challenges, and Responses," Ameneh Maghzi and Mark Gruchy take a historical approach to challenging the conventional belief that polygyny is compatible with the Islamic tradition. In doing so, they explore the origins of polygyny in the Arab and Islamic worldview and spell out why a historically-oriented interpretation of the *Quran* and the life of the Prophet Muhammad produce a compelling case for discontinuing the practice. They conclude that polygyny can be prohibited in light of the underlying sentiment and lessons of the *Quran* and the realities of modern gender relations.

In "The Need for a Sociological Perspective on Polyamory," Kristin McCarty makes the case that sooner rather than later, sociologists must undertake the study of polyamory with the enthusiasm that such an important but understudied topic deserves. She then examines the likely reasons why few sociologists have yet to do so: the newness of the term "polyamory," its reputation, and the troubled relationship between polyamory and public sociology. She concludes with a plea for sociologists to devote their time and skills to understanding polyamorous families.

In "Scrutinizing Polygamy: Utah's *Brown v. Buhman* and British Columbia's *Reference Re: Section 293*," Maura Strassberg explains that the social and individual harms of polygamy identified in *Reference* provide a compelling state interest sufficient to withstand the strict scrutiny deemed necessary by *Brown*. She then argues that the real target of the Utah statute are the multiple marital relationships present in all polygamy and not the religious motivation for polygamy characteristic of the actual Mormon Fundamentalist polygamy practiced in Utah. As such, the strict scrutiny called for by the *Brown* court under the *Hialeah* analysis is not justified. She concludes with some thoughts on how a statute that only criminalizes religiously motivated polygamy might be justified, based on the way in which polygamous religious communities funnel teenage girls into polygamous marriages by ensuring that they never have the chance to develop sufficient autonomy to truly choose for themselves, forcing reconsideration of both *Yoder* and the limits of free exercise of religion.

NOTES

1. Richard H. Thaler and Cass R. Sunstein, *Nudge: Improving Decisions About Health, Wealth, and Happiness*, revised and expanded edition (New York: Penguin Books, 2009), 225.

ONE

Obergefell and the Liberal Case Against Civil Marriage

Sonu Bedi

The principle of public reason or justification is a familiar one.[1] John Rawls famously defends a "political liberalism" that holds that the state must not justify its exercise of power by simply appealing to controversial religious or moral conceptions of the good.[2] Drawing from this framework, some recent work in contemporary political theory argues that civil marriage is inconsistent with liberal neutrality or anti-perfectionism.[3] This work highlights the fact that the institution of marriage problematically affirms a kind of intimate relationship as morally superior to other ways of living. I draw from *Obergefell v. Hodges*, the recent United States Supreme Court affirming a fundamental constitutional right to marry the person of one's choice, irrespective of their sex, to inform this critique. In doing so, I assume that bans on gay marriage are unjust.[4] If the state has provided the institution of marriage to straight couples, justice requires that gay couples also be able to avail themselves of it. What has gone largely undertheorized, and the focus of this chapter, is the relationship between the liberal argument for gay marriage and the liberal argument against marriage itself. *Obergefell* provides an opportunity to explore that relationship.

This chapter situates the liberal case against civil marriage in the context of the Court's argument. Justice Anthony Kennedy, writing for the majority, grounds his constitutional argument, in part, on the importance of marriage for gays and lesbians, providing a powerful objection to bans on same-sex marriage. I argue that in making this positive and indeed strong case for gay marriage, Kennedy unintentionally underwrites the core liberal case against marriage itself. This chapter is in two parts. First, I outline the core claims of liberal neutrality or anti-perfectionism. Second, and this is the main focal point, I explain how the Court's reasoning violates these claims in three ways: one, by affirming that marriage is a status, which is not reducible to the mere tangible benefits and responsibilities that flow from it, two, by arguing for the moral superiority of that status, and three, by making the desire to attain that status a significant component of gay identity.

LIBERAL NEUTRALITY

John Rawls famously proposes that "the limits imposed by public reason" apply to "'constitutional essentials and questions of basic justice."[5] The Supreme Court, according to Rawls, is an "exemplar" of public reason.[6] As he puts it: "our exercise of political power is fully proper only when it is exercised in accordance with a constitution the essentials of which all citizens as free and equal may reasonably be expected to endorse in the light of principles and ideas acceptable to them as reasonable and rational."[7] This consensus is not about some actual agreement but what reasonable individuals should accept. This commitment to public reason excludes those justifications that cannot in principle be accepted by all.

One variant of this principle of public justification is a commitment to anti-perfectionism or liberal neutrality, a commitment that holds the state must remain neutral among competing conceptions of the good life. Howard Schweber provides a defense of this kind of public reason or what he calls "public justification."[8] Such a theory of justification requires that democratic citizens proffer reasons that their fellow listeners could accept. This kind of justificatory constraint rules out those reasons from the realm of law making that do not meet this principle.[9] The implication is that the state may not pass laws and policies grounded in the belief that a particular way of life is intrinsically better than another. Lawrence Solum calls this approach an "exclusionary" account of public reason or public justification. It is "exclusionary" because it does not permit all justifications to count as legitimate.[10] For instance, reasons that invoke a conception of the good are non-public and as such, cannot be used. Ronald Den Otter expounds upon this "exclusionary" approach by arguing that it is "the best interpretation of an ideal of public justification."[11]

Central to anti-perfectionism or liberal neutrality, then, is the claim that reasons that derive from conceptions of the good life are not a morally legitimate basis for lawmaking. Rawls defines a conception of the good as what "is valuable in human life."[12] This definition covers beliefs about what counts as a good, appropriate, or worthwhile life. Thus, a conception of the good normally consists of more or less determinate scheme of final ends, that is, ends we want to realize for their own sake. . . .[13] Such a conception takes a position on what kind of life has "intrinsic or inherent value."[14] Often, these conceptions of the good are based on religious or moral doctrines. Anti-perfectionism contends that these conceptions are illegitimate grounds for legislation. Given the pluralistic nature of democratic bodies, a liberal state must not privilege one such conception over another, particularly in those areas concerning its members' personal lives. The state may not pass laws and policies grounded in the belief that a particular way of life is *intrinsically* better than another. These beliefs are perfectionist ones, because they point to what counts as a decent or virtuous existence. They seek to articulate how individuals can live more perfect lives. Precisely because individuals may disagree over the inherent worthiness of certain ways of living over others, such beliefs are not in principle shareable by all, especially under conditions of moral pluralism. For this reason, liberal neutrality eschews them as grounds for lawmaking.

OBERGEFELL AND LIBERAL NEUTRALITY

This idea of anti-perfectionism or liberal neutrality is controversial, challenged by some liberals and many non-liberals alike.[15] I do not seek to defend it here but only to illuminate its implications. Recent work by liberal scholars like Elizabeth Brake and Tamara Metz contends that civil marriage, in its current form, violates liberal neutrality. I draw from *Obergefell* to inform and deepen this argument.

Marriage as a Status

Central to Justice Kennedy's opinion is the claim that marriage is a status, not simply a contract, that brings with it legal benefits and responsibilities. And it is precisely this status that underlies the constitutional infirmity with bans on gay marriage. One way to elaborate upon this idea is to consider the distinction between civil union and marriage.

The distinction between marriage and civil union became central to the debate over same-sex marriage as a result of *Baker v. State,* a Vermont Supreme Court decision that struck down prohibitions on same-sex marriage under the Vermont constitution. The court held that by refusing to provide legal recognition to same-sex couples, the state of Vermont violated the equal benefits clause of the Vermont Constitution, that constitution's equal protection analog to the Equal Protection Clause of the Fourteenth Amendment. Finding a constitutional violation, the court gave the legislature two options: permit either same sex couples to marry or provide them civil unions or domestic partnerships:

> We hold only that plaintiffs are entitled under [the Vermont Constitution] to obtain the same benefits and protections afforded by Vermont law to married opposite-sex couples. We do not purport to infringe upon the prerogatives of the Legislature to craft an appropriate means of addressing this constitutional mandate, other than to note that the record here refers to a number of potentially constitutional statutory schemes from other jurisdictions. These include what are typically referred to as "domestic partnership" or "registered partnership" acts, which generally establish an alternative legal status to marriage from same-sex couples, impose similar formal requirements and limitations, create a parallel licensing or registration scheme, and extend all or most of the same rights and obligations provided by law to married partners.[16]

The Vermont legislature opted for civil union or domestic partnership laws that provide gay couples with all the legal benefits, burdens, and responsibilities that come with marriage while withholding the all-important label.

In explaining its decision to pass the Vermont Civil Union Statute of 2000, the lawmakers acknowledged that "while a system of civil unions does not bestow the status of civil marriage, it does satisfy the requirements of the Common Benefits Clause."[17] "Changes in the way significant legal relationships are established under the constitution should be approached carefully, combining respect for the community and cultural institutions most affected with a commitment to the constitutional rights involved."[18] One journalist covering the Vermont decision summed up the reaction of an unnamed minister as follows: "'I don't care what people do,' [the minister] insisted. 'Just don't call it marriage. It can't be marriage.'"[19] Even though gay couples would receive all the same benefits, burdens, and responsibilities that come with marriage, they would not receive the label of "marriage." Vermont granted all couples the status of marriage in 2009. The label of "marriage" is important inasmuch as it adds something symbolic to the relevant union, something that goes above and beyond the tangible benefits and burdens that accompany civil unions.

In *Maynard v. Hill*, the United States Supreme Court held that a state legislature might dissolve the bonds of marriage, because marriage is a public institution. Justice Stephen Field, writing for the Court, famously reasoned that marriage is a kind of status:

> [Marriage is] declared a civil contract for certain purposes, but it is not thereby made synonymous with the word "contract" employed in the common law or statutes. . . .The relation is always regulated by government. It is more than a contract. It requires certain acts of the parties to constitute marriage independent of and beyond the contract. It partakes more of the character of an institution regulated and controlled

> by public authority, upon principles of public policy, for the benefit of the community.[20]

Whereas civil unions are just a contract with no symbolic significance, marriage means more. As Janet Halley points out, "advocates and opponents [of same-sex marriage have] converge[d] on an image of marriage as status."[21] On one hand, gays and lesbians seek that status to affirm their relationships. On the other hand, detractors seek to protect it from alteration. This emphasis on status informs *Goodridge v. Dep't of Public Health*, the Massachusetts Supreme Judicial Court decision that invalidated Massachusetts' prohibition on same-sex marriage under the state's constitution. The decision clarifies that "[t]angible as well as intangible benefits flow from marriage."[22] This intangible quality is the public recognition that comes with declaring two individuals married. Writing positively in light of the *Goodridge* decision, Joseph Singer reasons that:

> After all, marriage is not just an ordinary contract; it is a status conferred by state officials who issue a license and conduct a ceremony in which they state: "By the authority invested in me by the Commonwealth of Massachusetts, I hereby declare you to be married."[23]

Citing *Maynard*, Justice Kennedy illuminates the nature of marriage as a status, explaining that marriage is "the foundation of the family and of society, without which there would be neither civilization nor progress."[24] Marriage, as Kennedy goes on to say, has long been "'a great public institution, giving character to our whole civil polity."[25] Marriage, for Kennedy, is "transcendent."[26] Although marriage importantly entails tangible benefits and responsibilities, it is also a "significant status,"[27] conferring "nobility" and "dignity."[28] This is the intangible feature that comes with the label of "marriage." Kennedy concludes that "[s]ame-sex couples, too, may aspire to the transcendent purposes of marriage and seek fulfillment in its highest meaning."[29]

Tamara Metz makes a powerful argument that this understanding of marriage cannot be squared with the idea that a liberal state must act in the realm of temporal affairs, not in the realm of morality or spirituality. Metz characterizes the putative liberal state in the following way:

> Traditionally, liberals have treated the commands of the state as limiting action (not belief) for the narrow purpose of ensuring social order, protecting citizens from harm, and guaranteeing political fairness [citation omitted]. Generally, the state confers legal status for instrumental convenience, not to alter self-understanding in any deep and enduring way. The familiar idea behind the limited state is that freedom consists, in large part, in individuals being free from interference to live according to their own design.[30]

Given this view of the liberal state, conferring the status of marriage seems to confound it. In declaring individuals married, the state alters "self-understanding."[31] Metz calls this the "expressive" or "constitutive" part of marriage[32] where marriage is "a unique kind of expressive good, the value of which exceeds the sum of the delineable benefits and burdens that attach to it."[33] This characterization informs Kennedy's description of marriage, as a "dynamic" that "becomes greater than just the two persons."[34] But it is precisely because this kind of legal status "alters self-understanding" in a "deep and enduring way," that renders it in conflict with a liberal state that is committed to neutrality.

The underlying constitutional issue in *Obergefell* is not simply about the denial of the tangible benefits and responsibilities that come with marriage. Kennedy's concern is that marriage also comes with intangible advantages including dignity and nobility. By denying this kind of status to same-sex couples, the state "demeans gays and lesbians" by "lock[ing] them out of a central institution of the Nation's society."[35] It leaves such couples without the ability to "aspire to the transcendent purpose of marriage and seek fulfillment in its highest meaning."[36]

The emphasis on how the very act of excluding gay couples demeans them makes sense because Kennedy, like many Americans do, ascribes so much significance to marriage. Marriage, unlike a civil union, is self-consciously about consecrating a relationship with mystical overtones. Denying gays and lesbians entry into this status rightly violates their dignity. Yet, this argument reveals what is so problematic with marriage itself (whether same or opposite sex) from a neutrality standpoint. By conferring the status of marriage, the state goes beyond temporal concerns of simply preventing harm and ensuring fairness.

Privileging a Particular Intimate Way of Life

It is not just that marriage is a status, irreducible to the tangible or legal benefits and responsibilities that come with it. Marriage also explicitly privileges a certain intimate way of life as superior to others. According to Kennedy, "[m]arriage responds to the universal fear that a lonely person might call out only to find no one there. It offers the hope of companionship and understanding and assurance that while both still live there will be someone to care for the other."[37] In privileging marriage in this way, Kennedy implicitly demeans those who are unmarried—the "lonely person." His doing so is all the more arresting because someone may be unmarried but far from alone. He or she may have a romantic partner or partners, a caretaker, friends, family, or a range of other relationships that he or she may find equally or more fulfilling.

In arguing that bans on gay marriage are unconstitutional, Kennedy states that marriage is a "keystone to our social order" and a "building block of our national community."[38] For Kennedy, marriage is "a two-person union unlike any other in its importance to the committed individuals."[39] Elizabeth Brake, in line with Metz, argues that marriage laws are ultimately based on the "belief that marriage and companionate romantic love have special value."[40] It consists:

> in the assumption that a central, exclusive, amorous relationship is normal for humans, in that it is a universally shared goal, and that such a relationship is normative, in that it should be aimed at in preference of other relationship types. The assumption that valuable relationships must be marital or amorous devalues friendships and other caring relationships, as recent manifestos by urban tribalists, quirkyaloners, polyamorists, and asexuals have insisted.[41]

This kind of belief about the morally superior status of marriage over other relationships fails liberal neutrality. In fact, David Estlund argues that a "more neutral, more liberal, liberalism" must reject marriage laws.[42]

The perspective of recent natural law theory is instructive in elucidating this special status. Robert George, one of the key figures in this tradition, argues that marriage is an "intrinsic" not merely "instrumental good."[43] It is the "one flesh union" that arises from procreative sex within marriage that constitutes this good:

> The central and justifying point of sex is not pleasure (or even the sharing of pleasure) per se, however much sexual pleasure is sought—rightly sought—as an aspect of the perfection of marital union; the point of sex, rather, is marriage itself, considered as an essentially and irreducibly (though not merely) bodily union of persons—a union effectuated and renewed by acts of sexual congress—conjugal acts.[44]

Under this view, the sex act within an opposite sex marriage usually is morally superior to sex acts that occur outside of it. George self-consciously and apologetically privileges this conception of the good, this way of living. He does not argue that this way of life is explicitly superior, because it provides benefits to others. Marriage is an intrinsic good. It is worthwhile for its own sake, providing a kind of good that other ways of living, including being unmarried, having "flings" or multiple partners or being with platonic friends cannot. This is the morally special status of marriage.

Now George's argument for marriage explicitly excludes same-sex couples. That's his purpose for making it. He would withhold the state's conferral of marriage to gays and lesbians. Gays and lesbians cannot fulfill the procreative part of his definition of marriage. But Kennedy rejects this procreative argument, and rightly so, concluding that states have not "conditioned the right to marry on the capacity or commitment to procreate."[45] Rather, marriage is about couples (either same or opposite sex) vowing to "support each other," where society "pledge[s] to support the couple, offering symbolic recognition and material benefits to protect and nourish the union."[46] Richard Posner also affirms a companionship model of marriage as:

between at least approximate equals, based on mutual respect and affection, and involving close and continuous association in child rearing, household management, and other activities, rather than merely the occasional copulation [of the procreative model]."[47]

Goodridge also adopts the companionate model of marriage:

> While it is certainly true that many, perhaps most, married couples have children together (assisted or unassisted), it is the exclusive and permanent commitment of the marriage partners to one another, not the begetting of children, that is the sine qua non of civil marriage."[48]

Or as Evan Wolfson puts it: "marriage is first and foremost about a loving union between two people who enter into a relationship of emotional and financial commitment and interdependence.[49] Marriage expresses their commitment to this kind of union. Marriage is about enjoying one's life with another. This model of marriage is, as William Eskridge suggests, "most similar to those that are typically valorized by most modern Western perspectives."[50]

By valorizing this kind of companionship, marriage confers a morally special status. By conferring it, the state tries to influence what ought to be each individual's personal decision about how to live. This is why Metz concludes that the state goes beyond its "limited" role of providing mere instrumental benefits in marrying individuals. In doing so, as she goes on to say, the state "assumes [through marriage laws] the role of *ethical authority* . . . violating the type of neutrality necessary for the state to secure liberty and equality in a diverse polity such as ours."[51] After all, individuals may very well reasonably disagree about the inherent worthiness of this kind of companionship model of marriage, one that sanctifies the special nature of such a union.

The Court concludes its decision by making clear that marriage is indeed the superior choice:

> No union is more profound than marriage, for it embodies the highest ideals of love, fidelity, devotion, sacrifice, and family. In forming a marital union, two people become something greater than once they were. [The hope of those who seek to marry] is not to be condemned to live in loneliness, excluded from one of civilization's oldest institutions.[52]

Kennedy places marriage as the "highest" type of relationship, devaluing "friendships and other caring relationships."[53] Indeed, for Kennedy, if one is not married, one is relegated to mere loneliness. And it is precisely the superior nature of this kind of legal status that requires the state to permit gay couples to marry. They, too, must be able to avail themselves of this "profound" kind of intimate relationship. But in making this argument, which appears to be so progressive, Kennedy also designates a certain way of life as superior, violating a core claim of liberal neutrality. This is something like natural law but with a gay spin.

Now perhaps this conclusion is too quick. Stephen Macedo maintains that marriage promotes "public welfare."[54] For instance, "[m]arried men (much evidence suggests) live longer, have lower rates of homicide, suicide, accidents, and mental illness than unmarried ones."[55] But even if we assume the accuracy of the public welfare claim, which may be empirically controversial,[56] it hardly proves that the state should stay in the marriage business. This is for three reasons. First, the state could accomplish such public welfare goals by simply making available a civil union status to everyone. For instance, if the purpose were to facilitate economic stability facilitating issues such as inheritance or child support, civil unions would be sufficient to accomplish it. Why deploy the label of "marriage"? It is not at all clear that downgrading marriage in this way would undermine any such benefits, assuming such benefits exist.

Second, it is entirely possible—even likely—that the reason why unmarried individuals may have higher rates of mental illness, suicide and the like is because their way of living is not privileged by the state. The state stigmatizes unmarried individuals by conferring the status of marriage only to those who incorporate marriage into life plan. By valuing one way of living, the state marks another as socially undesirable. This action, in turn, makes it more likely that those who undertake the "socially undesirable" option will suffer more than those who do not. This can turn out to be a self-fulfilling prophecy.

Similarly, it seems equally likely that fifty years ago, gays and lesbians had higher rates of suicide and mental distress than their straight counterparts (and this is probably true even today). Gays were (and of course sometimes still are) forced to hide their sexuality. But we would reject the conclusion that "being straight" somehow promotes the "public welfare" even if it is true that gays are individually worse off in society. The conclusion to draw from these facts is not that heterosexuality is the answer but that the state ought to cease privileging that kind of lifestyle. And in the same way, it ought to stop conferring the morally special status of marriage. Doing so marginalizes those who are not married, just as the myriad of laws and policies that banned gay sex and privileged heterosexuality stigmatize individuals for being gay.

Third, if the label of marriage has a religious underpinning, this ought to automatically rule it out as civil institution. Perry Dane argues that the "'secular' and 'religious' meanings . . . of marriage are so intermeshed in our history, legal and religious imagination" that we cannot "wall off" civil marriage from its "religious considerations."[57] Dane goes on to point out that "even a casual observer would, of course, notice that the laws of all the states recognize religious clergy or religious communities, in addition to various civil officials, as officiants in civil marriages. No other civil institution is structured quite this way."[58] Religious clergy have the power to finalize the legal status of marriage. Marriage is one of the most glaring exceptions to the principle of the separation of church and state.

For instance, Metz considers the case of baptism or a bar mitzvah.[59] These ceremonies may very well have important benefits for those who undertake them. Suggesting that we permit the state to establish or confer such practices (imagine a state-sanctioned "coming of age" ceremony) would unequivocally violate liberal neutrality. Again, this is because such a ceremony stands for a deeply moral, personal, and often religious decision, and one that is often central to an individual's conception of the good life.

Recent studies indicate that religious individuals are less likely than their non-religious counterparts to abuse drugs and alcohol, to be stressed, and to suffer from low self-esteem.[60] Even if this were evidence that individuals ought to consider becoming religious, it would be illegitimate for the state to establish a religion or act on such religious premises. Because religion, like marriage, is such a personal decision, so central to a conception of the good life, the state must remain neutral towards it in the name of anti-perfectionism.

Essentializing Gay Identity

Chief Justice John Roberts, in his dissenting opinion in *Obergefell*, raises the objection of plural marriage: "If not having the opportunity to marry "serves to disrespect and subordinate" gay and lesbian couples, why wouldn't the same "imposition of this disability," . . . serve to disrespect and subordinate people who find fulfillment in polyamorous relationships?"[61] One difficulty in drawing such a distinction is that prohibitions on same sex marriage, as written, do not explicitly discriminate against gays and lesbians as a class. After all, a gay man may marry a lesbian (and vice versa). The law tracks sex not sexual orientation. In this way, bans on both plural marriage and gay marriage seek to regulate behavior or desire: in one case the desire to marry more than one person and in the other the desire to marry someone of the same sex. How then do we distinguish between these desires?

Andrew Sullivan seeks to do so it in the following way:

> Almost everyone seems to accept, even if they find homosexuality morally troublesome, that it occupies a deeper level of human consciousness than a polygamous impulse. Even the Catholic Church, which believes that homosexuality is an "objective disorder," concedes that it is a profound element of human identity. It speaks of 'homosexual persons,' for example, in a way it would never speak of "polygamous persons." And almost all of us tacitly assume this, even in the very use of the term "homosexuals." We accept also that multiple partners can

> be desired by gays and straights alike: that polygamy is an activity, whereas both homosexuality and heterosexuality are states.[62]

Even if a prohibition on same-sex marriage does not explicitly invoke sexual orientation, it regulates desire that is, according to Sullivan, fundamental to who gays and lesbians are. Bans on plural marriage do not regulate behavior or desire that is central to who someone is. As Jonathan Rauch puts it, "Do homosexuals actually exist? I think so. . . By contrast, no serious person claims there are people constitutively attracted only to relatives, or only to groups rather than individuals."[63] Whereas the desire for someone of the same sex is constitutive of gay identity, the desire for more than one person or one's sibling is not.

This means that prohibitions on same-sex marriage strike at who gays and lesbians are. Although the Court may not do enough to respond to Roberts' rejoinder of plural marriage, Kennedy does say: "[f[ar from seeking to devalue marriage, the petitioners seek it for themselves because of their respect—and need—for its privileges and responsibilities. And their immutable nature dictates that same-sex marriage is their only real path to this profound commitment."[64] Whereas the desire to be in a plural marriage is not immutable, the desire to be in a same sex marriage is. Kennedy realizes that "psychiatrists and others recognized that sexual orientation is both a normal expression of human sexuality and immutable."[65] Those who seek to marry more than one person may be straight or gay or bisexual. Sexual orientation is more basic than the desire to be in a plural marriage. As Kennedy goes on to say, "The nature of marriage is that, through its enduring bond, two persons together can find other freedoms, such as expression, intimacy, and spirituality. This is true for all persons, whatever their sexual orientation."[66]

This language of immutability points to an important claim by proponents of gay marriage: that being gay is often central to one's sexual identity.[67] As David Richards argues, claims by gays and lesbians "are in their nature claims to a self-respecting personal and moral identity in public and private life through which they may reasonably express and realize their ethical convictions of the moral powers of friendship and love in a good, fulfilled, and responsible life."[68] This is why gay and lesbian organizations often deploy the locution of "sexual orientation" rather than "sexual preference."[69] Constitutive of gay and lesbian identity is the desire for those of the same sex. Bans on gay marriage therefore discriminate against a bona fide identity group or class. By contrast, limitations on numerosity do not strike at who plural marriage enthusiasts are. These limitations only regulate behavior. This may suggest that although bans on gay marriage are wrong, bans on plural marriage are not.

But this argument comes at a cost. It turns out to privilege certain kinds of gay lives over others. Sullivan and Rauch as well as Kennedy imply that the desire to marry someone of the same sex is crucial to being gay just as marrying someone of the opposite sex may be crucial to being straight—"This is true for all persons, whatever their sexual orientation." It is not enough to say that desiring someone of the same sex is central to gay identity. If that were the case, limiting marriage to opposite sex couples would clearly not frustrate it. After all, as long as individuals may choose to have sex with and live with individuals of the same sex—even setting up domestic partnerships or civil unions to that effect, current marriage laws would not strike at the core of gay desire.

As Roberts explains in his dissent, even with a ban on gay marriage, "[s]ame-sex couples remain free to live together, to engage in intimate conduct, and to raise their families as they see fit."[70] According to Roberts, sodomy laws, like the one the Court invalidated in *Lawrence v. Texas*, involve "government intrusion," even going so far as making gay sex a "crime."[71] These kinds of laws, then, do in fact strike at who gays and lesbians are, preventing them from acting on their desire or love for someone of the same sex, whereas prohibitions on same sex marriage do not. Such a prohibition does not frustrate a gay person's ability to love someone of the same sex. It merely frustrates their desire to *marry* the person they desire or love. In order for such a prohibition to discriminate against an identity group rather than behavior, as in the case of plural marriage, this desire must be constitutive of what it means to be gay or lesbian. Only then do limitations on same-sex *marriage* discriminate against gays and lesbians rather than simply a desire or behavior.

But of course, and this is the rub, there are many gays and lesbians, including this author, (as well as many heterosexuals to be sure) who do not desire to marry, who may even despise the idea. They may prefer non-monogamous, anonymous or multi-partner sex or choose to remain unmarried. To insist or even suggest that the desire to marry is fundamental problematically essentializes the notion of gay identity. It binds individuals to, what Kwame Anthony Appiah calls, identity "scripts," scripts that outline what it means to be a member of a particular group, in this case what it means to be gay.[72]

In particular, this kind of argument advocates a surprisingly traditional, hetero-normative depiction of human desire—one that privileges monogamy and commitment over being unmarried and sexually active with multiple partners. Those who choose to be unmarried are, under the terms of this argument, defective, "condemned to live in loneliness," in Kennedy's words. They are failing to live up to their essential nature as human beings to marry someone they love. Making the desire to marry fundamental straightforwardly marginalizes those—gay or straight—who choose to remain unmarried. This strategy to distinguish same-sex marriage from its plural counterpart brazenly views being unmarried as inferior.

This irony has not gone unnoticed. Self-described "queer theory" criticizes the mainstream gay and lesbian identity for reaffirming these values.[73] Darren Rosenblum argues that many self-proclaimed "queers" explore and celebrate other kinds of sexuality: "public sex (parks, tea rooms, "adult bookstores," backrooms), anonymous sex, group sex, promiscuity, sadomasochism, and role-playing."[74] Rendering marriage constitutive of gay identity essentializes it, makes it terribly boring, and marginalizes these non-hetero normative desires and behaviors. Ultimately, this argument (once again) privileges marriage over being unmarried. In conceptualizing gay identity in terms of marriage, Americans reinforce the idea that a life with a committed romantic partner is superior to a life without one.

CONCLUSION

Obergefell is indeed a landmark case, representing an important and necessary constitutional elaboration upon the fundamental right to marry. Its magisterial reasoning illuminates why denial of marriage licenses to gay couples demeans their dignity. But in making this kind of argument, the Court simultaneously makes clear why civil marriage itself is inconsistent with the claims of liberal neutrality. If Americans hold fast to the idea that a putative liberal state must remain neutral among competing conceptions of the good life, they must ultimately get out of the marriage business. The force of *Obergefell*'s reasoning suggests just that.

NOTES

1. See, e.g., Bruce Ackerman, *Social Justice and the Liberal State* (New Haven: Yale Press, 1980); Rainer Forst, *Contexts of Justice: Political Philosophy Beyond Liberalism and Communitarianism* (Berkeley: University of California Press, 2002); Gerald F. Gaus. *Justificatory Liberalism* (New York: Oxford University Press, 1996); Kent Greenawalt, *Private Consciences and Public Reasons* (New York: Oxford University Press, 1995); Jürgen Habermas, *Moral Consciousness and Communicative Action*, trans. Christian Lenhardt and Shierry Weber Nicholsen (Cambridge: MIT Press, 1990); Jürgen Habermas "Remarks on Legitimation Through Human Rights," in *The Postnational Constellation: Political Essays*, ed. and trans. Max Pensky (Cambridge: Polity Press, 2001); Charles E. Larmore, *Patterns of Moral Complexity* (New York: Cambridge University Press, 1987); John Rawls, *Political Liberalism* (New York: Columbia University Press, 1996).

2. Rawls, *Political Liberalism*.

3. See, e.g., Sonu Bedi, *Beyond Race, Sex and Sexual Orientation: Legal Equality without Identity* (New York: Cambridge University Press, 2013); Elizabeth Brake, *Minimizing Marriage: Marriage, Morality, and the Law* (New York: Oxford University Press, 2012); Martha A. Fineman, *The Neutered Mother, the Sexual Family and Other Twentieth Century Tragedies* (New York: Routledge, 1995); Tamara Metz, *Untying the Knot: Marriage, the State, and the Case for Their Divorce* (Princeton: Princeton University Press, 2010).

4. For arguments to that effect, see, e.g., Carlos A. Ball, *The Morality of Gay Rights: An Exploration in Political Philosophy* (New York: Routledge Press, 2003); Evan Gerstmann, *Same-Sex Marriage and the Constitution*, 2nd ed. (New York: Cambridge Press, 2008); Andrew Koppelman, *The Gay Rights Question in Contemporary American Law* (Chicago: University of Chicago Press, 2002); David A.J. Richards, *The Case for Gay*

Rights: From Bowers to Lawrence and Beyond (Lawrence: University of Kansas Press, 2005); Ralph Wedgwood, "The Fundamental Argument for Same-Sex Marriage," *Journal of Political Philosophy* 7 (1999): 225–242; Evan Wolfson, *Why Marriage Matters? America, Equality, and Gay People's Right to Mary* (New York: Simon & Schuster, 2004).

5. Rawls, *Political Liberalism*, 214.

6. Ibid., 216.

7. Ibid., 217.

8. Howard, Schweber. *Democracy and Authenticity: Toward a Theory of Public Justification* (New York: Cambridge University Press, 2012).

9. See generally Lawrence B. Solum, "Constructing an Ideal of Public Reason," *San Diego Law Review* 30 (1993): 729–762; see also Ronald Den Otter. *Judicial Review in an Age of Moral Pluralism* (New York: Cambridge Press, 2009).

10. Solum, "Constructing an Ideal of Public Reason," 729.

11. Den Otter, *Judicial Review in an Age of Moral Pluralism*, 139.

12. Rawls, *Political Liberalism*, 19.

13. Ibid.

14. Jonathan Quong, *Liberalism without Perfection* (New York: Oxford Press, 2011), 12; George Sher, *Beyond Neutrality: Perfectionism and Politics* (New York: Cambridge Press, 1997), 9.

15. See, e.g., Robert P. George, *Making Men Moral: Civil Liberties and Public Morality* (New York: Oxford Press, 1993); Robert George, "Same-Sex Marriage and Moral Neutrality," in *Homosexuality and American Public Life*, ed. Christopher Wolfe (Dallas: Spence Publishing, 1999): 141–153; William A. Galston, *Liberal Purposes: Goods, Virtues, and Diversity in the Liberal State* (Cambridge: Cambridge University Press, 1991); Alasdair MacIntyre, *After Virtue: A Study in Moral Theory*, 2nd ed. (Notre Dame: Notre Dame University Press, 1984); Joseph Raz, *The Morality of Freedom* (Oxford: Oxford University Press, 1986); George Sher, *Beyond Neutrality: Perfectionism and Politics* (New York: Cambridge Press, 1997); Michael Sandel, *Liberalism and the Limits of Justice* (Cambridge: Cambridge Press, 1982). But see Matthew Clayton, *Justice and Legitimacy in Upbringing* (New York: Oxford University Press, 2006); Steven Lecce, *Against Perfectionism: Defending Liberal Neutrality* (Toronto: Toronto Press, 2008); Quong, *Liberalism without Perfection*; Schweber, *Democracy and Authenticity*.

16. *Baker v. State*, 170 Vt. 224–225 (Vt. 1999).

17. An Act Relating to Civil Unions, No. 91, Section 1 (10).

18. Ibid, Section 1 (10).

19. Adrian Walker, "Give Partners the Right to Marry," *Boston Globe*, March 9, 2000.

20. *Maynard v. Hill*, 125 U.S. 212–213 (1888).

21. Janet Halley, "Behind the Law of Marriage (I): From Status/Contract to the Marriage System," *Unbound: Harvard Journal of the Legal Left* 6 (2010): 4.

22. *Goodridge v. Dep't of Public Health*, 440 Mass. 322 (Mass. 2003).

23. Joseph William Singer, "Same Sex Marriage, Full Faith and Credit, and the Evasion of Obligation," *Stanford Journal of Civil Rights and Civil Liberties* 1 (2005): 5

24. *Obergefell v. Hodges*, 135 U.S. 2584 (2015) (Kennedy, J., majority opinion).

25. Ibid., 2601.

26. Ibid., 2594.

27. Ibid., 2601.

28. Ibid., 2594.

29. Ibid., 2602.

30. Metz, *Untying the Knot*, 115.

31. Ibid., 93.

32. Ibid., 89–94.

33. Ibid., 36

34. *Obergefell v. Hodges*, 135 U.S. 2594 (2015).

35. Ibid., 2602.

36. Ibid.

37. Ibid., 2600.

38. Ibid., 2601.
39. Ibid., 2599.
40. Brake, *Minimizing Marriage*, 88
41. Ibid., 88–89.
42. David Estlund, "Shaping and Sex: Commentary on Parts I and II," in *Sex, Preference, and Family: Essays on Law and Nature* , ed. David M. Estlund and Martha C. Nussbaum (New York: Oxford Press, 1998): 164.
43. Robert P. George, "What's Sex Got to do with It? Marriage, Morality, and Rationality," *American Journal of Jurisprudence* 49 (2004): 63.
44. Ibid., 73.
45. *Obergefell v. Hodges*, 135 U.S. 2601 (2015).
46. Ibid.
47. Richard Posner, *Sex and Reason* (Cambridge: Harvard University Press, 1992), 45; see also, Ruth K. Khalsa, "Polygamy as A Red Herring in the Same–Sex Marriage Debate," *Duke Law Journal* 54 (2005): 1664.
48. *Goodridge v. Dep't of Public Health*, 440 Mass. 332 (Mass. 2003).
49. Evan Wolfson, "Crossing the Threshold: Equal Marriage Rights For Lesbians and Gay Men and the Intra-Community Critique," *New York University Review of Law and Social Change* 21 (1994): 579.
50. William N. Eskridge, Jr., "A History of Same-Sex Marriage," *Virginia Law Review* 79 (1993): 1436.
51. Metz, *Untying the Knot*, 115.
52. *Obergefell v. Hodges*, 135 U.S. 2608 (2015).
53. Brake, *Minimizing Marriage*, 88–89.
54. Stephen Macedo, "Sexuality and Liberty: Making Room for Nature and Tradition," in *Sex, Preference, and Family: Essays on Law and Nature* , ed. David M. Estlund and Martha C. Nussbaum (New York: Oxford University Press, 1997), 94.
55. Ibid., 94 (citing James Q. Wilson, *The Moral Sense* (New York: The Free Press, 1995), 178).
56. For an argument that unmarried individuals live happy and healthy lives, see Bella DePaulo, *Singled Out: How Singles are Stereotyped, Stigmatized, and Ignored, and Still Live Happily Ever After* (St. Martin's Griffin, 2006).
57. Perry Dane, "A Holy Secular Institution," *Emory Law Journal* 58 (2009): 1129.
58. Ibid, 1137.
59. Metz, *Untying the Knot*, 114–115.
60. Christopher G. Ellison, et al., "Religious Involvement, Stress, and Mental Health: Findings from the 1995 Detroit Area Study," *Social Forces* 80 (2001): 215–249; see also http://www.heritage.org/research/reports/2006/12/why-religion-matters-even-more-the-impact-of-religious-practice-on-social-stability
61. *Obergefell v. Hodges*, 135 U.S. 2622 (2015) (Roberts, CJ., dissenting). For a serious defense of a constitutional right to engage in plural marriage or polyamorous marriage, see Ronald Den Otter, *In Defense of Plural Marriage* (New York: Cambridge University Press, 2015).
62. Andrew Sullivan, "Three's a Crowd," in *Same-Sex Marriage: Pro and Con, A Reader*, ed. Andrew Sullivan (New York: Vintage Books, 1997): 278.
63. Jonathan Rauch, "Marrying Somebody," in *Same-Sex Marriage: Pro and Con, A Reader*, ed. Andrew Sullivan (New York: Vintage Books, 1997): 286.
64. *Obergefell v. Hodges*, 135 U.S. 2594 (2015).
65. Ibid., 2596.
66. Ibid., 2599.
67. See Emily R. Gill, "Beyond Immutability: Sexuality and Constitutive Choice," *The Review of Politics* 76 (2014): 93–117; David A.J. Richards, *Identity and the Case for Gay Rights: Race, Gender, Religion as Analogies* (Chicago: University of Chicago Press, 1999).
68. Richards, *Identity and the Case for Gay Rights*, 93.
69. Lambda Legal http://www.lambdalegal.org/issues/employment-workplace/; International Gay and Lesbian Human Rights Commission http://www.iglhrc.org/cgi-

bin/iowa/theme/2.html; Human Rights Campaign http://www.hrc.org/issues/workplace/equal_opportunity.asp; GLAD (Gay and Lesbians Advocates and Defenders) http://www.glad.org/rights/c/anti-lgbt-discrimination/

70. *Obergefell v. Hodges*, 135 U.S. 2620 (2015).

71. Ibid.

72. Kwame Anthony Appiah, *The Ethics of Identity* (Princeton: Princeton Press, 2005).

73. See generally Annamarie Jagose, *Queer Theory: An Introduction* (New York: NYU Press, 1997); Andrew Sullivan, "The Conservative Case for Gay Marriage," *Time*, June 30, 2003; Michael Warner, *The Trouble with Normal: Sex, Politics, and the Ethics of Queer Life* (Cambridge: Harvard Press, 1999).

74. Darren Rosenblum, "Queer Intersectionality and the Failure of Recent Lesbian and Gay 'Victories,'" *Law & Sexuality: Review Lesbian & Gay Legal Issues* 4 (1994): 108.

REFERENCES

Ackerman, Bruce. *Social Justice and the Liberal State*. New Haven: Yale University Press, 1980.

Appiah, Kwame Anthony. *The Ethics of Identity*. Princeton: Princeton University Press, 2005.

Baker v. State, 170 Vt. 194 (Vt. 1999).

Ball, Carlos A. *The Morality of Gay Rights: An Exploration in Political Philosophy*. New York: Routledge Press, 2003.

Bedi, Sonu. *Beyond Race, Sex and Sexual Orientation: Legal Equality without Identity*. New York: Cambridge University Press, 2013.

Brake, Elizabeth. *Minimizing Marriage: Marriage, Morality, and the Law*. New York: Oxford University Press, 2012.

Card, Claudia. "Against Marriage and Motherhood." *Hypatia* 11(1996): 1–23.

Clayton, Matthew. *Justice and Legitimacy in Upbringing*. New York: Oxford University Press, 2006.

Dane, Perry. "A Holy Secular Institution." *Emory Law Journal* 58 (2009): 1123–1194.

Den Otter, Ronald. *In Defense of Plural Marriage*. New York: Cambridge University Press, 2015.

_____. *Judicial Review in an Age of Moral Pluralism*. New York: Cambridge Press, 2009.

DePaulo, Bella. *Singled Out: How Singles are Stereotyped, Stigmatized, and Ignored, and Still Live Happily Ever After*. St. Martin's Griffin, 2006.

Ellison, Christopher G. et al. "Religious Involvement, Stress, and Mental Health: Findings from the 1995 Detroit Area Study." *Social Forces* 80 (2001): 215–249.

Eskridge, William N. Jr. *Gaylaw: Challenging the Apartheid of the Closet*. Cambridge: Harvard University Press, 1999.

_____. "A History of Same-Sex Marriage." *Virginia Law Review* 79 (1993): 1419–1513.

Estlund, David. "Shaping and Sex: Commentary on Parts I and II." In *Sex, Preference, and Family: Essays on Law and Nature* , edited by David M. Estlund and Martha C. Nussbaum. New York: Oxford University Press, 1998: 148–170.

Fineman, Martha A. *The Neutered Mother, the Sexual Family and Other Twentieth Century Tragedies*. New York: Routledge, 1995.

Forst, Rainer. *Contexts of Justice: Political Philosophy Beyond Liberalism and Communitarianism*. Berkeley: University of California Press, 2002.

Galston, William A. *Liberal Purposes: Goods, Virtues, and Diversity in the Liberal State*. Cambridge: Cambridge University Press, 1991.

Gaus, Gerald F. *Justificatory Liberalism*. Oxford: Oxford University Press, 1996.

George, Robert P. "What's Sex Got to do with It? Marriage, Morality, and Rationality." *American Journal of Jurisprudence* 49 (2004): 63–85.

_____. "Same-Sex Marriage and Moral Neutrality." In *Homosexuality and American Public Life*, edited by Christopher Wolfe. Dallas: Spence Publishing 1999: 141–153.

_____. *Making Men Moral: Civil Liberties and Public Morality*. New York: Oxford University Press, 1993.

Gerstmann, Evan. *Same-Sex Marriage and the Constitution*. 2nd ed. New York: Cambridge University Press, 2008.

Gill, Emily R. "Beyond Immutability: Sexuality and Constitutive Choice." *The Review of Politics* 76 (2014): 93–117.

Goodridge v. Dep't of Public Health, 440 Mass. 309 (Mass. 2003).

Greenawalt, Kent. *Private Consciences and Public Reasons*. New York: Oxford University Press, 1995.

Habermas, Jürgen. "Remarks on Legitimation through Human Rights." In *The Postnational Constellation: Political Essays*, edited and translated by Max Pensky Cambridge: Polity Press, 2001.

_____. *Moral Consciousness and Communicative Action*, Translated by Christian Lenhardt and Shierry Weber Nicholsen. Cambridge: MIT Press, 1990.

Halley, Janet. "Behind the Law of Marriage (I): From Status/Contract to the Marriage System." *Unbound: Harvard Journal of the Legal Left* 6 (2010): 1–58.

Jagose, Annamarie. *Queer Theory: An Introduction*. New York: NYU Press, 1997.

Khalsa, Ruth K. "Polygamy as a Red Herring in the Same-Sex Marriage Debate." *Duke Law Journal* 54 (2005): 1665–1693.

Koppelman, Andrew. *The Gay Rights Question in Contemporary American Law*. Chicago: University of Chicago Press, 2002.

Larmore, Charles E. *Patterns of Moral Complexity*. Cambridge: Cambridge University Press, 1987.

Lawrence v . Texas, 539 U.S. 558 (2003).

Lecce, Steven. *Against Perfectionism: Defending Liberal Neutrality*. Toronto: University of Toronto Press, 2008.

Macedo, Stephen. "Sexuality and Liberty: Making Room for Nature and Tradition." In *Sex, Preference, and Family: Essays on Law and Nature* , edited by David M. Estlund and Martha C. Nussbaum. New York: Oxford University Press, 1997: 86–101.

MacIntyre, Alasdair. *After Virtue: A Study in Moral Theory*. 2nd ed. Notre Dame: Notre Dame University Press, 1984.

Maynard v. Hill, 125 U.S. 190 (1888).

Metz, Tamara. *Untying the Knot: Marriage, the State, and the Case for Their Divorce*. Princeton: Princeton Press, 2010.

Obergefell v. Hodges, 135 S. Ct. 2585 (2015).

Posner, Richard. *Sex and Reason*. Cambridge: Harvard University Press, 1992.

Quong, Jonathan. *Liberalism without Perfection*. New York: Oxford University Press, 2011.

Rauch, Jonathan. "Marrying Somebody." In *Same-Sex Marriage: Pro and Con, A Reader*, edited by Andrew Sullivan. New York: Vintage Books, 1997: 285–288.

Rawls, John. *Political Liberalism*. New York: Columbia Press, 1996.

Raz, Joseph. *The Morality of Freedom*. Oxford: Oxford University Press, 1986.

Richards, David A.J. *The Case for Gay Rights: From Bowers to Lawrence and Beyond*. Lawrence: Kansas Press, 2005.

_____. *Identity and the Case for Gay Rights: Race, Gender, Religion as Analogies. Chicago*: University of Chicago Press, 1999.

Rosenblum, Darren. "Queer Intersectionality and the Failure of Recent Lesbian and Gay 'Victories'." *Law & Sexuality: Review Lesbian & Gay Legal Issues* 4 (1994): 83–122.

Sandel, Michael. *Liberalism and the Limits of Justice*. Cambridge: Cambridge Press, 1982.

Schweber, Howard. *Democracy and Authenticity: Toward a Theory of Public Justification*. New York: Cambridge University Press, 2012.

Sher, George. *Beyond Neutrality*: *Perfectionism and Politics* New York: Cambridge Press, 1997.

Singer, Joseph William. "Same Sex Marriage, Full Faith and Credit, and the Evasion of Obligation." *Stanford Journal of Civil Rights and Civil Liberties* 1 (2005): 1–50.

Solum, Lawrence B. "Constructing an Ideal of Public Reason." *San Diego Law Review* 30 (1993): 729–762.

Sullivan, Andrew. "The Conservative Case for Gay Marriage." *Time*, June 30, 2003.

_____. "Three's a Crowd." In *Same-Sex Marriage: Pro and Con, A Reader*, edited by Andrew Sullivan. New York: Vintage Books, 1997: 278–282.

Walker, Adrian. "Give Partners the Right to Marry." *Boston Globe*, March 9, 2000.

Warner, Michael. *The Trouble with Normal: Sex, Politics, and the Ethics of Queer Life*. Cambridge: Harvard Press, 1999.

Wedgwood, Ralph. "The Fundamental Argument for Same-Sex Marriage." *Journal of Political Philosophy* 7 (1999): 225–242.

Wilson, James Q. *The Moral Sense*. New York: The Free Press, 1995.

Wolfson, Evan. *Why Marriage Matters? America, Equality, and Gay People's Right to Mary*. New York: Simon & Schuster, 2004.

_____. "Crossing the Threshold: Equal Marriage Rights For Lesbians and Gay Men and the Intra-Community Critique." *New York University Review of Law and Social Change* 21 (1994): 568–615.

TWO

Progressive Polygamy in Western United States

Janet Bennion

In his dissent in *Lawrence v. Texas*, Justice Antonin Scalia warned that decriminalization of homosexual practices would lead in directions that no one had anticipated.[1] It would appear, based on the recent decision in *Brown v. Buhman*, that he was prescient.[2] If nationalization of same-sex marriage has put America on a slippery slope toward decriminalizing polygamy, what would be the relative costs to women and children, and society as a whole? Media images of Warren Jeffs's raping a 12 year old in Texas and Winston Blackmore's contracting "marriages" of 13 and 14 year olds in Canada has painted a rather disturbing picture of the polygamous lifestyle. However, these images are hardly representative of polygamous culture as a whole. In this chapter, I shall challenge the popular belief, which also is shared by many academics, that Fundamentalist Mormon polygyny necessarily subordinates women. Indeed, the data reveals a considerably more complicated picture of how certain polygynists live. At the very least, these findings not only challenge the conventional wisdom about Fundamentalist Mormon polygyny in the United States but also explain why such polygyny could become more progressive in the near future.

BRIEF LITERATURE REVIEW

Scholars have come at the question of the relative benefits and harms of polygamy from different angles. Social psychologist Irv Altman focused on the complexity of relationships among the Apostolic United Brethren (the Allredites), emphasizing how these families struggled to fit into a polygamous structure using Victorian psychological frameworks developed in a monogamous context.[3] William Jankowiak investigated the father-adoration concept in polygamous relationships in Colorado City (also known as Short Creek).[4] Anthropologists Philip Kilbride and Robin Fox were interested in showing the benefits polygamy offers in the context of the crises of American modernity; they emphasized how women choose alternative family forms as a way to cope with the socioeconomic obstacles they confront.[5] Kilbride applauded the adaptive measures polygamists took to share resources and protect themselves from the harsh realities of urban life. My early research explored the unexpected ascendance of women in rigid patriarchal communities, especially how women could gain autonomy and power during the prolonged absences of their husbands.[6] I recorded the experiences of female converts in the Montana Allredite order and found that many women are attracted to the commune because of the socioeconomic support it offers, replacing a rather difficult life in the mainstream where their status as divorcees, single mothers, widows, and "un-marriageable" limited their access to good men, and the spiritual affirmation that comes from a community of worship. I detailed substantial variability in the expressions of polygamy in *Polygamy in Prime Time,* finding that some Mormon women experience more individual satisfaction within the dynamics of a polygamous family than they could in any other marital form.[7] Kilbride's book *Plural Marriage for Our Time: A Reinvented Option* similarly states that plural marriage can help rebuild a strong sense of family for specific groups of Americans, particularly in times of socioeconomic crisis.[8]

HISTORY

Polygamy first arose in the Mormon context in 1831 with Joseph Smith's revelation to restore plural marriage to the earth. Smith, who married at least thirty-three women and had children with thirteen of them, was told to practice "celestial marriage" from the same source that commanded Abraham to bed his handmaid, Hagar, to produce a righteous seed and glorious progeny. Later, when the existence of polygamy blocked Utah's chances for statehood, Wilford Woodruff banned the practice, sending scores of poly families underground or to prison. The fundamentalists are a vestige of an original Council of Friends, led by Lorin C. Woolley, to preserve the old-time Joseph Smith doctrines of god-making, united order, and plural marriage. Those who join them must consecrate all their assets to be "worthy to have their names written in the book of the law of God" (LeBaron 1981, 166).[9]

Polygamy is practiced by only 2.5 percent of North Americans from a range of religious and national backgrounds, but the practice of plural marriage occupies a disproportionately large space in the public and legal imagination. Reality television shows like *Sister Wives, My Five Wives,* and *Polygamy, USA* normalize the polygamous unit, showing seemingly happy, thriving and relatively self-aware families with little apparent abuse or underage marriage. For the first time, the public is able to see the emergence of a new polygamy, depicting women as the decision makers who operate in the public sphere with careers and political ambitions, questioning the adage that polygamy per se uniformly causes harm. Although polygamy was the object of intense legal actions between the 1930s and 1950s, law enforcement made no effort to arrest polygamists between 1960 and 2001. In fact, as these reality programs illustrate, there is less verified child abuse among all the Utah churches and offshoots than among priests who passed through Cardinal Law's diocese in the city of Boston alone. This lack of interest in prosecuting polygamists causes many to question criminalization of polygamy and the validity of *Reynolds v. United States,* which still allows states to ban polygamy even in our era of modern religious freedom.[10] It has also become difficult to justify banning polygamy when so many other forms of marriage, intimacy, and sexuality are tolerated.[11] In December of 2013, U.S. District Court Judge Clark Waddoups ruled in *Brown v Buhman* that part of Utah's ban on polygamy was unconstitutional.[12] This change was brought about by a lawsuit filed by the Kody Brown family, one of the cases analyzed in this paper. While the law still prohibits holding more than one marriage license at a time, cohabitation with more than one consenting adult is now decriminalized in part of the United States. The ruling raises deeper questions about the relationship between "church and state" in western societies. It restructures the formation of marriage where religion retains a presence in the law so that polygamists will no longer be prosecuted for *religiously* based cohabitation. But their plural "marriages" are still considered unofficial, unrecognized. Although Kody Brown and his wives live polygamy for religious reasons, the state is determined to deny this right.

Justice Waddoups's decision in *Brown v. Buhman* is a mixed blessing. He crafted a rather Victorian understanding of marriage, limiting how marriage is legally defined. For him, the state's marriage license as the essential action or condition of marriage itself, regardless of religious ritual or intent. Through that action, the state holds a monopoly over marriage, dictating the terms of social recognition. Waddoups stated, "The one and only factor that is officially indicative of marriage is the marriage license which must be present before any kind of solemnization ritual has the legal effect creating a marriage, and fraudulently obtaining more than one license constitutes bigamy."[13] Thus, Waddoups's decision limits the use of religiously sanctioned marriage or any unions from past cultural and legal practice and restricts the possibilities of non-hetero and non-mononormative alternatives. In his ruling, Waddoups also disconnected the relationship between religion and marriage, ironically maintaining the legal boundaries of Christian-based monogamy. So, though the *Brown* decision was a victory for poly families who wish to avoid arrest, it is a pyrrhic one, as the greater battle is still to come—full legal recognition.

Could polygamy be considered as a viable tool for women to juggle careers and motherhood and for single women, who normally would not be able to marry, to find a solution to the so-called "lack of good men" dilemma? Or, is the recent verdict of the British Columbia polygamy trial in 2010 and what many feminist scholars, like Maura Strassberg, suggest is true: that polygamy itself is uniformly abusive to women and children?[14]

In the rest of this chapter, I provide evidence of the viability of the poly form by identifying five cases of progressive polygamy in Utah. In doing so, I examine the factors contributing to the emergence of such progressivity, which have not yet been appreciated. Antipolygamists often overemphasize the patriarchal nature of polygyny, stating that it is uniformly abusive to women and children and at its best, is incompatible with a commitment to gender equality. But there is considerable ethnographic evidence to the contrary; as it turns out, many forms of polygamy actually foster female empowerment and choice. These forms were ignored in the British Columbia trial of 2010 or said to be epiphenomenal, only standing for a minority of cases.[15] My research reveals that most of the polygamist families in North America represent a more benign version of poly, one where women and children are not abused, but live happy, productive, and relatively carefree, satisfying lives.

DEFINITION AND METHODS

I define progressive polygamy as a poly family that recently exited a rigidly patriarchal group, typically living in the Intermountain West, which then subsequently adopted a more feminine, holistic mindset where men have a reduced control over productive and reproductive resources, and women have implemented a strong female network to enable them balance their love of career, family, and a newly developed more generative, global ideology.

I used a purposive sample—drawn from 114 families associated with the Allred Group (Apostolic United Brethren, of Bluffdale, Utah)—who left the group in order to develop an intentionally progressive poly lifestyle. I targeted five extended families, whom I could access through participant observation, and who were also in the public eye (welcoming publicity in the form of a television program, news interview, or public speech). These were citizens who advertised themselves to the world as model, progressive, polygamists and exhibited the following progressive traits:

- women who are both highly educated and career-oriented
- a loosely based faith in the Mormon doctrine of celestial marriage (along with other Eastern ideologies)
- an absence of male supremacy, and an emphasis on female autonomy and economic networking

I used informal interview, participant observation, blogging, and prime time televised viewing to gather data about the lives of the five progressive families. With the exception of four of Alex Josef's wives, all the men and women (a total of 25 individuals) were affiliated in some way with both the Mormon Church and the Allred Group (AUB). Most of the women (14 of 24) had once been active members of the Mormon Church, but converted to polygamy from a lower status position in the mainstream, such as in the case of Robin, Kody Brown's latest wife, who was divorced with children. I compared these disenfranchised fundamentalist women with other marginalized Mormon women from the Utah mainstream described by social demographers Goodman and Heaton in their 1980–1990 study on divorce.[16] The 1986 sample included Mormon women who were divorced, abandoned, widowed, or unmarried. The similarities between the characteristics of my sample of 20 women and the 1986 sample are remarkable. In both cases, women were highly educated with career ambitions, had been trained in a post-feminist Mormonism (after the revelation by Ezra Taft Benson that gave women the right to covenant to God directly, and not through their husbands), and were accustomed to wearing the slimmer, more contemporary garment. They also more easily blended into the mainstream, wearing clothing and donning attitudes consistent with modern feminist Mormonism of the Salt Lake City region.

At the same time, the five polygynous cases surpassed the Goodman women in several ways. In all of my sample, there appeared to be a loosened or weakened patriarchal hold over women and children, women were accustomed to using female models of empowerment, and there was, in most cases, a lose adherence to Mormon doctrine, often accompanied by a "hippie," neo-pagan, and/or Eastern ideology.[17]

A CASE STUDY OF FIVE FAMILIES

The Rod Williams Family

Rod Williams is a disenfranchised polygamist and Nixon-era Secret Service agent. He left the Allred Group after its prophet, Owen Allred, died, chaffing at the more rigid policies of the new prophet, Lemoine Jensen. Rod took his three wives—Stella, Deana, and Nora—and nine children out of Utah, and now lives a non-fundamentalist lifestyle in the backwoods of the Olympic Peninsula of Washington, near Port Angeles. They reside in a 5000 sq. foot home consisting of three separate apartments for each of his three wives. Recently, after twenty years of marriage, Deana, his third wife, left him for another woman.

Rod and his wives do not follow a strict Mormon code. In fact, they drink wine occasionally, and sometimes coffee. They do not hold worship services, but still incorporate faith-based prayer and an occasional fast, when emergency requires it. When Deana came out of the closet as a lesbian, the family accepted her and arranged a way for her and her new lover to continue being part of the family, though they live in a separate dwelling. Rod's attitude in his family life is to promote the will and wants of his wives, often giving them the reins of business and domestic decisions. Nora, his third wife, manages all the finances and the family business, an immigrant information bureau. The family also has begun to separate their poly philosophy from Mormon doctrine, practicing instead a form of non-denominational Unitarian-style ideology, incorporating Native American, Eastern mystic, and libertarian/hippy concepts about living off the grid.

The Brady Williams Family

Rod's eldest son Brady Williams lives in Rocky Ridge, an Allred/AUB enclave near the town of Santaquin, Utah. Brady and his five wives recently came out to the world about their poly lifestyle in their TLC reality show *My Five Wives*, depicting the most progressive form so far, incorporating Eastern philosophies and feminism. They practice female priesthood and four of the five women have careers, as well as 24 children among them.

Brady and his five wives felt that the fundamentalist doctrine no longer fed them the spiritual and social food they needed to progress fully, as a family, and as individuals. Indeed, Brady and his wives believe so fervently in the actualization of selfhood that they have adopted a blend of Buddhism and liberal Mormonism, where the evolution of the soul and families are forever and both are revered. Brady and his family left the AUB a few years ago, claiming it also to be too rigid for his family. Still, they live in the order's housing (all construction projects belong to the AUB, even if the individual who occupies the home actually built it).

Brady views the recent attempts to decriminalize polygamy as a positive opportunity for his family to be accepted by the larger mainstream culture. As he puts it, "We are no longer considered criminals by the courts. Let's prove that we are deserving of that assessment by abandoning those darker practices of traditional polygamy that have haunted us for so long."[18] He and his wives condemn backwards polygamy, which incorporates child brides and arranged marriages, calling it a "damnable practice."

Brady and his family believe that women are equal to men, not a sub class to be used by men, but every bit men's superiors. They also feel that polygamy doesn't necessarily breed misogyny and patriarchy but can represent feminist ideologies, and empowerment for women, depending upon the beliefs, practices, and circumstances of the members of the family. The Williams are calling for a "New Polygamy" that embraces equality and freedom which can energize people to "new levels of awakening. Find the courage to transform yourselves into agents of change . . . become noble ambassadors of justice and peace in this world by embracing the ways love and equality as taught by our prime exemplar, Jesus Christ."[19]

The Joe Darger Family

Joe Darger married twin sisters—Vicki and Valerie—and their first cousin, Alina. The four spouses live in Salt Lake City, Utah with their 24 children. The family believes in empathy in accepting each other's loving feelings for each spouse, akin to what has now become known in anthropology as "compersion," the act of taking pleasure in—or at least empathy with—your companion's love of another.[20] Valerie, who joined the family 22 years after her twin had married Joe, said she knew Joe would be a good husband because he treated her sister so well. And, since the twins often liked the same type of man, it made sense that they both marry Joe. Alina and Joe courted back in the 1990s, and as she was close to the twins, it was an easy transition. In the end, it was a four-way friendship of respect and nurturance.

Joe was attracted to all three women (all of whom look nearly identical) and knew that individual relationships would develop in time. All three women have their own bedroom, and Joe alternates between the three rooms each evening. Because of their mutual respect, the women say they have no jealousies. They seek each other's happiness and all three wives were raised in a poly culture where it is not strange for siblings and cousins to share husbands.

A few years ago, the Dargers came out to their community as a poly family, fighting to decriminalize plural marriage. Although affiliated with the AUB, they became independent, hoping to show how their version of polygamy categorically differs from the type practiced by Warren Jeffs, who forced underage teens to marriage vastly older males against their will. The narrative of *Big Love*—written, interestingly, by two gay Mormon men—was, in part, inspired by the Darger family (and part by my depiction of the Rod Williams family), because of the family's emphasis on feminism and a more liberal version of fundamentalism. Together, the Dargers have 25 children, including five children from Valerie's other marriage.

The Kody Brown Family

Kody Brown and his family, like the Williams and Darger families, parallel the "progressive" philosophies of Bill Hendrickson in HBO's *Big Love* series in many ways.[21] Kody is an emotionally expressive, negotiator-type personality, just like Rod and Joe. He actively listens to his wives and implements their suggestions. Indeed, most of the time, he lets the women lead in household and family matters. All four families (including the fictive Hendricksons from *Big Love*) involve an independent polygynist leaving the larger group to provide his wives and children with a more liberal and open expression of fundamentalist life. Kody and his four wives—Meri, Janelle, Christine, and Robyn—and their 16 children, are progressive by contemporary political standards; they call themselves feminists, and are also in favor of gay marriage, female autonomy, and promoting career paths for women. The Browns came out to the world in their reality television show, *Sister Wives* with the hope that their children will find the experience liberating. Although the show alienated them from the AUB leadership, for the time being, the Browns have succeeded in overturning the ban on polygamy in Utah and continue to fight for poly family rights in terms of housing, employment, and putting an end to the stigma generated against them from the mainstream culture.

In the primetime show, viewers were able to see that many of these struggles were common to any monogamous marriage. The wives discuss infertility problems and teenage rebellion and jealousy issues. Kody and his wives manage a marriage that is both dyadic and communal; each wife has her own separate apartment in the same home. The wives often talk about the benefits of having sister wives. The arrangement allows Janelle to work long hours outside the home without having to worry about cooking and cleaning; it gives Meri the peace of mind that if anything should happen to her, the two other mothers will be there to raise her daughter; and it allowed Christine to stay home when she was pregnant and keep house without worrying about the need to generate more family income. "I never wanted to just be married to one man," says Christine, who recently had a baby. She is glad to be Kody's third wife because she never wanted to be alone with a husband and the third wife balances out the tension between the first two. "I always wanted sister wives," she says. "There's too many things I wanted to do, to be free for."[22] In sum, the Brown family represents many of the characteristics of a progressive American family: open ideas about religion and marriage, female networking and collaboration, and an absence of rigid patriarchy or a narrow gendered division of labor that is supposed to characterize all Fundamentalist Mormon polygamy.

The Alex Joseph Family

Alex Joseph, was the mayor of Big Water, Utah, married eight wives, and has 14 children. Although raised in the Greek Orthodox Church, he was baptized into Mormonism in his teens and joined the AUB in the 1970s. He married four college students of University of Montana (who were non-Mormon) and then left the AUB to live independently in Big Water, Utah, eventually taking four more wives. The careers of his wives include a registered nurse, a schoolteacher, a lawyer, a ski instructor, and a Kentucky beauty contest winner.

All his wives are college-educated and outspoken advocates of feminist ideals of autonomy and the female network. Elizabeth Joseph, for example, was an attorney and teacher, and is now a journalist. She was the keynote speaker at the National Organization of Women conference in 1997. Joseph's wives have full volition and choice, having been independent adults with their own ideas about how to change the world and contribute to their family. All wives entered into their marriages of their own accord rather than being coerced or designated by a paternal authority. Joseph actively encouraged his wives to be very independent. He was also open about his polygamist lifestyle, instead of being secretive, and welcomed media coverage, believing that it is his constitutional right and because "he wants public opinion on his side."[23]

PROFILE OF A PROGRESSIVE POLY FAMILY

What do all these families have in common? What factors contributed to the development of a more liberal, progressive framework? The most significant findings among the five extended polygynous families observed were that the women had selected liberally minded patriarchs/husbands who believed in female-led households, female autonomy, and a more relaxed version of priesthood power. All five husbands (Rod, Brady, Joe, Kody, and Alex) exhibited signs of ENFP personalities (extraverted feelers who operate on intuition and non-goal oriented processes) that took pleasure in their wives' control of the household and sexual matters.[24] Further, the family philosophy and faith-based worship incorporated a more liberal ideological interpretation of Mormonism, including Eastern mysticism, goddesshood, female priesthood, hypergamy, and polyandry.[25]

These families also encourage female ascendancy, exhibiting a lowered male supremacy or a tendency towards loosening the reins of priesthood power and allowing women to take charge of the budgeting, sexual rotation, and household maintenance. Many of these characteristics emerged due to the influence of Owen Allred, the current atmosphere of tolerance for alternative sexuality, the presence of feminism and the female network, and an emphasis on secular education.

Owen Allred and the Apostolic United Brethren

All of the progressives have operated under the influence of Owen Allred, a kind-hearted, urbane, and politically shrewd prophet of the Apostolic United Brethren, Utah's second largest polygamous group, a church with some 5,000 to 7,000 believers, located in Bluffdale, on the edge of Salt Lake City. Allred initiated an era of openness or "glasnost" in 1989 when he invited me to freely access his northern order and ask questions about the group. He accompanied this openness with a new rule about marriage: that no man could acquire a wife that was under 18 years of age and she (the new wife) had to give full consent and select her own husband out of the pool of married and unmarried men in the community. Additionally, Allred introduced no-fault, free release divorce in the community so that women could leave an unwanted husband. He promoted the Brigham Young rule of hypergamy so that women could marry up in the system, selecting a man with more money, better priesthoods, and more favorable wife companions. Allred also asked me to assist him in an internal investigation of child sexual abuse and domestic violence, requiring a survey to be distributed among extended families to flush out any inappropriate behaviors related to the Jay and Thompson years of abuse that left so much embarrassment. To this day, the only occurrence of an abusive case was when a man from Alaska intruded in on the Pinesdale community and attacked a young girl. He was arrested by the Sheriff of Ravaille County (with the cooperation of the Allredite leadership).

Under Owen Allred's tenure, the Allred group does not force men to become polygamous to attain priesthood glory, as do the FLDS and Kingston groups. In fact, most men are gratefully monogamous, recognizing how difficult the poly life can be, having watched their fathers struggle trying to please so many wives. Allred also condoned the practice of living in Babylon among Mormons and gentiles of the mainstream and obtaining a secular education. It is from this more open-minded Allredesque model that the five progressive families sprang.

Adoption of Feminism and New Age Philosophies

Another influence on the five progressive families is the cultural and political norm of embracing alternative sexuality and marriage. The Twenty-First Century is an era of "rights to privacy," modish "tolerance" and "multiculturalism," with special attention on feminist ideals. Many feminist scholars are now arguing for legalizing polygamy, saying it would actually help protect, empower, and strengthen women, children, and families.[26] Polygamist women are now labeling themselves as modern progressives and suggest that polygamy allows them freedom outside the home, providing the perfect feminist template. After all, many real monogamous intimate relationships are far from egalitarian in practice. Elizabeth Joseph, the journalist married to Alex Joseph mentioned in the last case, indicates that without polygamy, some modern American women would be deprived of personal choices. For her, polygamy provides an opportunity to maximize female potential without the tradeoffs and compromises that one finds in monogamy. She is friends with her co-wives and can work outside the home. With her co-wives to care for her husband and children, she is free to pursue her career. The Brown wives also find polygamy to be conducive to feminism, saying it is mutually beneficial. There is a strong sense of feminist cooperation and community. They have a built-in, reliable daycare system. The majority of the wives in the five cases are college-educated and outspoken.

All five cases exhibit a loose interpretation of the Mormon doctrine, sprinkled with various combinations of Buddhism and Native American ideologies, especially as they favor female empowerment and a close relationship to the earth. This new direction of liberal, progressive Mormon polygyny reflects female conversion from the more educated, more career-oriented Mormon mainstream community, which produces an excess of disenfranchised widows, divorcees, and un-marriageables that look to polygyny, ironically, for sources of empowerment, access to a liberal "Savior on Mt. Zion," female networking, and ideologies that give rise to Eastern concepts of the divine self. There also seems to be a connection between urban centers and progressive Mormon thought. For example, Salt Lake City is much more politically liberal than many rural areas, where the *Salt Lake Tribune* often criticizes conservative thinking. The exception, of course, is Utah Valley, housing the sprawling twin cities of Orem/Provo, where some of the most conservative, traditional values are espoused.

CONCLUSION

A new form of Mormon polygamy, which emphasizes progressive feminist values and New Age, secular ideologies, has emerged in the Intermountain States region of the United States in the last 25 years. This poly form owes its existence to the influx of disenfranchised female converts from mainstream orthodox Mormonism, the influence of Prophet Owen Allred, and increased urban-based secularization. The growth of the form varies directly with increases in the numbers of marginalized mainstream women in Salt Lake and Utah Counties.[27]

This study has implications for legalization of poly forms of marriage. It also raises questions about the variability in poly forms and the demographics of alienated women in American mainstream monogamy. While polygamy can sometimes be a source of oppression for women, to oversimplify the practice and construe it as necessarily generating abuse is not only inaccurate but unproductive. Instead, by attending to the nuances and variance of experience and relying on the diversity of women's voices, scholars and policymakers might be more successful in both rooting out the causes of harm, raising awareness, and increasing tolerance for alternative lifestyles that have little in common with the crimes of Warren Jeffs and Winston Blackmore.

NOTES

1. *Lawrence v. Texas*, 539 U.S. 558 (2003).
2. *Brown v. Buhman*, Case No. 2:11-cv-0652-CW (2013).
3. Irwin Altman and Joseph Ginat, *Polygamous Families in Contemporary Society* (New York: Cambridge University Press.
4. William Jankowiak and Emilie Allen, "The Balance of Duty and Desire in an American Polygamous Community," in *Romantic Passion: A Universal Experience*? ed. William Jankowiak (New York: Columbia University Press, 1995): 166-186.
5. Philip Kilbride, *Plural Marriage for Our Times: A Reinvented Option?* (Westport: Bergin and Garvey, 1994); Robin Fox, *Reproduction and Succession* (New Brunswick, NJ: Transaction Publishers, 1993).
6. Janet Bennion, *Women of Principle: Female Networking in Contemporary Mormon Polygyny* (Oxford: Oxford University Press, 1998).
7. Janet Bennion, *Polygamy in Primetime* (Waltham: Brandeis University Press, 2012).
8. Kilbride, *Plural Marriage for Our Times*.
9. Verlan LeBaron, *The LeBaron Story* (TX: Keels, 1981).
10. *Reynolds v. United States*, 98 U.S. 166 (1879).
11. *Obergefell* requires all states to issue marriage licenses to same-sex couples and to recognize same-sex marriages validly performed in other jurisdictions. *Obergefell v. Hodges*, 135 U.S. 2584 (2015).
12. Subsequently, Utah appealed the decision, hoping that the three-judge panel would reverse the trial court's decision.
13. *Brown v. Buhman*, Case No. 2:11-cv-0652-CW (2013), 58.
14. Maura Strassberg, "Why the U.S. Should Not Decriminalize Polygamy, but Should Not Criminalize Polyamory" (paper presented at the Polygamy, Polygyny, and Polyamory conference, Brandeis University, Waltham, Massachusetts, November 7, 2010).
15. Lori Beaman, "Opposing Polygamy: A Matter of Equality or Patriarchy?" in *The Polygamy Question*, ed. Janet Bennion and Lisa Fishbayn-Joffe (Logan: Utah State University Press, 2015): 42-61.
16. Kristen L. Goodman and Tim B. Heaton, "Divorce," in *Utah in Demographic Perspective,* ed. Thomas K. Martin et. al. (Salt Lake City: Signature Books, 1986): 121-144.
17. Granted, the sample was small; it was made up of only those willing to speak out about their lifestyles in primarily urban areas and not those still choosing to live quietly in rural settings. Further, the form of marriage is illegal and has consequences for losing employment and livelihood. Thus, a larger, more representative, sample could not have been obtained without duress and complications to lifestyles.
18. Although the Facebook post of 2013 has been altered recently, the quotation can also be found on the Williams' family website: http://www.bradyandwives.com/our-blog/time-to-grow-up-the-polygamist-dilemma.

19. Williams' family website: http://www.bradyandwives.com/our-blog/time-to-grow-up-the-polygamist-dilemma.

20. The reference of "compersion" is used widely at poly conventions but can be summed up as "the idea of our partner deriving pleasure separate from us and from another source." http://www.huffingtonpost.com/gracie-x/compersion-a-polyamorous-principle-that-can-strengthen-any-relationship_b_6803868.html.

21. In the last episode, right before he dies, Hendrickson's character, played by Bill Paxton, accepts his first wife's being part of the priesthood. While Kody Brown has not made this leap, Brady Williams, another reality television polygamist, already has mentioned his intention to do so.

22. Barbara Hall, "Preface to 'Summer'," *Canadian Diversity* 8 (2010): 3-5.

23. Sara Davidson, "The Man with Ten Wives," http://www.saradavidson.com/the-man-with-ten-wives.

24. See the "Myers-Briggs personality test," http://www.humanmetrics.com/cgi-win/jtypes2.asp

25. Hypergamy is where women are allowed to marry up in the system. In the case of fundamentalism, this means that wives can leave their husbands for a better man with more temporal and spiritual resources. Polyandry is where a woman can take more than one man as a husband/lover. In the case of Mormon-based polygamy, Joseph Smith provided a nineteenth-century template for convincing married women to marry either him, or another man of their choice. In fundamentalism, similar patterns exist: men allow their wives to have lovers or be wed to two men.

26. See Beaman, "Opposing Polygamy," 42-61; Bennion, *Polygamy in Primetime*; Angela Campbell, *Polygamy in Canada: Legal and Social Implications for Women and Children*, http://www.vancouversun.com/pdf/polygamy_021209.

27. I used the Pearson Correlation Coefficient to test the strength of a linear association between percentage of unmarried, divorced, widowed women—Goodman, Heaton 1986; Haight, 1984—and the growth of progressive-style polygamy, emerging in the last 25 years among independents and AUB members. The growth of disenfranchised mainstream women correlated with the growth in the number of progressive families (r=0.57).

REFERENCES

Al-Krenawi, Alean, et al. "Success and Failure among Polygamous Families." *Family Process* 45 (2006): 311–330.

Altman, Irwin, and Joseph Ginat. *Polygamous Families in Contemporary Society.* Cambridge: Cambridge University Press, 1996.

Bailey, Martha. "Dossier: Should Polygamy be Recognized in Canada? Ethical and Legal Considerations." *Printemps* 2 (2007):18–21.

Beaman, Lori. "Opposing Polygamy: A Matter of Equality or Patriarchy?" In *The Polygamy Question.* Edited byJanet Bennion and Lisa Fishbayn-Joffe, 42–61. Logan: Utah State University Press, 2015).

Bennion, Janet. *Women of Principle: Female Networking in Contemporary Mormon Polygamy.* Oxford: Oxford University Press, 1998.

_____. *Desert Patriarchy: Gender Dynamics in the Chihuahua Valley.* Tucson: University of Arizona Press, 2004.

_____. *Polygamy in Primetime.* Waltham: Brandeis University Press, 2012.

Campbell, Angela, et al. *Polygamy in Canada: Legal and Social Implications for Women and Children: A Collection of Policy Research Reports.* Ottawa: Status of Women Canada, 2005. http://www.vancouversun.com/pdf/ polygamy_021209.pdf.

Cook, Rebecca, and Lisa M. Kelly. *Polygyny and Canada's Obligations under International Human Rights Law.* Family, Children, and Youth Section Research Report. [Toronto]: Department of Justice of Canada, 2006. http://www.justice.gc.ca/eng/dept-min/pub/poly/poly.pdf.

Davidson, Sara. "The Man with Ten Wives ." http://www.saradavidson.com/the-man-with-ten-wives.

Davis, Adrienne. "Regulating Polygamy: Intimacy, Default Rules, and Bargaining for Equality." *Columbia Law Review* 110 (2010): 1955–1986.

Dixon-Spear, Patricia. *We Want for Our Sisters What We Want for Ourselves: African American Women Who Practice Polygyny by Consent.* Baltimore: Black Classic Press, 2009.

Dobner, Jennifer. "'Sister Wives' Family Investigated for Bigamy." *MSNBC,* September 29, 2010. http://today.msnbc.msn.com/id/39418047/ns/ today-entertainment/t/ sister-wives-family investigated-bigamy.

Driggs, Ken. "Twenty Years of Observations about the Fundamentalist Polygamists." In *Modern Polygamy in the United States: Historical, Cultural, and Legal Issues,* edited by Cardell Jacobson. New York: Oxford University Press, 2011: 77–100.

Duncan, Emily. "The Positive Effects of Legalizing Polygamy: 'Love Is a Many Splendored Thing'." *Duke Journal of Gender Law and Policy* 15 (2008): 315–337.

Fox, Robin. *Reproduction and Succession.* New Brunswick: Transaction Publishers, 1993.

Gage-Brandon, Anastasia J. "The Polygyny-Divorce Relationship: A Case Study of Nigeria." *Journal of Marriage and the Family* 54 (1992): 282–292.

Gordon, Sarah. *The Mormon Question: Polygamy and Constitutional Conflict in Nineteenth Century America.* Chapel Hill: University of North Carolina Press, 2001.

Hassouneh-Phillips, Dena. "Polygamy and Wife Abuse: A Qualitative Study of Muslim Women in America." *Health Care for Women International* 22 (2001): 735–748.

Jankowiak, William, and E. Allen. "The Balance of Duty and Desire in an American Polygamous Community." In *Romantic Passion: A Universal Experience?* edited by William Jankowiak. New York: Columbia University Press, 1995: 166–186.

Jankowiak, William, and Monique Diderich. "Sibling Solidarity in a Polygamous Community in the USA." *Evolution & Human Behavior* 21 (2000):125–139.

Kanazawa, Satoshi, and Mary Still. "Why Monogamy?" *Social Forces* 78 (1999): 25–50.

Keller, James. "Canada Should Legalize Polygamy: Study." *CTV News,* January 13, 2006.

Kilbride, Philip. *Plural Marriage for Our Times: A Reinvented Option?* Westport: Bergin and Garvey, 1994.

Malaysian Insider. "More Wives = Less Adultery and Prostitution?" *Malaysian Insider* November 19, 2009. http://www.themalaysianinsider.com/ litee/malaysia/article/ More-wives-less-adultery-and-prostitution.

Martin, Wednesday. "Co-Wife Conflict: Why It's Easy to Hate the 'Other Woman.'" *Psychology Today,* December 1, 2009.

Smith, Linda. "Child Protection Law and the FLDS Raid in Texas." In *Modern Polygamy in the United States: Historical, Cultural, and Legal Issues,* edited by Cardell Jacobson. New York: Oxford University Press, 2011: 301–330.

Song, Sarah. "Should the US Decriminalize Polygamy? Considerations from the Mormon Case." Paper presented at the conference "Polygamy, Polygyny, and Polyamory," Brandeis University, Waltham, Massachusetts, November 7, 2010.

Stacey, Judith, and Tey Meadow. "New Slants on the Slippery Slope: The Politics of Polygamy and Gay Family Rights in South Africa and the Unites States." *Politics & Society* 37 (2009): 167–202.

Strassberg, Maura. "Why the U.S. Should Not Decriminalize Polygamy, but Should Not Criminalize Polyamory." Paper presented at the conference "Polygamy, Polygyny, and Polyamory," Brandeis University, Waltham, Massachusetts, November 7, 2010.

Thornhill, Randy, and Craig Palmer. *A Natural History of Rape.* Cambridge: MIT Press, 2000.

Thornton, Arland. "The International Fight against Barbarism." In *Modern Polygamy in the United States: Historical, Cultural, and Legal Issues,* edited by Cardell Jacobson. New York: Oxford University Press, 2011: 259–300.

Turley, Jonathan. "Polygamy Laws Expose Our Hypocrisy." *USA Today*, October 4, 2004.

U.S. Census. 2010. "Families and Living Arrangements." *U.S. Census Bureau*. http://www.census.gov/population.

Zeitzen, Miriam K. *Polygamy: A Cross-Cultural Analysis*. Oxford: Berg Publishers, 2008.

THREE

Plural Marriage, Exemptions, and the Redundancy of the Free Exercise Clause

Ronald C. Den Otter

These days, lawmakers rarely intentionally discriminate against religious minorities.[1] In cases involving the meaning of the Free Exercise Clause (hereinafter, "FEC"), judges must decide whether a law of general applicability, which incidentally burdens religious behavior, merits an exemption.[2] According to the accommodationist view developed by Michael McConnell, any law that has that impact ought to be presumptively unconstitutional.[3] As a consequence, the state would have to grant an exemption from a generally-applicable law to a religious objector who could prove that he has sincere religious reasons for wanting to do (or not to do) something provided that the law in question also substantially burdens his proposed action.[4] For example, if a Fundamentalist Mormon could prove the sincerity of his belief that he has a religious duty to marry more than one person at the same time (or that she has a duty to marry someone who already is married), it would seem to follow that a law that does not permit polygamy is unconstitutional, unless the state could establish that it has an important interest in disallowing such a marital arrangement. The accommodationist view, which assumes that religion is special, provides considerable constitutional protection for religiously-motivated conduct, including the right to plural marriage.

However, a growing number of legal scholars reject this assumption.[5] As far as they are concerned, accommodationists have failed to adequately defend their position that religion merits more favorable treatment. After all, it appears that deeply-held but secular convictions can play the same role even for someone who is not religious, namely to guide the most important personal decisions and imbue her life with meaning. The accommodationist approach to constitutionally-required exemptions is vulnerable to the objection that a more inclusive term, such as "freedom of conscience," better captures the normativity of the FEC in a morally diverse society. A less narrow interpretation of "religion" has the advantage of treating more Americans, like atheists, agnostics, and the practitioners of non-theistic religions, fairly.

This chapter elaborates on why religion is not special by showing how accommodationists have not answered the most serious objection to their view: religion does not have to be defined so narrowly for purposes of exemptions. If religion is not special, then the religious nature of the personal reason of, say, a Fundamentalist Mormon for seeking a plural marriage does not differ from the non-religious personal reason of a polyamorist for wanting the same marital arrangement.[6] Constitutionally, they are equivalent. Both personal reasons could be distinguished in other ways, of course, like their sincerity, their epistemic support, or the intensity with which they are held, but their religious nature, or lack thereof, would be beside the point. The nature of the objector's personal reason for demanding an exemption, in other words, no longer would make any constitutional difference.

In the context of the coming debate over whether states may limit marriage to couples, the implication is that any state's only allowing religiously-motivated polygynists to marry would constitute unequal treatment. States must allow all plural marriage enthusiasts to marry, regardless of their personal reasons for wanting to do so, or they must deny all of them such a right.[7] As I shall argue, in terms of constitutionally-mandated exemptions, no independent free exercise of religion argument for a constitutional right to plural marriage exists. The FEC is redundant inasmuch as it cannot do any additional normative or legal work in explaining why states cannot limit marriage to couples. Advocates of plural marriage will have to look elsewhere for constitutional support.

This chapter shall be divided into the following sections. First, I discuss free exercise of religion doctrine to provide some background for my constitutional analysis. In doing so, I sketch the Court's most important free exercise decisions over the last fifty years and discern the themes that underlie them. Second, I give an overview of the *Reynolds* decision, make the case that it is not nearly as important as it initially appears to be, and begin to explain why those, who believe that a constitutional right to plural marriage exists, cannot rely on the FEC. Third, I describe the appeal of "freedom of conscience" as a less parochial alternative to "religion." I then share some thoughts on why a free exercise of religion argument, situated in the debate over legal recognition of plural marriage, really is a freedom of personal choice argument, when, for purposes of constitutionally-mandated "religion" exemptions, religious personal reasons are not special and ought not be treated as such.

FREE EXERCISE OF RELIGION DOCTRINE

The Short Life of Constitutionally-Mandated Religious Exemptions

The issues of how, why, and when to accommodate religiously-motivated conduct will continue to be salient as long as many Americans conceive of themselves as religious and want to act on their respective religious beliefs. Any liberal society is committed to tolerating at least some religious, moral, and cultural differences. One that does not make a serious effort to do so would be liberal in name only. Under such circumstances, a coherent approach, to deciding when lawmakers must make room for religiously-motivated behavior, is called for. The trouble is that formulating such an approach is easier said than done, as evidenced by the failure of lawmakers and judges to do so in the past. The doctrine surrounding the religion clauses is a patchwork and the issue of when to grant an exemption from a generally-applicable law is no exception.[8] Just about everyone agrees that every now and then, religious freedom ought to be sheltered from legislative encroachment, but there is nothing like a consensus with respect to real cases. The harder the case, the more reasonable disagreement becomes inevitable. Until 1990, the debate over how to understand the FEC and apply it to new fact patterns took the form of when religious practices had to be permitted, even when a particular religious group had not been intentionally targeted for discriminatory treatment.

At present, the FEC does not compel the federal government or states to accommodate religious conduct.[9] After *Sherbert v. Verner* in 1963, for the next twenty-seven years, the burden of proof was on the state to prove that it could not grant such an exemption.[10] In *Smith v. Employment Division*, better known as the peyote case, the Court returned the country to a pre-*Sherbert* regime in which government could grant such exemptions, if it so desired, but did not have to do so.[11] For most accommodationists, though, legislatively-created exemptions fail to sufficiently protect religious freedom. Indeed, they insist that the need for constitutionally-required exemptions may be greater than ever before in the midst of the proliferation of statutes, many of which overreach.[12] According to McConnell, government must remove legislative obstacles to a religious practice unless there is adequate justification for their existence.[13] In his view, the state should grant as many exemptions as possible without sliding so far down the slippery slope that the state must always accommodate, regardless of the strength of its countervailing interest. Additionally, this more generous approach in making exceptions to generally-applicable rules is more likely to shield religious minorities from indirect discrimination, understood as disparate impact. As he puts it, "A constitutional interpretation that *requires* [his emphasis] accommodations extends this treatment to religious faiths less able to protect themselves in the political area."[14]

Along similar lines, critics of *Smith* point out that a law that only indirectly interferes with religiously-motivated conduct is almost as troubling as a law that intentionally discriminates against a religious minority. In both instances, the effect is that people cannot act according to their sincere religious convictions without risking prosecution, making their lives worse than they otherwise would be. If a liberal society is supposed to tolerate most of the particular practices that follow from such convictions, then it is imperative that people be allowed to engage in religiously-motivated conduct without unnecessary interference by the state. Accommodationists seek to transfer the burden of proof from the individual demanding an exemption to the state to make the state demonstrate that it had no other choice but to ban the religiously-inspired behavior in question to achieve some important legislative goal.[15]

On its face, this request for an interpretation of the FEC that is less hostile to exemptions strikes many persons, even those who are not religious, as reasonable inasmuch as it is not hard to appreciate how religion continues to play a crucial role in so many Americans' lives. The truth of religion convictions is neither here nor there. Accommodationists are not absolutists who adhere to the untenable view that the state may not restrict religiously-motivated behavior under any circumstances. They concede that religious beliefs may lead to behaviors that undermine public health and safety or harm others or infringe upon their equally important rights to have worthwhile lives. Individuals may be convinced that their religion requires them to sacrifice animals, murder apostates, and beat their children. The application of a heightened standard of review is not designed to guarantee free exercise of religion at all costs. Because exemption cases tend to be fact-specific, judges must determine the relative importance of the religious reasons of the person who wants to be exempted and the reasons that the state offers in support of the legislation whose constitutionality is being challenged. After *Smith*, the ball, so to speak, is in the court of lawmakers. The federal government and many state governments responded to *Smith* by enacting RFRAs, which mitigated its adverse effects on religious freedom.[16]

On one end of the spectrum, then, lies anti-accommodationist position of Justice Antonin Scalia, whose majority opinion in *Smith* maintains that exemptions are not normally constitutionally required. On the other end is that of McConnell, who insists that government must do just about everything that it can do to accommodate religious practices.[17] As he sees it, intermediate scrutiny remains the appropriate standard of review in free exercise of religion cases.[18] The burden of proof would be on the state to justify its refusal to provide an exemption, and the outcome would turn on the importance of the state's interest. Other scholars, who disagree with both the reasoning and result of *Smith* have taken a different tack, arguing that the religion clauses of the First Amendment stand for the principle of religious equality.[19] For Martha Nussbaum, everyone should have an equal share of religious liberty and the equal distribution of such liberty would represent the equal standing of all persons in the political community.[20]

The Infamous Reynolds *Decision*

In this section, I shall show why *Reynolds v. U.S.* may not be nearly as important, as it initially appears to be, in answering the constitutional question of whether states must create the option of multi-person marital arrangements.[21] Plural marriage has deep roots in Mormon theology.[22] In his case, George Reynolds contended that his taking a second wife was a requirement of his religion.[23] Federal legislation aimed at eliminating the practice towards the end of the Nineteenth Century was intentionally discriminatory. Moreover, many people have criticized the reasoning employed in *Reynolds*, and no thoughtful person today would accept its racist claim that plural marriage is "odious among the northern and western nations of Europe."[24] As Sarah Song writes, "The *Reynolds* court both drew upon and reinforced . . . [a] discourse of racial and cultural superiority of whites over others, casting the American-born Mormon religion as foreign and other."[25] Referring to Chief Justice Morrison Waite, the author of the opinion, Nussbaum adds, "He seems eager . . . to tar polygamy by association with the bad practices of allegedly primitive races."[26]

Be that as it may, the Court constitutionalized an anti-polygamy position, which remains good law for the time being. Many years later, in making the constitutionally important distinction between belief and action, Scalia cited *Reynolds* for support.[27] Scalia fears that anarchy would result if each person, subject only to the dictates of her own conscience, would "become a law unto himself."[28] For him, the state has only two choices: permit all exemptions or none of them. Surely, though, this is a false choice. No one has ever held the indefensible view that reasons based on religious convictions are immune from criticism or always trump the most compelling countervailing state interests. For instance, one's sincere religious belief in the truth of white supremacy would not justify private forms of racial discrimination in public accommodations or excuse hate crimes. Even McConnell concedes that "The individual believer is not judge in his own case."[29] As Justice Blackmun notes, the exemption that Smith and Black had asked for was confined to the "ceremonial use of peyote" and thus, would not have directly undermine the "war on drugs."[30] Oregon had not bothered to prosecute them under its anti-drug laws.[31] If Oregon had exempted those who use peyote in religious ceremonies, it hardly follows that Oregon or any other state then would be compelled to create exemptions for everyone who wants to use illegal drugs for any purpose whatsoever.

From the accommodationist standpoint, the elimination of all exemptions is a draconian solution that does not sensibly balance the value of religious beliefs and actions premised upon those beliefs in the eyes of those who seek exemptions from generally-applicable laws. The essence of the criticism of *Smith* is that Scalia gives too much weight to the state's interest and not enough to that of Smith, Black, and others like them when their religion demands certain illegal actions as part of its sacraments. In his defense, Scalia is more drawn to the underlying institutional question, primarily concerning himself with whether such an exemption ought to be granted could be left to the political process.[32] As Kent Greenawalt comments, "The heart of Justice Scalia's opinion is that courts should not have to decide when religious claims of variant strength should triumph over state interest of variant strength."[33] According to the proper division of labor between lawmakers and the judiciary, such decisions are better left to the former. The political branches should decide whether an exemption for a religious minority is appropriate, as long as such an exemption does not run afoul of the Establishment Clause.[34] The Court permits the state to make this determination however it sees fit.[35] As a result, "legislative discretion is maximized."[36]

Whatever the merits of the above criticism of Scalia's majority opinion may be, the Court returned the country to rational basis standard of review for the vast majority of freedom of religion cases. The consequences of their doing so would have been even worse but for the aforementioned legislative response to the decision in the form of federal and state statutory exemptions found in RFRAs. The change in constitutional doctrine that *Smith* produced remains troubling for anyone who cares about the important place of religion in many individual lives because legislative majorities always can repeal RFRAs or limit their scope. The "religion blindness" approach advocated by Scalia is unlikely to work as expected in a world where government actions often affect religious practices.[37] *Smith* is a significant decision insofar as the Court distances itself from the approach laid out in *Sherbert* by abandoning strict scrutiny as the standard of review in free exercise cases. No one believes that *Smith* makes it easier for a litigant to win on free exercise grounds. At the same time, it is too easy to overstate its impact. A few defenders of *Smith* maintain that in practice, not much has changed.[38] Others, who oppose *Smith*, hold a similar view concerning its constitutional significance.[39] Even after *Sherbert*, the Court rarely granted exemptions to generally-applicable laws.[40] The kind of strict scrutiny that the Court applied was more often than not "Strict in theory, feeble in fact."[41]

FREEDOM OF CONSCIENCE AS A MORE INCLUSIVE ALTERNATIVE

The Problem

The consequence of empowering lawmakers to decide when to accommodate is not that judges will no longer have to figure out what "religion" means.[42] And if the Court were to overturn *Smith* or at least weaken it and return the country to a standard of review closer to a heightened form of scrutiny, as those who adhere to accommodationist views would prefer, it would be even more critical for the definition of "religion" to be appropriate under the conditions of moral pluralism that characterize contemporary America. At minimum, accommodationists must address the concern that their understanding of religion is parochial. The argument that supports their position may prove too much: when such exemptions are constitutionally required on free exercise grounds, the state also must extend the same favorable treatment to similar non-religiously-motivated conduct.[43] Accommodationists like McConnell may be employing an underinclusive definition of religion. For Christopher Eisgruber and Lawrence Sager, fairness lies "at the very heart of free exercise exemption controversies."[44] A much stronger presumption in favor of religious freedom, even when lawmakers have not singled out a particular religion for discriminatory treatment, may lead to a semi-libertarian regime of accommodations for anyone who has deeply-held convictions for his behavior, provided that others, whose lives are equally important, are not harmed or put at an unreasonable risk of such harm. If religion is not special, then the state either must cease granting any exemptions or it must extend the same favorable treatment to similar non-religiously-motivated conduct. There is no third way.

So far, despite their efforts, accommodationists have failed to explain why their definition of "religion" is fair to everyone, including those who have deep secular convictions and also want exemptions from generally-applicable laws. This concern about an indefensible double standard is not new. During the Vietnam era, in determining the scope of statutory exemptions from the Draft, the Court expanded its definition of "religion" to include deeply-held secular beliefs.[45] An alternative like "conscience," which is considerably more inclusive, seems to better capture the normative purpose of treating "religion" as special in the first place: to enable people to form, revise, and pursue their reasonable life plans without undue interference by the state. According to Andrew Koppelman, the appeal of conscience, as the basis of exemptions, comes from its capacity to reduce the tension between the two religion clauses.[46] Other constitutional law scholars are attracted to conscience as the most appropriate understanding of "religion" due to its apparent fairness.[47]

It is puzzling, then, why accommodationists continue to maintain religion is special, with respect to exemptions, when they could avail themselves of a more inclusive definition, like conscience, that would not have the effect of privileging religion over non-religion. That is not to say that accommodationists are unaware of this concern about unfairness or unwilling to concede some ground. Koppleman states that "I have never said that religion is the *only* [his emphasis] legitimate basis for accommodation, nor that conscience, as such, should never be accommodated."[48] Along similar lines, Thomas Berg expresses willingness to accommodate the views of atheists or agnostics.[49] Koppelman falls back on the view that while "religion" is not a perfect proxy, it is good enough and better than the alternatives.[50]

Unfortunately, this sort of response is unsatisfactory. Critics of the accommodationist position, who are convinced that conscience would be a better alternative, demand to know why personal religious reasons for an exemption still warrant more deference from the state. First, the value of a plural intimate relationship or marriage may be the same for a polyamorist as a religiously-inspired polygynist. No one denies that non-religious beliefs can be held with the same intensity. Next, and most importantly, for purposes of exemptions, "religion" can be defined in multiple ways. The metaphysics of religious and non-religious beliefs about the world and how to live in it can be a distraction when it overshadows the normative question of what the legal or constitutional meaning of religion should be.

When accommodationists defend their respective definitions of religion, they often appeal to what is (or is supposed to be) the case, common use of language, intuition, and public opinion. In his book, Koppelman maintains that we (or at least most of us) know religion "when we see it."[51] McConnell states that most Americans subscribe to some notion of what is religious.[52] Others turn to history. McConnell points out the authors of the First Amendment rejected the term "conscience."[53] It is true that the authors of the Constitution said "religion" and not "conscience" nor "deeply-held belief" in the text. McConnell emphasizes that the constitutional text "singles out" religion.[54] As he puts it, this didn't happen by accident.[55] In defending religious freedom, but not that of conscience more generally, accommodations insist that religion must be understood as being unique, compared with other belief systems, for constitutional purposes. Steven Shiffrin notes that religion and nonreligion are not equals "because religion itself is regarded as valuable."[56]

One of the problems with looking to American history for guidance is that the Court has never based its interpretation of the FEC on its historical meaning.[57] It would be anomalous, then, to adopt such an approach to discovering or constructing its meaning in a society that has moved beyond the relatively narrow, largely Protestant pluralism that existed at its inception. If the concern involves fairness, one option would be to deny all exemptions, which Eugene Volokh calls "equalizing up."[58] This solution would not leave accommodationists vulnerable to the charge that their view discriminates against non-religious persons. However, for accommodationists, that "solution" may come at too high a price; it would leave far too little room for religious freedom and put religious minorities at the mercy of legislative majorities that may be hostile or insensitive to their belief systems.

According to Ronald Dworkin, "religion" is an interpretive concept, meaning that that it has a normative core.[59] In many Americans' eyes, many non-theistic belief systems, like Buddhism, Jainism, Daoism, Confucianism, Falun Gong, Shinto, Unitarianism, would count "religions."[60] That view provides some support for the position that a definition of religion need not be so underinclusive. Alternatively, substituting "conscience" for "religion" would have the advantage of not singling out religion at the expense of other belief systems, like non-theistic ones, that are equally valuable. A more expansive understanding of conscience, one that is not limited to religion, would acknowledge the breadth and depth of pluralism that currently exists in American society, be a fairer basis for exemptions, and serve the contemporary normative purposes of the FEC. Especially in a more secular age, a commitment to protect only religious conscience seems unnecessarily parochial; it does not seem to get at what is morally wrong with the denial of free exercise of religion, namely interference with a person's living according to her most deeply-held convictions, religious or otherwise.

Of course, accommodationists can try to rely on original public meaning to defend their view that "religion" still means what it meant in 1791 when the Bill Of Rights was ratified. The most obvious rejoinder is that whatever the authors meant and the ratifiers understood religion to mean at the end of the Eighteenth Century carries little weight. Assuming that they had similar views, which is improbable, very few people would interpret constitutional language so narrowly in 2015.[61] After all, the Constitution says "speech" and not "expressive conduct"; "arms" and not "semi-automatic machine guns"; "probable cause" and not "reasonable suspicion"; "seizure" and not "arrest" or "detention"; "self-incrimination" and not a "right to remain silent." As a matter of constitutional practice, American lawmakers, judges, and lawyers have long been in the habit of going beyond the underdetermined constitutional text (and its original public meaning) in discerning the implications of abstract constitutional language. It is inconceivable that they could stop doing so in a common law country, like our own, that enables judges to make decisions that take into account how circumstances have changed. The point is not that most of us have a preference for a more expansive reading of certain constitutional provisions and not others to achieve what we are convinced are happy endings. Rather, a more literal reading of the text just is not possible more than two hundred years later. Even self-identified textualists like Scalia concede that interpreters must venture beyond the four corners of the document to discover the original meaning of constitutional provisions when the words are not clear enough.[62]

To construe "religion" narrowly, then, and not include conscience as well, cuts against the moral pluralism that characterizes contemporary American society. Despite its superficial appeal, the trouble with the view that the text settles the matter is not only that the text does not specify what "religion," "prohibition," and "free exercise" mean, elaborate on which kinds of interference would be permissible, or include any examples. More importantly, this approach does not account for the extent to which many crucial constitutional terms and phrases, over time, have been constructed to express their underlying principles. Today, no one would take seriously the unduly narrow view that the Equal Protection Clause only protects African-American males from purposeful discrimination by state governments. Likewise, the principle that underlies the FEC cannot be reduced to how most people would have understood the meaning of the word "religion" in 1791.[63] It is worth noting how little Scalia had to say about the original meaning of the religion clauses in his majority opinion in *Smith*. If such a narrow understanding of religion were to be adopted, it follows that many non-Western and all nontheistic religions would not be covered as well. In the end, the "privileging religion" argument, premised on constitutional language or on an originalist rationale, cannot stand on its own; it needs a supplementary normative argument that establishes why religion is entitled to better treatment than non-religion.

One way of framing this question is to inquire into whether religious reasons differ in some constitutionally significant way from their nonreligious counterparts. Epistemically, they do not appear to do so.[64] Both are subject to the same standards of evidence inasmuch as they are propositions and therefore, are subject to verification. Religious reasons may not be more motivationally-powerful than other sorts of reasons are.[65] Nor is it obvious that religious conscience binds a believer more than secular conscience does because religious duties are perceived to be non-optional. Henry David Thoreau's well-known non-religious but moral reasons for civil disobedience do not seem to be less adequate, as a source of moral motivation, than the religious reasons of other abolitions in the antebellum period. As Eisgruber and Sager state, "religious conscience is just one of many very strong motivations in human life, and there is no particular reason to suppose that it is likely to matter more in the run of religious lives generally than will other very powerful forces in the lives of both the nonreligious and the religious."[66] Many deeply-held secular beliefs have some, if not all, of the features that religious beliefs have, the moment that it is acknowledged that a religion does not have to be theistic.

But even if they did not, it is still not evident that constitutionally-mandated exemptions from generally-applicable laws may be so limited. When the state singles out for religion for special treatment, it would be making a judgment about the value of religion over non-religion. Apart from the fact that Establishment Clause may bar it, such a judgment raises concerns about the ability of the state to treat those who are subject to its authority fairly. In William Marshall's words, "Granting exemptions only to religious claimants promotes its own form of inequality: a constitutional preference for religious over non-religious belief systems."[67]

Probably no definition of "religion" could be perfect in the sense of including everything that should be included and excluding everything that should be excluded. The real issue is whether one definition, all things considered, does a better job than its rivals, as Koppleman notes above. Judges, lawyers, scholars, and the rest of us are bound to disagree over the meaning of "best" in this discursive context. The overinclusiveness problem, where too many behaviors receive constitutional protection, presents a less grave problem because any claim for an exemption is always subject to being balanced against the state's interest in prohibiting the behavior in question, irrespective of the personal reasons that underlie it. By contrast, the underinclusiveness problem, where some behaviors that should be protected are not, is more serious, because the state is denying personal freedom to people who ought to be able to do what they seek to do because of the importance of their convictions in their lives.

As a matter of constitutional principle, it is not evident that under the Free Exercise Clause, the state should be allowed to treat the religious reasons of its members differently than the non-religious reasons of others when "religion" can be expanded to include other beliefs systems. As a substitute for "religion," "freedom of conscience" does not discriminate against those who are religious; it only includes those who have previously been excluded. In doing so, it acknowledges the value of everyone's life. The only consideration that can trump a deeply-held reason, religious or secular, is one that involves a compelling or at least an important state interest under a heightened standard of review. As such, the constitutional status quo could become non-discriminatory. When accommodationists reject "freedom of conscience," they not only permit the state to favor religion over non-religion and in doing so, acquiesce to legislative interference in, say, an atheist's life that they would not stomach if he or she were a Christian, Jew, or Muslim. They also fail to respect the lives of those who are not religious, and never will be, by sending them an unambiguous message: as far as they state is concerned, your personal reasons for deciding how to live are not entitled to the same respect. The rationale that accommodationists offer on behalf of their position can only be accepted by those who already are inclined toward a religious understanding of the world and their place in it.

PLURAL MARRIAGE

Background

The implication of the view that religion is not special is that no free exercise argument exists when it comes to exemptions. There are only personal reasons that individuals have for wanting to engage in certain behavior, including being married. For constitutional purposes, a personal religious reason for wanting to marry more than one person at the same time is the same as a non-religious one. Both merit the same level of concern (or lack thereof). In the discursive context of whether states must issue marriage licenses to plural marriage enthusiasts, who meet all of the other valid requirements for eligibility, a personal religious reason for wanting some kind of multi-person marital arrangement, like a polygynous one, may be good or bad, but its religious nature has no relevance. A state should not treat it any differently than the personal reason of, say, a polyamorist.

One solution to the problem of the state's only allowing religious plural marriage enthusiasts to marry would be to eliminate civil marriage as a legal status, which is a kind of "equalizing up" solution if no one can marry or be granted a marriage-like status by the state. Because marriage is no longer a legal precondition for having sex or children, the rationale for the state's licensing it is weaker than it used to be.[68] Some scholars believe that civil marriage ought to be disestablished.[69] In their view, disestablishment means something like civil union status for everyone, which would be a kind of "equalizing down" solution. Disestablishment, understood as abolition, would mean that intimate relationships could be privatized in one way or another. The most extreme version of such a view involves replacing the legal status of marriage with private contracts that the state would enforce. There is more than something to be said in favor of some version of abolition. Removing the state from the marriage business would reduce the likelihood that the state would continue to be treating marital nonconformists, including plural marriage enthusiasts, and single persons, unequally.

Same-Sex Marriage

The end of the debate in this country over whether states must permit same-sex couples to marry is instructive because it clarifies the kinds of reasons that a state may not offer on behalf of its decision to only allow a man to marry a man and a woman to marry a woman. These days, one would be hard pressed to maintain that a state, which would limit marriage to opposite-sex couples if it were constitutionally permitted to do so, would not be conveying a message about the superiority of opposite-sex marriage. In this context, separate is not equal. Many critics of same-sex marriages do not simply ground their opposition in empirical claims about good or bad consequences for children or for the institution of marriage itself. They also reject the idea that such marriages are just as worthwhile as their opposite-sex counterparts. To state that a same-sex marriage is not marriage is not simply to refer to a definition or point out a contradiction. At least implicitly, to do so is make a moral judgment about same-sex relationships as well. In 2015, finally, it is no longer imprudent to inquire into whether same-sex marriages may be better than opposite-sex ones. Framing the constitutional debate over same-sex marriage in substantive due process and equal protection terms, while ultimately successful, comes at the cost of leaving unchallenged the assumption that everyone should aspire to the ideal that an opposite-sex marriage represents. If gays and lesbians wanted to be a part of the institution, they were supposed to be able to demonstrate that they could be like opposite-sex couples in the most important respects.

In the same-sex marriage debate, advocates for a change in the marital status quo endeavored to convince the public that such marriage only differed superficially from its opposite-sex counterpart. The objective was to avoid calling attention to difference so that straight persons, who constitute the vast majority of the electorate, would be convinced that gays and lesbians could be assimilated into the traditional institution of marriage without fundamentally changing it. The kind of equal protection analysis that judges used to invalidate laws that do not allow same-sex couples to marry confirms the belief that constitutionally, such couples are the same and ought to be treated as such. For the most part, this equal protection strategy, which underscores similarity, paid dividends. Even if gays and lesbians do not qualify as a suspect class, states failed to articulate why their interest in limiting marriage to opposite-sex couples was legitimate, which is what rational basis standard of review requires.[70] Heterosexism, the idea that opposite-sex attractions are the norm and therefore, are better than the alternatives , is much less socially acceptable than it used to be, and that change in attitude toward same-sex sexual relationships undoubtedly made judges more skeptical of the attempts by states to justify unequal legal treatment. *Romer*, *Lawrence*, and *Windsor* already eroded the foundations of the view that states may classify on the basis of sexual orientation.[71] *Obergefell* extends this line of reasoning by establishing that states may no longer deny marriage licenses to same-sex couples.[72]

Plural Marriage

It is important to keep in mind that some of the language of the majority opinion in *Obergefell* underscores the value of marital choice, which means that the state is not supposed to vet the kinds of personal reasons that consenting adults have for marrying each other, even if doing so were administratively feasible. This part of Kennedy's majority opinion should not be overlooked. Long before the same-sex marriage debate began, several U.S. Supreme Court decisions dealt with the extent to which states could interfere with the marital choices of a competent, consenting adult.[73] In the past, states have imposed few restrictions on marriage. As one commentator observes, "The law determines who is eligible for marriage . . . but it says almost nothing about what marriage itself consists in; it is a contract without content."[74] At the beginning of the Twenty-First Century, the only constitutionally acceptable rationales for permitting such interference were age, consanguinity, gender (a man could not marry another man and a woman could not marry another woman), and numerosity (a person could not marry another person if she already was married and a person could not marry another person who already was married to someone else). Otherwise, an adult could marry any other adult, for whatever personal reasons that she happened to have, with the exception of a non-citizen's marrying a citizen only for immigration purposes. At least for two-person marriages, lawmakers and judges agree that such a relationship does not have to be predicated upon any kinds of feelings or behaviors. The personal reason(s) of each person in the couple are considered to be sufficient.

However, when it comes to plural marriage, states take a noticeably different approach, as if it were obvious that numerical limitations, and the mononormativity that underlies them, need no defense.[75] In his dissent in *Obergefell*, Chief Justice John Roberts challenged those, who endorse the legal recognition of same-sex marriage, to explain why such legal recognition should not extend to multi-person relationships.[76] Someday, *Obergefell* may pave the way for more scrutiny of laws that privilege monogamy. Just like the reasons that American lawmakers used for years to discriminate against gays and lesbians, the reasons that lawmakers fall back upon to prevent polyamorists from forming their own marriages may turn out to be unsatisfactory. Marriage is laden with social meaning and for this reason alone, extensive state involvement with the institution raises constitutional concerns, particularly when the state promotes a particular conception of marriage on perfectionist grounds. Anything less the legal status of marriage is problematic. By analogy, to agree to anything less than the legal status of marriage for same-sex couples, like settling for civil unions, is to be complicit in circulating the pernicious view that marriage is only for straight persons. To not allow same-sex couples to marry is not only to deny them material benefits and legal privileges that married opposite-sex couples enjoy. Recognition of marriage by the state also validates intimate relationships and dignifies those who are permitted to marry.

The creation of an equal legal status for plural unions would inform the public that marital multiplicity could be better than the monogamist alternative for some people in some circumstances. As a number of scholars point out, the debate over same-sex marriage implicates the deeper question of why a state may continue to deny marriage licenses to plural marriage enthusiasts, including polyamorists.[77] In his dissent in *Obergefell*, Chief Justice John Roberts compares the legal recognition of same-sex marriage to that of plural marriage.[78] The idea of equal treatment, which colors so much of the debate, makes it easy to miss the fact that most Americans want the state to let them act on the basis of their own personal reasons in deciding whom to marry or whether to marry in the first place.

As it turns out, *Reynolds* may be more of a red herring than anything else; it does not have to be overturned, as the debate over legal recognition of plural marriage unfolds. The main reason why the Court reached the wrong conclusion is that under the Constitution, a state like Utah should not have denied Reynolds or his "wives" their constitutional right to marry whomever they pleased as long as all of them were adults that consented to the arrangement. That their personal reasons happened to be religious can be relegated to a footnote. Personal reasons for wanting to marry only are constitutionally significant because they are personal reasons that the state should not second-guess. There is plenty support in the case law for the view that the most personal of personal decisions, including marital ones, should be left to individual judgment. After all, under the marital status quo for opposite and same-sex couples, the state is indifferent to them. They could be terrible reasons but because they are hers, the state cannot reject them. Indeed, she need not articulate her reasons. Furthermore, people are allowed to form and stay in all kinds of bad or unhealthy personal relationships. That some or perhaps many marital choices are less than wise does not entail that either person should be denied the right to marry or that the state could force the couple to divorce. One does not have to be a libertarian to appreciate why some and probably most of the most critical personal choices must be left to the people who are most directly affected by them. Usually, they are in a better position to make such choices due to the likelihood that they know themselves and their personal needs better than anyone else does.

What is really doing the normative heavy lifting here is the importance that Americans, and their constitutional tradition, assign to marital choice. Marriage is one of those choices that almost everyone wants to make for themselves, even if encouraging them to do so is likely to produce bad consequences for themselves and society. The institution remains extremely important to the vast majority of Americans.[79] On average, it is likely to be, in one way or another, an essential component of their conception of the good. For some of them, it may be more important than anything else. Constitutionally, the issue ought to be whether competent adults should be free to choose such a marital relationship and not whether it would be wise for most people to do so, whether the legal recognition of different types of plural marriages would irreparably damage the traditional institution of marriage, or whether the licensing of only two-person marriages would produce better overall consequences. Here, as it should, paternalism on the part of the state—saving competent adults from poor marital decisions—has little appeal.

CONCLUSION

As I have tried to show in this chapter, the current definition of "religion" is not only outdated but too parochial to be fair to many Americans. One might conclude that the time has come to stop treating religion as special in deciding when exemptions from generally-applicable laws are constitutionally required. The only way, I believe, to continue to defend a more traditional, less inclusive definition of "religion" for constitutional purposes is to deny liberal neutrality, and its place in constitutional doctrine, and explicitly take the position that the state may discriminate by treating religious persons (and their convictions) more favorably. From this standpoint, the state could treat the religious reason of a Fundamentalist Mormon differently than that of a secular polyamorist. One then could argue that those who believe that polygyny is a religious duty have a constitutional right to marry more than one person at the same time (or marry someone who already is married).

However, under conditions of moral pluralism, if one is convinced that all lives count equally, it is not easy to walk this line. Simply put, equal treatment would entail that no one, for any reason, could marry more than one person at the same time, which is the marital status quo. The difference cannot be split. One of my objectives in this chapter is to entice those who subscribe to a strong accommodationist view to come to terms with the unfairness of using an unnecessarily narrow definition of religion as the basis of constitutionally-required exemptions, which, for far too long, have been discriminatory. The other is to link this debate to the emerging scholarship that concerns whether post-*Obergefell*, states have to legally recognize plural intimate relationships.

NOTES

1. For an exception, see *Church of the Lukumi Babalu Aye, Inc. v. City of Hialeah*, 508 U.S. 520 (1993).

2. Steven H. Shiffrin, *The Religious Left and Church-State Relations* (Princeton: Princeton University Press, 2009), 16.

3. "By exemption," I mean a constitutionally-required exception to a generally applicable law that has "the purpose and effect of removing a burden on, or facilitating the exercise of, a person's religion." I use the terms "exemption" and "accommodation" interchangeably.

4. Michael W. McConnell, "Accommodation of Religion: An Update and Response to the Critics," *George Washington Law Review* 60 (1992): 687.

5. See, e.g., Micah Schwartzman, "What If Religion Is Not Special?" *University of Chicago Law Review* 79 (2012): 1351–1427; Brian Leiter, *Why Tolerate Religion?* (Princeton: Princeton University Press, 2012).

6. Other religions either require or permit polygyny as well. In one interpretation of the Islamic tradition, men are allowed to marry up to four wives, subject to certain conditions. Those conditions include the consent of the wives and their being treated equitably. "Polygamy in Islam," accessed December 22, 2015, www.islamology.org/Overview/Women/Polygamy in Islam.htm.

7. Or more radically, states might get out of the marriage business, leaving the institution to private religious organizations like churches, synagogues, and mosques.

8. Martha C. Nussbaum, *Freedom of Conscience: In Defense of America's Tradition of Religious Equality* (New York: Basic Books, 2010), 24–25.

9. See McConnell, "Accommodation of Religion," 687.

10. Sherbert v . Verner , 374 U.S. 398 (1963); *see also* Wisconsin v . Yoder , 406 U.S. 205 (1972).

11. *Employment Division v. Smith*, 494 U.S. 872 (1990).

12. Douglas Laycock, "The Remnants of Free Exercise," *The Supreme Court Review* (1990): 68.

13. See McConnell, "Accommodation of Religion," 687–688.

14. Ibid., 693.

15. For a more thorough discussion of the "accommodationist" view, see McConnell, "Accommodation of Religion," 685–742.

16. The Religious Freedom Restoration Act (RFRA), Pub. L. No. 103–141, 107 Stat. 1488 (November 16, 1993), codified at 42 U.S.C. § 2000bb through 42 U.S.C. § 2000bb-4. The RFRA was invalidated by the U.S. Supreme Court in City of Boerne v. Flores , 521 U.S. 507 (1997) on federalism grounds. States responded by enacting their own RFRAs. At present, more than half of the states grant some exemptions for religious practices. Additionally, in 2000, Congress tried again, creating the Religious Land Use and Institutionalized Persons (RLUIPA), Public Law 106–274, codified at 42 U.S.C. § 2000cc et seq.

17. See McConnell, "Accommodation of Religion," 690–695.

18. Michael McConnell, "Free Exercise Revisionism and the *Smith* Decision," *University of Chicago Law Review* 57 (1990): 1128.

19. Nussbaum, *Freedom of Conscience*, 3.

20. Ibid., 19.

21. *Reynolds v. U.S.*, 98 U.S. 145 (1879).

22. See Joseph Bozzuti, "The Constitutionality of Polygamy Prohibitions After Lawrence v. Texas: Is Scalia a Punchline or a Prophet?" *Catholic Lawyer* 43 (2004): 417–418; see also Irwin Altman, "Polygamous Family Life: The Case of Contemporary Mormon Fundamentalists," *Utah Law Review* (1996): 367–370.

23. *Reynolds v. U.S.*, 98 U.S. 161–162 (1879).

24. Ibid., 164.

25. Sarah Song, *Justice, Gender, and the Politics of Multiculturalism* (New York: Cambridge University Press, 2007), 148–149.

26. Nussbaum, *Liberty of Conscience*, 196.

27. Employment Division v. Smith, 494 U.S. 879 (1990).

28. Ibid., 885.

29. Michael McConnell, "Free Exercise Revisionism and the *Smith* Decision," 1150.

30. Employment Division v. Smith, 494 U.S. 909–910 (1990).
31. Ibid., 911.
32. Joan Biskupic, *American Original: The Life and Constitution of Supreme Court Justice Antonin Scalia* (New York: Sarah Crichton, 2009), 139.
33. Kent Greenawalt, *Religion and the Constitution: Free Exercise and Fairness* (Princeton: Princeton University Press, 2009), 78.
34. For McConnell's response to those who maintain that all legislative exemptions from generally applicable laws violate the Establishment Clause, *see* McConnell, "Accommodation of Religion," 713–722.
35. Employment Division v. Smith, 494 U.S. 872 (1990).
36. See McConnell, "Accommodation of Religion," 696.
37. McConnell, "Accommodation of Religion," 692.
38. See, e.g., Mark Tushnet, "The Rhetoric of Free Exercise Discourse," *Bringham Young University Law Review* (1993): 118.
39. As William Marshall observes, the Court has never actually taken the compelling interest standard of review seriously in this context. William P. Marshall, "What Is the Matter with Equality? An Assessment of the Equal Treatment of Religion and Nonreligion in First Amendment Jurisprudence," *Indiana Law Journal* 75 (2000): 195–196; see also McConnell, "Free Exercise Revisionism and the *Smith* Decision," 1127.
40. Marshall, "What is the Matter with Equality?" 197.
41. Christopher L. Eisgruber and Lawrence G. Sager, "The Vulnerability of Conscience: The Constitutional Basis for Protecting Religious Conduct," *University of Chicago Law Review* 61 (1994): 1247.
42. See, e.g., Holt v. Hobbs 135 S. Ct. 853 (2015).
43. Steven D. Smith, *The Rise and Decline* of *American Religious Freedom* (Cambridge: Harvard University Press, 2014), 11.
44. Christopher L. Eisgruber and Lawrence G. Sager, *Religious Freedom and the Constitution* (Cambridge: Harvard University Press, 2010), 15.
45. See U.S. v. Seeger, 380 U.S. 163 (1965); Welsh v. U.S., 398 U.S. 333 (1970).
46. Andrew Koppelman, "Conscience, Volitional Necessity, and Religious Exemptions," *Legal Theory* 15 (2009): 217.
47. See, e.g., David A.J. Richards, *Toleration and the Constitution* (New York: Oxford University Press, 1986), 140–141.
48. Andrew M. Koppelman, "'Religion' as a Bundle of Legal Proxies: Reply to Micah Schwartzman," *San Diego Law Review* 51 (2014): 1082.
49. Thomas C. Berg, "Secular Purpose, Accommodations, and Why Religion is Special (Enough)," *University of Chicago Law Review Dialogue* 24 (2013): 36.
50. Koppelman, "'Religion' as a Bundle of Legal Proxies," 1083.
51. Andrew Koppelman, *Defending American Religious Neutrality* (Cambridge: Harvard University Press, 2013), 7.
52. Michael W. McConnell, "Why Protect Religious Freedom?" review of *Why Tolerate Religion?* by Brian Leiter, *Yale Law Journal* 123 (2013): 772.
53. Michael W. McConnell, "The Origins and Historical Understanding of Free Exercise of Religion," *Harvard Law Review* 103 (1990): 1488–1491.
54. Michael McConnell, "The Problem of Singling Out Religion," *DePaul Law Review* 50 (2000): 9.
55. McConnell, "The Problem of Singling Out Religion," 12–15.
56. Shiffrin, *The Religious Left and Church-State Relations*, 13–14.
57. See McConnell, "The Origins and Historical Understanding of Free Exercise of Religion," 1413.
58. Eugene Volokh, "Intermediate Questions of Religious Exemptions: A Research Agenda with Test Suites," *Cardozo Law Review* 21 (1999), 606.
59. Ronald Dworkin, *Religion Without God* (Cambridge: Harvard University Press, 2013), 7.

60. David Ramsay Steele, *Atheism Explained: From Folly to Philosophy* (Chicago: Carus, 2008), 7, 12–13.

61. Vincent Philip Munoz, *God and the Founders: Madison, Washington, and Jefferson* (New York: Cambridge University Press, 2009).

62. Antonin Scalia, *A Matter of Interpretation: Federal Courts and the Law* (Princeton: Princeton University Press, 1997), 23–25.

63. According to Greenawalt, originally, "liberty of conscience" had a different meaning than "free exercise," which referred to various kinds of behavior based on religious convictions. By contemporary standards, the founders had a narrow understanding of "religion" and "religious freedom." Greenawalt, *Religion and the Constitution: Free Exercise and Fairness*, 22–23.

64. Brian Leiter, "Foundations of Religious Liberty: Toleration or Respect?" *San Diego Law Review* 47 (2010): 943–951.

65. Eisgruber and Sager, "The Vulnerability of Conscience," 1263.

66. Ibid.

67. William P. Marshall, "In Defense of *Smith* and Free Exercise Revisionism," *University of Chicago Law Review* 58 (1991): 319.

68. Richard H. Thaler and Cass R. Sunstein, *Nudge: Improving Decisions About Health, Wealth, and Happiness* (New York: Penguin, 2009): 221.

69. See, e.g., Edward Zelinsky, "Strengthening Marriage by Abolishing Civil Marriage," last modified October 26, 2012, http://www.huffingtonpost.com/edward-zelinsky/abolish-marriage_b_1831271.html

70. In American equal protection doctrine, in some instances, this requirement means that a heightened standard of review is triggered. The state then has the burden of proof in trying to rebut the presumptive unconstitutionality of the legislative classification in question. A court is supposed to invalidate the law unless the state can prove that (a) its interest is sufficiently strong and (b) the legislative means, which the state employed, clearly serves the state's interest.

71. See *Romer v. Evans*, 517 U.S. 620 (1996); *Lawrence v. Texas*, 539 U.S. 558 (2003); *U.S. v. Windsor*, 570 U.S. _ (2013).

72. *Obergefell v. Hodges*, 135 S. Ct. 1039 (2015).

73. See *Loving v. Virginia*, 388 U.S. 1 (1988); *Zablocki v. Redhail*, 434 U.S. 374 (1978); *Turner v. Safly*, 482 U.S. 78 (1987).

74. Brook J. Sadler, "Re-Thinking Civil Unions and Same-Sex Marriage," *Monist* 91 (2008): 580–581.

75. The term "mononormativity" is found in Deborah Anapol, *Polyamory in the Twenty-First Century: Love and Intimacy with Multiple Partners* (Lanham: Rowman and Littlefield, 2010), 169.

76. *Obergefell v. Hodges*, 135 S. Ct. 1039 (2015) (Roberts, CJ., dissenting).

77. Sonu Bedi coined the term "plural marriage enthusiasts." Sonu Bedi, *Beyond Race, Sex, and Sexual Orientation* (New York: Cambridge University Press, 2014), 244.

78. *Obergefell v. Hodges*, 135 U.S. 2622 (2015) (Roberts, CJ., dissenting).

79. Martha C. Nussbaum, *From Disgust to Humanity: Sexual Orientation and Constitutional Law* (New York: Oxford University Press, 2010), 127.

REFERENCES

Altman, Irwin. "Polygamous Family Life: The Case of Contemporary Mormon Fundamentalists." *Utah Law Review* (1996): 367–391.

Anapol, Deborah. *Polyamory in the Twenty-First Century: Love and Intimacy with Multiple Partners*. Lanham: Rowman and Littlefield, 2010.

Bedi, Sonu. *Beyond Race, Sex, and Sexual Orientation*. New York: Cambridge University Press, 2014.

Berg, Thomas C. "Secular Purpose, Accommodations, and Why Religion is Special (Enough)." *University of Chicago Law Review Dialogue* 24 (2013): 24–42.

Biskupic, Joan. *American Original: The Life and Constitution of Supreme Court Justice Antonin Scalia*. New York: Sarah Crichton, 2009.

Bozzuti, Joseph. "The Constitutionality of Polygamy Prohibitions After Lawrence v. Texas: Is Scalia a Punchline or a Prophet?". *Catholic Lawyer* 43 (2004): 409–441.

Church of the Lukumi Babalu Aye, Inc. v. City of Hialeah. 508 U.S. 520 (1993).

Dworkin, Ronald. *Religion Without God*. Cambridge: Harvard University Press, 2013.

Eisgruber, Christopher L., and Lawrence G. Sager. *Religious Freedom and the Constitution*. Cambridge: Harvard University Press, 2010.

_____. "The Vulnerability of Conscience: The Constitutional Basis for Protecting Religious Conduct." *University of Chicago Law Review* 61 (1994): 1245–1315.

Employment Division v. Smith. 494 U.S. 872 (1990).

Greenawalt, Kent. *Religion and the Constitution: Free Exercise and Fairness*. Princeton: Princeton University Press, 2009.

Holt v. Hobbs. 135 S. Ct. 853 (2015).

Koppelman, Andrew M. "Conscience, Volitional Necessity, and Religious Exemptions." *Legal Theory* 15 (2009): 215–244.

_____. "'Religion' as a Bundle of Legal Proxies: Reply to Micah Schwartzman." *San Diego Law Review* 51 (2014): 1079–1084.

_____. *Defending American Religious Neutrality*. Cambridge: Harvard University Press, 2013.

Lawrence v. Texas. 539 U.S. 558 (2003).

Laycock, Douglas. "The Remnants of Free Exercise." *The Supreme Court Review* (1990): 1–68.

Leiter, Brian. *Why Tolerate Religion?* Princeton: Princeton University Press, 2012.

_____. "Foundations of Religious Liberty: Toleration or Respect?". *San Diego Law Review* 47 (2010): 935–959.

Loving v. Virginia. 388 U.S. 1 (1988).

Marshall, William P. "What Is the Matter with Equality? An Assessment of the Equal Treatment of Religion and Nonreligion in First Amendment Jurisprudence." *Indiana Law Journal* 75 (2000): 193–217.

_____. "In Defense of *Smith* and Free Exercise Revisionism." *University of Chicago Law Review* 58 (1991): 308–328.

McConnell, Michael W. "Why Protect Religious Freedom?" Review of *Why Tolerate Religion?* by Brian Leiter. *Yale Law Journal* 123 (2013): 770–810.

_____. "The Problem of Singling Out Religion." *DePaul Law Review* 50 (2000): 1–47.

_____. "Accommodation of Religion: An Update and Response to the Critics." *George Washington Law Review* 60 (1992): 685–742.

_____. "Free Exercise Revisionism and the *Smith* Decision." *University of Chicago Law Review* 57 (1990): 1109–1153.

_____. "The Origins and Historical Understanding of Free Exercise of Religion." *Harvard Law Review* 103 (1990): 1409–1517.

Munoz, Vincent Philip. *God and the Founders: Madison, Washington, and Jefferson*. New York: Cambridge University Press.

Nussbaum, Martha C. *Freedom of Conscience: In Defense of America's Tradition of Religious Equality*. New York: Basic Books, 2010.

_____. *From Disgust to Humanity: Sexual Orientation and Constitutional Law*. New York: Oxford University Press, 2010.

Obergefell v. Hodges. 135 S. Ct. 1039 (2015).

Reynolds v. U.S. 98 U.S. 164 (1879).

Richards, David A.J. *Toleration and the Constitution*. New York: Oxford University Press, 1986.

Romer v. Evans. 517 U.S. 620 (1996).

Sadler, Brook J. "Re-Thinking Civil Unions and Same-Sex Marriage." *Monist* 91 (2008): 578–605.

Scalia, Antonin. *A Matter of Interpretation: Federal Courts and the Law*. Princeton: Princeton University Press, 1997.

Schwartzman, Micah "What If Religion Is Not Special?" *University of Chicago Law Review* 79 (2012): 1351–1427.
Shiffrin, Steven H. *The Religious Left and Church-State Relations*. Princeton: Princeton University Press, 2009.
Sherbert v . Verner . 374 U.S. 398 (1963).
Song, Sarah. *Justice, Gender, and the Politics of Multiculturalism*. New York: Cambridge University Press, 2007.
Smith, Steven D. *The Rise and Decline* of *American Religious Freedom*. Cambridge: Harvard University Press, 2014.
Steele, David Ramsay. *Atheism Explained: From Folly to Philosophy*. Chicago: Carus, 2008.
Thaler, Richard H. and Cass R. Sunstein. *Nudge: Improving Decisions About Health, Wealth, and Happiness*. New York: Penguin, 2009.
Turner v. Safly. 482 U.S. 78 (1987).
Tushnet, Mark. "The Rhetoric of Free Exercise Discourse." *Bringham Young University Law Review* (1993): 117–140.
U.S. v. Seeger. 380 U.S. 163 (1965).
U.S. v. Windsor. 570 U.S. (2013).
Volokh, Eugene. "Intermediate Questions of Religious Exemptions: A Research Agenda with Test Suites." *Cardozo Law Review* 21 (1999): 595–662.
Welsh v. U.S. 398 U.S. 333 (1970).
Wisconsin v . Yoder . 406 U.S. 205 (1972).
Zablocki v. Redhail. 434 U.S. 374 (1978).
Zelinsky, Edward. "Strengthening Marriage by Abolishing Civil Marriage." Last modified October 26, 2012. http://www.huffingtonpost.com/edward-zelinsky/abolish-marriage_b_1831271.htm

FOUR

Robotic Marriage and the Law

Mark Goldfelder and Yosef Razin

The United States, and the world at large, is in the midst of a family law revolution that will fundamentally change our very conception of family. Ethical challenges to age-old ideas have prompted people to ask foundational questions, such as how and why our most important personal relationships evolved. In a country where same-sex marriage has been legalized, it is only natural to wonder who marriage may include in the future.

At the same time, we are also living in an age of unprecedented technological innovation. The rise of smart machines and the incredible advances in robotics over the last few decades highlight that the difference between science fiction and science is closing with the passage of time. Social robots spend time with the elderly[1] and the young.[2] Robots can even experience a form of childhood.[3] Robots now work in our factories[4] and mines,[5] and, career-wise, they can be anything from blue-collar prison guards[6] to white-collar financial traders.[7] Humans are already forming deep and meaningful relationships with their artificial friends, and indeed many humans are becoming intrigued by the possibility, and increasing reality, of human-robot romance. Films and television shows like *Her,*[8] *Ex Machina,*[9] *Humans,*[10] and *AI*[11] make up just a small sample of the dynamics of this relationship spectrum, ranging from platonic love to prostitution.

The question that this chapter deals with will extend these possibilities one step further with a simple thought experiment: Could it ever be possible for a human and a robot to *legally* wed in the United States? The second section addresses whether robots could be legal persons subject to marriage laws in the United States. The third section considers what it would mean for robots to be in loving relationships. The last sections analyze three threshold requirements for marriages—consent, understanding, and decision-making capacity—that robots would have to meet to qualify for a legal marriage. Our conclusion, which is laid out in the final section, is that when it comes to love and marriage, almost anything is possible, and robots and human beings could marry each other someday.

Background

To begin, two critical issues must be addressed. First, a robot must be a legal person to be eligible to marry. The meaning of legal personality differs from how ordinary people typically use the term "person." Legal personality makes no claim about morality, and does not in any way require sentience or vitality.[12] "In books of the Law, as in other books, and in common speech, 'person' is often used as meaning a human being, but the technical legal meaning of a 'person' is a subject of legal rights and duties."[13] To be a legal person, then, is to have the capability of possessing legal rights and duties within a certain legal system, such as the right to enter into contracts, own property, sue and be sued.[14] As Lawrence Solum notes, "[t]he question whether an entity should be considered a legal person is reducible to other questions about whether or not the entity can and should be made the subject of a set of legal rights and duties. The particular bundle of rights and duties that accompanies legal personhood varies with the nature of the entity."[15] According to Black's Law Dictionary, an artificial person is:

> An entity, such as a corporation, created by law and given certain legal rights and duties of a human being; a being, real or imaginary, who for the purpose of legal reasoning is treated more or less as a human being. An entity is a person for purposes of the Due Process and Equal Protection Clauses but is not a citizen for purposes of the Privileges and Immunities Clauses in Article IV § 2 and in the Fourteenth Amendment.[16]

Not all legal persons have the same rights and obligations, and some entities are only considered "persons" for some matters, but not others. Corporations, for instance, have the right to free political speech, but not the right to vote.[17] If the law creates legal persons, then legal "definitions of persons are prescriptive rather than descriptive, it follows that arriving at a satisfactory concept of personhood is a matter of decision not discovery."[18] The establishment of personhood is an assessment made by a legislature or a judicial body to grant an entity rights and obligations, regardless of how the entity looks and whether it could pass for human. The truth is that the:

> notion of personhood has expanded significantly, albeit slowly, over the last few thousand years. Throughout history, women, children, and slaves have all at times been considered property rather than persons.[19] The category of persons recognized in the courts has expanded to include entities and characters including natural persons aside from men . . . as well as unnatural or juridical persons, such as corporations, labor unions, nursing homes, municipalities and government units.[20]

So, can a robot be a person? Again, "personhood" as a legal concept arises not from the humanity of the subject but from the ascription of rights and duties to the subject.[21]

> The determination of whether an entity or being counts as a legal person is largely context-specific, and not necessarily consistently made. 'In the United States' common law tradition there is no discrete body of law containing all of the applicable provisions of legal personhood. Legal persons constitute a diverse community that includes various individuals, entities and collectives in different ways for different jurisdictions. To add to this diversity, the common law of legal personhood is disparate and diffuse, found in cases, statutes and treatises.'[22]

If an autonomous artificial being were capable "of accepting social responsibility, legal responsibility, or duties necessary for rights of legal personhood,"[23] then there is no reason why a robot could not be a legal person. Indeed, many scholars, noting that robots already serve as agents, make contracts, and commit torts and crimes, have started calling for the ascription of robotic personhood to those intelligent autonomous systems that seem to deserve it.[24]

Once the potential personhood of a robot is admitted, it is worth exploring the extent of such rights and duties that judges and lawmakers may decide to grant to these robots in the future. We may grant robots rights for their own safety as well as establish a duty to protect another person's safety.[25] We may also consider assigning them responsibility in regard to issues of custody and liability, rights to privacy, or even intellectual property.[26] Once we have established that at least *some* robots can or be a kind of "person" with some legal rights, the question becomes whether they should be the kind of person that also has the right to marry other persons.[27]

Before making such conclusions about robots, we must consider a more developed set of case law concerning the most common articulation of an artificial person: the corporation. In 1819, the U.S. Supreme Court in *Trustees of Dartmouth College v. Woodward* held that a corporation was entitled to protection under the Contracts Clause.[28] In 1853's *Marshall v. Baltimore and Ohio Railroad Company*, the Court also recognized corporations as citizens to establish jurisdiction. [29] In *Santa Clara County v. Southern Pacific Railroad*, the Court held that under the Fourteenth Amendment a corporation was a person.[30] Recently, corporate free speech was protected under the First Amendment in *Citizens United v. Federal Election Commission,*[31] as were corporate religious rights *in Burwell v. Hobby Lobby Stores, Inc.*[32] Corporations also may have Second, Third, Fourth, Fifth, and Sixth Amendment rights.[33] Thus, courts consider corporations to be persons under the Constitution, subject to laws and entitled to certain protections. If corporations can associate, and, indeed, can even be religious, it is not farfetched to push a little further and ask if *all* persons—including all corporations as juridical people—hold the specific right to marry.[34]

At least at first glance, the answer certainly seems to be yes. In *Loving v. Virginia,* the Court noted that the freedom to marry has long been recognized as a "vital personal right," finding that laws discriminating on the basis of race violated the Due Process Clause.[35] The Court in *Obergefell v Hodges* found that the fundamental right to marry is guaranteed to same-sex couples by both the Due Process Clause and the Equal Protection Clause of the Fourteenth Amendment.[36] As the Court noted, "The nature of marriage is that, through its enduring bond, two persons together can find other freedoms, such as expression, intimacy, and spirituality. This is true for *all persons,* whatever their sexual orientation."[37]

If this is true for all persons, then should natural persons differ from juridical persons? Or should we adopt the approach of Professor Hilary Putnam, who once wrote, regarding the concept of robotic personhood, that "discrimination" based on the "softness" or "hardness" of the body parts of a synthetic "organism" seems as silly as discriminatory treatment of humans on the basis of skin color. As Angelo Guisado notes:

> precluding a subgroup of persons, whether they are labeled homosexual, Latino, or artificial, is a classification that, should the State wish to exclude them from marriage rights, must be justified in the face of the Equal Protection Clause. Thus, [a corporation] could possibly find repose in an equal protection claim, even in light of the extensive case law indicating that marriage is a fundamental right and a liberty interest under the Fourteenth Amendment.[38]

It would seem, then, that a juridical person could marry a natural person, or another juridical person for that matter. In fact, on July 26, 2012, in King County (Seattle), Washington, Angela Marie Vogel became the first woman in America to legally marry a corporation.[39] The marriage was short-lived, as the County quickly reversed its decision and voided the license.[40] But the statement by Cameron Satterfield, a spokesperson for the County, was revealing:

> [W]hen either party to a marriage is incapable of consent then it's void, no longer valid, or not valid period. So that's the basis in which we went ahead and voided the application. We went ahead and did that ourselves within our office because by the time it would've gone to the

> state, they would've voided it anyways. So we just avoided that altogether and voided it here.

Here, the problem seems to lie in the finite and quite addressable area of "consent." Perhaps, corporations cannot consent, and maybe the division of power between shareholders, board members, a CEO, COO, President, and others makes unambiguous consent too much of an issue.[41] The question of whether an artificial person could actually express simple consent is answered in a subsequent section, but before then, the question of whether robots can love must be addressed.

Robotic Relationships

Humans are already involved in sexual, caring, and even loving—if, arguably, unilateral—relationships with robots.[42] How mutual or consensual these relationships are in fiction versus reality is a different story, and a far grayer area. These relationships may eventually have significant legal implications, and there is a rapidly growing need for a framework within which to conceive of these robot relationships. Marriage, as a fundamental social and legal institution, provides us a tool with which to start conceptualizing an approach to robot-human relationships. Such marriages have not escaped treatment in science fiction and generally fall under one of two categories. The first, as illustrated in the film *Bicentennial Man*, is a human-robot marriage, where a humanoid robot is also functionally acting like a human.[43] The second, as seen in *The Stepford Wives*, is where an artificial intelligence (AI) replaces the human brain but the human body remains intact.[44] While this chapter will only deal with the first situation, objections to both of these scenarios tend to be similar, as the questions that arise may include:

1. Can robots/AI love?
2. Can robots/AI choose to be with someone that they love?
3. Can robots/AI choose to actually take care of people that they love?

The first question implicates different kinds of love and "love" simply may refer to an amalgam of thoughts, feelings, and emotions, such as pleasure, concentrating on the object of affection, longing, butterflies, and so on.[45] Certainly, a robot can mimic love, and even artificially experience all or subsets of these experiences that are widely thought to constitute love.[46] Whether they can *actually* love is legally extraneous. After all, many marriages are not premised on romantic love, and no kind of love has to exist on the part of either participant for a marriage to be valid. So long as a robot could pass any of the various marriage fraud tests that we use to weed out so-called "sham marriages" in the areas of family law, tax law, social security law, welfare law, immigration law, military benefits, and pension and insurance law, amongst other areas, the union should be presumptively legally valid.[47]

The third question—Can robots provide care?—has been definitively answered in practice because robots already care for the sick and elderly, such as the PARO Therapeutic robot.[48] Robots that can drive,[49] fold laundry,[50] and cook.[51] There is no longer any need for them to demonstrate their remarkable capabilities.[52] This capacity and willingness to fulfill a caregiving role, though, is also not a requirement for marriage, as the division of labor in any marriage is left for the couple to decide.

Legally, and as confirmed by the King County spokesperson, the second question is most interesting: Can robots actually choose to be with someone with whom they are in love? From a legal perspective, marriage is fundamentally a right between two consenting adults to contract to live together as spouses.[53] The right is not absolute, due to the nature of consent, and by certain factors, like age and mental capacity. State law may limit the number of spouses and set the prohibited levels of kinship as related to marriage as well.[54] Persons who cannot consent thus cannot enter into a marital relationship.[55] The robot, as a legally-eligible person, would just need to be able to consent, then, to the marital contract to be married.

The Functional Criteria of Consent

While the exact definition of consent differs in each state, Black's Law Dictionary defines it as:

> A voluntary yielding to what another proposes or desires; agreement, approval, or permission regarding some act or purpose, esp. [especially] given voluntarily by a competent person; legally effective assent.[56]

In addition, in terms of marriage:

> consent has been defined as an assent then present in the parties, freely, voluntarily, and understandingly given, representing a mutual intention of marital relationship by competent contracting parties. . . . The consent to be married may be manifested in any form; thus it may be express, or implied from the parties' conduct.[57]

Legally, consent is composed of four distinct concepts: (1) understanding, (2) retention, (3) formulation of decision, and (4) communication. These concepts are further condensed into three fundamental requirements:

> [1] the parties must have the legal capacity to contract a marriage, [2] they must voluntarily assent to entering into the marital relationship, and [3] there must be at least substantial compliance with statutory requirements as to the formalities of a ceremonial marriage.[58]

The legal definitions of understanding do not comprise deep contemplation of every (or any) aspect of marriage. At most, a person must have minimal understanding of the nature of the legal relationship that she is about to form and need not be aware of the possible consequences if the marriage ends. As the Supreme Court of Arkansas understood it:

> Generally, a party lacks the mental capacity to enter into a contract for marriage if that party is "incapable of understanding the nature, effect, and consequences of the marriage." ("[T]he best accepted test . . . is whether there is a capacity to understand the nature of the contract and the duties and responsibilities which it creates.") . . . As a collateral point, immaturity of the parties is not sufficient to establish a party's inability to consent to marriage. Nor does the mental capacity necessary to enter into marriage require the ability to exercise "clear reason, discernment, and sound judgment."[59]

Simply put, to be valid, consent does not have to be particularly informed or well-reasoned, and the process of reaching a decision is not subject to second-guessing by the state.

> Although many different terms have been used to define the required mental capacity, the best-accepted test appears to be whether there is a capacity to understand the nature of the marriage contract and the duties and responsibilities it creates. In some states the test of the mental capacity to marry is the same as the test of the capacity to contract generally; in others less capacity is required for marriage than for ordinary contracts.[60]

Applying this concept to robots is straightforward. Retention stems from concepts of mental capacity in medicine,[61] which concern human's choices under failing memory. In this context, what matters is whether memory is retained long enough to make the relevant decision. Robots, like any computer-based system, can save any information that they collect or access in their memory, whether on an on-board memory chip, flash drive, or external servers. However, AI systems should track and log memory faults because they may "crash," resulting in memory "lapses." Automatically backing-up and restoring this data protects robots from amnesia, and their recall would only be limited to processing speed, which is likely much faster than for a human.[62] In order to decide to enter into the marriage contract, the parties in question must weigh their options. To do so, they must consider their goals, values, emotions and thoughts, and the reactions from family, friends, and society that will be caused by their choice. This process resembles understanding, but also incorporates and accounts for idiosyncratic goals and values. Their parents, mentors, or the surrounding culture may indeed have inculcated these values, but they are ultimately the values that an individual has adopted and incorporated into a personal identity. Sophisticated robots are more than capable of instrumental reasoning in the sense of performing cost-benefit analysis and deciding on the best way to further their own best interests.[63] A criterion for consent is communicating that decision. Like retention, the ability of robots to express themselves, whether verbally or non-verbally, is simply a technical issue of having an appropriate interface, whether auditory or visual.

Finally, robots would have to be free of coercion or threat, just like a human, so that the consent in question is genuine. If those forces taint any part of the decision-making process of the robot, whether explicitly programmed or taught via machine learning, then such consent would fail to be genuine and the contract would be void or voidable. Thus, a robot would have to be free to learn and to choose whether it wished to marry based on internally formed preferences.

Can Robots Understand the Concept of Marriage?

This issue raises the following two secondary questions: (1) Can robots extract relevant information? (2) Can robots infer the consequences of acting on that extracted information? Information extraction falls under the purview of natural language processing ("NLP"), which has been around since the late 1940s.[64] However, anyone who has dealt with an automated customer service representative recently knows that even after decades of technological advances, natural language is not always fully grasped. To combat this error, many systems confirm that they heard correctly (including a just-proposed to human, who might say, "Repeat that again."). One can also receive a written proposal of marriage, and this proposal might be a more natural and less error-prone way to talk to one's beloved 'bot. The information extraction itself may be carried out using key words or lexical affinity.[65]

Once the robot grasps that the question is whether it will enter a marriage, it must be able to identify what exactly that entails. This task goes beyond a simple definition of marriage, but falls precisely within the range of traditional NLP research. Both denotative and connotative understandings can be extracted from semantic networks and sentic computing.[66] Minimally inferring what it means to be married does not require applying the latest NLP results, a simple deductive first-order logic system,[67] or an inductive Production Rule (such as, grammar).[68] More recent work using statistical machine learning, with the massive corpus of knowledge available on the web, the entire topic of marriage, with all of its varied realizations, can be researched far more quickly and thoroughly than a human considering a marriage proposal.[69]

One might object that even though it is well within the capabilities of machines to carry out many of the NLP programs, a robot still does not really understand the meanings of the words. This problem was first described in the context of AI by John Searle in his famous "Chinese Room" thought experiment.[70] First, imagine a computer that passes the Turing Test; it is capable of convincing any human Chinese speaker that talks with it that it is another human Chinese speaker. Then, consider a person, who only speaks English, is locked in a room with writing implements and an English print-out of the Turing Test-proved program. Messages in Chinese are passed through a slot and the person follows the program's instructions and passes back the appropriate response. Yet, Searle asserts, the person clearly does not know Chinese, just how to follow English instructions on how to manipulate symbols. For Searle, real understanding requires what he terms "intentionality."

Philosophers and roboticists have formulated different responses to Searle's conclusion. For instance, while the person (or, in case of a very large program, millions of persons) in the room does not individually understand Chinese, the system as whole does, just as an individual, or clusters, of neurons do not understand Chinese but the mind understands, as a whole.[71] Or the property of understanding is not the system's but is an emergent property of a virtual mind.[72] Others insist that if the person was not trapped in a room, but was trapped inside a large robot body that can fully sense the world and then attach symbols to meanings ("externalist semantics"), then the person would be able to understand Chinese through empirical experience.[73]

Finally, how do humans know that other humans actually understand them during a conversation?[74] If communication was assessed by measuring and evaluating how a listener responds, then a robot that passes the Turing Test would in fact understand. Searle's general response to all of these concerns is that original intentionality requires consciousness, as opposed to the derivative intentionality ("meaningful content") that a listener, whether human or machine, ascribes to language input. His opponents contend that all intentionality is the same; its application in "original" intentionality is simply a heuristic, and we attribute it to persons because it allows for prediction of behaviors.[75] This is the case even when the mind is not conscious.[76]

As much as researchers in AI confront such issues, they tend to take either a strictly functionalist approach, like that of Daniel Dennett, or they must admit that there is "something . . . deep" or "infinitely more complex" about human consciousness and creativity that is simply unachievable.[77] An intriguing exception is Zhu,[78] who strengthens Dennett's Intentional Stance by developing an AI hermeneutic theory. Zhu theorizes that those systems (for example, humans, robots, animals, and so on) to which intentionality is ascribed have four components: (1) autonomy, (2) operational opacity, (3) relatable behavior, and (4) authorial intention. Agents are intentional when they are designed to act independently. That action arises from processes that are so hard to decipher (due to being hidden or complex) that they can only be explained through analogy to a human behavior. Samir Chopra brings this line of reasoning full circle by combining a similar hermeneutics with a functional framework to define knowledge.[79] Rather than viewing knowledge as true and justifiable belief,[80] Chopra claims that knowledge can be attributed to an agent when the knowledge is true, accessible, and the agent can act on it.

While philosophers continue to debate the nature of understanding, intentionality, and consciousness, AI and the law may present us with solutions. The legal doctrine of "attributed knowledge" is used to show that as long as an agent possesses knowledge it is attributed to a principal, even when that knowledge is obtained outside of the agency's scope, given that a capacity to communicate exists between the agent and the agency. This sort of attributed knowledge is true for persons, such as a human, who "knows" the time by wearing a watch, and a company that "knows" your address by storing it in a database. For legal purposes, knowledge should only be attributed to an AI person when that robot can access and act upon data stored in memory. We may even be able to ascribe to robots an intentional stance based on hermeneutics, if the way that they then use that data appears complex enough to be inscrutable yet relatable. In fact, case law has been slowly moving towards using that approach to equate the actions of autonomous machines with the actions of human beings when mental states must be considered for legal purposes.[81]

Can Robots Make Decisions?

Some requirements that may legally constitute what forms a decision are: the existence of a goal, the possibility of multiple courses of action to achieve that goal, the ability to pursue more than one of those courses, and the ability to evaluate the cost of pursuing those options. The decision to consent to marry should also be fully voluntary, but does it not have to be rational; it can even be impulsive.

The first set of these requirements has been studied and achieved for a wide-variety of situations with respect to artificial intelligent planning and scheduling. In the 1950s, dynamic programming, exemplified by Markov decision processes, began to apply techniques from mathematical optimization to complex decision-making.[82] A decade later, John McCarthy pioneered a complimentary approach based on predicate logic called situational calculus.[83] In 1971, the STRIPS automated planner, which would serve as the basis for most classical planning languages (ADL and PDDL) was introduced.[84] Decades of research have led to much more complex planners, which have expanded and integrated symbolic and stochastic approaches.[85] Still, even early AI planning systems could achieve the basics of decision-making, and they were aimed to achieve optimality and completeness far beyond any legal requirement that is currently required for humans.

However, critics may contend that a robot is just carrying out a calculation but the values (goals and constraints) are not arising from an internal system. Of course, not all human values spontaneously form in newborns, and only some values arise from biological needs. Other values must be imparted and reinforced by parents, teachers, mentors, media, and culture. Additionally, robots could be given a robotic survival imperative (maintain electrical charge, minimize damage, limit processor speed, and allocate sufficient memory), so that other values could be imparted. Such values could then be incorporated into a robot's cost function and goals when it is formulating a decision. Indeed, development of a system that incorporates learned values, goals, complex memory, emotional responses, and logical thinking already has begun.[86]

The presence of a robotic survival imperative, coupled with derived societal values, would enable a robotic agent to make decisions. At the same time, robots would be at risk of being influenced and even coerced. Any actor could oppose the internally-held values of a robot and try to induce it to make one decision instead of another.

On the one hand, some people might laud an education system where students could be programmed with societal values as easily as the AI systems described above. On the other hand, other people might argue that a person must internalize these values, by understanding them and incorporating them into a larger value system. Marvin Minsky's *Emotion Machine* illuminates how emotions help humans internalize such values from their *imprimers* (parents and mentors), and how we might approach developing an artificial emotion machine.[87] However, we do not require that humans who marry (or contract) to have a well-developed value system.[88] Also, it is unclear how the law could turn this development into a legal requirement, beyond requiring the participant to have sufficient mental capacity. Logic is circular when mental capacity is defined as the ability to formulate decisions.

The standard tests of legal competence and mental incapacity may prove useful in resolving this dilemma. Based on *Dusky v. United States*, competency is based on the ability to consult rationally with an attorney and understand the facts of related charges.[89] And in the case of execution, the capacity to understand the effect of such is mandatory.[90] Similarly, a cognitive definition of mental capacity simply requires one to understand the meaning and effect of the relevant words, whereas an affective definition requires the party to be able to act in a reasonable manner. A motivational approach holds that the party must be able to judge whether to enter into an agreement. Both capacity and competence are defined in a purely functional manner and current AI systems appear to meet such tests. An important difference is that humans are presumed to have mental capacity over a certain age, and from that point on, a right to a competency evaluation.[91] If we adopt similar tests for AI, it would not be unreasonable to presume a status quo that a given AI does not have mental capacity unless meeting the requirements of the test. However, once a robot's mental capacity and legal competence is established, it is presumed that they can freely consent, unless coerced or the robot's functionality is compromised.

CONCLUSION

How strong, then, is the case against allowing robots, who meet the appropriate requirements, to marry? In general, the law seems to favor an intentional approach to attributing intent to better predict outcomes.[92] Additionally, case law has been slowly moving towards using that approach to equate the actions of autonomous machines with the actions of human beings in considering mental states for legal purposes.[93] Conversely, if the claim of Professor Gary Marchant is considered: "Robot-human marriage is not about robot rights; it is about the right of a *human* to choose to marry a robot."[94] If that is the case, then, given how Western society is heading in the direction of adopting the view that if no one else is being harmed, then consenting people should be allowed to enter into any marital relationships that they freely choose.[95]

Thus, a robotic person capable of entering into contracts could certainly understand, decide, and express an intention to enter into a marital contract. Then assuming the parties were happy, or at least manifesting happiness,[96] the answer to the question posed by the thought experiment of this chapter is, theoretically, yes. Robots and humans could marry someday, and predictably, they will eventually do so with the blessing of the law.

NOTES

A version of this chapter originally appeared as an article entitled "Robotic Marriage and the Law" in the Journal of Law and Social Deviance, Vol. 10. (Fall 2015)

1. Mark Hay, "Why Robots Are the Future of Elder Care," Good, June 24, 2015, accessed January 9, 2016, http://magazine.good.is/articles/robots-elder-care-pepper-exoskeletons-japan.

2. Brandon Keim, "I, Nanny: Robot Babysitters Pose Dilemma," Wired, December 18, 2008, accessed January 1, 2016, ahttp://www.wired.com/2008/12/babysittingrobo/.

3. Jordan Pearson, "Watch This Robot Learn to Limp Like a Wounded Animal," Motherboard, May 27, 2015, accessed December 20, 2015, http://motherboard.vice.com/read/watch-this-robot-learn-to-limp-like-a-wounded-animal.

4. Connor Forrest, "Chinese Factory Replaces 90% of Humans with Robots, Production Soars," Tech Republic, July 30, 2015, accessed Novermber 3, 2015, http://www.techrepublic.com/article/chinese-factory-replaces-90-of-humans-with-robots-production-soars/.

5. Andrew Nusca, "The Mining Industry in 2016: Sensors, Robots, and Drones (Oh My!)," Fortune, August 15, 2015, accessed September 18, 2015, http://fortune.com/2015/08/25/internet-things-mining-industry/.

6. Lena Kim, "Meet South Korea's New Robotic Prison Guards," Digital Trends, April 21, 2012, accessed October 10, 2015, http://www.digitaltrends.com/cool-tech/meet-south-koreas-new-robotic-prison-guards/.

7. Lawrence Knight, "A Dark Magic: The Rise of the Robot Traders," BBC News July 8, 2013, accessed August 29, 2015, http://www.bbc.com/news/business-23095938.

8. *Her.* 126 min. Warner Brothers, 2013.

9. *Ex Machina.* 100 min. Universal Pictures, 2015.

10. *Humans.* AMC, 2015.

11. *A.I. Artificial Intelligence.* 146 min. Warner Brothers, 2001.

12. Samir Chopra and Lawrence F. White, *A Legal Theory for Autonomous Artificial Agents* (Ann Arbor: University of Michigan Press, 2011).

13. John Chipman Gray, *The Nature and Sources of the Law* (MacMillan, 1921). 27, quoted in Lawrence B. Solum, "Legal Personhood for Artificial Intelligences," North Carolina Law Review 70 (1992): 1231.

14. "Legal Personality," https://en.wikipedia.org/wiki/Legal_personality. and Lewis A. Kornhauser and W. Bentley MacLeod, "Contracts between Legal Persons," (National Bureau of Econmic Research, 2010).

15. Solum, "Legal Personhood for Artificial Intelligences." 1239. To be fair, Solum also notes that "[t]his statement is not quite correct. As Cristopher Stone points out, X may be given the legal status of personhood in order to confer rights on Y. Thus, giving a fetus the status of personhood might confer the right to sue in tort for injury to it on its parents. See Christopher D. Stone, *Earth and Other Ethics: The Case for Moral Pluralism* (Harper Collins Publishers, 1987).

16. Henry Campbell Black, "Person," in Black's Law Dictionary (2014).

17. But see John Celock, "Steve Lavin, Montana Legislator, Didn't Mean to Give Corporations the Right to Vote," *Huffington Post*, Feburary 25, 2013, accessed January 7, 2015, http://www.huffingtonpost.com/2013/02/25/montana-corporations-vote_n_2761209.html.

18. Ruth Macklin, "Personhood and the Abortion Debate," in *Abortion, Moral and Legal Perspectives*, ed. Jay L. Garfield and Patricia Hennessey (Amherst: University of Massachusetts Press, 1984): 85.

19. See, e.g., Susan A. Ross, *Anthropology: Seeking Light and Beauty* (Wilmington: MIchael Glazier, 2012).

20. Mark Goldfeder, "The Age of the Robots Is Here," *CNN Opinion*, June 10, 2014), accessed November 3, 2015, http://www.cnn.com/2014/06/10/opinion/goldfeder-age-of-robots-turing-test/.

21. Amadio v. Levin, 501 A.2d 1098 (1985).

22. "Matter of Nonhuman Rights Project, Inc. V. Stanley, No. 152736/15, 2015 Wl 4612340," (N.Y. Supreme Court, 2015).

23. 22 Carmody-Wait 2d. N.Y. Prac. §139:76.

24. See, for example, Chopra and White, *A Legal Theory for Autonomous Artificial Agents.*

25. Gabriel Hallevy, *When Robots Kill: Artificial Intelligence under Criminal Law* (Northeastern University Press, 2013).

26. J.F. Weaver, *Robots Are People Too: How Siri, Google Car, and Artificial Intelligence Will Force Us to Change Our Laws* (ABC-CLIO, 2013).

27. Note that this question is quite different than debates about, say, abortion or end of life issues. Those debates focus on the outer limits of natural personhood, and when (and until what time) a natural person is human. This question fundamentally assumes that robots are not human, but can still be unnatural persons.

28. Guisado, Angelo. "When Harry Met Sallie Mae: Marriage, Corporate Personhood, and Hyperbole in an Evolving Landscape." *University of San Francisco Law Review* 49 (2015): 127. and160 citing *"Trs. Of Dartmouth Coll. V. Woodward," in 17 U.S. (4 Wheat.) 518 (1819).* 706;"U.S. Constitution," (1789). art. I, §10, cl. 1 ("No State shall . . . pass any . . . Law impairing the Obligation of Contracts. . . .").

29. "Marshall V. B&O R.R. Co.," in *57 U.S. 314,* 328 (1853). cited in "When Harry Met Sallie Mae: Marriage, Corporate Personhood, and Hyperbole in an Evolving Landscape," 130.

30. "When Harry Met Sallie Mae: Marriage, Corporate Personhood, and Hyperbole in an Evolving Landscape." 130 n.52 quoting "Santa Clara County V. S. Pac. R.R. Co.," in *118 U.S. 396* (1886). ("The court does not wish to hear argument on the question whether the provision in the Fourteenth Amendment to the Constitution, which forbids a State to deny to any person within its jurisdiction the equal protection of the laws, applies to these corporations. We are all of opinion that it does.")

31. Citizens United v. Federal Election Commission, 558 U.S. 310 (2010).

32. Burwell v. Hobby Lobby, 573 U.S. ___ (2014).

33. "When Harry Met Sallie Mae: Marriage, Corporate Personhood, and Hyperbole in an Evolving Landscape," 137–141.

34. The authors are aware that this is an oversimplification of the laws of corporations, and that there are multiple theories of corporate personhood, many of which rely on the fact that the corporation is really just an aggregate of multiple natural people. This Article is not meant to argue that corporations or robots should be able to marry, just that under some understandings it would be possible. For the purposes of the thought experiment, then, we are comfortable choosing the understanding that would best fit our question.

35. *Loving v. Virginia,* 388 U.S. 12 (1967).

36. *Obergefell v. Hodges*, 135 S. Ct. 2604 (2015).

37. Ibid., 2599.

38. Guisado, "When Harry Met Sallie Mae: Marriage, Corporate Personhood, and Hyperbole in an Evolving Landscape," 147.

39. Vogel, an activist, did this to try and draw attention to the U.S. Supreme Court's recognition of corporations as people in the controversial *Citizens United* decision in 2010; see Jake Ellison, Evan Hoover, and Mallory Kaniss, "Why King County Nixed Woman's Marriage to a Corporation in Seattle," *KPLU 88.5 News* (2012), http://www.kplu.org/post/why-king-county-nixed-woman-s-marriage-corporation-seattle.

40. Ibid.

41. Guisado, "When Harry Met Sallie Mae: Marriage, Corporate Personhood, and Hyperbole in an Evolving Landscape," 148–156.

42. See generally, David Levy, *Love and Sex with Robots: The Evolution of Human-Robot Relationships* (New York: HarperCollins, 2007).

43. Chris Columbus, "Bicentennial Man," (1999).

44. Frank Oz, "The Stepford Wives," (2004).

45. John Searle, The Rediscovery of Mind (Cambridge: MIT Press, 1992).

46. Jean Thilmany, "The Emotional Robot. Cognitive Computing and the Quest for Artificial Intelligence," EMBO Reports 8, no. 11 (2007).

47. See generally, Kerry Abrams, "Marriage Fraud," *California Law Review* 100 (2012): 1–67.

48. "Paro Theraputic Robot," PARO Robots U.S., Inc., http://parorobots.com/.

49. J. Rojo et al., "Spirit of Berlin: An Autonomous Car for the Darpa Urban Challenge-Hardware and Software Architecture," in *Technical semifinalist paper of DARPA Urban Challenge* (2007).

50. Karthik Lakshmanan et al., "A Constraint-Aware Motion Planning Algorithm for Robotic Folding of Clothes," in *13th International Symposium on Experimental Robotics (ISER)* (2012).

51. "Moley," Moley Robotics, http://www.moley.com/.

52. Mary Jo Webster, "Could a Robot Do Your Job?," *USA Today News*, October 28, 2014), accessed July 30, 2015, http://www.usatoday.com/story/news/nation/2014/10/28/low-skill-workers-face-mechanization-challenge/16392981/

53. See, for example, Minn. State Ann. §517.01, (West).: "A civil marriage, so far as its validity in law is concerned, is a civil contract between two persons, to which the consent of the parties, capable in law of contracting, is essential." Most states have very similar statutory definitions.

54. The free consent of the parties is essential to a valid ceremonial marriage. 36 Am. Jur. Proof of Facts 2d. 441, (1983).

55. The capacity to consent has always been part of the definition of the marriage contract. See, for example http://legal-dictionary.thefreedictionary.com/marriage.
56. Henry Campbell Black, "Consent," in Black's Law Dictionary (2014).
57. 52 Am. Jur. 2d. Marriage §28, (2011).
58. 36 Am. Jur. Proof of Facts 2d 441.
59. Porter v. Arkansas Dep't of Health & Human Services, 286 S.W.3d 696 (2008).
60. 36 Am. Jur. Proof of Facts 2d. 441
61. "Mental Capacity Act 2005," ed. Queen Elizabeth II (2005).
62. *Her*. 126 min. Warner Brothers, 2013.
63. Wendell Wallach and Colin Allen, Moral Machines: Teaching Robots Right from Wrong (New York: Oxford University Press, 2008).
64. Karen Sparck Jones, "Natural Language Processing: A Historical Review," in Current Issues in Computational linguistics: in Honour of Don Walker (Springer, 1994): 3–16.
65. Erik Cambria and Bruce White, "Jumping Nlp Curves: A Review of Natural Language Processing Research," in IEEE9.2 (2014).
66. Erik Cambria and Amir Hussain, Sentic Computing: Techniques, Tools, and Applications, vol. 2 (Springer Science & Business Media, 2012).
67. Jon Barwise, "The Realm of First-Order Logic," in Handbook of Mathematical Logic, ed. Jon Barwise (New York: North Holland, 1977).Dictionary.com. *The Free On-line Dictionary of Computing*. Denis Howe. http://dictionary.reference.com/browse/first-order logic (accessed: January 09, 2016).
68. Noam Chomsky, "Three Models Ofr the Description of Language," IRE Transactions on Information Theory 2 (1956), 113–124.
69. The ultimate goal of this research, in general, is to formulate a program that passes the Turing Test, where a human is unable to discern if he or she is speaking with a human or an AI.
70. John Searle, "Minds, Brains, and Programs," Behavioral and Brain Sciences 3 (1980): 417–457.
71. Margaret Boden, "Escaping from the Chinese Room." In *The Philosophy of Artificial Intelligence*. Edited by Margaret Boden New York: Oxford University Press, 1990: 238–251.
72. Marvin Minsky, "Decentralized Minds," Behavioral and Brain Sciences 3 (1980): 439–440.
73. Frank Jackson, "Epiphenomenal Qualia," Philosophical Quarterly 32 (1982): 127–136).
74. Terry Horgan, "Original Intentionality Is Phenomenal Intentionality," *Monist* 96 (2013): 232–251.
75. Daniel C. Dennett, The Intentional Stance (Cambridge: MIT Press, 1989).
76. David J. Chalmers, *The Conscious Mind: In Search of a Fundamental Theory* (New York: Oxford University Press, 1996).
77. Kelvin Kelly, "By Analogy: A Talk with the Most Remarkable Researcher in Artificial Intelligence Today, Douglas Hofstadter, the Author of Gödel, Escher, Bach," Wired (1995), http://www.wired.com/1995/11/kelly/.
78. Jichen Zhu, "Intentional Systems and the Artificial Intelligence (Ai) Hermeneutic Network: Agency and Intentionality in Expressive Conputational Systems" (Georgia Institute of Technology, 2009).
79. Samir Chopra, Laurence F. White, and Rue Franklin. "Attribution of Knowledge to Artificial Agents and Their Principals." *International Joint Conference on Artificial Intelligence* 19 (2005): 635–639.
80. Plato, "Theaetetus," (369 BCE).
81. United States v. Flowerday, in 28 M.J. 705, 707–08 (A.F.C.M.R., 1989).: "holding that [w]e perceive no legal significance in the difference between an operator who has been "programmed" to perform certain actions to effectuate telephone service upon receipt of specified "input" from a customer and an electronic device programmed to perform those same functions upon receipt of similarly specified input from that cus-

tomer," and "Thrifty-Tel, Inc. V. Bezenek," in 46 Cal. App. 4th 1559, 1567–68 (1996).: "The Bezeneks maintain they cannot be liable for fraud because the computer machinations did not constitute a misrepresentation and there was no evidence of reliance by Thrifty–Tel . . . misrepresentation is only one element of a fraud cause of action; the plaintiff must also have relied on the misrepresentation to its detriment. True, no human at Thrifty–Tel received and acted on the misrepresentation. . . . We view Thrifty–Tel's computerized network as an agent or legal equivalent."

82. Stuart Dreyfus, "Richard Bellman on the Birth of Dynamic Programming," *Operations Research* 50 (2002): 48–51.

83. John McCarthy, *Programs with Common Sense*. Fort Belvoir : Defense Technical Information Center, 1963: 300–307.

84. Richard E. Fikes, and Nils J. Nilsson, "Strips: A New Approach to the Application of Theorem Proving to Problem Solving." *Artificial Intelligence* 2 (1972): 189–208.

85. Avrim Blum and John C. Langford, " Probabilistic Planning in the Graphplan Framework," in 5th European Conference on Planning (1999). and H. Geffner and B. Bonet, "High-Level Planning and Control with Incomplete Information Using Pomdps," in Fall AAAI Symposium on Cognitive Robotics (1998).

86. Jean Thilmany, "The Emotional Robot. Cognitive Computing and the Quest for Artificial Intelligence," *EMBO Reports* 8 (2007): 992–994.

87. Marvin Minsky, *The Emotion Machine: Commonsense Thinking, Artificial Intelligence, and the Future of the Human Mind* (New York: Simon and Schuster, 2007).

88. Consider, for example, the fact that the Supreme Court upheld the right of incarcerated prisoners to marry: "Taken together, we conclude that these remaining elements are sufficient to form a constitutionally protected marital relationship in the prison context." in Turner v. Safley, 482 U.S. 96 (1987).

89. Dusky v. United States, 362 U.S. 402 (1960).

90. Ibid. and Ford v. Wainright, 477 U.S. 399 (1986).

91. But see Carmen M. Cusack, "Kent Make-up Their Minds: Juveniles, Mental Illness, and the Need for Continued Implementation of Therapeutic Justice within the Juvenile Justice and Criminal Justice Systems," *American University Journal of Gender Social Policy and Law* 22 (2013): 149–166.

92. Solum, "Legal Personhood for Artificial Intelligences," 1231.

93. Ibid, Part IV.

94. Gary Marchant, "A.I. Thee Wed: Humans Should Be Able to Marry Robots," Slate, August 10, 2015, accessed September 2, 2015, http://www.slate.com/articles/technology/future_tense/2015/08/humans_should_be_able_to_marry_robots.html.

95. *See, e.g.*, Baskin v. Bogan, 12 F. Supp. 3d 1144 (S.D. Ind.). *aff'd*, "766 F.3d 648 ", (7th Cir., 2014). *cert. denied*, "Walker V. Wolf," in 135 S. Ct. 316 (2014). *cert. denied sub nom.* ibid.

96. Not because we need them to be happy but as a first protection against coercion. For instance, see the interview with "Zoltan," a robosexual inventor in Addy Dugdale, "Technosexual: One Man's Tale of Robot Love," Gizmodo (2008), http://gizmodo.com/367698/technosexual-one-mans-tale-of-robot-love.

REFERENCES

Abrams, Kerry. "Marriage Fraud." California Law Review 100 (2012): 1–67.

Amadio v. Levin, 501 A.2d 1085, 1098 (1985).

Barwise, Jon. "The Realm of First-Order Logic." In Handbook of Mathematical Logic, edited by Jon Barwise. New York: North Holland, 1977.

Baskin v. Bogan, 12 F.Supp.3d 1144 (S.D. Ind. 2014).

Bicentennial Man. 132 min. Touchstone Pictures and Columbia Pictures, 1999.

Black's Law Dictionary, 10th ed. Edited by Bruan A. Garner, Eagan: Thomson-West, 2014.

Blum, Avrim, and John C. Langford. "Probabilistic Planning in the Graphplan Framework." In Lecture Notes in Computer Science 2000: 319–332.

Boden, Margaret. "Escaping from the Chinese Room." In The Philosophy of Artificial Intelligence. Edited by Margaret Boden, 238–251. New York: Oxford University Press, 1990.

Burwell v. Hobby Lobby, 573 U.S. ___ (2014).

Cambria, Erik, and Amir Hussain. *Sentic Computing: Techniques, Tools, and Applications*. Vol. 2: Springer Science & Business Media, 2012.

Cambria, Erik, and Bruce White. "Jumping Nlp Curves: A Review of Natural Language Processing Research." In Institute of Electrical and Electronics Engineers IEEE9.2, 2014.

Celock, John. "Steve Lavin, Montana Legislator, Didn't Mean to Give Corporations the Right to Vote." Feburary 25, 2013. Acessed January 7, 2015. http://www.huffingtonpost.com/2013/02/25/montana-corporations-vote_n_2761209.html.

Chalmers, David J. *The Conscious Mind: In Search of a Fundamental Theory*. New York: Oxford University Press, 1996.

Chomsky, Noam. "Three Models of the Description of Language." IRE Transactions on Information Theory 2 (1956): 113–124.

Chopra, Samir, Laurence F. White, and Rue Franklin. "Attribution of Knowledge to Artificial Agents and Their Principals." International Joint Conference on Artificial Intelligence 19 (2005): 635–639.

Chopra, Samir, and Lawrence F. White. *A Legal Theory for Autonomous Artificial Agents*. Ann Arbor: University of Michigan Press, 2011.

Citizens United v. Federal Election Commission, 558 U.S. 310 (2010).

Cusack, Carmen M. "Kent Make-up Their Minds: Juveniles, Mental Illness, and the Need for Continued Implementation of Therapeutic Justice within the Juvenile Justice and Criminal Justice Systems." *American University Journal of Gender Social Policy and Law* 22 (2013): 149–166.

Dennett, Daniel C. *The Intentional Stance*. Cambridge: MIT Press, 1989.

Dreyfus, Stuart. "Richard Bellman on the Birth of Dynamic Programming." Operations Research 50 (2002): 48–51.

Dugdale, Addy. "Technosexual: One Man's Tale of Robot Love." Accessed January 7, 2015. http://gizmodo.com/367698/technosexual-one-mans-tale-of-robot-love.

Dusky v. United States, 362 U.S. 402 (1960).

Ellison, Jake, Evan Hoover, and Mallory Kaniss. "Why King County Nixed Woman's Marriage to a Corporation in Seattle." KPLU 88.5 News, July 18, 2012. http://www.kplu.org/post/why-king-county-nixed-woman-s-marriage-corporation-seattle.

Fikes, Richard E., and Nils J. Nilsson. "Strips: A New Approach to the Application of Theorem Proving to Problem Solving." Artificial Intelligence 2 (1972): 189–208.

Ford v. Wainright, 477 U.S. 399 (1986).

Forrest, Connor. "Chinese Factory Replaces 90% of Humans with Robots, Production Soars." Tech Republic, July 30, 2015. http://www.techrepublic.com/article/chinese-factory-replaces-90-of-humans-with-robots-production-soars/.

Ex Machina. 100 min. Universal Pictures, 2015.

Geffner, H., and B. Bonet. "High-Level Planning and Control with Incomplete Information Using Pomdps." In Fall AAAI Symposium on Cognitive Robotics, 1998.

Goldfeder, Mark. "The Age of the Robots Is Here." CNN Opinion (6/10/2014). http://www.cnn.com/2014/06/10/opinion/goldfeder-age-of-robots-turing-test/.

Gray, John Chipman. *The Nature and Sources of the Law*. New York: Macmillan, 1921.

Guisado, Angelo. "When Harry Met Sallie Mae: Marriage, Corporate Personhood, and Hyperbole in an Evolving Landscape." University of San Francisco Law Review 49 (2015): 123–160.

Hallevy, Gabriel. *When Robots Kill: Artificial Intelligence under Criminal Law*. Boston: Northeastern University Press, 2013.

Hay, Mark. "Why Robots Are the Future of Elder Care." Good, June 24, 2015. http://magazine.good.is/articles/robots-elder-care-pepper-exoskeletons-japan.
Her. 126 min. Warner Brothers, 2013.
Horgan, Terry. "Original Intentionality Is Phenomenal Intentionality." Monist 96 (2013): 232–251.
Humans. 46 minutes. American Movie Classics, 2015.
Jackson, Frank. "Epiphenomenal Qualia." Philosophical Quarterly 32 (1982): 127–136.
Jones, Karen Sparck. "Natural Language Processing: A Historical Review." In Current Issues in Computational linguistics: in honour of Don Walker: Springer, 1994: 3–16.
Keim, Brandon. "I, Nanny: Robot Babysitters Pose Dilemma." Wired (12/18/2008). http://www.wired.com/2008/12/babysittingrobo/.
Kelly, Kelvin. "By Analogy: A Talk with the Most Remarkable Researcher in Artificial Intelligence Today, Douglas Hofstadter, the Author of Gödel, Escher, Bach." Wired (1995). http://www.wired.com/1995/11/kelly/.
Kim, Lena. "Meet South Korea's New Robotic Prison Guards." Digital Trends (4/21/2012). http://www.digitaltrends.com/cool-tech/meet-south-koreas-new-robotic-prison-guards/.
Knight, Lawrence. "A Dark Magic: The Rise of the Robot Traders." BBC News (7/8/2013). http://www.bbc.com/news/business-23095938.
Kornhauser, Lewis A., and W. Bentley MacLeod. "Contracts between Legal Persons." National Bureau of Econmic Research, 2010.
Lakshmanan, Karthik, Apoorva Sachdev, Ziang Xie, Dmitry Berenson, Ken Goldberg, and Pieter Abbeel. "A Constraint-Aware Motion Planning Algorithm for Robotic Folding of Clothes." In 13th International Symposium on Experimental Robotics (ISER), 2012.
"Legal Personality." https://en.wikipedia.org/wiki/Legal_personality.
Levy, David. Love and Sex with Robots: *The Evolution of Human-Robot Relationships*. New York: Harper Collins, 2007.
Loving v. Virginia, 388 U.S 1 (1967).
Macklin, Ruth. "Personhood and the Abortion Debate." In Abortion, Moral and Legal Perspectives 1984: 81–102.
Marchant, Gary. "A.I. Thee Wed: Humans Should Be Able to Marry Robots." Slate, August 10, Accessed Septmer 2, 2015. 2015.http://www.slate.com/articles/technology/future_tense/2015/08/humans_should_be_able_to_marry_robots.html.
Marshall v. B&O R.R. Co., 57 U.S. 314, 328 (1853).
Matter of Nonhuman Rights Project, Inc. v. Stanley, No. 152736/15, 2015 Wl 4612340. N.Y. Supreme Court, 2015.
McCarthy, John. Programs with Common Sense. Fort Belvoir: Defense Technical Information Center, 1963: 300–307.
"Mental Capacity Act 2005." edited by Queen Elizabeth II, 2005.
Minsky, Marvin. *The Emotion Machine: Commonsense Thinking, Artificial Intelligence, and the Future of the Human Mind*. New York: Simon and Schuster, 2007.
_____. "Decentralized Minds." Behavioral and Brain Sciences 3 (1980): 439–440.
"Moley." Moley Robotics, http://www.moley.com/.
Nusca, Andrew. "The Mining Industry in 2016: Sensors, Robots, and Drones (Oh My!)." Fortune, August 15, 2015. http://fortune.com/2015/08/25/internet-things-mining-industry/.
Obergefell v. Hodges, 135 S. Ct. 2584 (2015).
"The Stepford Wives." 2004.
"Paro Theraputic Robot." PARO Robots U.S., Inc., http://parorobots.com/.
Pearson, Jordan. "Watch This Robot Learn to Limp Like a Wounded Animal." Motherboard, May 27, 2015. http://motherboard.vice.com/read/watch-this-robot-learn-to-limp-like-a-wounded-animal.
Plato. "Theaetetus." 369 BCE.
Porter v. Arkansas Department of Health and Human Services, 286 S.W.3d 686, 696 (2008).

Prac., 22 Carmody-Wait 2d. N.Y.
Rojo, J., R. Rojas, Gunnarsson K., M. Simon, and F. Wiesel. "Spirit of Berlin: An Autonomous Car for the Darpa Urban Challenge-Hardware and Software Architecture." In Technical Semifinalist Paper of DARPA Urban Challenge, 2007.
Ross, Susan A. *Anthropology: Seeking Light and Beauty*. Wilmington, Michael Glazier, 2012.
Santa Clara County v. Southern Pacific Railroad Co., 118 U.S. 396 (1886).
Searle, John. "Minds, Brains, and Programs." Behavioral and Brain Sciences 3 (1980): 417–457.
_____. *The Rediscovery of Mind*. Cambridge: MIT Press, 1992.
Solum, Lawrence B. "Legal Personhood for Artificial Intelligences." North Carolina Law Review 70 (1992): 1231–1290.
A.I. Artificial Intelligence. 146 min. Warner Brothers, 2001.
Stone, Christopher D. *Earth and Other Ethics: The Case for Moral Pluralism*. New York: Harper Collins, 1987.
Thilmany, Jean. "The Emotional Robot. Cognitive Computing and the Quest for Artificial Intelligence." EMBO Reports 8 (2007): 992–994.
Thrifty-Tel, Inc. v. Bezenek, 46 Cal. App. 4th 1559, 1567-1568 (1996).
Trustees of Dartmouth College v. Woodward, 17 U.S. (4 Wheat.) 518 (1819).
Turner v. Safley, 482 U.S. 78 (1987).
United States v. Flowerday. In 28 M.J. 705, 707–08: A.F.C.M.R., 1989.
Walker v. Wolf, 135 S. Ct. 316 (2014).
Wallach, Wendell, and Colin Allen. *Moral Machines: Teaching Robots Right from Wrong*. Oxford University Press, 2008.
Weaver, J.F. *Robots Are People Too: How Siri, Google Car, and Artificial Intelligence Will Force Us to Change Our Laws*. ABC-CLIO, 2013.
Webster, MaryJo. "Could a Robot Do Your Job?" USA Today News, October, 28, 2014. http://www.usatoday.com/story/news/nation/2014/10/28/low-skill-workers-face-mechanization-challenge/16392981/.
Zhu, Jichen. "Intentional Systems and the Artificial Intelligence (Ai) Hermeneutic Network: Agency and Intentionality in Expressive Conputational Systems." Georgia Institute of Technology, 2009.

FIVE

A Friendship Model of Sex, Polyamory, and Plural Marriage

Diane Klein

What if, instead of treating sexual intimacy as conferring a *sui generis* status on relationships, we understood sexual relationships as a part of our voluntary connections, subject to the same basic principles and norms as those others? Would this destroy "romance"? Or would it liberate us? What if we treated our lovers more like our friends, and our sexual relationships more like our friendships? One of the first consequences—though far from the only one—is that we might allow ourselves to have more than one of them simultaneously, and even think of that as a good thing for everyone involved. We might do this, that is, *without* thinking it demonstrates weakness of character, ungovernable appetites, or lack of commitment. We do not think it is wrong to have more than one friend. Why, then, do so many people think it is wrong to have more than one lover? In part, I suspect, because of a usually unstated and unquestioned assumption of radical discontinuity between friendships and relationships of sexual intimacy, an assumption I suggest we might benefit from examining more closely.

The method I employ is simply to set out these observations, explore them, and speculate a bit about the consequences of applying them to sexually intimate relationships. What follows is not an argument "for" a friendship model of sex, in the sense of being an argument intended to persuade people to adopt this model. It is instead a challenge designed to suggest that the burden of proof should rest upon those who *reject* this model (typically without even having considered it), and instead treat relationships of sexual intimacy as a *sui generis* form of human relating, to which ordinary rules of interpersonal relationship, including friendship, do *not* apply. The considerations presented here are designed to highlight the underlying structural similarity, morally speaking, between friendship and relationships that include sexual intimacy, and therefore to undergird the claim that it is both psychologically possible and morally acceptable to be a part of multiple simultaneous relationships that include sexual intimacy. My goal is not to persuade those committed to either a monogamous or a *sui generis* approach to sexuality that their approach is wrong, so much as to suggest that those ways of thinking are not the only ones available, and should therefore not be regarded as the sole presumptive norms of sexual conduct. There are alternatives.

PRELIMINARY THOUGHTS ON THE FRIENDSHIP MODEL

The impetus for the development of this model came from noticing that, for many of us, friendship works better than sex. We have an easier, less fraught, time making new friends, keeping them, and letting them go, than we do finding lovers or negotiating the end of sexual relationships without trauma. A person may go years at a time without a stable sexually intimate partnership, while maintaining a few, several, or numerous non-sexual friendships simultaneously. Many, maybe most, of us are able to create and sustain healthy, mutually fulfilling friendships that last many years, and draw away from friendships that have ceased to serve us well, with a minimum of drama, emotional injury, confusion, and hurt. Many, maybe most, of us exist with relative ease in a complex network of friends, some near, some far, some who are close to one another and some who have never met, some we communicate with very frequently and others we see only once in a while. No two people arrange their "friendship lives" in quite the same way. And yet, somehow, it all works. In fact, for most of us, our friendships are some of the best things in our lives. Friendships nourish and sustain us, make good times more joyful and bad ones bearable. Normally, we neither suffer nor inflict significant damage at the hands of our friends.

A friendship model of sex begins with the idea of treating or thinking about sexual relationships in a way more closely resembling non-sexual friendships, and guiding our sexual lives in accordance with the same principles that guide our friendships. But the friendship model is also a heuristic, which can be used to evaluate the behavior of lovers (including ourselves) as if they were friends. Is there conduct we tolerate (or engage in) in sexual relationships that we would never stand for among friends? And if so, can that difference be justified?

Driving this inquiry is the thought that it is regrettable that so little of what we know of friendship is carried over into sexual relationships. We know how to find, and be, good friends. The successful practice of friendship has given us skills with respect to voluntary two-person relationships of varying degrees of psychological intimacy. Over a lifetime, we learn a great deal in and about friendship—even if we don't know that we know it!—both in general and for each of us specifically. Reflecting on friendship allows us to identify some "considered convictions," in John Rawls's technical sense of the term,[1] that have some unappreciated implications for relationships of sexual intimacy. I hope and intend that most of these will seem obviously true, even trite, set in the context of friendship, and failing that, at least plausible on reflection.

A Wittgensteinian Theory of Meaning as Applied to "Friend" and "Friendship"

It might be thought that a friendship model of sex cannot proceed without a very clear definition of "friendship." I think that is a mistake, but not an obvious one. It is right to say that not just *any* relationship can rightly be called a "friendship." For instance, we cannot simply purchase friends, as if they were commodities. But neither are there certain essential characteristics any and every relationship *must* have in order to qualify as a friendship, that we must identify in advance before proceeding.

Wittgenstein's philosophy of language presses us to examine a word's various uses to illuminate its meaning (his example is the word "game"), and in so doing, we "can see how similarities crop up and disappear. And the result of this examination is: we see a complicated network of overlapping and criss-crossing: sometimes overall similarities, sometimes similarities of detail."[2] This is his notion of a "family resemblance" that obtains between different uses of a word.

In explicating this idea, Wittgenstein instructs the reader to "look and see whether there is anything common to all. . . . For if you look at them you will *not* [my emphasis] see something that is common to all, but similarities, relationships, and a whole series of them at that. To repeat: don't think, but look!"[3] Look, that is, at everything to which we apply the word "game," rather than *thinking about* games and trying to identify what they all have in common (which, on his view, is nothing).

For Wittengenstein, then, the meaning and proper use of a word like "game" are conveyed by ostension:

> And this is just how one might explain to someone what a [friend/friendship] is. One gives examples and intends them to be taken in a particular way. . . . I do not, however, mean by this that he is supposed to see in those examples that common thing which I—for some reason—was unable to express; but that he is now to employ those examples in a particular way. Here giving examples is not an indirect means of explaining—in default of a better. For any general definition can be misunderstood too. The point is that this is how we play the game. (I mean the language-game with the word ["friend"/ "friendship"].)[4]

The language-game involves using the word successfully, understanding each other, without our knowing or identifying—and indeed, without there *being*—something every proper use has in common.

To take some easy examples, what one person might think of as a "friend" is another's mere "friendly acquaintance," one's "old friend" is another's "former friend." Are Facebook "friends" actually *friends*? It is possible for people to disagree about whether a relationship under consideration (real, fictional, online, etc.) is properly denominated a "friendship" or not, without undermining anyone's confidence in our ability to use the words intelligibly. All that obtains is this metaphorical "family resemblance" among our relationships with those we would call our "friends," and that is enough.

Wittgenstein also encourages us—urges us, even—to become more comfortable with the notion of unclear boundaries around concepts or words. "Friend" and "friendship" are no exception. He says, "We do not know the boundaries because none have been drawn. To repeat, we can draw a boundary—for a special purpose. Does it take that to make the concept usable? Not at all!"[5]

At this point, it might be objected that a Wittgensteinian approach proves too much: that with a "family resemblance" analysis, we *already* can see our sexually intimate relationships as a kind (albeit a special kind) of friendship. As voluntary relationships of affinity (an "overall similarity"), friendships and sexual relationships do of course have a great deal in common, including also many "similarities of detail." But to the extent that statements about friends and friendship do *not* seem readily to apply to, or accurately to describe, our sexually intimate relationships, that suggests a "boundary" has been crossed. "Let's just be friends" connotes an intention to not have any kind of sexual intimacy. If the application of these statements to sexual relationships produces surprising results, we have clearly taken the words beyond their familiar meanings and uses. Whether that happens, and what we think if it does, of course, remains to be seen.

Observations about Friendship and Sexual Relationships

The observations that follow do not constitute a "theory," much less a complete theory, of friendship. Instead, they highlight certain aspects of friendship I believe have special relevance to our thinking about relationships including sexual intimacy. Several of them derive from understanding friendship as a good in itself, with no other *telos*, so we may begin there.

Friendship is not teleological. There is something strange about asking the purpose of friendship, not because friendship does not serve various purposes or meet various needs, but because one who needs to ask seems to have missed the point. Friendship is constitutive of the good life. It is not merely instrumental in the satisfaction of other needs or desires. Nor do we tend to ask ourselves about a friendship, "But where is this relationship *going*?" A friendship is not a promissory note, to be redeemed at some future time, when what we put up with now will "pay off." We do not stay in a friendship because of what we think or hope or believe it will someday be.

We might express a closely related point more colloquially, by saying friendships "pay their own way." What this means is that in evaluating whether a friendship is "working," we look at the present state of the relationship. Is time spent together fun, pleasant, satisfying, worthwhile? Are the demands that it makes of us worth it? Do we feel "seen" and genuinely present in the relationship? Do we feel supported and affirmed (even if lovingly criticized)? When we allow ourselves to be vulnerable with this person, do they react responsibly? Do we feel this person has our best interests at heart, and is able to understand our best interests as *we* see them, even if that differs from how they might see them? Does this person sympathize, empathize, and motivate us, in the right balance for where we are in life right now? Will they accept our flaws? Forgive our mistakes?

A multiplicity of friends is widely regarded as healthy and developmentally appropriate at all stages of life. Consider a person (of almost any age beyond earliest childhood) who was able to maintain only one friendship (or one at a time). Such a person would be the proper object of our pity if not our scorn. This emotional or psychological limitation would reflect emotional poverty and stuntedness, along with, perhaps, over-attachment or over-investment in just one other person. We might think the person lacked imagination—about him/herself as well as others—in failing to find and recognize more than one person with whom he could share a recognizable relation of friendship. If the person had in fact *correctly* judged that he or she was unable to meet the friendship needs of more than one person, we would see this, I suspect, as an unenviable constriction of affection (even if the person was behaving in a morally responsible way in not taking on obligations of friendship he or she would later be unable to fulfill).

A person with only one friend would clearly be missing out on many of the benefits of friendship, including the way different sides of ourselves are called upon and called forth in friendships with different people. Having multiple friends also helpfully shares the "friendship labor." We do not depend solely upon one person to do all the things for us that a friend might do.

It would be worse yet if a person of this type, the "friendship monogamist," demanded the same of his or her only friend, even if the other person were perfectly capable (emotionally, psychologically, and otherwise) of maintaining multiple friendships. Would this demand to forego other friendships be an appealing sign of "commitment"? Or would this condition seem like an unloving, ungenerous requirement to accommodate one person's needs or insecurities at the cost of another's happiness and engagement with the world?

Mightn't we say the same about the sexual monogamist? The inability or unwillingness to have more than one lover, and the demand that one's partner do the same, may reflect some of the same limitations. They are perhaps real and widespread, but neither universal nor praiseworthy. If, when it comes to friendship, emotional exclusivity seems out of place, could that also be the case for at least some sexual relationships?

The "right number" of friends can vary both between people and over the life course. Some people have a lot more friends than others, and many of us have more friends at some times in our lives than at others. Some people can host a party and invite "100 of their closest friends." Others react to the very idea with incredulity. Some people are quite happy with just a few friends, and find further commitments unnecessary and unappealing. Others would feel terribly isolated or disconnected without a quantity of friends others would find overwhelmingly burdensome. Some people who want more from their friendships tend to deepen existing relationships, while others prefer to acquire varied new friends.

How many friends one has or wants to have can also vary over time. Some people make their closest friends early in life, and keep them, only rarely or occasionally adding new friends, while others may make new friends everywhere they go. Some find it easier to cultivate friendships while in college, because of all the unstructured time compared to working, while others find the work environment more congenial than academia for friendship formation. Some find it easier to keep up lots of friendships before becoming a parent, while for others, parenthood turns a more solitary person into one who craves adult companionship and reaches out to make more friends.

Whether our actual number of friends at a given time feels like the "right" number depends on many factors. Some people have more time and energy for the cultivation of non-family and non-work relationships; some people attract friends more easily; some people are disposed to use their discretionary time to make and cultivate friends, rather than on more solitary pursuits. There is a logistical dimension to finding the right number of friends, but part of it is also psychology, disposition, inclination, and even luck.

But the point is not only that there is wide variation on this front. It is that it would seem bizarre to judge people morally on the basis of where they fall on this spectrum. Surely, what is important, morally, is to be a good friend to the friends you have, be they few or many. That some of us are more sociable, more emotionally available for, or alternatively more in need of, the friendship of many people, is just one of the ways in which we interestingly differ from one another.

So, too, with lovers. For some people, it might be the case that they are incapable of creating and sustaining a healthy relationship of sexual intimacy with more than one person at a time. If so, it would be irresponsible for them to be multiply involved. (But of course, some people are incapable of doing this with even *one* person, and they are also irresponsible, yet rarely criticized on this basis.) But for those who *are* capable of it, it seems as pointless and counterproductive to suggest they should refrain from multiple involvements, as to suggest the same about a person who would like to have more friends.

If the number isn't one, some people interested in or drawn to polyamory might naturally wonder what the "right" number of lovers is. The friendship model suggests not an actual answer, but an unconventional way of thinking about the question in the first place. What is the "right" number of friends to have? The answer is, "the number that suits you, and them. The number that enables you to meet your obligations to them, while getting your own needs met in a way that does not place undue demands on others." Most people answer this in a practical way, without ever explicitly formulating the question or answer to themselves. A person who is feeling a little lonely, or in need of more companionship or different companions or more variety in companions, may seek to deepen existing friendships, meet new people, and so on, while a person feeling overextended, bored, frustrated, or misused may withdraw from or dial back those relationships that either have become too demanding, or are not significant or nourishing enough to warrant the time or attention they are taking away from more important (if more demanding) friendships or other commitments.

Like friends, the "right" number of lovers, and the intensity and duration of one's relationship with them, also tend to vary among people and change in response to circumstances. Even if, as may well be the case, one *is* the right number at some times and for some people, that does not show the principled superiority of that number over others; it only reveals what is suitable at that particular moment. The friendship model also counteracts some simple-minded idea that those who reject sexual exclusivity simply think more is better. Finding the right number of friends or lovers for oneself is not a matter of "friendship promiscuity" or unselectiveness, simply because the number may be 5 or 10 or 20.

Someone with many friends can be friends with a person who has just a few. A person with very few friends may be one of another person's many friends. Somebody else with just three or four friends can be friends with someone who has twenty friends, as long as the relationship reasonably meets each of their needs. Nor must the friends occupy *precisely* the same place in one another's informal hierarchy of friends, while perhaps too great an asymmetry would be hard to sustain. When one person is a much more important friend to the other, it may put the relationship under some strain. But some people have the sort of personality that makes others feel close to them, even if that feeling is not entirely reciprocated. If a person has a lot of time and energy for friendship, or simply delivers a quality of attention, listening, concern, and so on, such that many people feel genuinely close to her although she does not necessarily feel as close to them, then this situation is sustainable and might suit everyone involved very well.

The desire for the company of others is not a symptom of a problem in a friendship. Wanting a new friend is not evidence of a deficiency in any existing friend or friendship (and certainly not in oneself!). It may suggest something is missing in one's life, but not in a way that is a criticism of anyone. And nothing at all needs to be missing, in order to wish to add a new friend to one's circle.[6] Meeting someone and finding oneself desirous of becoming friends with that person is not a symptom that one's "friend life" is in trouble or that one's other friends are falling short in some way.

By contrast, for those operating in a monogamous/sexual exclusivity model, the mere *desire* (especially but not limited to sexual desire) for a person other than one's committed partner demonstrates a deficiency in the existing relationship, in the existing partner, in oneself ("weakness," incontinence, lack of "commitment," selfishness, immaturity)—or all of the above. Conversations around this aspect of monogamy center around struggle. The (almost inevitable) desire for others is a temptation to be "resisted," "fought," and hopefully, "overcome." A person of principle, who desires and decides to be sexually involved with a new partner, *must* end the prior relationship, or is inevitably "cheating."[7] This is a consequence of a kind of normative sexual essentialism, which posits that sexual desire *should* properly have only one object (or one at a time). This is the claim that Dan Savage expresses (critically) as, "[w]here there's love, monogamy should be easy."[8] Thus, when it isn't "easy," it must be because of a lack of "love." On this view, non-monogamy is therefore inherently loveless. This entire line of reasoning is foreign to a friendship model.

In friendship, we do not assume that novelty and variety must be sacrificed for depth. We can seek both novelty and variety, on the one hand, and depth on the other. Except at some outer limit of practicality (which may be reached at different numbers for different people), these are not deeply in tension with one another, and certainly not treated as mutually exclusive. Nor, in friendship, is depth regarded as a product or effect of exclusivity. The depth and intimacy of a friendship is not measured by how many *other* friends each person has or, as the case may be, *doesn't* have. A dearth of other friends does not, in itself, contribute to the depth of any particular friendship (or recommend someone as a friend, frankly).

Ultimately, each of our friendships enriches us, and in turn is enriched and supported by our other friendships. Obviously, it is not simply that one may have a variety of genuinely deep friendships, or that one may have deep friendships and an array of newer and/or more superficial ones, without either one jeopardizing the other. It is better than that. Ideally, each friendship actively nourishes the others. A person's ability to be a good friend develops over the whole life course, and one brings to new friendships a life-history of friendship experience. To have known some people well, over many years, allows one to see a new friend with a longer, better-rounded view of how people change and grow over a lifetime. At the same time, long-term friendships may fall into a rut or grow stagnant, with the friends locked into old roles or patterns. New connections offer new perspectives, new interests, and make each friend more interesting to the other.

Friendships do not generally threaten one another. At best, they enhance and strengthen each other. But even at worst, friendships do not generally even interfere with, much less threaten, jeopardize, or undermine, other friendships. One important exception or limitation simply relates to time and attention. Some friends and friendships are more demanding of time and attention, and thus will implicitly compete with other friendships and commitments, just as work and family may do. If these demands are occasional and generally manageable, they will not meaningfully disrupt other relationships. At least until we approach the limit of our time and attention, and barring certain kinds of simultaneous crises in the lives of various friends, one friendship should not threaten another.

Friends with constant "drop everything" sorts of crises are a different story, of course, and may involve some degree of explicit competition with other relationships and responsibilities. This phenomenon leads to the second important exception, which is perhaps more common early in life though not unknown among adults. Being forced (however explicitly) to "choose" between friends may happen when a rupture between two people makes it very difficult or impossible to go on being friends with both of them. For adults, a divorce or romantic break-up provides the most common example, with former friends of the couple "taking sides" after the split. For children and teenagers, "loyalty" to one friend or another may seem to require breaking off a friendship with a third party who is now an "enemy" of the other friend. But setting these to one side, the impact of one friendship on another generally ranges from neutral to benign to very positive.[9]

Because most of us do not practice friendship exclusivity, there is, in a general way, no such thing as "friendship cheating." That is to say, merely *having* multiple friends is not regarded, by anyone, as problematic, nor is making new friends a problem *vis-a-vis* old friends, as such, assuming one can continue to meet the needs of existing friends in a mutually satisfactory way. "You're so busy with your new friends you don't have any time for me!" is certainly a lament many of us have made or heard, though probably more frequently before adulthood, and it may be a fair one. If the person at whom the complaint is directed really did not intend to distance himself or herself from the complainer, that person may be finding themselves a little over-extended, friendship-wise. It may signal a need to reconfigure one's friend group a bit, a process that is not necessarily entirely painless, especially early in life. But this situation tends to be temporary. The point remains that it is not the mere *having* of multiple or new friends that is seen as the problem.[10]

If it would be disloyal to one friend to be or remain friends with another, that friendship cheating problem is posed because of the relationship *between* those two other people, neither of whom presumably begrudges the third person other friends in a general way. The problem is *that particular* other friend. This situation is fundamentally structurally dissimilar to the sexual cheating situation, which might be aggravated by the identity of the "other woman" (or man), but arises from the multiplicity of sexual involvements itself.[11]

Friendship is a flexible and capacious relation whose participants can largely define it for themselves. In contrast to sexually intimate relationships which typically carry with them well-defined roles and expectations, a long list of "shoulds" apparently culturally imposed and beyond question, in each friendship, the friends effectively make their own rules. What people need and want from friendships, what they expect from their friends and what they offer them, is as individualized as the people involved. It can evolve, change, and be negotiated, without either person bringing a great deal of baggage to that process. Each friendship has its own unique history, or perhaps more aptly, its own biography, allowing friendships to vary greatly in intimacy, duration, and scope.

Friendships can exist stably along the widest possible spectrum of intimacy. The metaphor of a circle of friends is a familiar one, with the very closest people in our lives, our "chosen family," in the center, and a widening circle of other, more distant, friends and acquaintances. At the core of our circle of friends are the people we know and like best, who know us best, and who we care most about, among our voluntary acquaintances. At the outer reaches are people we are happy to see when we encounter them, who we wish well, but who we don't necessarily go out of our way to see or get to know better. Of course, "closeness" is itself a metaphor, not measured by any single metric, like geographic proximity or frequency of contact. In some ways friends with whom we are in daily or near-daily contact are "closer" than those we communicate with less often, but we also have friends we may rarely talk to, but when we do, it is about things that matter, and we readily re-connect at a deep level.

Some friendly acquaintances may become real friends in time, but others do not, and not because of any particular "problem." Friendships do not "stagnate" if they do not become more and more intimate over time. On the contrary, many—and maybe most—friendships work best at a particular level of contact and intensity, and will suffocate from too much and starve on too little. It is perfectly intelligible and even common to have a friend one sees once a month or once a week, who would drive one crazy interacting on a daily basis. We might think of this as friendships "finding their own level."[12]

Thus we know, from our friendship lives, that it is possible to like someone enough to want to see or talk to them once a week, or once a month, but not every day. Yet this is dramatically more difficult to enact in a romantic relationship, which is seen as falling apart if it does not "move forward" in a highly conventional way. If two people do not want to see more and more of each other, it is regarded as the beginning of the end, a reaction we simply do not have in the friendship context, as a friendship finds its own level of closeness. Because there *are* so many acceptable levels of closeness in a friendship (just one of the ways it is such a flexible relationship), this is much more readily available.

A friendship that becomes less "intimate" is not necessarily a friendship that is ending, and how close a friendship is over time cannot necessarily be tracked in a straight line. It is possible for a high school or college friendship, for example, with daily in-person interaction often for hours at a time, plus technology-enabled contact, to transition as the friends go off to college, graduate school, or jobs in different cities, only to re-engage over vacations or should the friends relocate to the same place. Friends who travel together may be much closer during and shortly after the trip, but then re-settle into a lower level of intimacy some time later. Not only do these changes not signal a crisis in the friendship, they are often relatively smooth and painless.

Friendships develop organically, in other words, at a pace that suits both people. At certain times of life, and in certain situations, fast friendships can be formed very quickly. This happens to some people during times of intense stress or "hazing," or because circumstances put people together who just "click" or "connect." Some people are more disposed to make close friends quickly, whether because they have an intuitive judgment about people, or simply as a matter of personal style. Other friendships grow more slowly, over months or even years. These patterns are not "right" or "wrong." There is no hidden timeline along which things are expected to progress. "Is this friendship moving too fast?" is not a question we tend to ask ourselves.

Some friendships are brief, others are lasting. A friendship is no less genuine because it does not last forever. A friendship has not "failed" because it has ended. A person who was an important and dear friend at a particular time of life may cease to be that a year or five years later, for a variety of reasons unrelated to anyone's misconduct or failure. People's life course may take them apart. As individuals develop they may come to have less in common, and various events may cause a rupture.

The closeness and intensity of a friendship can ebb and flow over time, without ending, sometimes over decades. This is another way in which friendships find their own level. One may fall out of touch with a person who was a very close friend at one time of life, and then reconnect, by chance, at an event or because of a shared life experience. Put another way, the (perhaps temporary) waning of a friendship need not signal its impending end. Some friendships grow closer over time. Yet a friendship can also fade to the margins of one's life, without ending, and later re-emerge into more significance. As the friends' needs and circumstances change, the role the friendship plays in their respective lives also changes. How much better off might we be if we did not regard romantic/sexual liaisons as "all or nothing" affairs and instead it were possible to dial back or "de-escalate" a romance or sexual involvement, as we do a friendship, without ending it once and for all (and without necessarily transitioning to a post-romance friendship, although those are also very valuable). And how much better off would we be, if we could react to lovers or prospective lovers who decline to pursue (or intensify) relationships with us with the same equanimity, not untinged with disappointment sometimes, that we feel when a friendship doesn't quite gel. Most of us would rather remain friends with someone we wish we were closer to, than cut things off entirely (and needlessly).

Another way friends and friendship styles vary is in how demanding they are. Some people are, or prefer, "low demand" or "high demand" friends. Others are so demanding as friends that they make it difficult to be friends with others (or with as many others as one might prefer), and it is one of the many ways that people vary: how demanding they are of their friends, and how demanding they wish their friends to be, of them. What is for one person an appealingly low-demand ("easy") friend or friendship, is for another too distant to be psychologically satisfying. At the other end of the spectrum, one person's style of closeness might be experienced as a suffocating, overwhelming degree of "neediness" to another. A mismatch here is one way a friendship may "fail," even between people who basically like one another, and so part of finding the right friends is striking a good, or at least workable, balance in this respect.

We do not usually need "friendship break-ups" (and why we don't usually need them). As noted above, friendships can wax and wane, but sometimes they actually do end. Take a moment to think about a friendship from your past. How did it end? The relationship you brought to mind might be one that ended dramatically, like in big fight, a betrayal, a "blow out." There is no question that this is a large-scale emotional trauma. And yet, I would still suggest that this is atypical of the way friendships end. Think instead of someone who used to be your friend, but who you would say you are not really friends with any more, even though there was no dramatic end to the relationship. What happened? It may be hard to say. You simply grew apart. Maybe one of you moved or changed jobs or graduated, and neither of you were strongly motivated to stay in touch. Or perhaps one of you *did* try to stay in touch, but the other didn't respond. The relationship may have found a new (albeit lower) level—"friends on Facebook," or friends who exchange holiday or birthday greetings. But even with respect to a friendship genuinely over, apart from some low-level feelings of hurt, awkwardness, or regret (depending on which "side" you were on), your continuing feelings may well be mostly positive. You genuinely wish the person well, would be glad to be closer if circumstances facilitated it, and would be happy at a chance encounter. But your emotional energies are now elsewhere.

Precious few romances end this way, with a gradual, comparatively painless, mutual diminution of interest, or recalibration at a lower level of intimacy and involvement. Much more frequently, a violent rupture occurs, with deeply hurt feelings, insults delivered or received, pent up resentments unleashed, and tears. The rejection is taken as personal, and it may trigger or reignites deep feelings of unworthiness or un-loveability. We may find ourselves ruminating on the end of the relationship for months or even years afterwards.

The non-exclusivity of friendship is central to this standard reaction. Because we do not practice friendship exclusivity, the loss of one particular friend, when painful, can be cushioned by other friendships. Although every relationship, of every kind, is unique, a changing circle of friends protects the emotional well-being of everyone involved. If one must "break up" or "break off" a friendship explicitly, it is generally *not* because this is somehow a prerequisite to engaging in or continuing other friendships.

However, equally important, the absence of a need for friendship break-ups (and the dreaded break-up conversations!) reflects a more subtle and nuanced view of relationships, which sexual exclusivity does not permit. To want to be less close to someone, to see less of them or have them less entangled in one's own life, is not, at all, to wish to be rid of someone completely. This Manichean all-or-nothing approach does not have very much to do with friendships, which ebb and flow more naturally. The radical rupture introduced into a presumptively sexually exclusive relationship by the definitive end of its sexual component, for most people practicing sexual exclusivity, makes a post-breakup friendship or relationship of any kind exceedingly difficult to maintain, despite everyone's best intentions. The loss of a lover is, all too often, and regrettably, also the loss of a friend, though often a friendship can be salvaged or reconstructed some time later.

We can have—and be—"special purpose" friends. A "special purpose" friend is a genuine friend with whom one shares one or a few activities, but not more. This is distinct from what Aristotle derisively regards as a friendship based on utility.[13] A special purpose friend might be a poker buddy, a tennis partner, a trusted work colleague or mentor, or someone who shares our taste in restaurants or theater. Another parent of one of our children's friends might be this type of friend, such as another parent at the Lamaze class, the toddler group, the co-op kindergarten, the dance studio, the baseball team. Some "work friends" fall into this category as well. If we didn't work together (or if our kids weren't friends), we'd be unlikely to be friends, and if we cease working together (or the kids go off to different schools and drift apart), the friendship will probably evaporate. The relationship does not extend beyond its special purpose. This is not the person we call in the midst of a personal or life crisis, or with whom we share our deepest secrets; we don't invite them to our family events or expect to be invited to theirs. We might never visit one another's homes, or meet members of one another's families (or even know much about them). But the friendship is genuine; that is, the shared pleasure is real, the regard is real, and the preference for this person's advice or company over going it alone or with a different person, equally so.

A lover can be a special purpose friend too. Sexual intimacy can be the setting for a special-purpose friendship. In making this suggestion, I do not mean, at all, to minimize the distinctive aspects of sexual intimacy (nor to suggest that this is the only way a friendship model conceives of a sexually intimate relationship). There are a variety of activities in which we engage which are "intimate" in the sense that we are "opened up" and made vulnerable, physically, psychologically, and maybe most especially, in both of those ways at the same time. A conversation is an intimate one to the extent that the speaker makes him/herself vulnerable to the listener's opinion, reaction, judgment, and so on. Typically, an intimate conversation does not expose one to *physical* risk, although of course it might, as the disclosure of certain facts or sentiments might, in the immediate, medium, or long term, provoke physical violence in one's listener (consider confessions of infidelity or of transgender status). Coordinately, many physically intimate activities (a dental or gynecological exam, a surgical procedure) involve specifically physical risks, typically of pain or injury. Very few activities combine the psychological and physical aspects of intimacy as sexuality does. But intimacy is not only about risk of harm. The benefits of intimacy to human beings are vast, and for many, maybe most, of us, a life lived without any form of psychological or physical intimacy is a kind of wasteland. The very closeness that puts us at risk also makes possible the deepest forms of love, connection, and trust of which human beings are capable. Intimate relationships with these characteristics—sexual or otherwise—are so precious as to be "sacred" (for those to whom that term has a meaning).

At the same time, the conventional (sexual essentialist) wisdom, which not only equates sexual intimacy with psychological or emotional intimacy, but places sexual intimacy on a kind of pedestal among intimate connections, is not supported by experience. Those of broader sexual experience know, often all too well, that many of our non-sexual friendships are dramatically more intimate in virtually every way than some of our more casual sexual connections. It is perhaps unfortunate, but undeniable, that sex does not *necessarily* create or support intimacy beyond the transitory physical contact involved. To be sure, sexuality *can* be an arena for the development and expression of intimacy, but nothing about sexuality ensures that this is the case. This converts the sexual essentialist claim, in effect that sexuality is the "royal road" to intimacy,[14] from the genuinely descriptive to the normative/prescriptive.

Non- or antiessentialism about sex and its meaning fits into a larger view on which activities do not have, as it were, semantic content ("meaning"). The meaning of a human activity resides not in the activities, but in us, for meaning-giving is yet another human activity, engaged in by individuals and groups in a complex manner that is neither arbitrary and subjective, nor fixed and deterministic. The rejection of sexual essentialism therefore clears the way for us to consider whether sexuality even needs to be (or be treated as) the most intimate form of relating, and whether sex that is not intimate is less desirable or even abusive as a result (as is commonly thought). We are freed to think about intimacy and sexuality each on their own terms, have more realistic expectations, and question whether intimacy is even a characteristic of the best sex *qua* sex, for a given person. The anti-essentialism of a friendship model of sex is not only liberating but allows us to begin to ask these questions, rather than foreclosing them.

A Friendship Model of Sex and Polyamory/Plural Marriage

The friendship model of sex presented here neither entails, nor is entailed by, polyamory or plural marriage. It has no necessary implications about how many sexual partners a person might ideally have. Nor is this model the only, or even the most common, way of thinking about polyamory or polygamy. A person might have multiple sexual or marital partners, and still regard those sexual relationships as fundamentally different in kind from all other relationships. Both traditional polygamy and contemporary defenses of "open" relationships often subscribe to such a view.[15] Conversely, one might have a friendship model of sex yet be singly-partnered.[16] Although the friendship model is therefore not coextensive with polyamory, it quickly becomes clear that many of the most striking differences between friendship and romance, conventionally understood, derive directly or indirectly from the assumption of exclusivity in sexual relationships, which polyamory rejects. The suggestion that we think about relationships of sexual intimacy as a species of friendship, rather than as *sui generis* relations guided by a unique set of rules or principles, is intended at the very least to de-naturalize that essentialist view, and free us from what appear as its inescapable and even at times, unhealthy consequences.

Despite the lack of entailment, then, the friendship model supports sexual non-exclusivity in at least two ways. First, it provides an intelligible, morally credible, and familiar model of responsible multiple involvements.[17] Second and equally important, the friendship model contributes to that critique of sexual exclusivity/monogamy that centers on its disingenuous, essentialist, and dishonest view of sex, sexual attraction, and the relationship between sex, intimacy, and emotional commitment. To the extent that sexual exclusivity/monogamy is justified as the highest or best form of intimacy, as reflecting something about the essential nature of the sexual connection, or as requiring the fullest development of the human character ethically and psychologically, a careful reflection on both sex and friendship belies and thus weakens those claims.[18]

It might be argued that no one is capable of responsible multiple sexual involvements, either because of human nature, or because of the nature of sexual involvements (sexual essentialism *redux* or in a more historicized formulation—the nature of sexual involvements "for us" or "here and now"). Here, one is reminded of Kant's famous essay, "On the Common Saying: 'This may be True in Theory, but it does not Apply in Practice,'" an argument that has been thrown in the face of philosophers for more than two centuries. Presented with a theory that falls short in practice, Kant responds, "It is . . . not the fault of the theory if it is of little practical use in such cases. The fault is that there is *not enough* theory: the person concerned ought to have learnt from experience."[19] While conceding that perhaps only a philosopher would say that the cure for a bad theory is more theory, where sexual intimacy is concerned, what have we, in the Kantian phrase, "learnt from experience"? Surely not that sexual exclusivity succeeds, or best suits every person. Precisely what is suggested here is that our theory of what is best in sexually intimate relationship be informed by our experience of another emotionally intimate voluntary relationship, that of friendship, an arena in which, it seems safe to say, many of us are more successful and more satisfied than in our "love lives."

This chapter has asked the reader simply to consider what it might be like if we treated our lovers more like our friends. Some possibilities emerge from this clearing. We might allow ourselves to have more than one lover at a time. We might acknowledge that desiring another partner or relationship need not reflect a deficiency in an existing relationship, or in the character of the person who has such desires. We might treat our intimate sexual partners—and expect and demand that they treat *us*—in accord with the same ethical principles that guide our other close relationships. We might bring to our sexually intimate relationships the same creativity and flexibility enjoyed in our friendships. Finally, we might allow these relationships to ebb and flow more naturally, and end less cataclysmically. In short, we might love better, and suffer less, if we treated our lovers more like our friends.

NOTES

My thinking on these subjects has been greatly enhanced by conversations over many years with, among others, Eben Moglen, Zach Cohen, and David Weinstein.

1. John Rawls, *A Theory of Justice* (Cambridge: Belknap Press, 1971). Rawls actually describes two kinds of considered convictions, which factor into the state of "reflective equilibrium" at which he aims: "[those] which we now make intuitively and in which we have the greatest confidence" (these are also referred to as "provisional fixed points"), and those about which we are "in doubt . . . given with hesitation," and as to which we seek "a resolution which we can affirm on reflection." My intention here is to offer statements about friendship which fall primarily into the first category; in other words, what is contentious, if anything, is their application to sexually intimate relationships. If any fall into the second category, I hope my explanatory remarks serve to make them more plausible.
2. Ludwig Wittgenstein, *Philosophical Investigations*, 3rd ed., trans. G.E.M. Anscombe (Englewood Cliffs: Prentice-Hall, 1958), 31–32.
3. Ibid.
4. Ibid., 34.
5. Ibid., 33.
6. This of course goes double for children. Wanting to enlarge one's family is not evidence of a deficiency in the existing family (much less in one's existing children!). While certainly *sometimes* people have another child for bad reasons, for example, in an attempt to cure a relationship problem, people of course can have a *first* child for equally bad reasons.
7. Even an "open marriage" or "swinging" relationship, in which both partners consent to the other being multiply involved, would be seen by monogamists (I posit) as a sort of "licensed cheating," rather than as not cheating at all. In other words, this conduct would be seen as having all the detrimental consequences of cheating *other than* those that stem exclusively from secrecy and lying.
8. Dan Savage, "On Swinging and Monogamy," https://www.youtube.com/watch?v=Fm9Bwpxy4V0&feature=youtu.be (2009).
9. The polyamory literature is replete with discussion of a neologistic emotion or virtue called "compersion," defined as "[a] feeling of joy when a loved one invests in and takes pleasure from another romantic or sexual relationship," the opposite of jealousy. See, e.g., "Compersion," accessed July 10, 2015, http://www.urbandictionary.com/define.php?term=Compersion; https://fetlife.com/groups/574/group_posts/7393551?escape=false&utm_campaign=notifications&utm_medium=email&utm_source=new_group_discussion. I confess to a certain agnosticism about the sentiment, but to the extent it might exist, it would fit within a friendship model.
10. Similarly, an example of something like "friendship cheating" might occur if two friends have agreed (tacitly or expressly) to engage in some specific activity together, and then one goes off and does it with a third party, like seeing a particular movie or visiting a particular restaurant. And this sort of cheating is a potential problem in a friendship.
11. The identity of that person is often a sort of "adding insult to injury" factor—you cheated on me with my sister?!? with my best friend?!? And so on.
12. Thanks to R. Alan Berman for this phrase.
13. In Book VIII of the *Nicomachean Ethics*, Aristotle refers to a sort of quasi or pseudo-friendship based on the usefulness of persons to one another. Aristotle, *The*

Ethics of Aristotle: The Nicomachean Ethics, trans. J.A.K. Thomson (London: Penguin Classics, 1988), 262.

14. As Freud believed, dreams were the "royal road to the unconscious." Sigmund Freud, *The Interpretation of Dreams: The Complete and Definitive Text*, translated by James Strachey (New York: Basic Books, 2010).

15. See, e.g., Dan Savage, "Dan Savage on Swinging and Monogamy," https://www.youtube.com/watch?v=Fm9Bwpxy4V0&feature=youtu.be (posted 2009), discusses "opening" a relationship as requiring that care be taken of the more insecure partner by giving that person control over the "outside" sexual activities of the other partner ("you have to cede that control" (2:28); "they have the reins" (2:32)). This is entirely foreign to a friendship model. In a friendship setting, this would be considered abusive or just bizarre. In intimate relationships, one partner demanding "veto power" and "control" over whom the other may see or be friends with is a classic precursor to domestic violence and abuse.

16. Arguably, many successful long-term marriages function very much like friendships with a sexual component.

17. So do family relationships, of course, in which multiple siblings, multiple children, two parents, four grandparents, and so on, are common. There are certainly ways in which the experience of coming to love more than one child, in particular, has interesting implications for the psychological and emotional dimensions of having more than one lover. However, family relationships also involve consanguinity and the absence of chosenness, two features entirely at odds with the voluntaristic model of friends and lovers in which an unrelated stranger becomes an intimate. Although the experience of coming to love more than one child has a great deal to teach us about truly loving more than one person simultaneously, it is beyond the scope of the argument made here.

18. Within this narrow scope, this is a Heideggerian move, related to Heidegger's notion of "existential possibility"—not what is merely physically or logically possible, but what it makes sense to do. As Hubert Dreyfus explains, the "sensibility of a culture" and its "norms . . . allow[] in any specific situation an open-ended but limited range of possible activities to show up as sensible," and more specifically, "the range of possible actions available in this current situation, not to the full range of possibilities available in the culture." Hubert Dreyfus, *Being-in-the-World: A Commentary on Heidegger's Being and Time* (MIT Press, 1991), 19. In this Heideggerian terminology, "Put generally, the shared practices into which we are socialized provide a background understanding of what counts as things, what counts as human beings and what it makes sense to do, on the basis of which we can direct our actions towards particular things and people. Thus, the understanding of being creates what Heidegger calls a clearing (*Lichtung*). Heidegger calls the unnoticed way that the clearing both limits and opens up what can show up and what can be done, its 'unobtrusive governance' (*Waltens*)." Hubert Dreyfus, "Being and Power: Heidegger and Foucault," http://socrates.berkeley.edu/~hdreyfus/html/paper_being.html.The pervasive normative sexual essentialism into which we are socialized, an aspect of which is its self-presentation as merely descriptive, exercises just this sort of governance over what it makes sense to do, in our intimate lives. A different understanding creates a different "clearing," in which different ways of relating can show up, and different styles of behavior make sense.

19. Immanuel Kant, "On the Common Saying 'This May be True in Theory, but it Does Not Apply in Practice'," in *Kant: Political Writings*, ed. Hans Reiss (Cambridge: Cambridge University Press, 1991), 61.

REFERENCES

Aristotle, The Ethics of Aristotle: The Nicomachean Ethics. Translated by J.A.K. Thomson. London: Penguin Classics, 1988).

Dreyfus, Hubert. Being-in-the-World: A Commentary on Heidegger's Being and Time. Cambridge: MIT Press, 1991.
_____. "Being and Power: Heidegger and Foucault." http://socrates.berkeley.edu/~hdreyfus/html/paper_being.html.
Freud, Sigmund. The Interpretation of Dreams: The Complete and Definitive Text. Translated by James Strachey. New York: Basic Books, 2010.
Kant, Immanuel. "On the Common Saying 'This May be True in Theory, but it Does Not Apply in Practice'." In Kant: Political Writings. Edited by Hans Reiss. Cambridge: Cambridge University Press, 1991, 61.
Rawls, John. A Theory of Justice. Cambridge: Belknap Press, 1971.
Savage, Dan. "Dan Savage on Swinging and Monogamy," https://www.youtube.com/watch?v=Fm9Bwpxy4V0&feature=youtu.be (posted 2009).
Wittgenstein, Ludwig. Philosophical Investigations. 3rd Edition. Translated by G.E.M. Anscombe. Englewood Cliffs: Prentice-Hall, 1958.

SIX

Public Reason, Liberal Neutrality, and Marriage

Andrew Lister

One response to the claim that God defined marriage as opposite-sex-only is simply to deny that this is what God did. A second response is to assert that, whether true or false, religious views are not legitimate grounds for public policy in a pluralistic society. The idea behind the latter, "sophisticated"[1] response is not that the views in question are false, and to be repudiated, as we would say about racist doctrines. Nor is it that the views in question are simply irrelevant to the definition of civil marriage, as with theories about gravity or continental drift. The idea is rather that we should consider irrelevant certain reasonable but also reasonably-rejectable claims, claims that otherwise would have bearing on decisions about marriage. The result is to leave as grounds for political decisions only reasons that are generally acceptable—public reasons.

The central principle of public reason is that we should exercise political power only in ways that are publicly justifiable, meaning justifiable to every person. The phrase "justifiable to every person" means "acceptable to all reasonable persons without such persons having to give up the religious or philosophical doctrine they reasonably espouse." The demand for public justifiability is thus an idealized but still multi-perspectival unanimity requirement—what David Estlund refers to more generically as a "qualified acceptability requirement."[2] Public justification figures importantly in the "political liberalism" of John Rawls,[3] but has its roots in the response of the social contract tradition to early modern religious pluralism.[4]

In the wake of the U.S. Supreme Court's decision compelling states to recognize same-sex marriage, the idea of public reason is likely to receive renewed attention. According to Micah Schwartzman, Richard Schragger, and Nelson Tebbe, the *Obergefell* decision will "put an end to lawmaking solely on the basis of religious reasons."[5] Because the only plausible reasons on the anti-same-sex marriage side of the argument were religious, nonrecognition of same-sex marriage ran afoul of constitutional prohibition against religious an establishment of religion, as well as its demand for equal treatment of people with different religious beliefs. This exclusion of religious reasons from political decision-making has the structure of a public reason principle. As a constitutional matter, the principle might be interpreted narrowly, as the view that restrictions on *basic liberties* cannot be based *solely* on religious reasons, allowing that other kinds of policies might be based partly on religious reasons (and perhaps that controversial philosophical but non-religious doctrines could figure as legitimate grounds for *any* kind of decision). When we turn from jurisprudence to political philosophy, however, the idea of public reason is generally understood to apply more strictly, to a broader range of decisions, and to exclude a wider range of considerations. Since reasonable people will disagree about the good life, as well as about salvation, we should exclude from political decision-making reasonably contestable moral or ethical views as well as specifically religious (or anti-religious) views, realizing a kind of neutrality in political life between rival "comprehensive doctrines."[6]

When specified in this way, the principle of public reason calls into question the legitimacy of civil marriage itself, same-sex or otherwise, as well as the limitation of marriage to couples. Marriage is not just a contract; it is a public status that seems to privilege one particular ideal of intimate life, an ideal not shared by all reasonable points of view. Can we criticize arguments against same-sex marriage for appealing to controversial religious doctrines while at the same time defending marriage within the limits of public reason? If opposite-sex-only marriage violates the state's duty of neutrality with respect to conceptions of the good, why doesn't civil marriage (or its limitation to two parties) violate neutrality? These are the questions I address in this paper.[7] I will avoid constitutional issues, because they depend on questions about the proper institutional roles of courts and legislatures in a democratic society that are tangential to my main concern. I will instead focus on questions of moral and political principle that arise for citizens in any jurisdiction. I hope to show that different conclusions about the justifiability of marriage presuppose different conceptions of neutrality and different models of public reason. More controversially, I claim that there are reasons to be skeptical of models that build in strongly individualist requirements that would rule out most if not all policies justified by generalizations.

Section 2 analyzes four different forms of neutrality—difference-splitting, inaction, exclusion, and equal treatment—and explains their relationships with public reason. The main claim here is that the demand for qualified acceptability can be applied to reasons for decisions with a default of exclusion, or to laws and policies directly, with a default of inaction or equal treatment. Section 3 illustrates how these different ways of conceiving of neutrality and public reason apply to the issue of civil marriage. Public reason is inhospitable to civil marriage when the principle is framed as a constraint on state action directly, with a default of inaction or equality. When framed as a constraint on reasons for decisions, the principle's implications are not obvious, because there are plausible arguments for and against civil marriage. However, the case for having an institution of marriage (and for not extending it to include polygamy) depends on statistical generalizations. Section 4 argues that marriage is threatened not by the exclusion of non-public reasons but by a strongly individualist interpretation of a particular version of public reason, namely equal treatment. The ultimate purpose of the paper is to distinguish public reason from the requirement of individualized treatment, and to suggest that we should be wary of extending this requirement of individualized treatment outside of its natural home in policing and criminal law.

NEUTRALITY AND PUBLIC REASON

Principles of neutrality must specify at least the following parameters:

1. *Force* (vs. other principles): whether the principle consists of a *pro tanto* reason (something that is important other things equal, but not necessarily determinative), or a stricter moral requirement that trumps (most or all) other considerations.
2. *Subject* (who): to what agent the principle applies (for example, legislators, judges, citizens, etc.).
3. *Object* (what): in what domain or to what issues the principle applies (for example, constitutional rights, coercive laws, all policy decisions, etc.).
4. *Constituency* (between whom): between what parties or positions the agent in question must remain neutral (for example, points of view passing some minimal threshold of rationality and moral motivation, or a more demanding standard involving acceptance of certain core liberal commitments).
5. *Metric*: what the neutral point consists in, given the parties' different positions.

My interest is in the last dimension. Therefore I will simply assume that the principle generates a strong but defeasible reason (1), and that whatever its exact scope (2 and 3), it applies to decisions about the legislative definition of civil marriage. We will see that different accounts of the constituency of justification (4) can yield different conclusions about the justification of (same-sex) marriage. For the most part, though, I will assume (improbably!) that there is agreement on the range of perspectives between whom neutrality is required. If we hold constant the principle's force, subject, object, and constituency, what different forms might neutrality take?

Suppose that the state must be neutral on some issue of public policy with respect to a range of points of view. Each point of view consists of a set of premises (beliefs and values or principles), as well as some conclusions about the ideal policy, in the given domain. In a simple case, point of view 1 supports policy P on the basis of reasons X, Y, and Z, while point of view 2 supports Q on the basis of X, Y, and Z. Neutrality with respect to these points of view for the given domain could mean at least four different things:

(1) *Splitting the Difference on Conclusions*: adopting the course of action that splits the difference between the conflicting policy preferences. In our simple case, this is the policy that is equidistant from P and Q. If there are more than two distinct positions there will not be any policy that is equally distant from all ideal points (for example, Left, Center, and Right). The generalization of difference-splitting is to choose the policy that minimizes the total distance between the set of ideal points. Assuming each point of view counts equally and that we are not weighting by number of adherents, minimizing the total distance means finding the point that is closest to equidistant from the various policy preferences. Either/or choices pose a problem for this definition of neutrality, while aggregating multiple binary choices allows for intermediate combinations. Increasing the range of qualified points of view does not affect the neutral point, on this account, so long as the increase is symmetrical.

(2) *Inaction / Non-intervention*: not acting or intervening unless there is unanimous support for doing so (or for selecting from within the set of options agreed to be better than inaction). In the simple case, this means identifying one of P or Q as the active option, then counting it as legitimate only if both points of view accept it as preferable to the alternative, the inactive option. Increasing the range of qualified points of view shrinks the range of legitimate action, on this account, unless acceptance of certain policies is made a criterion of qualification.

(3) *Excluding Contested Premises*: adopting a course of action based only on premises accepted by all. In the simple case, this means making the decision between P and Q based only on reasons X and Y. The resulting policy need not be equidistant between P and Q. Increasing the range of qualified points of view shrinks the set of legitimate grounds for decision, on this account, unless acceptance of particular reasons is made a criterion of qualification.

(4) *Equal Treatment*: treating the parties the same. Neutrality in this sense involves a presumption against differential treatment rather than against inaction. Equal treatment is not equivalent to splitting the difference between policy preferences, because people might disagree about the interpretation of equality, or about its weight relative to other values. They may therefore adopt a range of positions, some of them inconsistent with truly equal treatment.

A lot more could be said about each of these notions of neutrality, but I will only make one comment about the meaning of equal treatment, before turning to the relationship between neutrality and public reason. Neutrality can't just refer to treating people the same; we need to know which parties have to be treated the same, in what respects. Every answer to this question implies differential treatment of other sets of parties in some other respects. For example, taxing individuals with the same income at the same rate implies taxing households with the same income at different rates, because some households have two earners and others one. Therefore there can be no presumption against differential treatment in general, but only a presumption against specific kinds of problematically unequal treatment. "Unequal treatment" must mean treating someone differently than someone else in a way that is *pro tanto* a bad thing, from the point of view of equality, even if possibly justifiable all things considered.

What is the relationship between public reason and these four forms of neutrality? The exclusion-of-reasons form of neutrality just is the idea of public reason, assuming an appropriate limitation of the range of points of view between which neutrality is required. The original Rawlsian conception of public reason assumes that citizens need not agree on conclusions, but that (at least on fundamental matters[8]) they must make decisions based on reasons everyone can reasonably be expected to accept. Excluded from political deliberation, therefore, are the various comprehensive doctrines that, while perfectly legitimate as guides to living one's own life, are not appropriately invoked in public decisions. On this view, it is the reasons that lie behind our decisions that must pass the qualified acceptability test. Otherwise, we exclude the reasons in question from our political decision-making. The resulting policies need not split the difference between people's policy preferences.

There is an alternative conception of public justification, however, according to which it is the laws themselves that must pass the qualified acceptability test, or else we refuse to enact any law, in the domain in question. I associate this model of public reason with the work of Gerald Gaus.[9] This revisionist conception of public reason construes neutrality as inaction, or at least as non-coercion—not having a common enforced rule, but leaving each free to follow his or her own conscience—and is thus potentially more libertarian (though not necessarily so, for reasons explained below). That the two principles are distinct can be seen from the fact that one can be satisfied while the other is not. The balance of shared reasons might be positive, even if some qualified point of view rejects state action based on its total balance of reasons. Conversely, all qualified points of view might support state action, each based on its own total balance of reasons, even if the balance of shared reasons is negative.

The relationship between public reason and equal-treatment neutrality can be understood in two ways. The first is to view equal treatment as a particular public reason, and to think of neutrality as encompassing both exclusion of reasons and equal treatment. The rationale for this interpretation is that there are policies that seem intuitively non-neutral but that satisfy neutrality of justification. State establishment of religion seems like the quintessentially non-neutral policy, because it treats members of different religions differently, but in some circumstances it might be necessary to avoid civil war, which is obviously a valid public concern.[10] Thus, it may be said that the idea of liberal neutrality goes beyond that of public reason, to the extent that it is animated by a strong *pro tanto* objection to unequal treatment. People can be treated unequally, but only if there are valid public grounds for this unequal treatment.

The second way of integrating equal treatment with public reason is to make it part of the principle itself. The demand for qualified acceptability may be applied to state action directly but with a default of equality rather than inaction. The principle would be that unequal treatment needs to be justifiable to each and every one of those treated unequally. Equal treatment is the default; unequal treatment is permissible only if it is acceptable to everyone, such as, acceptable to all those treated worse than others. However, each proposed law will treat *some* group differently than others in *some* respect; this is the problem of multiple inequalities discussed above. Therefore, the equal-treatment framing of the principle requires some substantive notion of equality to serve as the default. It must be problematically unequal treatment that demands reasonable acceptability, not just any differential treatment. The question then arises as to how a given form of treatment could count as substantively unequal, if it was in fact justifiable to everyone. The answer is that a form of treatment may be locally unequal, in a way that is bad *ceteris paribus*, but justified on the whole, in the context of other policies.

The idea of a unanimity condition on departures from equality is familiar from the intuitive line of reasoning that leads to Rawls's difference principle (i.e., the one presented in §11–17 of *A Theory of Justice*, not the original position argument from §26).[11] Inequalities between social positions must be acceptable to everyone, even the worst-off. However, in this argument, acceptability is determined by a standardized set of interests—the share of social primary goods of the representative member of the lower position—not rival doctrines. Rawls never argued that inequalities had to be acceptable to the full range of reasonable doctrines that members of the lowest social position might hold. Such an interpretation of public reason would give the most extreme egalitarian view that is still reasonable a veto over deviations from equality, even where these deviations promise to benefit the worst-off. The result would be a normative dictatorship of the barely reasonable egalitarian.

By the same token, the coercion model may seem implausibly libertarian, if not anarchist, in its practical implications. This is not necessarily so, however, for two reasons. First, when the set of policy choices is not binary, one can argue that any policy is legitimate if it is unanimously preferred as opposed to no-policy (inaction, leaving each to follow the dictates of his or her own conscience), and if it is chosen by some reasonable decision-procedure (for example, majority vote). Second, the qualified acceptability criterion can be applied to packages of policies, at a high level of aggregation, rather than to single policies, finely individuated. At a high level of aggregation, the inactive option may be very unappealing, since as more issues are lumped together, it will approach the state of nature. Whether there are principled grounds for these moves is controversial.[12]

MARRIAGE WITHIN THE LIMITS OF PUBLIC REASON'S NEUTRALITY

The lesson of the previous section is that neutrality can mean different things, and that principles of public reason can realize different forms of neutrality. This section explains how these differences play out in debates on marriage.[13]

Difference-Splitting

The difference-splitting form of neutrality appears in Jeff Jordan's argument that recognition of same-sex marriage is non-neutral.[14] Jordan reaches this surprising conclusion by assuming the relevant parties are those who think homosexual conduct wrong, and those who do not. According to Jordan, splitting this difference involves permitting homosexual conduct, but not recognizing same-sex unions as marriages. This argument has met with vigorous criticism,[15] but what interests me is to clarify the conditions under which it would be valid. These are (1) the interpretation of neutrality as difference-splitting, and (2) the appropriate identification of the positions between which the difference must be split. The implications of the principle of maximally accommodating rival policy preferences obviously depends on what views are taken to mark the ends points of the spectrum of legitimate or reasonable disagreement. "I think *hetero*sexuality is immoral," someone might object, "but I am prepared to split the difference, and allow both same and opposite-sex couples to marry, as a compromise that gives as much as possible to all sides." "I think marriage immoral," someone else might say, "but I am prepared to split the difference, and allow people to marry privately, as a compromise between the policy of having civil marriage as a public institution, and the policy of forbidding anyone to marry, even privately."[16] Of course, to some extent, every conception of neutrality is going to be sensitive to the way its constituency of justification is identified. It's also true that compromise may be advisable, in particular situations, in the name of prudence. Yet splitting the difference cannot in general be a moral requirement, irrespective of the content of the views at stake. Most discussions of public reason and marriage have not adopted this conception of neutrality.

Inaction

The issue of marriage is easily resolved if one assumes that public justification (or neutrality) requires that state action be acceptable to all qualified points of view. On this account of public reason, civil marriage must be acceptable on the basis of each qualified point of view's total balance of reasons. Otherwise, we default to not having any such institution. All it takes is for one reasonable point of view to reject civil marriage (from the right or the left), and we have to abolish the institution.

The coercion model of public reason is implicit in a number of discussions of neutrality and (same-sex) marriage, although in some cases it takes some work to disentangle it from the reasons-for-decisions model. For example, Michael Sandel has argued that the question of same-sex marriage reveals the illusory nature of the liberal aspiration to ethical neutrality, because the definition of civil marriage has unavoidable implications for the spiritual and ethical status of same-sex relationships.[17] From this perspective, recognizing same-sex unions as marriages implies that doctrines rejecting same-sex marriage are false, while failing to recognize same-sex marriage implies that the views of proponents are false. On the reasons-for-decision framing of public reason, however, this implication does not hold. If the balance of public reasons supports same-sex marriage, we ought to recognize same-sex unions as civil marriages even if homosexuality is not fully spiritually and ethically equivalent to heterosexuality. A decision in favor of same-sex marriage does not imply that this view about the ethical status of sexual orientation is false, just that it is reasonably contestable and hence, not public. At least if we frame public reason as a constraint on reasons for political decisions, the principle involves an exclusion of contested premises, not a refusal to adopt any law that some reasonable doctrine disagrees with on the basis of its total balance of reasons.

Sandel's real claim is not that the question of same-sex marriage is undecidable, on public grounds, but that public reason requires the abolition of marriage. If the state truly wanted to be neutral, he argues, it would get out of the marriage business.[18] The advantage of abolishing civil marriage is that "it does not require judges or citizens to engage in the moral and religious controversy over the purpose of marriage and the morality of homosexuality."[19] Since he doesn't canvass the reasons that exist on either side of the debate, Sandel can't simply be claiming that the balance of public reasons tilts in the direction of abolishing marriage. Rather, he is assuming that neutrality involves the state not doing anything that some reasonable point of view rejects. Since there are reasonable points of view that reject same-sex marriage, but also reasonable points of view that reject opposite-sex-only marriage, we should default to abolishing civil marriage (even though there are reasonable points of view that oppose abolition; this is what it means for inaction to be the default). If it is reasonable for someone to prefer no civil marriage over same-or-opposite-sex marriage, but it is also reasonable to reject opposite-sex-only marriage, we must default to not having a public institution of marriage.

The same model of public reason is at work in Kyla Ebels-Duggan's discussion of same-sex marriage. Ebels-Duggan suggests that for issues such as same-sex marriage, there may be no neutral resolution, other than abolition of civil marriage. Recognizing only opposite-sex unions would presume the falsehood of certain reasonable worldviews, but recognizing both same-sex unions would presume the falsehood of others. "Either way," as she puts it, "The policy is not justified to some reasonable citizens." The solution is "to get the state out of the marriage business altogether."[20]

The inaction default also is found in Clare Chambers' recent defense of a marriage-free state. Although marriage can be endorsed by a variety of conceptions of the good, it is not a neutral institution, Chambers argues, "since it is not endorsed by everyone with a reasonable conception of the good."[21] Chambers identifies a dilemma for proponents of civil marriage: unreformed, patriarchal, heteronormative marriage is compatible with the views of orthodox Catholics and the conservative strands of the other major theisms, but is incompatible with a wide range of more liberal views. If it is reformed so as to include same-sex couples, though, civil marriage would conflict with the views of traditionalists. Any state recognition of marriage is "inescapably non-neutral," Chambers concludes.

At this point a defender of a Rawlsian conception of public reason might object that if there is a good public case for retaining a reformed institution of civil marriage, then state recognition *is* neutral, in the relevant justificatory sense, and that those who insist on making decisions about policy based on their total balance of reasons should not count as reasonable, since they do not respect the demand for public justification. However, this allegation of unreasonableness ignores the possibility of interpreting neutrality as inaction. On the revisionist account, public reason demands that state action be unanimously acceptable, on the part of reasonable views, for whatever reasons, not necessarily the same ones (hence my reference to a reasonable doctrine's "total balance of reasons"). Even if the balance of public reasons supports reformed civil marriage, some reasonable doctrines maintain that it is preferable not to have any institution of civil marriage at all. Marriage therefore fails the qualified acceptability test, on this model, even if the balance of shared reasons favors retaining some less exclusive and less privileged form of the institution.

Exclusion of Reasons

If we approach the question of marriage from the perspective of public reason framed as a constraint on reasons for decision, we can reach a different result. In this section, I will try to show that there are plausible public reasons in favor of retaining civil marriage, and that it is at least not obvious that these reasons are outweighed by considerations that favor abolition.

One preliminary question about the principle of public reason, so construed, is whether reasons must be unanimously acceptable among the qualified points of view that exist in a particular society, at a particular point in time, or to all possible views that would meet the standard of qualification. For the purposes of this paper, I would like to avoid choosing between these models or making any very specific claims about the bounds of the reasonable. To illustrate the framing of the principle in terms of reasons-for-decisions, I hope it will be sufficient to sketch what I think is a plausible and plausibly public case for civil marriage, as well as some of the considerations on the other side of the question.

A second preliminary concerns the definition of marriage. The case for civil marriage requires some account of what "marriage" is, and what policies its recognition in law would involve. Civil marriage, I will assume, consists primarily of a set of mutual rights and obligations. It is a public legal status that has a somewhat vague but not indefinite social meaning. People who are married are generally involved in, or have been involved in, an ongoing sexual or romantic relationship that involves a commitment to mutual care. The existence of such a status encourages social norms that govern the treatment of married couples, for example, that one ought not use a low point in a marriage to try to pry someone away from their partner. I will assume that marriage also involves some rights with respect to third parties, rights that foster and facilitate such relationships, for example, visitation rights in hospitals, immigration rights, testimonial privilege in courts, and a right to leave from work to care for one's spouse. However, marriage ought not involve any special tax treatment or financial bonus. Nor should benefits that ought to be available to all citizens such as health care be available only to married couples, via an employed spouse (although it is of course better than they be available in this way than not at all). I will assume that marriage is open to both same and opposite-sex couples, but only to couples. The existence of marriage does not rule out that there could be other, distinct personal relationship statuses, such as domestic partnership, nor does it rule out contractual re-creation of marriage-like relationships.

One reason for having the institution of marriage is that it helps people communicate to others certain general facts about the nature of their relationship.[22] Getting married is a way of signalling to others that the relationship involves a long-term commitment to mutual care and cooperation generally involving sexual intimacy. A relationship need not have these characteristics to count as a legal marriage, but it is common knowledge that people who marry normally intend their relationship to have this character, and expect others to understand that if married, their relationship probably has or aspires to have these features. It facilitates a range of social interactions for people to be able to communicate these facts about their relationship easily, without others having to ask, particularly in a pluralistic society where religious and cultural conceptions of marriage will vary around this core.

A second reason for marriage is that the existence of the public status solves a kind of collective action problem. One of the things people typically seek, in marriage, is intimacy, meaning a high degree of openness of one's self to another, and a blurring of the boundaries of one's self and the other.[23] It may be self-defeating to negotiate the legal terms of such a relationship in advance, for example, via a prenuptial agreement. Negotiations encourage people to think of themselves as separate individuals with distinct interests, but in this case the parties involved are trying to get themselves into a relationship based on shared interests (such as, interests defined in part by their being shared). Marriage therefore helps solve a kind of market-failure, and so can be justified on the neutral ground that it helps satisfy unobjectionable preferences rather than the perfectionist grounds of promoting what some believe to be truly valuable.

Third, civil marriage may encourage stable, two-parent childrearing, which is likely to benefit children in ordinary ways. Abolishing marriage would be expected to work against the goal of encouraging adults to team up in the raising of children. The question of the effects of family structure on child outcomes is of course highly controversial.[24] Is family structure the cause of worse outcomes, or is it the result of factors that independently diminish chances of success for children? Is family structure itself to blame, or is it the greater incidence of economic hardship on the part of single parents (typically women)? Would allegedly inferior types of family still be harmful if they weren't stigmatized by society's valorization of the intact biological family? If we socialized childrearing, adults could enter and exit relationships as they pleased without major risks of harm to children. In the context of private childrearing, however, liberty for adults is in tension with well-being for children. Although many different combinations of parenting and intimate relationships can work fine, the question is what combinations are likely to work best, in a society unwilling to socialize childrearing except in very limited ways.

There are reasons on the other side of the argument as well. One of the most prominent concerns is that marriage disadvantages women, undermining their autonomy and equality with respect to men. This was certainly true when "coverture" meant that a married women had no legal existence independent of her husband.[25] Even after women gained civil and political rights, non-enforcement within marriage of laws against rape and assault meant that marriage created a "zone of partial lawlessness," in the words of Anita Bernstein.[26] And even with improved enforcement, economic dependence within marriage creates obstacles to exit from abusive relationships.[27] According to Claudia Card, marriage promotes "murder and mayhem" by encouraging people to blend their lives, binding themselves together in ways that create resentment and reduce autonomy, by making it harder to leave.[28] From this perspective, private marriage should at best be tolerated, not encouraged by the creation of a public status.

Yet men can also be violent and women economically dependent in unmarried intimate relationships. Women might be better off if not involved with men at all, but if they will be cohabiting and raising children with them anyway, it may be beneficial for them to have the option of marrying. Marriage can provide some protection against the vulnerabilities that arise in intimate relationships. Even without marriage many people will still fall in love, move in together, and have children, creating emotional, psychological, and economic interdependence. While it can provide security and mutual support, this interdependence is also risky since it can be unequal, due to differences in affection, attitudes towards risk, possession of marketable skills, and so on. People make decisions about children, work, place of residence, hoping for permanency, but in ways that may leave them unequally vulnerable if the relationship breaks down. One response is to impose some of the mutual rights and obligations of marriage on unmarried couples who cohabit in a conjugal relationship for a certain period of time.[29] Yet this policy means that people no longer have the option of cohabiting without these rights and obligations. There is thus a case for preserving a status that makes available an egalitarian package of mutual rights and duties that protect people in intimate relationships.

I have only sketched a public case for marriage, and some of the objections it faces. I do not claim that this case is conclusive, just that it is plausible, and plausibly public, and that there is a debate to be had about where exactly the balance of public reasons lies. The reason for making this point is to illustrate the consequences of framing the principle of public reason as a constraint on reasons for decisions. As described in the previous section, many people have thought that only the abolition of civil marriage could satisfy the demand for state neutrality. That is true if neutrality is understood as inaction, and if public reason is framed as a constraint on state action directly, with a default of inaction. It is not true when the principle is framed as a constraint on reasons for political decisions. The question of the justifiability of civil marriage within the limits of public reason is not open and shut.

Equality

In Section 2, I argued that the principle of public reason cannot plausibly be framed as a constraint on state action with a default of equal treatment. Equal treatment is nonetheless an important public reason. Unequal treatment can only be justified by sufficiently weighty public reasons.

The equality objection to civil marriage is obviously powerful when marriage is not open to same-sex couples. True, under the regime of opposite-sex-only marriage, everyone is allowed to marry someone of the opposite sex, even if they are gay, while no one is allowed to marry anyone of the same sex, even if they are heterosexual. So we can imagine worse regimes, for example, one in which proof of heterosexuality was required in order to marry. Still, in order to see the force of the equality objection to opposite-sex-only marriage, one only needs to imagine a situation in which only same-sex couples could marry, be they gay or straight. Would heterosexuals not complain of unequal treatment?

The equality objection is also powerful if the state treats marriage as a privileged status, to be supported by a range of tax benefits intended to encourage people to marry (by penalizing the unmarried). However, if marriage is treated primarily as a prepackaged set of mutual rights and duties, including only a limited set of rights with respect to third parties, the objection is less pressing, and may be outweighed by the public reasons in favor of civil marriage.

The equality objection may be more powerful than it initially appears, though, if it is understood to require individualized treatment. By "individualized treatment," I mean treatment based on characteristics of the individual, as opposed to treatment based on average characteristics of a group to which the individual belongs. Examples of treatment that is not individualized include racial profiling in policing, different car insurance rates for men and women, and perhaps also having a mandatory retirement age. Each of these policies involves differential treatment based on an imperfect correlation between an observable characteristic (race, sex, age) and an underlying variable of interest (crime, accidents, productive ability). These policies are based on averages, in the sense that they are justified by statistical generalizations.

A good example of the application of individualized treatment to family law is provided by the Law Commission of Canada's 2001 report *Beyond Conjugality*. The report argues that the state ought not use broad relationship types as a criterion for regulating behavior or delivering benefits, but focus instead on relationships that have the characteristics that are ultimately of interest given state objectives.[30] Of course, it would be irrational to use characteristics wholly unrelated to legislative objectives; the issue is about use of characteristics that are only statistically related to outcomes of interest. "Relational equality" and "relational autonomy" are said to be compromised when the state gives more support (or penalties) to one relationship status than to others.[31] This demand for neutrality with respect to relationship status does not mean that government must treat all relationships the same, but only that laws must be framed in terms of "the qualitative attributes of relationships,"[32] for example, the presence of violence within the relationship, but not conjugality. Thus, relational neutrality rules out policies on based on imperfect correlations, or proxies.

Not all of the arguments for civil marriage depend on generalizations about the consequences of relationship types. The communicative argument does not maintain that civil marriage encourages a relationship-type that is independently beneficial. Rather, it maintains that the existence of the public status helps satisfy unobjectionable personal preferences on the part of those who would be in such relationships anyway. The facilitative argument depends on the claim that the public status makes it easier for those who seek intimacy to obtain it, not that intimate relationships should be promoted because they are generally beneficial.

However, some of the elements of the public case for civil marriage that I sketched above clearly do depend on generalizations. The argument based on children's interests was that given private childrearing, children generally do better when raised by parents in a stable, long-term relationship (and that the existence of marriage as a labelled package of mutual rights and obligations encourages such relationships). The protective argument was that conjugal relationships carry risks, when they break down, and that having a default set of rights and obligations provides some protection against such risks. These arguments depend on claims about average consequences of broad types of relationships; they are not claims about what is true in each case.

Some arguments for limiting the scope of the right to marry also depend on generalizations. One of the main grounds for not recognizing polygamous relationships as valid civil marriages is that such relationships are predominantly polygynous, such as, one man and two or more women, and that such relationships tend to undermine the autonomy and equality of women. In his critique of Chief Justice Roberts' attempt to link legal recognition of same-sex marriage to legal recognition of plural marriage in his dissent in *Obergefell*, Stephen Macedo says that plural marriage is "strongly associated" with patriarchy.[33] A second argument is that the increased prevalence of such relationships has other negative social consequences. Jonathan Rauch quotes a 2012 study as finding "significantly higher levels" of crimes such as murder and assault in polygynous cultures (mainly due to reduced access to marriage on the part of young men without wealth or status).[34]

One problem with policies based on averages is that they are less effective than policies targeted more narrowly at the variable of fundamental interest. Yet it may be costly or impossible to observe this variable, making the policies in question effective relative to the feasible alternatives. The other main problem with policies based on averages is that they may violate individual rights. The arguments against polygamy cited above are consequentialist. Whether people will have the legal right to marry more than one person at a time is to be determined on the basis of the aggregate social consequences. There is a tension, however, between arguing for same-sex marriage as a right, and resisting polygamy on utilitarian grounds, as John Holbo puts it.[35] Of course, the reason for concern about gender inequality is not only that it diminishes utility. Nevertheless, the argument is consequentialist, in the sense that it bases the decision about whether people will have the right to marry more than one person based on the aggregate consequences of recognizing the right, rather than on intrinsic considerations that apply in each case. In response to Rauch, Fredrik de Boer asks "are we really rights consequentialists?"[36]

One general point to make about objections to consequentialism is that the problem they raise for the institution of marriage does not stem from the principle of public reason but from a commitment to specific rights. The perceived flaw in the gender equality objection to polygamy is that it is inconsistent with rights-based arguments for same-sex marriage, not that it depends on non-public reasons.

A second point is that we need to be clear about what right is in question. If there is a right to plural marriage, it could not be defeated by the negative consequences with which it is statistically associated. But that is the question; is there such a right? The argument might be that there is a right to marry, and that limits on this right can't be based on consequentialist considerations. However, it's not obvious that there is a moral right to marry (as distinct from a constitutional right). I do not believe that we would wrong anyone if we abolished civil marriage, in favor of a system private relationship contracts and purely associational marriage, though in my view such a policy would be suboptimal from the point of view of well-being.[37] Even if there is a right to marry, it's not clear that limits on whom one can marry must be justified in each particular case, disregarding average effects across multiple instances. The idea that rights trump considerations related to general welfare does not imply that social consequences are irrelevant to delimiting the scope of a right. The stringent kind of priority moral rights enjoy would be implausibly demanding if any limitation in the scope of a right counted as an infringement that made all non-rights consequences irrelevant. I have a right to vote, but that doesn't mean that cost is irrelevant in setting up a voting system. Otherwise, there might be no money left over for education and health care. My right to life should not be sacrificed for the sake of the comfort of *n* others, no matter the size of *n*, but that cannot mean that any reduction in the probability of assault is always more important than any other social benefit, regardless of cost.[38] Our basic rights and liberties must be specified in terms of a "central range of application,"[39] so that not just any limitation counts as an infringement. Individual rights never are absolute; they can only plausibly be trumps over aggregate consequences if their content is appropriately delimited.

Instead of appealing to a right to marriage, though, proponents of plural marriage may appeal to a right to equal treatment, which can be understood in at least two different ways. On the first account, individuals have a right not to be treated by the state in ways that are stigmatizing and that contribute to their status as second-class citizens (people generally perceived and treated as having lesser worth). Citizens may also have a right to positive actions that prevent, protect against or correct such a status. So understood, the right to equal treatment involves a conception of equality defined by what Cass Sunstein calls the "the anti-caste principle."[40]

The second way of understanding the right to equality is as a right to being treated equally as an individual, based on one's individual characteristics, rather than on the basis of the average characteristics of the group to which one belong. Policies based on averages impose burdens on some because of the conduct of others, conduct for which they are not responsible. Such policies are discriminatory, in a sense, even where the group in question is not marginalized or oppressed. Anti-discrimination law has its origins in the concern about ending the subordination of marginalized groups, but may also be understood to involve a guarantee of individualized treatment.

Anti-caste equality provides an important objection to some policies based on averages. Even when based on accurate statistical generalizations, such policies may stigmatize the group targeted, contributing to its members' status as second-class citizens (for example, with respect to police profiling of visible minorities). The two conceptions of equality can conflict, however, because in some cases, policies involving differential treatment based on average group characteristics can advance the goal of eliminating social hierarchy (for example, affirmative action).[41]

The application of the anti-caste conception of equality to the issue of marriage involves answering a number of different questions. First, how big or significant is the inequality that the policy involves? Second, to what extent is the group that suffers the unequal treatment a group that is generally marginalized or oppressed? Third, to what extent does the policy in question directly or indirectly contribute to the group's subordinate status? The answers to these questions will vary depending on whether we are concerned with limits on marriage as to race, sex, or number. My sense is that on the first dimension, it is a greater inequality to be denied the opportunity to marry anyone one could genuinely love (in the way that marriage is normally understood to involve), than it is to be denied the opportunity to marry everyone one loves, or even to be denied the opportunity to marry outside one's race. On the second dimension, however, the ban on interracial marriage supported (and was commonly understood to support) a system of racial hierarchy. The same can be said for nonrecognition of same-sex marriage, because it was part of a general system of discrimination against gays and lesbians. Members of polygamous religious groups have also suffered discrimination. As Ronald Den Otter argues, "the persecution of Mormons for unconventional marital arrangements should not be papered over on the assumption that it obviously pales in comparison to what racial and sexual minorities and women have gone through and, consequently, merits no concern."[42] Whether the concern with equal status is great enough with respect to nonrecognition of polygamy to outweigh worries about consequences for gender equality I am not sure.

It is true, though, that non-recognition involves differential treatment based on the average characteristics of a relationship type. As I will explain in the following section, such policies may be seen to violate a right people have to be treated equally as individuals, or what I am referring to as individualized treatment.

INDIVIDUALIZED TREATMENT AND MARRIAGE

The idea of individualized treatment plays an important role in arguments for recognition of plural marriage that appeal to consistency. For example, Cheshire Calhoun argues that refusing to recognize plural marriage on the ground that it is sometimes oppressive to women involves "a clear failure to exercise neutrality," because monogamous marriage is sometimes oppressive too.[43] Similarly, Elizabeth Brake argues that the problems associated with polygyny ("social pressure to marry, lack of exit options, economic dependency") are also problems associated with patriarchal monogamy. "By parity of reasoning," we should refuse to recognize traditional marriages as well.[44] However, the claim opponents of polygamy make is not that it is "sometimes" oppressive, but that it is more likely to be oppressive, and that its social prevalence has harmful effects on third parties. The reason for the state not to recognize plural unions is suitably neutral, or public, albeit based on statistical generalizations. It may turn out, of course, that these generalizations are mistaken.

Even if they are accurate, however, they are still generalizations, differences between average group characteristics, not factors that apply in each individual case. Just because some polygynous relationships are dysfunctional, Den Otter writes, that doesn't mean all are.[45]

The argument from gender equality does not claim that monogamy is always or intrinsically superior, just that in present circumstances it tends to be. Elizabeth Emens points out that not all multiparty conjugal relationships are abusive, or even patriarchal, and that some are more egalitarian than typical two-person marriages. In her words, "The charge that polygyny [the form of polygamy involving one man and many women] is oppressive is contingent; the validity of the charge depends on the individual relationship, just as in monogamous marriage."[46] However, an effect that holds only on average and might be attenuated in different circumstances is still real here and now. The consequentialist case against recognition of plural marriage only requires that such relationships are more likely to have harmful effects. Parity of reasoning does not similarly condemn recognition of monogamous marriage, if its average effects are not as negative, compared to the likely alternatives—not unless the demand for individualized treatment applies. (If there isn't even an effect on average, then the issue I'm highlighting about policies based on generalizations doesn't arise.)

Recent work by Andrew March on polygamy and incest also reveals a commitment to individualized treatment. March is explicitly concerned with the arguments that can be made "from public reason," consistent with "the obligation to justify public coercion and exclusion in terms accessible and fair to all members of morally and culturally diverse society."[47] However, March does not deny that female autonomy is a public reason. Instead, he questions whether the argument from female autonomy is strong enough to justify prohibiting all forms of polygamy in order to prevent the subset that is harmful to women.[48] What is doing the work in this case is not the restriction of the grounds of decision making to public reasons but the requirement of individualized treatment. This requirement is no doubt appropriate with respect to criminal law. If the question is whether to prohibit people from living together in conjugal-type relationships with more than one other person, then everyone's liberty interest is paramount. I am focusing on the issue of whether to recognize relationships as valid civil marriages, however, not whether to criminalize private relations. The objection based on individualized treatment can also be raised with respect to nonrecognition. How can it be right not to recognize *any* plural relationships, just because (so it is claimed) they are more likely to be objectionable? Refusal to recognize any plural relationships as valid civil marriages on the basis of statistical claims about the increased incidence of harms to women or third parties burdens all of the members of the broader class because of features present in a subset, or because of other indirect consequences, for which the individuals involved aren't responsible.

There may be a deeper connection between public reason and individualized treatment, however, if we apply the demand for reasonable acceptability to state action directly, with a default of inaction or equal treatment. On these models, any limits or inequalities imposed by the state would have to be justified *to* each and every one of those constrained/treated unequally. March seems to be relying on this premise in his discussion of innocent incest.[49] Although some instances of incest are obviously wrong, others are not, for example, two siblings raised apart who meet as adults. This is a case "where it is simply the state telling two autonomous persons 'You can't do that.' And they will demand a reason. What do we say?"[50] March concludes that the arguments within public reason for prohibiting / not recognizing incestuous relationships are "quite weak." [51] The problem is not that the best arguments against incest appeal to nonpublic reasons, but that they violate an implicit right to individualized treatment. What we can say to the people involved, in order to justify *to each and every one of them* nonrecognition of their particular relationship? Even if the policy of not recognizing incestuous relationships as civil marriages has beneficial social consequences, those involved in innocent incestuous relationships can object that it is not fair that they bear the cost of generating these benefits. In this way, the demand that the exercise of political power be justifiable *to* each person can provide the basis for a right to individualized treatment. This right can be grounded in the principle of public reason if the requirement of reasonable acceptability is applied directly to state action, with a default of inaction *or* equal treatment. Thus we reach the surprising conclusion that the demand for public justification of unequal treatment can provide a powerful obstacle to state action (at least if it is assumed that inaction involves no treatment, and *a fortiori* no unequal treatment).

CONCLUSION

Neutrality can take different forms: difference-splitting, inaction, exclusion of reasons, and equal treatment. Public justifiability can refer to the exclusion of reasons that fail the general acceptability test, but it can also refer to the illegitimacy of laws or policies that are not generally preferred to no-policy, or to equal treatment. There is a plausible public case for having an institution of civil marriage, but it is not so strong as to be conclusive, such as, not reasonably rejectable. Moreover, even on the reasons-for-decisions model, equality is an important public reason, and it can be understood to require equal treatment as an individual, or what I have called individualized treatment. The demand for individualized treatment is appropriate with respect to the criminal prohibition of conduct and the application of the criminal law. Applied more generally, however, it would greatly restrict the sphere of legitimate political authority, limiting our ability to advance important public objectives, objectives such as equality for women. The question is how far we should extend the requirement of individualized treatment outside the field of policing and criminal law, and to groups other than marginalized and oppressed ones.

NOTES

1. Michael Sandel, "Moral Argument and Liberal Toleration: Abortion and Homosexuality," *California Law Review* 77 (1989): 521. For examples of "naive" and sophisticated arguments from the Canadian Parliament's 2003 hearings on same-sex unions, see Andrew Lister, *Public Reason and Political Community* (London: Bloomsbury, 2013), 2–5.

2. David M. Estlund, *Democratic Authority: A Philosophical Framework* (Princeton: Princeton University Press, 2008), 40–65.

3. The idea of public justification shows up under different guises, in Rawls's theory: the "criterion of reciprocity," the "liberal principle of legitimacy," and the "ideal of public reason" with its associated duty of civility. John Rawls, *Political Liberalism* (New York: Columbia University Press, 1996), xliv, xlvi, l, li, 217, 226. While these ideas play distinct roles in his theory, I am lumping them together because they all in some way involve reasonable or qualified acceptability.

4. Gerald F. Gaus, "Public Reason Liberalism," in *The Cambridge Companion to Liberalism*, ed. Steven Wall (New York: Cambridge University Press, 2015), 112–140.

5. Micah Schwartzman, Richard Shragger, and Nelson Tebbe, "Obergefell and the End of Religious Reasons for Lawmaking" June 29, 2015, http://religionandpolitics.org/2015/06/29/obergefell-and-the-end-of-religious-reasons-for-lawmaking/.

6. Rawls, *Political Liberalism*, 13. Rawls's idea of a comprehensive doctrine is best understood as meaning "not political," rather than "all encompassing," since a doctrine might be narrow in the range of topic it addresses, but not aspire to any kind of multiperspectival acceptability. In order to count as political, in Rawls's technical sense, a doctrine must be (1) about the basic structure of a political society (not the whole of life), and (2) acceptable to (or based on reasons acceptable to) all reasonable religious and philosophical points of view. A doctrine can therefore count as comprehensive despite not having something to say about everything.

7. Other attempts to answer these questions include: Ralph Wedgwood, "The Fundamental Argument for Same-Sex Marriage," *Journal of Political Philosophy* 7 (1999): 225–42; Tamara Metz, "The Liberal Case for Disestablishing Marriage," *Contemporary Political Theory* 6 (2007): 196–217; Elizabeth Brake, "Minimal Marriage: What Political Liberalism Implies for Marriage Law," *Ethics* 120 (2010): 302–37; Tamara Metz, *Untying the Knot: Marriage, the State, and the Case for Their Divorce* (Princeton: Princeton University Press, 2010); Elizabeth Brake, *Minimizing Marriage : Marriage, Morality, and the Law* (New York: Oxford University Press, 2012); Ralph Wedgwood, "Is Civil Marriage Illiberal?" in *After Marriage: Rethinking Marital Relationships*, ed. Elizabeth Brake (New York: Oxford University Press, 2015), 29–50; Clare Chambers, "Political Liberal Neutrality, Public Reason, and State-Recognized Marriage," in *New Directions in Public Reason*, ed. Kevin Vallier and Jeremy Williams (New York: Oxford University Press, forthcoming).

8. Rawls said that the limits of public reason did not apply to all political questions but only those involving "constitutional essentials" and "questions of basic justice." Rawls, *Political Liberalism*, 214. His reasons for limiting the scope of the principle in this way were not fully clear, however, and have been challenged. See, e.g., Jonathan

Quong, "The Scope of Public Reason," *Political Studies* 52 (2004): 233–50. If the definition of civil marriage counts as non-fundamental, then public reason cannot threaten marriage, but it can also not be used to rebut religious arguments against recognizing same-sex marriage. I will therefore assume that either marriage counts as fundamental, or that the principle applies to all public decisions.

9. See Gerald F. Gaus and Kevin Vallier, "The Roles of Religious Conviction in a Publicly Justified Polity: The Implications of Convergence, Asymmetry and Political Institutions," *Philosophy and Social Criticism* 35 (2009): 51–76; Gerald F. Gaus, "Coercion, Ownership, and the Redistributive State: Justificatory Liberalism's Classical Tilt," *Social Philosophy and Policy* 27 (2010): 233–275. The distinction between these two models of public reason is sometimes referred to by contrasting consensus justification with convergence justification. For further discussion, see Kevin Vallier, "Convergence and Consensus in Public Reason," *Public Affairs Quarterly* 25 (2011): 261–80; Andrew Lister, "Public Justification of What? Coercion vs. Decision as Competing Frames for the Basic Principle of Justificatory Liberalism," *Public Affairs Quarterly* 25 (2011): 349–367. The account of public justification Gaus presents in *The Order of Public Reason* (New York: Cambridge University Press, 2011) is more complex, because in this work the principle applies first to the claims of authority Gaus thinks are implicit in everyday social morality, and only secondarily to coercion on the part of the state. For a summary of Gaus's argument, and some tentative criticisms, see Andrew Lister, "The Classical Tilt of Justificatory Liberalism," *European Journal of Political Theory* 12 (2013): 316–326.

10. Alan Patten, *Equal Recognition: The Moral Foundations of Minority Rights* (New York: Oxford University Press, 2014), 111–19.

11. John Rawls, *A Theory of Justice* (Cambridge: Harvard University Press, 1999).

12. For further discussion of aggregation/individuation, see Lister, *Public Reason and Political Community*, 81–104.

13. This section of the paper draws upon arguments from Chapter 6 of my *Public Reason and Political Community*.

14. Jeff Jordan, "Is it Wrong to Discriminate on the Basis of Homosexuality?" *Journal of Social Philosophy* 25 (1995), 45.

15. David Boonin, "Same-Sex Marriage and the Argument from Public Disagreement," *Journal of Social Philosophy* 30 (1999): 251–259; Jason A. Beyer, "Public Dilemmas and Gay Marriage: Contra Jordan," *Journal of Social Philosophy* 33 (2002): 9–16.

16. I am thinking here of views attributed to the school of feminist thought dubbed "radical feminism," associated with the work of Andrea Dworkin, Adrienne Rich, and Catherine Mackinnon. Their main claim was not that opposite-sex sex was intrinsically immoral, but that under present social conditions, heterosexuality is constituted by relations of sexual subordination. Feminist criticisms of heterosexuality are therefore not symmetrical with religious views that condemn same-sex sexual relations in principle, under all possible social conditions. Still, if these feminist views are counted as reasonable, splitting the difference will not justify the status quo of opposite-sex-only marriage, as Jordan hoped.

17. Michael Sandel, *Justice: What's the Right Thing to Do?* (New York: Farrar, Straus and Giroux, 2009), 253; see also Carlos A. Ball, "Moral Foundations for A Discourse on Same-Sex Marriage: Looking Beyond Political Liberalism," *The Georgetown Law Journal* 85 (1997): 1893, citing Sandel, "Moral Argument and Liberal Toleration," 1778.

18. Sandel, *Justice*, 257.

19. Sandel, *Justice*, 256.

20. Kyla Ebels-Duggan, "The Beginning of Community: Politics in the Face of Disagreement," *Philosophical Quarterly* 60 (2010), 65–66.

21. Chambers, "Political Liberal Neutrality, Public Reason, and State-Recognised Marriage."

22. This paragraph summarizes the argument of Wedgwood, "The Fundamental Argument for Same-Sex Marriage," 225–242, and Wedgwood, "Is Civil Marriage Illiberal?" 29–50.

23. Milton C. Regan, *Family Law and the Pursuit Of Intimacy* (New York: New York University Press, 1993), 95–96.

24. William Galston, "A Liberal-Democratic Case for the Two-Parent Family," *The Responsive Community* 1 (1990): 14–26; Iris Marion Young, "Mothers, Citizenship and Independence: A Critique of Pure Family Values," *Ethics* 105 (1995): 535–579; David Blankenhorn, *Fatherless America* (New York: Basic Books, 1995); David Popenoe, *Life Without Father* (New York: Martin Kessler Books, 1996); Judith Stacey, *In the Name of the Family* (Boston: Beacon Press, 1996).

25. Brake, *Minimizing Marriage*, 112–113.

26. Anita Bernstein, "For and Against Marriage: A Revision," *Michigan Law Review* 102 (2003): 129–212.

27. Brake, *Minimizing Marriage*, 114–116.

28. Claudia Card, "Against Marriage and Motherhood," *Hypatia* 11 (1996): 1–22.

29. Miron v. Trudel, [1995] 2 S.C.R. 418, May 25, 1995. csc. lexum.com/scc-csc/scc-csc/en/item/1264/index.do.

30. *Beyond Conjugality: Recognizing and Supporting Close Personal Adult Relationships.* Government of Canada (2001), 14.

31. Ibid., 13, 18.

32. Ibid., 19.

33. Stephen Macedo, "John Roberts' Gay Marriage Dissent Is Wrong About Polygamy-and the Constitution," June 30, 2015, www.slate.com/blogs/outward/2015/06/30/supreme_court_gay_marriage_john_roberts_dissent_is_wrong_about_polygamy.html.

34. Jonathan Rauch, "No, Polygamy Isn't the Next Gay Marriage," June 30, 2015. http://www.politico.com/magazine/story/2015/06/polygamynotnextgaymarriage-119614.html#.VbY6GXhUQXc, citing Joseph Henrich, Robert Boyd, and Peter J. Richerson, "The Puzzle of Monogamous Marriage," *Philosophical Transactions of the Royal Society* 367 (2012): 657–669; see also Nicholas Bala, *An International Review of Polygamy: Legal and Policy Implications for Canada* (Ottawa: Research Directorate, Status of Women Canada, 2005).

35. John Holbo, "Polygamy and Polyamory," July 8, 2015, http://crookedtimber.org/2015/07/08/polygamy-and-polyamory/.

36. Fredrik de Boer, "Every Bad Argument Against Polygamy, Debunked," July 1, 2015, http://fredrikdeboer.com/2015/07/01/every-bad-argument-against-polygamy-debunked/.

37. However, for a defense of the claim that a heavily reformed institution of marriage *is* a requirement of justice, *see* Brake, *Minimal Marriage*, 171–185.

38. Colin Farrelly, "Justice in Ideal Theory: A Refutation," *Political Studies* 55 (2007): 844–864.

39. Rawls, *A Theory of Justice*, 54; for further discussion, see Samuel Freeman, *Rawls* (New York: Routledge, 2007), 64–72.

40. Cass Sunstein, "The Anticaste Principle," *Michigan Law Review* 92 (1994), 2411.

41. Sunstein, "The Anticaste Principle," 2417–18.

42. Ronald C. Den Otter, "Three May Not Be a Crowd: The Case for a Constitutional Right to Plural Marriage," *Emory Law Journal* 64 (2015): 2027.

43. Cheshire Calhoun, "Who's Afraid of Polygamous Marriage? Lessons for Same-Sex Marriage Advocacy from the History of Polygamy," *San Diego Law Review* 42 (2005): 1040–41; see also Den Otter, "Three May Not be a Crowd," 1990.

44. Brake, *Minimizing Marriage*, 198–199.

45. Den Otter, "Three May Not be a Crowd," 1986.

46. Elizabeth Emens, "Just Monogamy?" in *Just Marriage*, ed. Mary Lyndon Shanley (New York: Oxford University Press, 2004), 77.

47. Andrew March, "Is There a Right to Polygamy? Marriage, Equality and Subsidizing Families in Liberal Public Justification," *Journal of Moral Philosophy* 8 (2011): 271, 247.

48. Ibid., 260.

49. Andrew March, "What Lies Beyond Same-Sex Marriage? Marriage, Reproductive Freedom and Future Persons in Liberal Public Justification," *Journal of Applied Philosophy* 27 (2010): 44.
50. Ibid., 45.
51. Ibid., 54.

REFERENCES

Beyond Conjugality: Recognizing and Supporting Close Personal Adult Relationships. Ottawa: Government of Canada, 2001.

Miron v. Trudel, [1995] 2 S.C.R. 418. May 25, 1995. http://scc-csc.lexum.com/scc-csc/scc-csc/en/item/1264/index.do.

Bala, Nicholas. "An International Review of Polygamy: Legal and Policy Implications for Canada." Ottawa: Research Directorate, Status of Women Canada, 2005.

Ball, Carlos A. "Moral Foundations for A Discourse on Same-Sex Marriage: Looking Beyond Political Liberalism." *The Georgetown Law Journal* 85 (1997): 1870–1943.

Bernstein, Anita. "For and Against Marriage: A Revision." *Michigan Law Review* 102 (2003): 129–212.

Beyer, Jason A. "Public Dilemmas and Gay Marriage: Contra Jordan." *Journal of Social Philosophy* 33 (2002): 9–16.

Blankenhorn, David. *Fatherless America: Confronting Our Most Urgent Social Problem*. New York: Basic Books, 1995.

Boonin, David. "Same-Sex Marriage and the Argument from Public Disagreement." *Journal of Social Philosophy* 30 (1999): 251–259.

Brake, Elizabeth. "Minimal Marriage: What Political Liberalism Implies for Marriage Law." *Ethics* 120 (2010): 302–37.

_____. *Minimizing Marriage: Marriage, Morality, and the Law*. New York: Oxford University Press, 2012.

Calhoun, Cheshire. "Who's Afraid of Polygamous Marriage? Lessons for Same-Sex Marriage Advocacy from the History of Polygamy." *San Diego Law Review* 42 (2005): 1023–1042.

Card, Claudia. "Against Marriage and Motherhood." *Hypatia* 11 (1996): 1–22.

Chambers, Clare. "Political Liberal Neutrality, Public Reason, and State-Recognised Marriage." In *New Directions in Public Reason*, edited by Kevin Vallier and Jeremy Williams. New York: Oxford University Press, forthcoming.

De Boer, Fredrik. "Every Bad Argument Against Polygamy, Debunked." July 1, 2015, http://fredrikdeboer.com/2015/07/01/every-bad-argument-against-polygamy-debunked/.

Den Otter, Ronald C. "Three May Not Be a Crowd: The Case for a Constitutional Right to Plural Marriage." *Emory Law Journal* 64 (2015): 1979–2046.

Ebels-Duggan, Kyla. "The Beginning of Community: Politics in the Face of Disagreement." *Philosophical Quarterly* 60 (2010): 50–71.

Emens, Elizabeth. "Just Monogamy?" In *Just Marriage*, edited by Mary Lyndon Shanley, 75–80. New York: Oxford University Press, 2004.

Estlund, David M. *Democratic Authority: A Philosophical Framework*. Princeton: Princeton University Press, 2008.

Farrelly, Colin. "Justice in Ideal Theory: A Refutation." *Political Studies* 55 (2007): 844–864.

Freeman, Samuel. *Rawls*. New York: Routledge, 2007.

Galston, William. "A Liberal-Democratic Case for the Two-Parent Family." *The Responsive Community* 1 (1990): 14–26.

Gaus, Gerald F. "Coercion, Ownership, and the Redistributive State: Justificatory Liberalism's Classical Tilt." *Social Philosophy and Policy* 27 (2010): 233–275.

_____. *The Order of Public Reason*. New York: Cambridge University Press, 2011.

_____. "Public Reason Liberalism." In *The Cambridge Companion to Liberalism*, edited by Steven Wall, 112–40. New York: Cambridge University Press, 2015.

Gaus, Gerald F. and Kevin Vallier. "The Roles of Religious Conviction in a Publicly Justified Polity: The Implications Of Convergence, Asymmetry and Political Institutions." *Philosophy and Social Criticism* 35 (2009): 51–76.

Henrich, Joseph, Robert Boyd, and Peter J. Richerson. "The Puzzle of Monogamous Marriage." *Philosophical Transactions of the Royal Society* 367 (2012): 657–669.

Holbo, John. "Polygamy and Polyamory." July 8, 2015. http://crookedtimber. org/2015/07/08/polygamy-and-polyamory/.

Jordan, Jeff. "Is It Wrong to Discriminate on the Basis of Homosexuality?" *Journal of Social Philosophy* 25 (1995): 39–52.

Lister, Andrew. "Public Justification of What? Coercion vs. Decision as Competing Frames for the Basic Principle of Justificatory Liberalism." *Public Affairs Quarterly* 25 (2011): 349–367.

_____. *Public Reason and Political Community*. London: Bloomsbury, 2013.

_____. "The Classical Tilt of Justificatory Liberalism." *European Journal of Political Theory*, 12 (2013): 316–26.

Macedo, Stephen. "John Roberts' Gay Marriage Dissent Is Wrong About Polygamy—and the Constitution." June 30, 2015. www.slate.com/blogs/outward/2015/06/30/supreme_court_gay_marriage_john_roberts_dissent_is_wrong_about_polygamy.html

March, Andrew F. "What Lies Beyond Same-Sex Marriage? Marriage, Reproductive Freedom and Future Persons in Liberal Public Justification." *Journal of Applied Philosophy* 27 (2010): 39–58.

March, Andrew F. "Is There a Right to Polygamy? Marriage, Equality and Subsidizing Families in Liberal Public Justification." *Journal of Moral Philosophy* 8 (2011): 244–270.

Metz, Tamara. "The Liberal Case for Disestablishing Marriage." *Contemporary Political Theory* 6 (2007): 196–217.

Metz, Tamara. *Untying the Knot: Marriage, the State, and the Case for Their Divorce*. Princeton: Princeton University Press, 2010.

Patten, Alan. *Equal Recognition: The Moral Foundations of Minority Rights*. New York: Oxford University Press, 2014.

Popenoe, David. *Life Without Father: Compelling New Evidence That Fatherhood and Marriage are Indispensable for the Good Of Children and Society*. New York: Martin Kessler, 1996.

Quong, Jonathan. "The Scope of Public Reason." *Political Studies*, 52 (2004): 233–50.

Rauch, Jonathan. "No, Polygamy Isn't the Next Gay Marriage." June 30, 2015. http://www.politico.com/magazine/story/2015/06/polygamy-not-next-gay-marriage-119614

Rawls, John. *Political Liberalism*. New York: Columbia University Press, 1996.

Regan, Milton C. *Family Law and the Pursuit of Intimacy*. New York: New York University Press, 1993.

Sandel, Michael. *Justice: What's the Right Thing to Do?* New York: Farrar, Straus and Giroux, 2009.

Sandel, Michael. "Moral Argument and Liberal Toleration: Abortion and Homosexuality." *California Law Review* 77 (1989): 521–538.

Schwartzman, Micah, Richard Shragger, and Nelson Tebbe. "Obergefell and the End of Religious Reasons for Lawmaking." Accessed June 29, 2015. religionandpolitics.org/2015/06/29/obergefell-and-the-end-of-religious-reasons-for-lawmaking/.

Stacey, Judith. *In the Name of the Family*. Boston: Beacon Press, 1996.

Sunstein, Cass. "The Anticaste Principle." *Michigan Law Review* 92 (1994): 2410–2455.

Vallier, Kevin. "Convergence and Consensus in Public Reason." *Public Affairs Quarterly* 25 (2011): 261–80.

Wedgwood, Ralph. "The Fundamental Argument for Same-Sex Marriage." *Journal of Political Philosophy* 7 (1999): 225–242.

Wedgwood, Ralph. "Is Civil Marriage Illiberal?" In *After Marriage: Rethinking Marital Relationships,* edited by Elizabeth Brake, 29–50. New York: Oxford University Press, 2015.

Young, Iris Marion. "Mothers, Citizenship and Independence: A Critique of Pure Family Values." *Ethics* 105 (1995): 535–579.

SEVEN

The Dialectic of Islam and Polygyny

Ameneh Maghzi and Mark Gruchy

By putting polygyny and the *Quran* in its historical context, this chapter makes the case that Islam contains the seeds for discontinuing the practice. These seeds have been present from Islam's earliest days and are finally germinating. Further, Islamic nations throughout the world are incrementally moving towards complete prohibition of the practice in a fashion consistent with Islamic thought. Polygamy is the marrying of more than one spouse simultaneously, as opposed to monogamy, where each person has only one spouse at a time. The most common form of polygamy and the only one that is currently practiced in the Muslim world is polygyny, where a man, and only a man, can have multiple wives. Polygyny, which dates back to ancient times, existed before the advent of Islam in Arabia and continued to be practiced in the region after the rise of Islam. In illuminating the origins of polygyny in the Arab and Islamic worldview, this chapter will explain how the underlying themes of Islamic thought, coupled with a historically-oriented interpretation of the *Quran,* with a focus on the apparent contradictions between Islamic theology and the Prophet Muhammed's life, provide the necessary support for the elimination of polygyny. Major steps in this direction have been ongoing for many years. This conclusion—that polygyny can be prohibited in a fashion consistent with Islamic theology—not only reflects the spirit of the *Quran;* it also takes into account the contemporary realities of gender relations and corrects misleading but commonly held views of Islam as a structure inherently resistant to what ostensibly are major social changes.

A BRIEF HISTORY OF POLYGAMY

The institution of polygamy tends to be remote from the perspective of the average modern westerner situated in cultures where monogamy is the norm. However, polygyny may have been the prevailing mode of marriage in the so-called primitive world.[1] Polygynous marital arrangements were well-known throughout the ancient world, far beyond what would become the Islamic world, ranging from the ancient Near East to the ancient British Isles. Polygynous behaviors were documented extensively by ancient historians, like Herodotus to Josephus.[2] Also, many Abrahamic prophets were polygamists. Jacob, David, Solomon, Muhammed and even Abraham himself all engaged in various forms of polygamy throughout their lives.[3] Polygamy was no mere social aberration; it was once a widespread, legitimate institution.

The question of how this state of affairs came to be is difficult to answer. Some explanations attempt to provide a functional analysis. Early thinkers were prone to providing "explanations" associated with matters that modern readers would find extraneous, such as the theory that hotter climates produce a surplus of mature women because women reach sexual maturity faster than men do.[4] Those from warmer climates were perceived to be less than civilized, while those from cooler areas were supposed to be temperate as a result of their living conditions. Today, such thinking is an embarrassment; it is tainted by the worst kind of cultural superiority found in the western scholarship of an earlier era.

Other explanations call attention to reproductive economy and exchange. In Islamic scholarship, ideas that women's intermittent sexual inaccessibility due to menstruation, mixed with the window of reproductive ability, may have conspired to promote polygamy as a practical matter.[5] Notions of unbalanced sexual ratios, leading to polygamy, also appear as explanations in Islamic scholarship.[6] The tendency of women to outnumber men in the context of early Muslim polygamy was a consequence of higher male death rates from stereotypical masculine activities and perceived masculine susceptibility to disease.[7] The idea is that the society deliberately optimized reproduction by apportioning women to the smaller population of surviving males.[8] Perhaps more compelling an explanation are claims that polygamy performed economic structures. Resource disparity, the viewing of multiple wives and large numbers of children as economic assets and signs of power, economic emphasis on labor-intensive activities like agriculture, and the importance of the economic benefits of a large extended family probably had the cumulative effect of fostering and maintaining polygamy as an institution.[9]

Political, social and cultural dimensions beyond economic ones also cannot be ignored. Polygyny may have served as a way of dealing with the social strains generated by an excess of women and controlling the behavior of single women who were unable to find mates. In addition, by expanding the range of a man's political alliances, he had a better chance of achieving and exercising political power. Finally, polygyny may have enabled men to navigate complex social norms involving post-partum sexual taboos, something common to Abrahamic religions.[10] Polygyny is more likely to appear in societies with relatively onerous divorce regimes.[11]

All of these explanatory variables are patriarchal in one way or another. Similarly patriarchal is the idea that polygyny existed originally in a context where wealthy, powerful men dominated society so completely that they could deprive average men of the opportunity to marry and reproduce. This argument, which is a component of the "male compromise" theory of polygyny, claims that the practice declines in response to democratic developments that reduce socioeconomic stratifications among men.[12] In this view, the prohibition of polygamy ensures the maximum number of males have a vested interest in their society by equalizing their reproductive potential, thereby reducing conflict between them.[13]

Related to these approaches is the "female choice" theory where women can be expected to engage in or at least support polygamy when resource distribution among males is so skewed that it benefits them more to be a member of a polygamous family than not. This theory incorporates the above referenced impacts of patriarchal social and political structures on the decision to enter into a polygynous arrangement.[14] One does not have to look any farther than the reality of the child bride phenomena to appreciate how outside factors, which have nothing to do with love, shape (and limit) marital options. There is often an age difference of decades between a second or third wife and her husband, and child brides are essentially acquired like possessions. This evidence indicates that polygyny comes about in circumstances that put into doubt whether the arrangement is genuinely consensual.[15]

POLYGYNY IN ARAB SOCIETY

Addressing any aspect of the question of polygyny in the Islamic world necessitates a basic understanding of the culture that produced and initially developed Islam: the culture of the Arabian Peninsula. We should also consider the traditional way in which Islamic thinkers approached understanding the pre-Islamic era and be aware how the same considerations could compromise our objectivity as well. While cultures may appear to change abruptly, as the result of the emergence of a new form of thought or living, broad cultural continuity with the period before the development is to be expected. This is so with respect to pre-Islamic Arab culture and post-Islamic Arab culture. Islam accommodated inherently patriarchal structures in the economic system, family structure, and politics even when they appeared to contradict its principles.[16]

Additionally, Arabia was influenced by the rest of the near east, from Egypt to Iran, and these lands would ultimately contribute to the forms that Islam would take. However, there were meaningful differences in between the periods with respect to the rights and status of women.[17] Traditional Islamic scholarship refers to the Pre-Islamic era as al-Jahiliyah or "The Days of Ignorance." Such an evocative title should immediately alert the reader that a non-trivial moral judgement is being made by such scholars. The standard narrative is to present the period as a state of uncivilized, semi-anarchy that ends with the emergence of Islam.[18] The term al-Jahiliyah occurs four times in the *Quran*.[19]

Unsurprisingly, reliable historical sources substantiating this supposed barbaric society are hard to come by. The reason is simple enough. These Arabs left little historical record of their society, while post-Islamic Arabs and others worked to erase the pre-Islamic past of Arabia while simultaneously striving to justify their faith and ideology by utilizing to a semi-imagined past. The Days of Ignorance, then, function more as a theological device than as an historical one.[20] The result is a problem common to understanding Islamic history: equating the Islamic interpretation of events with the indisputable truth obscures the central role that political and social reasons played in its development. Scholarship which focuses on the *Quran* and *Hadith* are particularly prone to this kind of interpretive error because the document is prescriptive; it does not aspire to presenting the pre-Islamic world as accurately as possible.[21]

What we little know of the earlier era comes by way of surviving oral traditions from pre-Islamic Arabia. Poetry is a particularly important source of information inasmuch as it came to be the primary cultural means of transferring cultural information across generations, often serving as the "sole medium of expression." These sources allow us to reach some general conclusions.[22] The ecology of the Arabian Peninsula, with its inherent scarcity of resources, especially in its northern regions, engendered a tribal structure that fluctuated from a state of decentralization to a state of relative cohesion and then back again. The southern part of Arabia was tribally organized but more settled, while the north was similarly tribal but relatively fluid. The peninsula saw a long running series of ever-shifting alliances between tribes which promoted a cluster of norms and values, strengthening tribal identity and regulating tribal behavior.[23]

In this fluid context both matrilineal and patrilineal variations of marriage emerged. While traditional Islamic scholarship depicts the state of women in pre-Islamic Arabia as abysmal, documenting female infanticide as commonplace, the reality is far murkier. The *Quran* posits the banning of infanticide as an example of the liberation of women.[24] Indeed, Islam's self-presentation as a liberator of women animates its self-concept. In this narrative, Pre-Islamic Arabia was a barbaric place that was hostile to women. However, in fact, certain tribes, like the Quraish, had high regard for women's rights.[25] Women could hold relatively high social positions, freely choose husbands, propose marriage, divorce, and could return to their own tribe if they were mistreated.[26] In some places, women could be regarded as inspired poets and warriors and equals to men. [27]

The existence of major female deities in the pre-Arabian Islamic pantheon further corroborates the claim that the traditional Islamic narrative distorts the reality.[28] Scholars have taken the view that much of pre-Islamic Arabia was matrilineal and that Islam converted Arabia to a patrilineal system. The trouble with this view is that women enjoyed greater social status prior to the emergence of Islam, with some tribal variance.[29] Matrilineal and patrilineal systems co-existed but eventually, the patrilineal system, under Islam, supplanted the matrilineal one.[30]

Matrilineal marriage norms manifested themselves in a form of marriage known as *sadiqa* marriage. These unions formed by mutual consent. A woman in such an arrangement retained the ability to dismiss her husband. Children of the union belonged to the woman's tribe. By contrast, the patrilineal system inverted this arrangement, giving the power of divorce to the husband and underscoring his authority over the woman. Indeed, these marriages could come into being as a result of "capture" or "purchase." These competing forms of marriage also co-existed before the emergence of Islam.[31] Polygamy also appeared in pre-Islamic Arabia and flexible sexual unions were common, including polyandry.[32] This flexibility would ultimately be curtailed to a large extent with the emergence of Islam, and oddly enough, would be presented subsequently as proof of Islam's commitment to female well-being.

The complex reality of the social position of women in pre-Islamic Arabia comes into focus with the presence of strong female figures in Islamic theology, notably Khadijah, Muhammed's first wife. Khadijah was Muhammed's benefactor, an independently wealthy and politically powerful woman who used her influence to make Muhammed's ascent to leadership possible.[33] She is the antithesis of the image of a repressed woman and stands at the very origin of Islam. Reconciling the reality of Khadijah with what would come next for women in Islam points to the usurping of the role of women in the faith by the incremental imposition of increasingly severe patriarchal norms. These norms were not necessarily engrained in pre-Islamic Arabian culture in the manner the *Quran* traditionally alleges.[34] Muhammed would ultimately have twelve (documented) wives, with as many as nine simultaneously playing the role. None would be as independent, autonomous, or as powerful as Khadijah. The story of Muhammed's acquisition of wives, prior to his emergence as the prophet and leader of Islam, and their treatment, parallels the imposition of patriarchal norms upon pre-Islamic Arabia as the Islamic system evolved.

POLYGAMY AND THE *QURAN*

The *Quran* may permit polygyny, but its structure unequivocally reveals that the status is less than morally desirable. The source of the majority of rules and customs on polygamous marriage is found in the fourth *Sura* of the *Quran*, An-Nisa (The Women). The conditions that polygyny is subject to appear in verses 3 and 129:

> People, be mindful of your Lord, who created you from a single soul, and from it created its mate, and from the pair of them spread countless men and women far and wide; be mindful of God, in whose name you make requests of one another. Beware of severing the ties of kinship: God is always watching over you [4:1].[35]

> Give orphans their property, do not replace [their] good things with bad, and do not consume their property with your own–a great sin [4:2].[36]

> If you fear that you will not deal fairly with orphan girls, you may marry whichever [other] women seem good to you, two, three, or four. If you fear that you cannot be equitable [to them], then marry only one, or your slave(s): that is more likely to make you avoid bias [4:3].[37]

Traditionally, these verses have been construed to permit polygyny. It is evident, though, that something more complex is underway. First, there is an exhortation to respect the common identity and humanity of men and women bestowed by divine action. Second, there is another exhortation to treat "orphans," the possible subject of polygyny in the verse that follows, with great humanity and respect. Third, there is yet another exhortation to never take more than one wife unless one can do so with great fairness and an absence of bias between or among them in one's affections.[38] The act of engaging in polygyny risks sinfulness. After all, few men could hope to morally navigate it. Additionally, the reader is warned to avoid the practice if they merely "fear" they cannot be equitable to their spouses.[39] Technically, these verses restrict the number of wives to four. Equally importantly, they strongly discourage all men from entertaining the idea of having more than one.

The matter is complicated further by verse 129 of the *Sura*:

> You will never be able to treat your wives with equal fairness, however much you may desire to do so, but do not ignore one wife altogether, leaving her suspended [between marriage and divorce]. If you make amends and remain conscious of God, He is most forgiving and merciful [4:129].[40]

This verse can be read as allowing for a man's heart to be naturally inclined towards one wife or the other, while creating a duty for him to act toward each of them with the same regard, independent of his emotions. The failure to treat one's spouses equally constitutes more than a minor sin. Once again, the practice of polygyny, ostensibly permitted by the *Quran*, is rendered so practically difficult as to almost be impossible in the real world. Indeed, it would seem that a sufficiently humble, introspective person would think twice about ever engaging in the practice.[41]

The moral content of the message resembles the pronouncements of Jesus concerning the concept of marriage found in the *Book of Matthew*. In *Matthew 19*, Jesus stated that while divorce was something that could be claimed to be done by men, it would not matter in the eyes of God. This provoked a comment from his followers it was better not to marry at all, leading to him to nudge them not to do so if possible. In other words, the status of marriage was presented as acceptable in theory, just like the status of polygyny in Islam, but serious spiritual warnings were attached to its consequences. Jesus presented celibacy as the preferred moral state. Structurally, then, it appears the *Quran* treats the concept of polygyny similarly to how the Christian bible treats marriage generally; it presents an option, but how it qualifies, by presenting as a moral dilemma, it should deter the thoughtful reader from actually selecting it.

In this manner, polygyny is rendered unattractive for a man who does not want to put himself in such a dangerous situation. After all, very few men could spiritually handle it, and those who display willingness to take on its burdens must perceive the institution as a moral duty and not one that is designed for his own pleasure. For the same reason, seeing polygyny as sensuous is inherently sinful; it is supposed to be depicted as a functional, austere, and limited institution.[42] The best interpretation of these verses suggests that polygyny ought to be prohibited; it is a moral duty that not only rarely, if ever, can be lived up to, in light of the universal responsibility of Muslims to act humbly and moderately, and it carries serious spiritual risks. This is exactly the rationale that multiple Islamic states, including Turkey and Morocco, use to prohibit the practice: "If injustice is feared, polygyny is forbidden."[43] Today, it is not uncommon for scholars to argue that these verses provide the moral authority for rulers of nations to ban polygyny in the name of the *Quran*.

This verse was originally narrated by Aisha, a post-Khadija wife of Muhammed, who revealed that it was solely intended to deal with the moral problem of a guardian who was seeking to exploit the wealth of an orphan under his care. This issue arose in early Islam due to a long history of factional violence. The idea is that having to mutually support up to four women justly is better than the act of dispossessing one orphan unjustly. The passage may be simply a way of dramatizing how problematic the issue of treating the vulnerable unjustly is. When taken in context, it need not be read as a serious endorsement of polygyny in all circumstances. Certainly, it does not speak to women *simplicter* as wives but only to orphans.[44]

Further, this verse seems to limit the number of wives available to a man to four. Prior to this declaration, no such limit of potential spouses was stipulated. As such, the *Quran* can be construed as trying to almost completely eliminate, not facilitate, the practice of polygyny. The verses require complete equity between the spouses if the moral purpose of polygyny is to be accomplished.[45] The *Quran* deals only with polygyny. Polyandry is not permitted. As noted, this practice existed in pre-Islamic Arabia, but was done away with under Islam.[46] In light of the diversity of sexual unions, such as polyandry in pre-Islamic Arabia, and in light of Muhammed's 12 wives, why then do we find such limitations imposed on polygyny by the *Quran*?

Muhammad and Polygamy

It is possible the answer may be found in the life of Muhammed himself. Muhammed ultimately had twelve wives, fully eight beyond what would be deemed permissible by the *Quran*. Muhammed is something of a special case, the traditional view being his marriages were by God's command and were necessary for various purposes beyond himself. From this standpoint, he was not a sensual or physical man. His long 24 year relationship with Khadijah, a woman markedly older than he when he was in his prime, is offered as confirmation. Mohammed remained monogamous with her until after her death.[47] That women in Khadijah's time did not wear a restrictive form of what would become known as *hijab*, as a sign of modesty, is supposed to prove that Muhammed could resist sexual temptation. His ability to restrain himself in the face of the openness of women of his day, then, implied his virtue. During the time he was married to Khadijah, plural marriage was customary, yet he remained monogamous.[48]

Only after her death did things change. At the age of fifty, in a short period, Muhammed accumulated eleven wives, all but one were virgins. The trouble with Muhammed's exceeding his wifely limit is addressed in the following Quranic verse. Muhammed, it seems, was an exception to all other men:

> Prophet, We have made lawful for you the wives whose bride gift you have paid, and any slaves God has assigned to you through war, and the daughters of your uncles and aunts on your father's and mother's sides, who migrated with you. Also any believing woman who has offered herself to the Prophet and whom the Prophet wishes to wed–this is only for you [Prophet] and not the rest of the believers: We know exactly what We have made obligatory for them concerning their wives and slave-girls—so you should not be blamed: God is most forgiving, most merciful [33:50].[49]

This should be the first indication that a certain imbalance was creeping into early Islam respecting polygyny. Muhammed had been monogamous for most of his days, and was now suddenly practicing polygyny in apparent contravention of established norms.

Muhammed's relationship with Zaynab Bint Jahash poses the most complex interpretative problem. The *Quran* provides an account that reveals that Muhammed may have felt lust when he desired to marry Zaynab. The passage describes how he saw her scantily-clad, sexually desired her, and ultimately, by using his public moral authority to undermine her marriage, provoked her divorce from his adopted son, Zayd. Thus, we have a marriage possibly inspired by lust, coupled with the double taboo of an adopted son being the preceding husband, which was looked upon by his contemporaries as overtly immoral.[50]

The answer to this problem came in the form of a divine revelation recorded in the *Quran*:

> God does not put two hearts within a man's breast. He does not turn the wives you reject and liken to your mothers' backs into your real mothers; nor does He make your adopted sons into real sons. These are only words from your mouths, while God speaks the truth and guides people to the right path [33:4].[51]

> When you [Prophet] said to the man who had been favoured by God and by you, 'Keep your wife and be mindful of God,' you hid in your heart what God would later reveal: you were afraid of people, but it is more fitting that you fear God. When Zayd no longer wanted her, We gave her to you in marriage so that there might be no fault in believers marrying the wives of their adopted sons after they no longer wanted them. God's command must be carried out [33:37].[52]

> the Prophet is not at fault for what God has ordained for him. This was God's practice with those who went before—God's command must be fulfilled— [33:38].[53]

This episode has become one of the most heavily criticized (and difficult to interpret) events of Muhammed's life inasmuch as it appeared to be incestuous.[54] Muhammed has been both demonized for this action and the subject of apologists' writings. The fact remains the event was out of character, morally problematic on multiple levels, and in stark contrast to the austere definitions of polygyny articulated elsewhere in the *Quran*. One could conclude that Muhammed's human nature got the better of him, and that an institutional response was necessary in the form of limiting the institution of polygyny going forward. This is, of course, only one interpretation. So much of what Muhammed did in his life to protect and elevate women from their "Days of Ignorance" status cannot easily be squared with this episode. The explanations and justifications are unconvincing and would have no doubt troubled his contemporaries. It could be argued this episode, at the highest level of Islamic society, cast into sharp relief the need for strict, ongoing practical regulation of polygyny lest it cause social damage. Muhammed the reformer appears here to be Muhammed the sometimes self-serving human being.

Ironically, it is precisely the conception of Muhammed as a moral reformer dedicated to elevating the status of women and humanity generally that advocates now make use of to get rid of polygyny within Islamic structures. The contemporary reality is that polygyny, while permissible in many Muslim nations, is either strongly discouraged or prohibited.[55]

A MODERN PERSPECTIVE ON POLYGAMY

Fifty countries today permit polygamous marriages to be performed within their jurisdictions.[56] National practice in Muslim nations with regard to polygamy is what one would expect in light of the treatment of the matter in the *Quran*: the practice is sometimes tolerated, albeit with non-trivial qualifications. Some societies, like Tunisia, have completely banned polygyny and see doing so as being consistent with the spirit of the *Quran*. In fact, Tunisia goes so far as to evoke the verses of the *Quran* in support of its policies.[57]

In another secular country of the Muslim world, Turkey, polygamy is illegal in any form, even though polygamy is still practiced secretly in many rural parts of Turkey.[58] In Iran, while polygamy is legally permitted, a man before taking an additional wife, must obtain the official consent of his existing wife. In 2008, the Iranian government proposed a Family Protection Law in which a man could marry a second wife if he could prove at a hearing that he is financially capable of supporting both wives. The proposal was rejected by the parliament as a result of a wave opposition from women.[59] This opposition reflected the concern that such a custom does not conform to Iranian social circumstances and can undermine women's rights. Politically, the proposal could be perceived as a government attempt to more deeply enshrine its strict Islamic interpretation into law.

While polygamy is allowed in the *Quran*, according to the traditional interpretation, most Muslims, particularly female ones, reject polygamy. Many of them now believe that polygamy is an unacceptable form of discrimination against women that has no place in a modern society. For them, the practice is nothing but a relic of a distant past that no longer serves a worthwhile moral, social, or economic purpose. The practice still favors, and always will favor, powerful men. After all, the most prominent man in the history of the Islamic world, Muhammed, once found himself at the center of such a controversy. At present, we continue to see such a moral reaction to similar situations.[60] Muslim states, in the process of modernization, often have struggled to minimize the discriminatory impact of traditional Islamic law on women. While no state has been completely successful given the continued clout of traditional Islamic law, reformers have succeeded in significantly reducing the impact of such discrimination.[61]

All of this must be viewed in the context of the tension that still surrounds the issue. Polygamy has been justified as a practice that is allowed by *Quran*, and countries that do not criminalize polygamy consider it permissible. As noted, the *Quran* subjects the custom to requirements that are nearly impossible to satisfy. The effect is an ongoing cultural struggle to come to grips with the apparent contradictions. Apart from being incompatible with modern and emerging norms of gender equality, some research indicates polygyny may harm families. Academic achievement of children from polygynous families has been found to be inferior to those of children from monogamous families.[62] Polygamous families also have higher levels of interfamilial conflict, translating into further educational difficulties and self-esteem issues for children.[63] Wives in polygamous families have been found to have worse mental health.[64] The effect can be particularly pronounced on the first wife in a union, who must adjust to the entry of subsequent wives.[65]

The normative implication of this information, coupled with changing cultural views of women in the Islamic world, is that the liberalization of Islamic society ought to continue. The removal of polygyny is a central component of this process. This may be counterintuitive to a western observer who is unfamiliar with the history of polygyny in the Islamic world. Its patriarchal nature has compromised the autonomy and agency of women for generations.

In confronting the future of polygyny in the Islamic world, two interpretative approaches emerge. One takes a very religious-oriented, God-based view while the other, historicism, calls for an interpretation of Islamic law in the context in which it arose. The former looks at society as an immutable entity created by God (akin to a natural law view). By contrast, the latter begins by placing that society in a phase of its development. [66] Interestingly, both can be argued to support the conclusion that polygyny should be discontinued. According to the natural law view, the relations between men and women, their rights, and their social and family status are rooted in nature, an objective pre-existing state. Because by nature they are morally and physical different, laws must accommodate their differences. God ensures justice among humans by authoritatively describing in the *Quran* which rights are good for women and men.[67] Muslim Faqih (jurisprudence) operates on this basis, and practicing polygamy is an example of this view.

Historicism takes a very different view, emphasizing that the norms of one's own society embody fundamental truths that must be reformulated in the midst of new circumstances. One must understand the historical foundations of Islamic practices, what economic and political realities the practices responded to, and how the underlying theme of Islamic principles expressed in the matter were remedied by the practice.[68] Although historicism still insists on some moral and physical differences between men and women, the application of religious principles must take into account contemporary circumstances.[69] From this standpoint, the *Quran* is seen as a moral admonition in total, not merely a legal code or list of rules, containing a general moral message that must be adhered to. In this sense, it bears much in common with a liberal interpretation of the Christian Bible, which informs faiths such as modern Anglicanism.[70]

Contemporary women have the same political and social responsibilities as men have, and discriminatory family laws cannot be applied to them.[71] The practice of polygamy may have been more justifiable in an age where men had the most important responsibilities in the familial, political, and social realms. Polygamy may have been well-suited for the familial needs of a primitive society, but such conditions no longer obtain. As a result, we cannot continue applying the same principles to contemporary women who now have the same responsibilities and status as men.[72] In other words, polygamy has outlived its usefulness. For Shabestari, it is better to have a historically-informed view of women's rights and status, because the true mission of Muhammad was to liberate women from pre-Islamic oppression.[73] In his view, Muhammad changed the status of women in pre-Islamic Arabia and tried to modify their situations based on the way he could make such adjustments within existing traditions. Shabestari maintains that all Muslims should follow his mission and change the laws incrementally to meets the demands of contemporary society.[74]

This notion of the Mission of Muhammed is fascinating. What we are seeing is a new reading of Islam to support an incremental liberation narrative, embodied by the person of Muhammed and his moral teaching, notwithstanding the human flaws he may have possessed as exhibited by his aforementioned episode with Zaynab. The person of Muhammed is being held up as a positive force to promote reform in the area of polygyny, notwithstanding that certain aspects of the example of his life may discourage such change.

The practice of polygyny, as defined by the *Quran*, should not be sustained in contemporary circumstances. As noted, the *Quran* itself appears to discourage the practice strongly by subjecting it to many onerous conditions. In the face of this scriptural authority, the response in the Muslim world is the increasingly widely-held view that the practice is immoral and damages families. It seems advisable, then, to continue with "Muhammed's Mission," defined by Shabestari, to put an end to polygyny. Both a historicist and religiously-based approach can be of service here. There is no need to choose one form of engagement over the other and risk alienating sections of the Muslim world's demographics. The seeds for reform can be found within Islam itself and the life of Muhammed.

CONCLUSION

Modernity is already putting considerable pressure on the strictly culturally-regulated Muslim observance of polygyny. The development of laws in Muslim nation states that prohibit or regulate the practice reveals the Muslim world is slowly but surely eliminating polygyny. For centuries, the practice has existed in the penumbra generated by the relevant Quranic verses. The question is now whether modernity will operationalize the potential of those verses to make polygyny disappear. A further question is whether those future Muslims, who may succeed in doing so, will realize they stood on Muhammed's shoulders to get there.

NOTES

1. Will Durant, *The Story of Civilization Vol. 1, Our Oriental Heritage* (New York: Simon and Schuster, 1976), 61.
2. Robison Blaine, "Polygamy," last modified December 19, 2014, http://www.blainerobison.com/concerns/polygamy.htm.
3. Gen 16:1– 3; 25:1– 6), Jacob (Gen 29:23– 28; 30:4, 9), David (1Sam 25:42– 44; 2 Sam 3:13– 14; 5:13; 6:20– 23; 12:8), and Solomon (1 Kgs 11:3).
4. Charles de Secondat Montesquieu, *The Spirit of the Laws*, trans. Anne M. Cohler (Cambridge: Cambridge University Press, 1989), 289.
5. Naser Makarem Shirazi, *Tafsir Namoneh* (Tehran: Darul Kotob al–Islamia Fi Tehran, 1992), 329; Morteza Motahhari, *The Rights of Women in Islam* (Hamburg: World Organization for Islamic Services, 1981), 127–161; Seyed Mohammad Hossein Tabatabai, *Al-Mizan fi Tafsir al-Quran* (Qom: Office of the Islamic Publications of Society of Seminary Teachers of Qom, 1996), 291–298.
6. Motahhari, *The Rights of Women in Islam,* 127–161; Sherif Abdel Azeem, *Women in Islam versus Women in the Judaeo-Christian Tradition: The Myth & the Reality* (World Islamic Network), http://www.al-islam.org/women-islam-versus-women-judaeo-christian-tradition-myth-reality-sherif-muhammad-abdel-azeem.
7. Motahhari, *The Rights of Women in Islam*, 139.
8. Ibid, 140.
9. Siahyonkron Nyanseor, "Polygyny (Polygamy) Is Already A Practice," Accessed January 30, 2016, http://www.theperspective.org/polygyny.html.
10. Martha Bailey et al., *Expanding Recognition of Foreign Polygamous Marriages: Policy Implications for Canada* (Kingston: Queen's University Legal Studies Research Paper, 2006), 2.
11. Ibid, 2.
12. Ibid, 3.
13. Ibid.
14. Ibid, 4.
15. Ibid.
16. Gunawan Adnan, *Women and the Glorious Quran: An Analytical Study of Women-Related Verses of Sūra An-Nisa'* (Göttingen: Universitätsverlag Göttingen, 2004), 23–24.
17. Jonathan Porter Berkey, *The Formation of Islam: Religion and Society in the Near East, 600–1800* (New York: Cambridge University Press, 2003), 39.

18. Peter Webb, "Al-Jāhiliyya: Uncertain Times of Uncertain Meanings." *Der Islam* 91 (2014): 69–94.

19. 33:33, 48:26, 5:50 and 3:154.

20. Berkey, *The Formation of Islam*, 39; Sita Ram Gole, *Hindu Temples: What Happened to Them; Part II the Islamic Evidence* (New Delhi: Voice of India, 1991), http://voiceofdharma.org/books/htemples2/; James E. Lindsay, *Daily Life in the Medieval Islamic World* (Westport: Greenwood Publishing Group, 2005), 179; Edward A. Kolodziej ed., *A Force Profonde: The Power, Politics, and Promise of Human Rights* (Philadelphia, University of Pennsylvania Press, 2013), 60; Elie Elhadj, "In Defense of Pre-Islamic Arabian Culture." August 2007, http://www.daringopinion.com/Islam--In-Defense-of-Pre-Islamic-Arabian-Culture.php.

21. Adnan, *Women and the Glorious Qur'ān*, 26.

22. Adnan, *Women and the Glorious Qur'ān*, 26; Elhadj, "In Defense of Pre-Islamic."

23. Nihal Sahin Utku, "Arabia in the Pre-Islamic Period," June 13, 2013, http://www.lastprophet.info/arabia-in-the-pre-islamic-period; Adnan, *Women and the Glorious Qur'ān*; Berkey, *The Formation of Islam*, 27–28.

24. Leila Ahmed, *Women and Gender in Islam: Historical Roots of a Modern Debate* (New Haven: Yale University Press, 1992), 41.

25. Adnan, *Women and the Glorious Qur'ān*, 25.

26. Ibid, 29.

27. Ibid, 29.

28. Goel, *Hindu Temples.*

29. James E. Lindsay, *Daily Life in the Medieval Islamic World* (Westport: Greenwood Publishing Group, 2005), 179.

30. Fatima Mernissi, *Beyond the Veil: Male-Female Dynamics in Modern Muslim Society* (Bloomington: Indiana University Press, 1987), 73–74; Susanne Monahan, William Andrew Mirola, and Michael O. Emerson, ed., *Sociology of Religion: A Reader* (Pearson College Division, 2001),102; Ahmed, *Women and Gender*, 41.

31. Mernissi, *Beyond the Veil*, 75.

32. Ibid, 78.

33. Ahmed, *Women and Gender*, 42–43.

34. Ahmed, *Women and Gender*, 42–43; Kolodziej, *A Force Profonde*, 60–61; Goel, *Hindu Temples.*

35. Abdel Muhammad Haleem, trans., *The Quran* (Oxford: Oxford University Press, 2005), 50.

36. Ibid.

37. Ibid.

38. Nasr Hamid Abu Zayd, "The Quranic Concept of Justice," http://them.polylog.org/3/fan-en.htm.

39. M. M. M. Shafi, *Ma'ariful Qur'an: A Comprehensive Commentary on the Holy Quran* (Karachi: Maktaba-e-Darul-Uloom, 2004), 1–14; Makarem Shirazi, *Tafsir Namoneh*, 325–336; Tabatabai, *Al-Mizan fi Tafsir al-Quran*, 291–298; Abdullah Yusuf Ali, *The Meaning of the Glorious Qur'an (Text, Translation and Commentary)* (Cairo: Dar al-Fatah al-Masri, 2012), 51–63; Muhammad Saed Abdul Rahman, *Tafsir Ibn Kathir Juz' 4 (Part 4): Ali-Imran 93 To An-Nisaa 23* (London: MSA Publication Limited, 2009), 119–124; Morteza, *The Rights of Women in Islam*, 127–160.

40. Haleem, *The Quran*, 63.

41. Shafi, *Ma'ariful Qur'an*, 1–14; Makarem Shirazi, *Tafsir Namoneh*, 325–336; Tabatabai, *Al-Mizan fi Tafsir al-Quran*, 291–298; Abdul Rahman, *Tafsir Ibn Kathir*, 119–124.

42. Motahhari, *The Rights of Women In Islam*, 127–160.

43. Mernissi, *Beyond the Veil*, 46–47.

44. Adnan, *Women and the Glorious Qur'ān*, 177–178; Abdul Rahman, *Tafsir Ibn Kathir*, 119–124.

45. Motahhari, *The Rights of Women In Islam*, 127–160; Ali, *The Meaning of the Glorious Qur'an*, 51–63; Muḥammad Ḥusayn Haykal, *The Life of Muhammad* (Kuala Lumpur: Islamic Book Trust, 1994), 315–316.

46. Ahmed, *Women and Gender*, 43.

47. Yahiya Emerick, *The Life and Work of Muhammad* (New York: Penguin, 2002), 136.

48. Justice Mufti Muhammad Taqi Usmani, *Discourses on Islamic Ways of Life*, trans. Iqbal Hussain Ansari (Karachi: Darul Isha, 1999), 240; Caesar E. Farah, *Islam: Beliefs and Observances* (Hauppaug: Barron's Educational Series, 1970), 69.

49. Haleem, *The Quran*, 270.

50. William Montgomery Watt, *Muhammad: Prophet and Statesman* (London: Oxford University Press, 1996), 157–159; Edward Sell, *The Historical Development of the Qurán*, http://onlinebooks.library.upenn.edu/.

51. Haleem, *The Quran*, 266.

52. Ibid., 269.

53. Ibid.

54. Watt, *Muhammad*, 157–159.

55. Pohl, Florian, *Modern Muslim Societies* (Marshall Cavendish, 2010), 32–35.

56. These are either Muslim countries or in Africa (either Muslim countries or non-Muslim): Afghanistan, Algeria, Bahrain, Bangladesh, Brunei, Burkina Fasco, Cameroon, Chad, CAR, Comoros, Congo, Djibouti, Eritrea (Sharia districts), Egypt, Gabon, Gambia, India (Muslim states), Iran, Iraq, Jordan, Kuwait, Lebanon, Libya, Malaysia, Maldives, Mail, Mauritania, Morocco, Myanmar, Niger, Nigeria (Sharia states), Oman, Pakistan, Palestine (Gaza Strip and West Bank) Qatar, Saudi Arabia, Senegal, Sierra Leone, Singapore, Somalia, Sri Lanaka, Sudan, Syria, Tanzania, Tago, Uganda, UAE, Yemen, Zambia. World Heritage Encyclopedia, http://www.worldheritage.org.

57. Florian Pohl, *Modern Muslim Societies* (Singapore: Marshall Cavendish, 2010), 32–35.

58. Dan Bilefsky, "Polygamy Fosters Culture Clashes (and Regrets) in Turkey," *New York Times*, July 10, 2006, http://www.nytimes.com/2006/07/10/world/europe/10turkey.html.

59. Sahar Sepehri, "Women Fight Polygamy Proposal," February 3, 2010, http://www.wluml.org/node/5929.

60. Adnan, *Women and the Glorious Qur'ān*, 176.

61. Priscilla Offenhauer and Alice R. Buchalter, *Women in Islamic Societies: A Selected Review of Social Scientific Literature* (Federal Research Division, Library of Congress, 2005).

62. Adesehinwa Olayinka Adenike, "Effects of Family Type (Monogamy or Polygamy) on Students Academic Achievement in Nigeria," *International Journal of Psychology and Counselling* 5 (2013): 153–156.

63. Alean Al-Krenawi and Ernie S. Lightman. "Learning Achievement, Social Adjustment, and Family Conflict Among Bedouin-Arab Children from Polygamous and Monogamous Families," *The Journal of Social Psychology* 140 (2000): 345–355; Donatus Ojiakudiniro Owuamanam,"Adolescents' Perception of Polygamous Family and Its Relationship to Self-Concept," *International Journal of Psychology* 19 (1984): 593–598.

64. Alean Al-Krenawi, John R. Graham, and Fakir Al Gharaibeh, "A Comparison Study of Psychological, Family Function Marital and Life Satisfactions of Polygamous and Monogamous Women in Jordan." *Community Mental Health Journal* 47 (2011): 594–602.

65. Alean Al-Krenawi, "Mental Health and Polygamy: The Syrian Case." *World Journal of Psychiatry* 3 (2013): 1.

66. Mojtahed Shabestari, *Naqdi Bar Qira'at-e Rasmyi Din [A Critique of the Official Reading of Religion]* (Tehran: Tahre-no, 2000), 53–70.

67. Shabestari, *A Critique of the Official Reading of Religion*, 54.

68. Suad Joseph, et al. *Women and Islamic Cultures: Disciplinary Paradigms and Approaches: 2003–2013* (Leiden: Brill, 2013), 318–325.

69. Shabestari, *A Critique of the Official Reading of Religion*, 56.

70. Yushau Sodiq, *An Insider's Guide to Islam* (Bloomington: Trafford Publishing, 2010), 294.

71. Shabestari, *A Critique of the Official Reading of Religion*, 57.

72. Ibid, 60.
73. Ibid, 67.
74. Ibid, 69.

REFERENCES

Abdul Rahman, Muhammad Saed. *Tafsir Ibn Kathir Juz' 4 (Part 4): Ali-Imran 93 To An-Nisaa 23*. London: MSA Publication Limited, 2009.

Abu Zayd, Nasr Hamid. "The Quranic Concept of Justice." http://them.polylog.org/3/fan-en.htm.

Adenike, Adesehinwa Olayinka. "Effects of Family Type (Monogamy or Polygamy) on Students Academic Achievement in Nigeria." *International Journal of Psychology and Counselling* 5 (2013): 153–156.

Adnan, Gunawan. *Women and the Glorious Quran: An Analytical Study of Women-Related Verses of Sūra An-Nisa'*. Göttingen: University of Göttingen, 2004.

Ahmed, Leila. *Women and Gender in Islam: Historical Roots of a Modern Debate*. New Haven: Yale University Press, 1992.

Ali, Abdullah Yusuf. *The Meaning of the Glorious Qur'an (Text, Translation and Commentary)*. Cairo: Dar al-Fatah al-Masri, 2012.

Al-Krenawi, Alean, and Ernie S. Lightman. "Learning Achievement, Social Adjustment, and Family Conflict Among Bedouin-Arab Children from Polygamous and Monogamous Families." *Journal of Social Psychology* 140 (2000): 345– 355.

Al-Krenawi, Alean, John R. Graham, and Fakir Al Gharaibeh. "A Comparison Study of Psychological, Family Function Marital and Life Satisfactions of Polygamous and Monogamous Women in Jordan." *Community Mental Health Journal* 47 (2011): 594–602.

Al-Krenawi, Alean. "Mental Health and Polygamy: The Syrian Case." *World Journal of Psychiatry* 3 (2013): 1.

Azeem, Sherif Abdel. *Women in Islam Versus Women in the Judaeo-Christian Tradition: The Myth and the Reality*. Alexandria: Conveying Islamic Message Society, 1995.

Bailey, Martha, et al. *Expanding Recognition of Foreign Polygamous Marriages: Policy Implications for Canada*. Kingston: Queen's University Legal Studies Research Paper 07–12 (2006).

Berkey, Jonathan Porter. *The Formation of Islam: Religion and Society in the Near East, 600–1800*. New York: Cambridge University Press, 2003.

Bilefsky, Dan. "Polygamy Fosters Culture Clashes (and Regrets) in Turkey." *New York Times,* July 10, 2006, http://www.nytimes.com/2006/07/10/world/europe/10turkey.html.

Durant, Will. *The Story of Civilization Vol. 1, Our Oriental Heritage*. New York: Simon and Schuster, 1976.

Elhadj, Elie. "In Defense of Pre-Islamic Arabian Culture." August 2007. http://www.daringopinion.com/Islam--In-Defense-of-Pre-Islamic-Arabian-Culture.php

Emerick, Yahiya. *The Life and Work of Muhammad*. New York: Penguin, 2002.

Farah, Caesar E. *Islam: Beliefs and Observances*. Hauppauge, NY: Barron's Educational Series, 1970.

Goel, Sita Ram. *Hindu Temples: What Happened to Them; Part II the Islamic Evidence*. New Delhi: Voice of India, 1991.

Gottlieb, Roger S. *Liberating Faith: Religious Voices for Justice, Peace, and Ecological Wisdom*. Lanham: Rowman & Littlefield, 2003.

Haleem, Abdel Muhammad, trans. *The Quran*. Oxford: Oxford University Press, 2005.

Haykal, Muḥammad Ḥusayn. *The Life of Muhammad*. Kuala Lumpur: Islamic Book Trust, 1994.

Joseph, Suad et al. *Women and Islamic Cultures: Disciplinary Paradigms and Approaches: 2003–2013*. Leiden: Brill, 2013.

Kolodziej, Edward A., ed. *A Force Profonde: The Power, Politics, and Promise of Human Rights*. Philadelphia: University of Pennsylvania Press, 2013.
Lindsay, James E. *Daily Life in the Medieval Islamic World*. Westport: Greenwood Publishing Group, 2005.
Mernissi, Fatima. *Beyond the Veil: Male-Female Dynamics in Modern Muslim Society*. Bloomington: Indiana University Press, 1987.
Montesquieu, Charles de Secondat. *The Spirit of the Laws*. Edited and Translated by Anne M. Cohler, Basia Carolyn Miller, and Harold Samuel Stone. New York: Cambridge University Press, 1989.
Monahan, Susanne C., William Andrew Mirola, and Michael O. Emerson, eds. *Sociology of Religion: A Reader*. Pearson College Division, 2001.
Makarem Shirazi, Naser. *Tafsir Namoneh*. Tehran: Darul Kotob al-Islamia Fi Tehran, 1992.
Motahhari, Morteza. *The Rights of Women in Islam*. Hamburg: World Organization for Islamic Services, 1981.
Nyanseor, Siahyonkron. "Polygyny (Polygamy) Is Already a Practice." http://www.theperspective.org/polygyny.html.
Offenhauer, Priscilla, and Alice R. Buchalter. *Women in Islamic Societies: A Selected Review of Social Scientific Literature*. Federal Research Division, Library of Congress, 2005.
Owuamanam, Donatus Ojiakudiniro. "Adolescents' Perception of Polygamous Family and its Relationship to Self-Concept." *International Journal of Psychology* 19 (1984): 593–598.
Pohl, Florian. *Modern Muslim Societies*. Singapore: Marshall Cavendish, 2010.
Robison, Blaine. "Polygamy." http://www.blainerobison.com/concerns/polygamy.htm.
Sell, Edward. *The Historical Development of the Qurán*. onlinebooks.library.upenn.edu/.
Sepehri, Sahar. "Women Fight Polygamy Proposal." Accessed February 3, 2010, https://iwpr.net/global-voices/women-fight-polygamy-proposal.
Shafi, M. M. M. *Ma'ariful Qur'an: A Comprehensive Commentary on the Holy Quran*. Karachi: Maktaba-e-Darul-Uloom, 2004.
Shabestari, Mojtahed. *Naqdi bar qira'at-e rasmyi din [A Critique of the Official Reading of Religion]*. Tehran: Tahre-no, 2000.
Sodiq, Yushau. *An Insider's Guide to Islam*. Bloomington: Trafford Publishing, 2010.
Tabatabai, Seyed and Mohammad Hossein. *Al-Mizan fi Tafsir al-Quran*. Qom: Office of the Islamic Publications of Society of Seminary Teachers of Qom, 1996.
Usmani, Justice Mufti Muhammad Taqi. *Discourses on Islamic Ways of Life*. Translated by Iqbal Hussain Ansari. Karachi: Darul Isha (1999).
Utku, Nihal Sahin. "Arabia in the Pre-Islamic Period." June 13, 2013. http://www.lastprophet.info/arabia-in-the-pre-islamic-period.
Watt, William Montgomery. *Muhammad: Prophet and Statesman*. London: Oxford University Press, 1961.
World Heritage Encyclopedia. http://www.worldheritage.org.
Webb, Peter. "Al-Jāhiliyya: Uncertain Times of Uncertain Meanings." *Der Islam* 91 (2014): 69–94.

EIGHT

The Need for a Sociological Perspective on Polyamory

Kristin McCarty

Surprisingly, few sociologists have made a serious effort to study polyamory.[1] This failure on their part is troubling as the demographics of the American family continue to evolve. In order to fully understand the nature and extent of these ongoing changes, sociologists must not exclude any individual family form, especially one like polyamory, which is becoming more prevalent. In what follows, I will explore the way polyamory is situated in the sociological literature as well as the likely reasons for the current lack of research on this particular intimate relationship structure. In doing so, I explain why it is imperative for more sociologists to begin to study the topic with the kind of care that it deserves. Otherwise, the public may continue to believe, without justification, that it threatens the family, instead of being an alternative form that has unique benefits. Sociologists can be a part of removing the stigma associated with polyamory by elevating it to the level of social phenomenon, thereby allowing Americans to have a more sophisticated discussion about it, free from misconceptions of what polyamory is and what polyamorists are like.

This chapter will be divided into the following sections. First, I begin by elaborating on why sociologists can no longer neglect the topic of polyamory. Second, I give an overview of sociological research on this topic, paying close attention to why sociologists are hesitant to contribute to the growing interdisciplinary literature on the various contemporary forms of multi-person intimate relationships. Third, I conclude with some thoughts on what they can do to fill the gap so that the public, policymakers, and scholars are not deprived of the knowledge that they need to make informed decisions.

SOCIOLOGY OF THE FAMILY

Some of the obstacles facing polyamory research result from the fact that polyamory is new in the sense that many people, including scholars, have never heard of it or are confused about its meaning. Sadly, the term often has an unfavorable reputation among other sexual minority groups, and most sociologists tend to favor research practices that align with the philosophy of pure sociology, as opposed to public or applied sociology. It is unknown exactly how many Americans practice polyamory. A survey published by *Loving More Magazine* estimates that 500,000 Americans are polyamorous; nearly two-thirds of them would seek legal recognition if they could; and more than 90 percent think that their relationships should be accorded the same rights, privileges, and responsibilities as two-party marriages.[2] Furthermore, some polyamorists believe that they are discriminated against in housing, employment, and child custody.[3] At present, the law still fails to recognize all families' worth, even in the midst of greater tolerance of same-sex intimate relationships. Anti-discrimination laws are supposed to uphold the legal right of all Americans to be treated equally, yet few scholars or activists are terribly concerned about the difficulties that polyamorists face.[4] In a morally pluralistic society, laws and social norms ought not discriminate against any family and make their lives more difficult than they have to be.

Instead, a liberal state is supposed to support the diverse family structures in which all members prosper.[5] The implications of this are numerous, not only for polyamorous families, but for all American families and members of nontraditional relationship groups, despite their minority status. It is imperative for sociologists to determine exactly how far these issues reach and whom they most affect so that professionals can provide adequate services to polyamorous adults, their children, and other dependents. As noted, few sociologists have ventured into the unchartered waters of polyamory. One notable exception is Elisabeth Sheff. Her book, *The Polyamorists Next Door: Inside Multiple-Partner Relationships and Families*, is the first comprehensive treatment of the dynamics of polyamorist families, including childcare issues.[6] Hopefully, it will not be the last.

As in the past, the family continues to evolve in a rapidly changing world. Sociologists are interested in explaining how the institution of family persists and what purposes it serves while weathering serious national and global events such as war, economic recessions, and industrialization. Americans are living in a historic time when same-sex marriage finally is an option in all states and families look less uniform than ever before.[7] A single concept of "the family" does not exist. Rather, sociologists focus on the plural "families" to underscore their variance. Scholars such as Talcott Parsons, Friedrich Engels, Judith Stacey, Nancy Cott, and many others have analyzed the institution of family and how it has evolved over time. Moreover, "alternate family forms" has become a recognizable subfield of the sociology of the family and one that has direct links to the study of polyamory. In 1960, if I were to ask you to imagine the typical American family, you might describe something that would resemble the world of Ward and June Cleaver—two kids and a white picket fence. Many scholars have noted that the predominant concept of family in the United States still conjures "an image of a married, monogamous, heterosexual pair and their progeny."[8] Fast-forward to 2015 and while some families still may be described as such, the typical family model has changed dramatically.[9]

The existing data portrays the "typical" American family as differing from families of the past. Americans have begun to name, identify, and employ a breadth of family structures that more accurately represent what is actually going on in families across the United States. There are adoptive families, single-parent families, blended families, and families that include stepparents. Within the last decade, the definition of family has expanded to include same-sex-parent families.[10] Nowadays, it is very likely for an American family to fall into one (or more) of these categories. As it should be, the American definition of "family" is more expansive than ever before.

Nevertheless, it is possible that few sociologists have yet pushed the concept of family far enough to mediate the consequences of legal and social discrimination suffered by some nontraditional families. Family law in many states seems incapable of keeping up with the reality of how so many people live. There are nontraditional families that are not covered by the social or legal definitions of what it means to be a family. As a result, they may not be treated equally. As these kinds of family become even more common, "professionals from counselors and therapists or educators and clergy to medical staff and lawyers will need factual information based in sound research to help them serve this growing client base."[11] This need must be addressed sooner rather than later. Sociologists are precisely the social scientists that can rise to the challenge by providing the data that makes informed decision-making possible. Sociology investigates the way that groups of people, such as polyamorists, interact to create the social worlds in which they exist. As a discipline, it incorporates the insights of many other social science fields, such as anthropology and economics, in order to paint the richest picture. This method of examining the social world is the most promising technique for illuminating the lives of polyamorists. In the next several years, as the United States continues to discuss marriage equality and its implications, access to this kind of knowledge will be critical.

Polyamorous families may encounter daily complications because American society lacks a more inclusive definition of family that would enable them to live healthy and happy lives, described by Nancy Polikoff to cover "economic well-being, legal recognition, emotional peace of mind, and community respect."[12] These potential shortcomings in our social and legal systems should prompt sociologists to study the potential adverse effects of discrimination. A comprehensive understanding of these social problems should inform and complicate our notion of what is going on in various intersecting social worlds. Grasping these nuances, which may be misunderstood or not understood at all, is what good sociology is all about. Without accurate data, public deliberation about polyamorous relationships, and whether they should be accorded some kind of legal status, is bound to suffer from the kinds of pathologies that characterized the debate over same-sex marriage in this country over the last decade.

BRIEF RESEARCH HISTORY

Polyamory is often defined by comparing it to what it is not. By definition, polyamory is not polygamy because all of those involved in polyamorous relationships are not necessarily married. In countries where plural marriage is illegal, like America, it is common for two of the people in the polyamorous relationship to be legally/civilly married to each other and then be "married" to other partners. Additionally, polyamory is not polygamy, understood as traditional polygyny, because it not only allows for but also aspires to gender equality. In much of the world, often for religious and cultural reasons, polygamy is practiced as polygyny, which is when one man is married to multiple women.[13] In these instances, the women do not have access to multiple partners and are not allowed to have sexual relationships with each other.[14]

Polyamory differs from infidelity or swinging as well. Polyamory is not cheating, as it is normally understood, because in keeping with its definition, all parties are aware of and consent to the structure of the relationship, which extends to bringing in new partners. A person may claim to be polyamorous but their relationship is not actually polyamorous if the people they are dating believe that the arrangement is sexually and emotionally monogamous. Polyamorous relationships often contain elements of negotiation and rules to which each party agrees. Similarly, polyamory is not swinging because of the emphasis placed on emotional and romantic intimacy, even though it is non-exclusive. Polyamory is not just about sex, in other words, whereas swinging is often intended to provide more sexual variety, excitement, and pleasure for an otherwise monogamous couple. At most, there is some overlap between polyamory and swinging. As a practice and way of life, polyamory contains both emotional and sexual preferences—as many romantic relationships do. Since the 1960s and 1970s, when the sexual revolution was in its prime, the ways in which Americans conduct themselves while engaged in intimate relationships never has been static.[15] During this time, open and non-monogamous relationships were on the rise. As a result, scholars began to study swinging and open marriages.[16]

According to Richard Parker, in the late 1970s and early 1980s, sexuality and "the ways in which we interpret and understand that experience" started to be understood as a product of social construction.[17] Something that is socially constructed is shaped by social and cultural systems and is dependent on aspects of our social identities. To say something is socially constructed is not to deny its existence; it is to express the thought that had we been a different society with different values and conditions, we might not have created the same phenomenon that appears to be normal or natural. Not only have the meanings of sexuality been called into question, but "this focus on the social construction of sexual identities has also been associated with an increasing emphasis on the organization of distinct sexual communities."[18]

Intentional communities and communes share a common ancestor with polyamory.[19] Perhaps most broadly, intentional communities can be defined as a group of people who have agreed to participate collectively in a "social structure greater than the nuclear family."[20] Patrick Conover states, "if . . . intentional communities . . . are seen as the building block institutions of the alternate culture, as the nuclear family is for establishment culture, then it must be judged that the alternative culture can become institutionalized in the meeting of domestic functional necessities without giving up distinctive values."[21] Just as different societies construct sexuality differently, they also construct relationship and familial systems differently, producing a wide range of legal and social needs.[22]

Much of the sociological literature presents a framework with built-in assumptions that still do not make enough room for extended notions of family, identity, sexuality, and marriage. The term "family" encompasses a variety of definitions and sociologists must be flexible enough to acknowledge them or risk excluding the experiences of numerous people and thereby, failing to grasp the nuances of the phenomenon in question. In the last couple of decades, the sociology of family literature has put into some doubt the explanatory power of the traditional idea of family. Although this is a good start, considerable work remains to be done. After all, the social world never remains inert. In conducting their research, sociologists must use a more encompassing definition of the family. Otherwise, they cannot be confident about the validity of their findings.

That is not to say that all scholars have missed the mark. A few of them have done an exemplary job at exposing the fallacies of this one-size-fits-all family model. According to Judith Stacey, the marriage promotion movement promoted an ideology, which "censors premarital sex and stigmatizes single parents, worsening the plight of women across the class spectrum, but disproportionately African American women, who face a dearth of marriageable suitors."[23] She debunks three influential principles of the contemporary marriage promotion movement: (1) "that marriage is a universal and necessary institution" (2) "that the ideal family structure for raising children is a married man and a woman and their biological or adopted children" and (3) "that children generally, and boys particularly, need both a father and a mother to turn out well."[24] Scholarship that takes issue with commonly accepted notions of family, like that of Stacey, is desperately needed in a time when much of our daily lives are impacted by our status and position within a family unit.[25]

In earlier literature, feminist scholars "challenged the ideology of the 'monolithic family,' which had elevated the nuclear family with a breadwinner husband and full-time wife and mother as the only legitimate family form. They did this in order to dislodge beliefs that any specific family arrangement is natural, biological, or 'functional' in a timeless way."[26] Other scholars have proposed that it would be possible and preferable to formulate a better working definition of the term "family." At the same time, feminist scholars are wary of essentializing anything and are skeptical of trying to posit anything like a static entity.[27] Despite their differences, all feminist perspectives converge on the view that "the family" must be conceptualized as the diversity of family structures that exist in our contemporary world to avoid the fallacy of only studying the most familiar forms.

Feminist research has paid close attention to relationships between men and women and female sexuality for a very long time because of how identities change, in response to gendered power relations, and the notion of what it means to be a woman.[28] It is especially concerned with how women are framed in these contexts—most often in a subordinate role, such as the caregiver. Recently, the concept of sexual fluidity is gaining some momentum in feminist thinking. Although such fluidity may play a huge part in some women's lives, it may play little or no part in others. Examining polyamory through a feminist lens does not attempt to reify an idea but focuses on exploring diversity and understanding all the different forms that relationships and sexuality can take, without judgment. Some feminist scholars even see polyamory as a way to empower women.[29]

A discussion of this topic wouldn't be complete without mentioning the few scholars who seek to comprehend the phenomenon of polyamory without reducing it to something else. As noted, Sheff has produced perhaps the most significant sociological analysis of polyamory to date in *The Polyamorists Next Door*.[30] In several of her scholarly works, Sheff demonstrates that polyamory can be linked to the literature of various other sexual movements and intentional communities. Research in intersecting fields of study—intentional communities, queer studies, monogamy, and heterosexuality—provides an agenda for future polyamory research. Sheff is the exception and not the rule, though.

The field of psychology has been more enthusiastic about studying the different aspects of polyamorist relationships. Meg John Barker is one of these psychologists and an open polyamory activist. In their view, polyamory challenges three main components in the composition of intimate relationships: (1) that a relationship should be between a male and a female (2) that relationships should be monogamous and (3) that the male is usually the active participant and the female is expected to be passive.[31] Roger Rubin analyzed three popular marriage and family textbooks and found that they rarely referred to alternative relationships: "It is like a family secret. Everyone is aware of it, but no one acknowledges it."[32] Sociologists must expand the conceptual vocabulary of what it means to be a family in order to understand the growing diversity of family forms. This refusal is inexcusable for scholars who pride themselves on the quality of their research and the accuracy of their data. If that were not enough, the failure on the part of sociologists to treat the study of polyamory with the care that it deserves is a disservice to polyamorous families, who have the same worth as other, more conventional families.

POLYAMORY AND SOCIOLOGY

What, then, explains sociologists' reluctance to treat polyamory as a legitimate form of the family or intimate relationship worthy of serious attention? It is my belief that this neglect is due to three intermingled causes. First, the term "polyamory" itself is new and thus, researchers may not be aware of its existence or have misconceptions about the practice.[33] Second, polyamory's placement within the LGBT+ community is unstable, at best. Third, the field of sociology quietly opposes public sociology and I will discuss why a scholarly work of this nature often is derisively labeled as public sociology.

Its Newness

Some sociologists have studied plural marriage, polygyny, swinging, and their resultant relationship forms, but as noted, with an exception every now and then, not polyamory itself. The exact time and place that "polyamory" was coined is not agreed upon within the polyamory community.[34] The term seems to have grown out of a need for language that accurately described the type of ethical non-monogamy in which members of this group engaged. Dropping it casually in conversation often gets me a few blank stares or nods but rarely thoughtful questions, which causes me to wonder whether the person is actually paying attention. I prefer fielding questions because it is my experience that even if people have heard the term before, they don't actually understand its meaning.[35]

I have a personal anecdote to back up these claims. As a graduate student, I am around very well-educated folks on a daily basis but I have had awkward encounters even with people I know and respect. For example, I was discussing some statistical topic and somehow the phrase "three-way interaction" became a part of the conversation. The actual meaning of this term is not relevant. Just know that it is a statistical expression relating to quantitative research. The person I was conversing with proceeded to make a joke about how "three-ways are my thing, aren't they?" I'm sure no offense was intended and it may have even been an awkward way of coping with a certain level of discomfort. Nevertheless, not only was this comment inappropriate, it also illuminated how misunderstood the term polyamory is. What I can gather from this communication is that this person doesn't understand that (1) conflating research interests with personal interests or biography is a precarious assumption to make and (2) polyamory is much more complex than threesomes, quads, or moresomes. People can go to sex clubs, sex parties, and have open relationships without coming close to qualifying as polyamorous. The joke stems from an unfortunate misunderstanding that I doubt is as uncommon as it ought to be in the rest of sociology. In fact, this wasn't my first experience of this kind and I doubt it will be my last. I use this as an example of just how new this concept is for most people, even for scholars, and how it may threaten their norms and values. While it certainly isn't new for those who practice the many forms of ethical non-monogamy that exist, it isn't yet well understood by outsiders. Hopefully, this state of affairs will change in the foreseeable future.

What is much more familiar to sociologists is polygamy. In my time in higher education, I have more than once encountered the mistaken assumption that what I study is polygamy. In the United States, people tend to have very strong negative feelings about polygamy. A public opinion poll conducted by Gallup in 2014 found that more than 70 percent of Americans find polygamy highly morally unacceptable.[36] However, this number is changing. Compared to a survey in 2006, Gallup found that public acceptance of polygamy rose from 5 percent to 14 percent.[37] This is a promising statistic and may be due to the surge of more positive representations of multiple-partner relationships in the popular culture, such as on the hit television shows *Big Love* and *Sister Wives*, featuring Fundamentalist Mormon families. It may hint that Americans are slowly becoming more tolerant of cultural and moral differences as they relate to family.

Our nation has a long and dramatic history pertaining to polygamy, and in recent years those feelings have been brought to the surface by well-publicized scandals involving men like Warren Jeffs.[38] Events such as these are what most people point to when arguing against acceptance of polyamorous practices. What most Americans don't appreciate is that polyamory is not the same as polygamy (or polygyny) other than the fact that each involves more than two participants. Not by definition and not in practice. For those who research polyamory, equal access to multiple partners and ethical non-monogamy render polyamory significantly different than other multi-person intimate relationships. These differences mean that, regardless of gender, each partner should have the same access to multiple partners in the polyamorous relationship, is aware of its sexual and emotional non-exclusivity, and is over the legal age of consent. Equally importantly, each member of a polyamorous unit is supposed to participate in all aspects of the group's decision making. As Sheff puts it, "The relationships have been negotiated with rules to structure scheduling and safer-sex agreements."[39]

Whether this confusion surrounding polyamory stems from a lack of sociological research on the topic, fear of difference, or pernicious stereotypes, is difficult to tell. Polyamory may not be a hot sociological topic just yet, but the mainstream has seen an influx of news reports and interviews about polyamory in the last few years, indicating that in the future it may not remain so hidden.[40] If the public is becoming more interested in the topic, then why are sociologists still ignoring it?[41]

THE REPUTATION OF POLYAMORY

The second possibility that I put forth as an explanation for why polyamory has been relatively excluded from sociological research concerns its uncertain status as a sexual orientation. That fact alone may dissuade some researchers from including it in their agendas. Controversy exists over polyamory's place within the LGBT+ community. As it stands, many gender and sexuality researchers and members of the LGBT+ movement do not consider polyamorists to be a part of the queer community, while some maintain that they are in a gray area.[42] Whether polyamory is a sexual orientation or a lifestyle choice seems to lie at the center of this discussion, as well as whether their being included in the LGBT+ community would benefit polyamorists. There are researchers on both ends of the spectrum that either support or disapprove of incorporating polyamory into the categories of sexual orientation. Ann Tweedy states:

> Because polyamory appears to be at least moderately embedded as an identity, because polyamorists face considerable discrimination, and because non-monogamy is an organizing principle of inequality in American culture, anti-discrimination protections for polyamorists are warranted. Moreover, polyamory shares some of the important attributes of sexual orientation as traditionally understood, so it makes con-

> ceptual sense for polyamory to be viewed as part of sexual orientation.[43]

By contrast, Christian Klesse claims that, "The incorporation of polyamory into sexual orientation frameworks is more likely to damage radical politics of non-monogamy and polyamory than to enhance accurate representations of the diversity of erotic experience."[44] For Klesse, including polyamory in the definition of sexual orientation would do more harm than good. He goes on to state that sexual orientation is often used to police people's desires and to enforce boundaries on sexual identity and the communities that form around them. Klesse maintains that if scholars were to apply the sexual orientation model to polyamorous people and consider them a distinct sexual minority, it would undermine the ability of polyamorists to ally themselves with other non-monogamous groups who are facing oppression.[45] This is an important point to consider. By conflating polyamory with sexual orientation, scholars may be unnecessarily limiting the discussion and elevating polyamory above other non-monogamous relationship groups that may otherwise support the polyamorous agenda.

From a sociological perspective, the following question arises: Why does it matter whether polyamory or any other form of sexual expression is a choice or not? I often raise this question with respect to homosexuality and now express the same concern in the case of polyamory as well. I have a hard time understanding why Americans are only allowed to stand up for the rights of people who "don't have a choice," as if that were the only relevant consideration. Even if being gay were a choice, would that fact justify treating same-sex couples unequally when it comes to civil marriage? According to developmental psychologist Lisa Diamond, "gay rights shouldn't depend on how a person came to be gay, and we should embrace the fact that sexuality can change."[46] Edward Stein states that from a legal perspective "advocates of LGB rights should avoid making arguments from etiology in court, in legislative contexts, and in public discourse. The arguments are neither valid nor persuasive and they have potential risks associated with them."[47] Even if someone chose to be gay or lesbian, it does not follow that legal discrimination would be acceptable.

I have several other problems with the "born this way" conceptualization of sexuality, with apologies to Lady Gaga. The first and most important is that if we presuppose that sexuality isn't a choice, and if that is the reason it shouldn't be allowed, what we are implying is that if it were a choice, then it wouldn't be acceptable. The legality of a particular sexual expression should not be determined by its achieved or ascribed status. In a liberal society like ours, which prides itself on tolerating difference, everyone is allowed to choose their identities. Regardless of whether polyamory is a choice, that shouldn't be a determining factor in whether polyamorists receive equal treatment.

As a social researcher, I don't concern myself with whether a genetic cause explains why some people choose to engage in relationships. Perhaps there is such a gene that can explain relationship preferences, but that information wouldn't, and shouldn't, change the way that Americans ought to look at equality and discrimination. As inevitably social beings, humans cannot be reduced to their genome or biology. Nor are they experimental subjects that can be poked and prodded so that the rest of humanity can feel more comfortable with their own existences. By asking questions like this one, we are using the wrong language, which is in turn sending the wrong message. At the end of the day, it doesn't matter whether sexual identity is a choice. To make this question the focal point is to paper over the tremendous variety of sexual experiences that many people have and to demean them and their lives inasmuch as what they do isn't "normal."

Most sociologists would agree that at least some part of sexual identity is socially constructed. Standards and beliefs about sexual behaviors are dictated through the interaction of culture, power, the self, the state, and many other social institutions. In that same vein of thought, the second issue that I have with the "born this way" conceptualization of sexual orientation is that essentializing sexual identities is an incongruous practice. This essentialization reifies ideas about these sexual identities, which can be problematic when a researcher misses the inherent variance of the individual and his or her experience. According to many experts on the topic, sexuality is fluid in that it fluctuates over the course of one's life. It is not innate, fixed, or static.[48] By essentializing sexuality, we are oversimplifying the issue. A key criticism of this type of essentialism in queer theory is that it "assume[s] the existence of homosexuality as an innate, or early acquired, *sexual orientation*. The development of a homosexual identity, in this view, simply entails a gradually developing awareness and acceptance of one's real, pre-existing self. Sexual identity development is conceptualized either as a process of natural unfolding, albeit dependent on environmental interactions, much like any other process of development, or as a voyage of discovery."[49] This way of thinking about sexual identity fails to capture the truly dynamic nature of human sexuality.

This criticism can be applied to the way that polyamory is often portrayed. If the argument is that certain types of sexual and emotional desires are only acceptable because the participants were "born that way," then we are distorting the process of the development of human sexuality beyond recognition. Some people may be born with a predisposition toward nonmonogamy, but that shouldn't undercut the experiences of other individuals who may reach that point in their sexual and emotional desires through a "voyage of discovery."[50] Both are valid human experiences, meriting the same amount of concern.

The even more serious issue is that many groups who are a part of the queer community, namely monogamous, homosexual men and women, do not wish to include polyamory under the LGBT+ umbrella. I suspect that many people believe this inclusion would threaten the LGBT+ political agenda. In his dissenting opinion of *Obergefell v. Hodges*, Chief Justice John Roberts states, "The majority . . . offers no reason at all why the two-person element of the core definition of marriage may be preserved while the man-woman element may not. Indeed, from the standpoint of history and tradition, a leap from opposite-sex marriage to same-sex marriage is much greater than one from a two-person union to plural unions, which have deep roots in some cultures around the world."[51] Thus, with this Supreme Court decision in place, it is more difficult to see the legal difference between the right to same-sex marriage and plural marriage.[52]

Gay rights activists have worked very hard to secure same-sex marriage rights. Activists have been fighting for decades and still have quite a battle ahead of them when it comes to other forms of discrimination based on sexual identity. Even with the ruling in *Obergefell*, enactment and enforcement of anti-discrimination laws, which protect sexual minorities, cannot be taken for granted. In fact, some clerks in some counties still are refusing to issue marriage licenses to same-sex couples.[53] There is still no federal law that protects people from discrimination on the basis of sexual orientation in public accommodations, employment, and so on. At most, in some places, a state law or ordinance may provide them with a legal remedy, assuming they can prove such discrimination in the first place. No one could reasonably fault the queer community for not wanting to embark on another odyssey through the American legal system, given how conservative opponents of same-sex marriage have tried to make the slope as slippery as possible.

Still, I speculate that a likely explanation for why polyamorists have encountered so much pushback from the queer community is that polyamorists are seen as extremists that could threaten their recent achievements. For instance, when Alex Greenwich of the Australian Marriage Equality group was asked whether he felt that plural marriage would devalue the worth of his gay, monogamous marriage, he said: "I will not support three people in a marriage at all."[54] If the queer community were to make common cause with the polyamorous community, they would likely be in for even more stigmatization and potentially another several decades fighting for polyamorous rights and maybe even putting some of their new and hard-fought gains in jeopardy. This is a risk that a lot of members of the queer community are just not willing to take, which is more than understandable. That said, in my experience researching polyamory communities in California, there seems to be noticeable overlap between the queer and polyamory communities insofar that it is probable that someone who identifies as gay, lesbian, or bisexual also knows someone who is polyamorous or practices polyamory to some degree themselves.

Although polyamorists are a sexual minority just like the rest of the queer community, they continue to fight to be accepted by queer activist groups. In other words, the question remains open whether a "P" should be added to LGBT. Regardless of the exact position that a person takes, polyamory remains at the outer edges of sexuality studies. Its status as a "fringe" alternative lifestyle may translate to a lack of funding for this kind of research and may partially explain the current lack of sociological research on the topic.[55] Moreover, without the resources and support of the LGBT+ community, polyamory battles to gain legitimacy, as a sexual experience, identity, and way of life.

Both inside and outside the LGBT+ community, polyamory has a long history and reputation as a primarily white, upper-class practice. According to a large and continually growing body of research, white professionals and college graduates dominate the community.[56] Someone working minimum wage or living below the poverty line may not have the time, resources, or energy to carry on multiple romantic relationships. Access to the kind of polyamory community that is most likely to facilitate multiple relationships demands the ability to travel to large, metropolitan cities where these kind of communities flourish, which may exclude those who don't live in these cities or have easy access to them. Also, people from more conservative areas or cultures may not be able to take the social risk of being associated with such a nontraditional lifestyle and its commitment to gender equality. This is especially salient when considering the few legal protections that polyamorous people have. For those researchers who are aware of polyamory and are curious about it, this reputation of demographic inequality in combination with its exclusion from the LGBT+ community may be enough to dissuade them from pursuing further study. While it is true that it is a privilege to be financially, socially, and physically able to love freely, I'm not sure that it should be in a society that is committed to treating everyone fairly and values personal choice. Perhaps the better question is "Why do we place limits on love?" or "Why are we preoccupied with numbers and structures of family?" Under the status quo, the likely answer is because, from an early age, we have internalized the normativity of monogamy. However, that doesn't mean we should accept this norm as static or conclude that nobody possibly could be happy in a polyamorous arrangement.

POLYAMORY AND PUBLIC SOCIOLOGY

The third and perhaps the most compelling reason for the lack of research on polyamory is the disdain the broader field of sociology tends to feel toward public sociology. There can be adverse consequences for pursuing such research. In 2004, Michael Burawoy, the president of the American Sociological Association, made a presidential address at the American Sociological Association's annual meeting, which was printed in the *British Journal of Sociology* and discusses the role of public sociology in modern sociological inquiry.[57] Long story much shorter, Burawoy is a proponent of pure sociology, that is, the view that sociology should be pure in the sense that sociologists should only pursue lines of inquiry from a scholarly, objective stance to further the understanding of a topic. They believe in creating knowledge for the sake of knowledge and eschewing areas of research that have political implications. That anyone would undertake sociological study with the hopes of influencing policy or enacting any change is unthinkable for sociologists that hold these traditional views.

Proponents of pure sociology will sometimes contend that in order to remain as objective as possible, social scientists must not enter into their inquiry with any assumptions or biases. Any normative commitments on their part are bound to compromise their objectivity as scholars and lead to less-then-reliable results. True, this may be ideal in order to produce results that are as close to those of a hard science as possible. Usually, no one cares whether a chemist is a Democrat or Republican. At the same time, many proponents of public sociology dispute this belief and state that research, particularly social science research, is never value-free. It is impossible to strip a human of all their human-ness, which always includes normative beliefs that a researcher holds about how the world ought to be. Every single researcher was born and raised in a particular context and socialized to have certain values and beliefs. That is exactly what sociology aims to study.

Of course, no one would deny that sociologists should strive to do their research as conscientiously as possible. There are many different checks in place on each review committee from the institutional review board to article reviewers, which endeavor to ensure the validity of scientific results. However, I don't agree that pursuing lines of research with real, foreseeable policy implications are necessarily to be avoided. Perhaps scholars should not only be open-minded to pursuing research with such implications, but actively pursuing it and being forthright about their political preferences in the name of full disclosure. In short, there is a way to do this kind of research while still remaining as objective as possible. Sociologists can do this by disclosing any possible biases and structuring their methodologies to account for them. Funding for social science research is difficult to come by and yet is a necessary evil. It is difficult for me to imagine a situation in which a researcher wouldn't be required by a grant committee to formulate a methodology that accounts for possible biases unless they were dishonest about them. What's more, it is possible, and in fact wise, to do research on a topic that, as a researcher, one feels especially passionate about. To pretend that everyone who does sociological research is completely disinterested when she pursues her research agenda is to be disingenuous. All of us have opinions about what is and what ought to be the case in a perfect world. It must be possible to do objective research while holding even a firm opinion. Otherwise no ethical research would ever be done. I would argue that most sociologists that research race and ethnicity hold the view that racism is not only an unpleasant reality but also morally wrong and needs to be eradicated. This doesn't mean they cannot conduct ethical research about race and ethnicity.

When conducting research about polyamory, a researcher will inevitably encounter many opinions from outsiders. As previously mentioned, polyamory has a tenuous place in the legal and social systems of the United States. Any research pertaining to polyamory, assuming it reaches the public at all, is likely to come with a healthy dose of skepticism. Not only do researchers have to combat public opinion, but because of the preference for pure sociology among professionals within the field, researchers must also contend with the opinions of their own colleagues, not all of which are kind. Polyamory research often lends itself best to public sociology because it has implications for public and private spheres: for family, for businesses (such as healthcare), for schools, and for politics, among many others. By investigating questions around polyamory that may inevitably land on the doorstep of social justice, sociologists would be inviting public sociology over for dinner. The problem is that I doubt that many are quite ready for that invitation.

Thus, those researchers who are bold enough to pursue this topic in any major detail tend to feel especially passionate about it for one reason or another. At least in my case, it is difficult to put your blood, sweat, and tears into research that you anticipate that no one except the ten other experts in your field will care about or even be aware of. Add to that the disparagement you may receive from the public for broaching a topic that is taboo or from your colleagues for the way you approach your research. In such a situation, it could be difficult to find any real motivation to do this work unless you believe that it has the potential to make some kind of real impact in the lives of the people you're studying.

The future of sociological study may depend on the willingness of scholars to persist despite the scorn that they may face by aligning themselves with public sociology. Other fields, such as psychology and anthropology, are keeping up with the times. They are the ones attempting research that gets at the provocative and real-life issues facing contemporary American families. They do research that both the public and the academic sectors are interested in, and if their work is being published in reputable journals, they're doing it while maintaining the ethical and methodologically sound research practices that their fields demand of them. I have pleaded that at least some sociologists must get on a train that has left the station. If they continue to exclude polyamorist families, sociologists are putting themselves in jeopardy of becoming irrelevant inasmuch as their contributions have no impact beyond the increasing smaller number of American families who still retain the traditional family form. Blockbuster educational budget cuts and a political climate that, while devaluing scholarship in the social sciences and humanities, puts particular emphasis on the STEM fields have created a world in which everything must serve a purpose. If sociologists cannot figure out a way to do research with a public purpose, something that public sociology promotes, then "sociologist" may not remain a job title for many more decades.

CONCLUSION

I have proposed three possible explanations for the noticeable lack of sociological research pertaining to polyamory: (1) the term "polyamory" is brand new and researchers may not be aware of its existence (or how it differs from polygamy) (2) polyamory has a fragile place within the LGBT+ community, and (3) the field of sociology largely looks down on public sociology. As I mentioned, I see this chapter as a call to action. There are scholars in several social scientific fields that are eager to do the kind of research that reflects the complexity of the lives of even the most "different" Americans. Polyamorists deserve the same kind of attention that same-sex couples have received. Sociologists should not leave themselves out of these exciting, new developments. After all, they are uniquely equipped to investigate these kinds of questions to develop a body of knowledge that aims to understand phenomena such as social order/disorder and social change with respect to the dynamics of family life. No one doubts that these forms have changed and will continue to change over time. Sociologists cannot disregard topics of inquiry just because they may threaten conventional ideas, even within their own field. These topics should be of the upmost importance in the near future because to understand them is to have nothing less than a more complete understanding of the social world. Sociologists will pay a high price when too many of them refuse to include polyamorists in their research agendas.

NOTES

1. According to Elisabeth Sheff, polyamory is defined as "consensual openly conducted, multi-partner relationships in which both men and women have negotiated access to additional partners outside of the traditional committed couple." Elisabeth Sheff, *The Polyamorists Next Door: Inside Multiple-Partner Relationships and Families* (Lanham: Rowman & Littlefield Publishers, 2014), 1–3.

2. Jim Fleckenstein, Curtis Bergstrand, and Derrell Cox. "What Do Polys Want? Results of the 2012 Loving More Polyamory Survey," http://www.lovemore.com/polyamory-articles/2012-lovingmore-polyamory-survey/.

3. Elaine Cook, "Commitment in Polyamorous Relationships," Master's Thesis at Regis University, Kinsey Institute, http://www.kinseyinstitute.org/library/e-text/Cook_Elaine.pdf.

4. See Civil Rights Act of 1964; Age Discrimination Act of 1975; Americans with Disabilities Act of 1990; *Romer v. Evans*, 517 U.S. 620 (1996); *Lawrence v. Texas*, 539 U.S. 558 (2003); *U.S. v. Windsor*, 570 U.S. __ (2013).

5. Sheff, *The Polyamorists Next Door*, 273.

6. Ibid.

7. *Obergefell v. Hodges*, 135 S. Ct. 2071 (2015).

8. Judith Stacey, *Unhitched: Love, Marriage, and Family Values from West Hollywood to Western China* (New York: New York University Press, 2011), 4.

9. According to Gretchen Livingston, less than half (46%) of U.S. kids younger than 18 years of age are living in a home with two married heterosexual parents in their first marriage. This is a marked change from 1960, when 73% of children fit this description, and 1980, when 61% did. Livingston, Gretchen. "Less than Half of U.S. Kids Today Live in a 'Traditional' Family." Pew Research Center. http://www.pewresearch.org/fact-tank/2014/12/22/less-than-half-of-u-s-kids-today-live-in-a-traditional-family/.

10. See Stacey, *Unhitched*; Judith Stacey, *Brave New Families: Stories of Domestic Upheaval in Late Twentieth Century America* (New York: Basic Books, 1990); Judith Stacey. *In the Name of the Family: Rethinking Family Values in the Postmodern Age* (Boston: Beacon Press, 1996).

11. Sheff, *The Polyamorists Next Door*, xi.

12. Nancy D. Polikoff, *Beyond Straight and Gay Marriage: Valuing All Families under the Law* (Boston, MA: Beacon Press, 2008), 8.

13. Philip Kilbride, *Plural Marriage for Our Times: A Reinvented Option?* (Westport: Bergin & Garvey, 1994).

14. For a full discussion of the term "polyamory," see Sheff, *The Polyamorists Next Door*, 1–22.

15. Lillian B. Rubin, *Erotic Wars: What Happened to the Sexual Revolution?* (New York: Farrar, Straus, & Giroux, 1990).

16. See Gilbert D. Bartell, *Group Sex: A Scientist's Eyewitness Report on the American Way of Swinging* (New York: Van Rees Press, 1971); Albert Ellis, "Group Marriage: A Possible Alternative?," in *The Family in Search of a Future: Alternative Models for Moderns*, ed. Herbert A. Otto (New York: Appleton-Century-Crofts, 1970).

17. Richard Parker, "Sexuality, Culture and Society: Shifting Paradigms in Sexuality Research," *Culture, Health & Sexuality* 11 (2009): 255.

18. Ibid., 258.

19. Intentional communities are groups of people who have chosen to live together so that they may create a lifestyle that supports their shared values. In popular culture, they are often referred to as cooperative housing or communes.

20. Jefferson Selth, *Alternative Lifestyles: A Guide to Research Collections on Intentional Communities, Nudism, and Sexual Freedom* (Westport: Greenwood Press, 1985), 3.

21. Patrick Conover, "An Analysis of Communes and Intentional Communities with Particular Attention to Sexual and Genderal Relations," *The Family Coordinator* 24 (1975): 462.

22. Tracey Steele, "'Doing It': The Social Construction of S-E-X," in *Sex, Self, and Society: The Social Context of Sexuality*, ed. Tracey Steele (Boston: Cengage Learning, 2005): 13–22.

23. Stacey, *Unhitched*, 186.

24. Ibid., 4.

25. For a lengthier discussion of this issue, see Nancy D. Polikoff, *Beyond Straight and Gay Marriage: Valuing All Families Under the Law* (Boston: Beacon Press, 2008).

26. Barrie Thorne, "Feminism and the Family: Two Decades of Thought," in *Rethinking the Family: Some Feminist Questions*, ed. Marilyn Yalom and Barrie Thorne (Boston: Northeastern University Press, 1992), 4.

27. Jane Collier, Michelle Rosaldo, and Sylvia Yanagisako, "Is There a Family? New Anthropological Views," in *Rethinking the Family: Some Feminist Questions*, ed. Marilyn Yalom and Barrie Thorne (Boston: Northeastern University Press, 1992).

28. Judith Butler, *Gender Trouble: Feminism and the Subversion of Identity* (New York: Routledge, 1990).

29. Daniel Cardoso, Carla Correia, and Danielle Capella, "Polyamory as a Possibility of Feminine Empowerment" (paper presented at the Ninth Congress of the European Sociological Association, Lisbon, Portugal, 2009).

30. Sheff, *The Polyamorists Next Door.*

31. Ani Ritchie and Meg John Barker, "'There Aren't Words for What We Do or How We Feel So We Have To Make Them Up': Constructing Polyamorous Languages in a Culture of Compulsory Monogamy," *Sexualities* 9 (2006): 584–601.

32. Roger H. Rubin, "Alternative Lifestyles Revisited, or Whatever Happened to Swingers, Group Marriages, and Communes?" *Journal of Family Issues* 22 (2001): 723.

33. Polyamory is a portmanteau term that combines the Greek "poly," meaning several or many, and the Latin "amor," meaning love.

34. Elisabeth Sheff, "Evolution of the Term Polyamory," http://elisabethsheff.com/2012/10/08/evolution-of-the-term-polyamory/.

35. Robyn Trask, "Real Polyamorous Families," http://www.lovemore.com/media-react/real-polyamorous-families/.

36. Rebecca Riffkin, "New Record Highs in Moral Acceptability," Gallup, May 30, 2014, http://www.gallup.com/poll/170789/new-record-highs-moral-acceptability.aspx.

37. Ibid.

38. See Elissa Wall and Lisa Pulitzer, *Stolen Innocence: My Story of Growing up in a Polygamous Sect, Becoming a Teenage Bride, and Breaking Free of Warren Jeffs* (New York: Harper Collins Publishers, 2009).

39. Sheff, *The Polyamorists Next Door*, 1.

40. Polyamory received a publicity boost when self-help author, Steve Pavlina, announced he was going to try polyamorous relationships in 2009.

41. For example, Showtime aired a reality television series from 2012–2013 called *Polyamory: Married & Dating*.

42. Michael Carey, "Is Polyamory A Choice?" *Slate*, October 16, 2013, http://www.slate.com/blogs/outward/2013/10/16/is_polyamory_a_choice.html.

43. Ann Tweedy, "Polyamory as a Sexual Orientation," *University of Cincinnati Law Review* 79 (2011): 1514.

44. Christian Klesse, "Polyamory: Intimate Practice, Identity or Sexual Orientation?" *Sexualities* 17 (2014): 95.

45. Ibid., 95.

46. Lisa Diamond, "Sexuality Is Fluid – It's Time to Get past 'Born This Way'," *New Scientist*, July 22, 2015, https://www.newscientist.com/article/mg22730310-100-sexuality-is-fluid-its-time-to-get-past-born-this-way/.

47. Edward Stein, "Born That Way? Not a Choice? Problems with Biological and Psychological Arguments for Gay Rights," *Social Science Research Network Electronic Journal* (2008): 73.

48. Celia Kitzinger and Sue Wilkinson, "Transitions from Heterosexuality to Lesbianism: The Discursive Production of Lesbian Identities," *Developmental Psychology* 31 (1995): 95–104.

49. Ibid., 96.

50. Ibid.

51. *Obergefell v. Hodges*, 135 S. Ct. 2071 (2015) (Roberts, J., dissenting).

52. Ronald Den Otter, "No Constitutional Difference Between Plural and Same-Sex Unions," *New York Times*, December 17, 2013, http://www.nytimes.com/roomforde-

bate/2013/12/17/should-plural-marriage-be-legal/no-constitutional-difference-between-plural-and-same-sex-unions.

53. Elliot McLaughlin and Catherine Shoichet, "Kim Davis Stands Firm on Same-sex Marriage; the Kentucky Clerk Stays in Jail," *CNN*, September 3, 2015, http://www.cnn.com/2015/09/03/politics/kentucky-clerk-same-sex-marriage-kim-davis/.

54. David Frum, "Gays Against Polyamory," *The Daily Beast*, May 30, 2012, http://www.thedailybeast.com/articles/2012/05/30/gays-against-polygamy.html.

55. Rubin, "Alternative Lifestyles Revisited," 711–726.

56. Sheff, *The Polyamorists Next Door*, 31–36.

57. Michael Burawoy, "2004 American Sociological Association Presidential Address: For Public Sociology," *The British Journal of Sociology* 56 (2005): 259–294.

REFERENCES

Burawoy, Michael. "2004 American Sociological Association Presidential Address: For Public Sociology." *The British Journal of Sociology* 56 (2005): 259–294.

Butler, Judith. *Gender Trouble: Feminism and the Subversion of Identity*. New York: Routledge, 1990.

Cardoso, Daniel, Carla Correia, and Danielle Capella. "Polyamory as a Possibility of Feminine Empowerment." Paper presented at the Ninth Congress of the European Sociological Association. Lisbon, Portugal: 2009.

Carey, Michael. "Is Polyamory A Choice?" *Slate*, October 16, 2013. http://www.slate.com/blogs/outward/2013/10/16/is_polyamory_a_choice.html.

Collier, Jane, Michelle Rosaldo, and Sylvia Yanagisako. "Is There a Family? New Anthropological Views." In *Rethinking the Family: Some Feminist Questions*, edited by Marilyn Yalom and Barrie Thorne. Boston: Northeastern University Press, 1992.

Conover, Patrick. "An Analysis of Communes and Intentional Communities with Particular Attention to Sexual and Genderal Relations." *The Family Coordinator* 24 (1975): 453–64.

Cook, Elaine. "Commitment in Polyamorous Relationships." Master's Thesis at Regis University, Kinsey Institute. http://www.kinseyinstitute.org/library/e-text/Cook_Elaine.pdf.

Den Otter, Ronald. "No Constitutional Difference Between Plural and Same-Sex Unions." *New York Times*, December 17, 2013. http://www.nytimes.com/roomfordebate/2013/12/17/should-plural-marriage-be-legal/no-constitutional-difference-between-plural-and-same-sex-unions.

Diamond, Lisa. "Sexuality Is Fluid—It's Time to Get Past 'Born This Way'." *New Scientist*, July 22, 2015. https://www.newscientist.com/article/mg22730310-100-sexuality-is-fluid-its-time-to-get-past-born-this-way/.

Fleckenstein, Jim, Curtis Bergstrand, and Derrell Cox. "What Do Polys Want? Results of the 2012 Loving More Polyamory Survey." http://www.lovemore.com/polyamory-articles/2012-lovingmore-polyamory-survey/.

Frum, David. "Gays Against Polyamory." *The Daily Beast*, May 30, 2012. http://www.thedailybeast.com/articles/2012/05/30/gays-against-polygamy.html.

Kilbride, Philip. *Plural Marriage for Our Times: A Reinvented Option?* Westport: Bergin & Garvey, 1994.

Kitzinger, Celia, and Sue Wilkinson. "Transitions from Heterosexuality to Lesbianism: The Discursive Production of Lesbian Identities." *Developmental Psychology* 31 (1995): 95–104.

Klesse, Christian. "Polyamory: Intimate Practice, Identity or Sexual Orientation?" *Sexualities* 17 (2014): 81–99.

Livingston, Gretchen. "Less than Half of U.S. Kids Today Live in a 'Traditional' Family." Pew Research Center. http://www.pewresearch.org/fact-tank/2014/12/22/less-than-half-of-u-s-kids-today-live-in-a-traditional-family/.

McLaughlin, Elliot and Catherine Shoichet. "Kim Davis Stands Firm on Same-Sex Marriage: The Kentucky Clerk Stays in Jail." *CNN*, September 3, 2015. http://www.cnn.com/2015/09/03/politics/kentucky-clerk-same-sex-marriage-kim-davis/.

Parker, Richard. "Sexuality, Culture and Society: Shifting Paradigms in Sexuality Research." *Culture, Health & Sexuality* 11 (2009): 251–66.

Polikoff, Nancy D. *Beyond Straight and Gay Marriage: Valuing All Families Under the Law.* Boston, MA: Beacon Press, 2008.

Riffkin, Rebecca. "New Record Highs in Moral Acceptability." Gallup. May 30, 2014. http://www.gallup.com/poll/170789/new-record-highs-moral-acceptability.aspx.

Ritchie, Ani, and Meg John Barker. "'There Aren't Words for What We Do or How We Feel So We Have To Make Them Up': Constructing Polyamorous Languages in a Culture of Compulsory Monogamy." *Sexualities* 9 (2006): 584–601.

Rubin, Lillian B. *Erotic Wars: What Happened to the Sexual Revolution?* New York: Farrar, Straus, & Giroux, 1990.

Rubin, Roger H. "Alternative Lifestyles Revisited, or Whatever Happened to Swingers, Group Marriages, and Communes?" *Journal of Family Issues* 22 (2001): 711–26.

Selth, Jefferson. *Alternative Lifestyles: A Guide to Research Collections on Intentional Communities, Nudism, and Sexual Freedom.* Westport: Greenwood Press, 1985.

Sheff, Elisabeth. *The Polyamorists Next Door: Inside Multi-Partner Relationships and Families.* Lanham: Rowman and Littlefield, 2014.

Stacey, Judith. *Unhitched: Love, Marriage, and Family Values from West Hollywood to Western China.* New York: New York University Press, 2011.

Steele, Tracey. "'Doing It': The Social Construction of S-E-X." In *Sex, Self, and Society: The Social Context of Sexuality*, edited by Tracey Steele. Cengage Learning, 2005.

Stein, Edward. "Born That Way? Not a Choice?: Problems with Biological and Psychological Arguments for Gay Rights." *Cardozo Legal Studies Research Paper*, no. 223 (2008): 1–76.

Thorne, Barrie. "Feminism and the Family: Two Decades of Thought." In *Rethinking the Family: Some Feminist Questions*, edited by Marilyn Yalom and Barrie Thorne. Boston: Northeastern University Press, 1992.

Trask, Robyn. "Real Polyamorous Families." http://www.lovemore.com/mediareact/real-polyamorous-families/.

Tweedy, Ann. "Polyamory as a Sexual Orientation." *University of Cincinnati Law Review* 79 (2011): 1461–1515.

NINE

Scrutinizing Polygamy: Utah's *Brown v. Buhman* and British Columbia's *Reference Re: Section 293*

Maura Strassberg

The constitutionality of criminalizing[1] polygamy was once an easy decision for the courts. In 1879, the United States Supreme Court confined its substantive discussion of polygamy to two paragraphs in *Reynolds v. United States*,[2] and the Court has never seriously reconsidered the conclusions it reached.[3] However, modern readers of *Reynolds* find the Court's conclusory and vague claims about the negative effects of polygamy on social order and political organization[4] unconvincing and tainted by the Court's disparaging association of polygamy with "Asiatic and . . . African people."[5] As same-sex relationships have become decriminalized [6] and legally recognized,[7] many have also found it difficult to understand why and how polygamy could continue to be criminalized. With the ground appearing to shift under what had previously been unquestioned rejection of polygamy, two recent major court decisions have tackled the issue head-on and have come out on opposite sides of the question.

In Canada, the British Columbia Supreme Court, addressing a constitutional reference to the court by the government of British Columbia, upheld the continued criminalization of polygamy under the Canadian Charter of Rights and Freedoms (Charter).[8] The trial in *Reference re: Section 293 of the Criminal Code of Canada* (*Reference*), under Canadian law,[9] was able to be brought in the absence of a "case or controversy."[10] It involved forty-two days of hearings,[11] ninety affidavits and expert reports,[12] and "Brandeis Brief materials . . . . compris[ing] several hundred legal and social science articles, books and DVDs."[13] Under Canadian law, limits on a right protected by the Charter must be justified by a purpose that is "pressing and substantial."[14] As such, a large part of the decision in *Reference* was concerned with identifying the harms of polygamy and determining whether they were pressing and substantial.[15] In 2011, the court issued a comprehensive 228-page opinion setting out the psychological, sociological, and political impacts of polygamy, finding that this was an objective that was pressing and substantial[16] and concluding that the law was consistent with the Charter, despite the way in which it infringed upon liberty and freedom of religion.[17]

In the United States, in a case brought by the reality TV stars of *Sister Wives*, Kody Brown and his four wives (Meri, Janelle, Christine, and Robyn) and litigated by Professor Jonathan Turley of George Washington University Law School, the United States District Court for the District of Utah found Utah's criminalization of polygamy unconstitutional.[18] *Brown v. Buhman* was decided on summary judgment based on twenty-two undisputed facts[19] with the State failing to submit any admissible evidence on the social harms of polygamy and largely failing to substantively oppose the constitutional claims.[20] In its long and complex 2013 opinion in *Brown*, the Utah federal court held that parts of Utah's criminal bigamy statute[21] failed to pass either strict, heightened, or rational basis scrutiny.[22] The court upheld the statute insofar as it prohibited multiple legal marriages but struck down the statute's application to a practice of polygamy that involved multiple religious marriages for which a license and legal recognition was not sought.[23] Subsequently, the Court of Appeals for the Tenth Circuit vacated the district court decision on the grounds that the case was moot, due to the relocation of the Browns to Nevada combined with the Utah county attorney's non-prosecution of the Browns and adoption of a policy limiting bigamy prosecutions to cases involving fraud, minors, or abuse.[24] The practical impact of this policy is to informally decriminalize polygamy because criminalization is believed to be either unconstitutional or unnecessary. Furthermore, since the Tenth Circuit's opinion did not address the merits of the district court's holding that at least some criminalization of polygamy is unconstitutional, the reasoning employed may be persuasive, even if not precedent, on the question of the constitutionality of criminalizing polygamy. Thus, it remains worthwhile to examine the reasoning of the district court in *Brown* and compare it with the reasoning in *Reference*.

Although the focus of this Article is not on the comparative advantages or disadvantages of a constitutional reference versus a case or controversy approach, it is notable that the presence of an adversarial "case" in *Brown* failed to produce the expected full exploration of the issues; it was not equally litigated on both sides. In contrast, the law in *Reference* was both strongly defended and attacked: the Attorneys General of British Columbia and Canada took the position that the polygamy law was constitutional, an 'Amicus' appointed by the court opposed the law,[25] and eleven groups were granted Interested Person status,[26] four of whom opposed the law and seven of whom supported it.[27] The impact of the incomplete litigation in *Brown* was significant; the court failed to appreciate the extent of the harm sought to be avoided by criminalizing polygamy. At the same time, this failure can also be traced to the vague justifications given for criminalizing polygamy in cases that preceded *Brown*, starting with *Reynolds* and ending more recently with one Tenth Circuit and two Utah Supreme Court cases upholding Utah's polygamy law against constitutional attack: *Potter v. Murray City*[28] in 1985, *State v. Green*[29] in 2004, and *State v. Holm*[30] in 2006.

The failure to appreciate the harm of polygamy had an impact on all phases and levels of the constitutional scrutiny in *Brown*. It allowed the court to claim a crucial distinction between polygamy understood as multiple licensed marriages and polygamy understood as multiple unlicensed marital relationships. As a result, the *Brown* court held that the decision in *Reynolds* was controlling only as to licensed polygamy because the facts of *Reynolds* did not involve multiple nonunlicensed marital relationships.[31] *Brown* therefore upheld the Utah polygamy law insofar as it prohibits multiple legal marriages without engaging in any scrutiny, even as the court suggested that this prohibition too was unjustified.[32] This then left the court free to subject the law's prohibition against entering into multiple unrecognized marital relationships by itself to a rigorous, contemporary constitutional analysis. However, it was exactly this isolation of unlicensed polygamy from licensed polygamy that allowed the court in *Brown* to justify strict scrutiny of the law as an impermissible "religious gerrymander" under the free exercise analysis set out in *Church of the Kukumi Bablu Aye, Inc. v. City of Hialeah.*[33] Later in the opinion, the court's isolation of unlicensed polygamy from licensed polygamy made it possible to dismiss the most significant state interest in the prohibition of polygamy, protecting monogamous marriage, as not even a rational basis,[34] let alone a compelling one,[35] for criminalizing multiple unlicensedmarital relationships.

However, with the deeper understanding of the negative social and political consequences of polygamy *Reference* provides, it becomes clear that tolerating polygamous relationships is no less problematic than recognizing them as legal marriages. Indeed, as has been the case with the move from decriminalizing same-sex relationships to recognizing same-sex marriage, tolerance may well be a step toward legal recognition. If *Reynolds* can be rehabilitated by this modern understanding of the social and political impacts of polygamy versus monogamy, then all three of the moves that allowed the *Brown* court to conclude that parts of the Utah polygamy law were unconstitutional will be foreclosed. Not only should the law not be subjected to strict scrutiny, but it should survive even if it is so scrutinized.

This chapter will summarize the findings of the court in *Reference* that reveal more clearly the harms of polygamy, as well as its inverse relationship to monogamy. This will create a foundation for an analysis and critique of the reasoning in *Brown*, both as to its findings that strict scrutiny was justified and its holding that there was no state interest sufficient to justify the law's application to legally unrecognized polygamous marriages.

WHAT ARE THE HARMS OF POLYGAMY?

The *B r own* court found that the harms of polygamy identified in *Reynolds, Potter, Green,* and *Holm* could not survive rational basis, heightened, or strict scrutiny. In large part this was because the only credible harm of polygamy that was identified was a possible association of abuse of women and children with polygamy; however, the evidence of a connection between abuse and polygamy seemed to be anecdotal at best. Whether this possible connection should have been found insufficient to justify the law under rational basis scrutiny is arguable, but it is certainly less so for heightened or strict scrutiny. To survive the strict and heightened scrutiny requirement that the polygamy law be narrowly tailored to prevent the harms of polygamy, the State needed to show that there were specific harms that were more than tangentially connected to polygamy. However, the State of Utah largely rested its arguments on prior opinions that had failed to go beyond vague claims about a presumed relationship between forms of marriage and larger social relations. The court in *Reference* remediates these failures by identifying wide ranging, inherent harms of polygamy that make blanket criminalization the only effective way to avoid these harms.

The Harms Identified in the British Columbia Reference

The *Reference* court identified the pressing and substantial objectives of the Canadian statute criminalizing polygamy as "the prevention of harm to women, to children and to society"[36] and "the preservation of monogamous marriage."[37] Ultimately, the court found that there was an inverse relationship between polygamy and monogamy:[38] monogamy benefits women, children, and society in precisely all the ways polygamy harms them.[39] Furthermore, in light of the court's finding that decriminalization of polygamy would result in a non-trivial increase in the practice of polygamy in Canada,[40] decriminalization would directly threaten the practice of monogamy itself.[41]

This in turn would erode the benefits of monogamy to individuals and society, even as it expanded the harms of polygamy to individuals and society. The findings of the court concerning the harms of polygamy were based on empirically grounded expert testimony as well as both positive and negative personal accounts from individuals who had lived in polygamous households.[42] The three main expert witnesses providing evidence of the harms of polygamy, benefits of monogamy, or both, were Dr. Joseph Henrich, an evolutionary psychologist[43] who conducted "an extensive review of the academic literature on polygyny in the sciences and social sciences"[44] for the reference; Dr. Shoshana Grossbard, an economist[45] with a special expertise in the economic effects of polygyny, who presented economic analyses of polygyny using data collected by others;[46] and Dr. Rose McDermott,[47] a political scientist who engaged in both a review of the academic literature on polygyny and produced an original statistical analysis undertaken specifically for the reference.[48] Dr. McDermott's work is also the subject of a separate article in this Issue. Dr. McDermott's statistical analysis was based on a unique dataset, WomanStats Project Database, with ten years of data about women and children from 171 countries along with separate data on their nation states.[49]

Dr. McDermott's statistical analysis demonstrated that "the harms of polygyny do not depend upon a particular regional, religious or cultural context. They can be generalized, and they can be expected to occur wherever polygyny exists."[50] The court noted that the "convergence of the evidence on the question of harm, from high level predictions based on human evolutionary psychology, to the recurring harms identified in intra-cultural and cross-cultural studies, to the 'on the ground' evidence of polygyny in contemporary North America . . . . [is] striking."[51] The court concluded that the harms of polygyny are "endemic [and] . . . inherent."[52] They "are not simply the product of individual misconduct; they arise inevitably out of the practice."[53] As a result, not only did the evidence show "a reasoned apprehension of harm"[54] sufficient to meet the Canadian legal standard for criminalizing an activity,[55] the court found that it also met a higher standard of "demonstrat[ing] 'concrete evidence' of harm."[56]

The Cruel Arithmetic of Polygamy

Any understanding of the harms arising from polygamy must begin with an appreciation of the "'cruel arithmetic' of polygamy":[57] "when some men are able to have multiple wives simultaneously, other men will be unable to find wives."[58] In particular, it is likely to be low-status men who will be most likely to be unable to marry,[59] as they will be the least attractive marriage partners to potential wives and their families.[60]

A simple model of a polygynous society developed by Dr. Henrich shows how even a low level of polygamy leads to a considerable pool of unmarried men:

> Imagine a society of 40 adults, 20 males and 20 females . . . Suppose those 20 males vary from the unemployed high-school drop outs to CEOs, or billionaires . . . Let's assume that the twelve men with the highest status marry 12 of the 20 women in monogamous marriages. Then, the top five men (25% of the population) all take a second wife, and the top two (10%) take a third wife. Finally, the top guy takes a fourth wife. This means that of all marriages, 58% are monogamous. Only men in the to [sic] 10% of status or wealth married more than two women. The most wives anyone has is four. The degree of polygynous marriage is not extreme in cross-cultural perspective . . . but it creates a pool of unmarried men equal to 40% of the male population.[61]

Dr. McDermott found that "polygyny causes the proportion of young unmarried men [to unmarried women] to be high, up to a ratio of 150 men to 100 women."[62]

Harm to Polygynous Wives and Women in General

The harm to women from polygamy begins with the fact that polygamy causes greater competition between men for wives, which "creates pressure to recruit increasingly younger brides into the marriage market."[63] In polygynous societies, women are more likely to "marry before age 18, or be 'promised' in marriage prior to age 18."[64] At the same time, these polygynous wives will have more children than monogamous wives.[65] The harmful effects of "early sexual activity, pregnancies and childbirth [and] . . . . [s]hortened inter-birth intervals"[66] include health impacts such as a greater likelihood of dying in childbirth and living a shorter life.[67] Early marriage also means that the socioeconomic development of polygynous wives is limited[68] as a result of less education,[69] lower literacy levels, and less participation in the labor force.[70]

The competition for wives also "causes men (as fathers, husbands, and brothers) to seek to exercise more control over the choices of women, increasing gender inequality and undermining female autonomy and rights. This is exacerbated by larger age disparities between husbands and wives."[71] Women become "viewed as commodities."[72] This control and commodification is reflected in numerous effects on women, widely ranging from a lack of reproductive autonomy,[73] leading to higher fertility,[74] lower levels of divorce,[75] and greater levels of domestic violence,[76] sex trafficking, genital mutilation,[77] and "discrimination under the law."[78] In addition, women in polygynous relationships also have to deal with "co-wife conflict,"[79] high rates of marital dissatisfaction and low levels of self-esteem,[80] inadequate financial support "as resources may be inequitably divided or simply insufficient,"[81] and "higher rates of depressive disorders and other mental health issues."[82]

Harm to Children of Polygynous Families

Children, too, were found by the court to have worse outcomes in polygamous families because polygamy causes men to "reduce investment in wives and offspring as they spread their resources more thinly across larger families and increasingly channel those resources into obtaining morewives."[83] The court found that harm to children included the following:

> higher infant mortality . . . more emotional, behavioural and physical problems, as well as lower educational achievement . . . . [arising out of] higher levels of conflict, emotional stress and tension in polygynous families . . . . inability of fathers to give sufficient affection and disciplinary attention to all of their children [and] . . . . enhanced risk of psychological and physical abuse and neglect.[84] Lack of educational opportunities due to limited financial resources are not limited to girls but also affect boys in polygynous families.[85]

For young men and boys, "[t]he sex ratio imbalance inherent in polygyny means that young men are forced out of polygamous communities to sustain the ability of senior men to accumulate more wives. These young men and boys often receive limited education . . . few life skills and little social support."[86] As a result, these young men and boys achieve lower levels of employment.[87]

General Social Harms

Many of the individual impacts of polygyny on women, men, and children can also be seen to have larger social consequences. We have seen that the cruel arithmetic of polygamy creates a pool of unmarried men, who are likely low status. In highly polygynous closed communities, this results in "[u]p to half of the boys . . . [being] ejected from their communities."[88] Considering that these boys are minimally educated but must support themselves, they are likely to become either an economic burden or drag on the society they end up in. To the extent that this pool of men cannot be dumped on a non-polygynous society but would remain within their original polygynous society, they are "incentivized to take substantial risks so they can eventually participate in the mating and marriage market."[89] Statistically, this can be shown to take the form of increased levels of violence, crime, and other antisocial behaviors.[90]

On a larger social level, Dr. Henrich more speculatively predicted that the pool of unmarried men could lead to greater military aggression towards other communities or nations.[91] This aggression could arise from a perceived need to prevent competition for existing unmarried women from men outside the community or as providing a source of new potential wives or resources that would allow the acquisition of wives. Alternatively, war may simply be a way for rulers to direct the antisocial tendencies of these men outside the community, while at the same time reducing their numbers through casualties.[92] These speculations were supported to some extent by Dr. McDermott's findings that "[s]tates with higher levels of polygyny spend more money per capita on defence, particularly on arms expenditures."[93] This leads to less spending on "domestic infrastructure and projects geared toward health and education."[94]

Polygynous societies will have greater levels of familial poverty.[95] This is due to a number of factors. Women's ability to support their children is reduced due to high fertility[96] and minimal education.[97] Furthermore, the gender inequality that is associated with polygyny is not only a harm to individuals but harmful to society itself.[98] At the same time, men's investment in their wives and children is reduced as described above.[99] Societies where basic needs are not met do not have the human resources necessary to grow and may also be less stable politically, requiring more authoritarian government.[100] Dr. McDermott's analysis showed that "[s]tates with higher levels of polygyny display fewer political rights and civil liberties for both men and women than those with less polygyny."[101] Theoretical economic models using data from highly polygynous states showed that the imposition of monogamy would increase per capita GDP because men "save and invest in production and consumption" instead of saving for and investing in additional wives.[102]

Finally, the court in *Reference* found polygamy harmful to society because it directly threatens the practice of monogamy, even in a country such as Canada.[103] This could occur in four ways. First, the court found that decriminalizing polygamy would make immigration to Canada by polygamists from other counties more attractive.[104] Second, decriminalization would allow those already in Canada who are familiar with and comfortable with the practice to take it up.[105] Third, decriminalization would remove a brake on the natural tilt of human beings "towards a polygynous mating system."[106] Fourth, the increased fertility of polygamous wives will cause the population of those raised in polygamy to increase faster than the population of those raised in monogamy.[107] As the practice of polygamy increases, the benefits of monogamy decrease. The court found the specific benefits of monogamy to be as follows:

> [E]xclusive and enduring monogamous marriage is the best way to ensure paternal certainty and joint parental investment in children. It best ensures that men and women are treated with equal dignity and respect, and that husbands and wives (or same sex couples), and parents and children, provide each other with mutual support, protection and edification through their lifetimes.[108]

Summary

No conclusion about strict, heightened, or rational basis scrutiny of the Utah bigamy law can be made on the basis of the constitutional analysis in *Reference,* as it was operating both with a different criminal law and under a distinctly Canadian standard of constitutional review. However, the more detailed and empirically supported harms of polygamy articulated there should be more than sufficient to pass ordinary rational basis scrutiny. The overbreadth arguments made in *Reference* were largely identical to those made in *Brown*[109] but were strongly countered by the exceedingly broad harmful impacts of polygamy. Thus, there is reason to think that the Utah bigamy law could pass heightened or strict scrutiny as well. However, the viability of the law would be greatly increased if strict or heightened scrutiny was not found to be appropriate. Thus, the second half of this Article turns to the arguments made in *Brown* to justify strict and heightened scrutiny.

NEITHER STRICT NOR HEIGHTENED SCRUTINY OF THE UTAH BIGAMY LAW WAS JUSTIFIED IN *BROWN*

After the first episode of TLC's reality television show *Sister Wives* aired, Utah state officials started a criminal investigation of the Brown family featured in the show, consisting of Kody Brown and his wives Meri, Janelle, Christine, and Robyn. The Browns are members of the Apostolic United Brethren, who believe that "polygamy is a core religious practice."[110] Although the Browns moved to Nevada to avoid a possible prosecution, Utah officials continued the investigation. As a result, the Browns filed an action in the United States District Court for the District of Utah challenging the constitutionality of Utah's statute criminalizing polygamy on multiple grounds, including under the Free Exercise Clause, the *Smith* Hybrid Rights Analysis framework, and the Due Process Clause.[111] After the Browns moved for summary judgment, it does not appear that the State mounted a strong defense, as the court noted that it was "intrigued by the sheer lack of response in Defendant's filing to Plaintiffs seven detailed constitutional claims."[112] The court granted summary judgment to the Browns, finding the bigamy statute unconstitutional as applied to Brown's religious polygamous marriage under strict scrutiny, heightened scrutiny, or rational basis scrutiny.

Strict Scrutiny of Polygamy Law under Hialeah's Free Exercise Analysis

Hialeah

Brown's determination that the bigamy statute should be subject to strict scrutiny[113] arose out of a free exercise analysis under *Church of the*

Lukumi Babalu Aye, Inc. v. City of Hialeah, the Supreme Court evaluated several ordinances prohibiting and regulating animal sacrifices passed in response to the establishment of a Santeria Church.[114] The Santeria religion engages in animal sacrifice as part of its rituals, after which the animal is often but not always eaten.[115] While *Employment Division v. Smith*[116] had found that "a law that is neutral and of general applicability need not be justified by a compelling governmental interest even if the law has the incidental effect of burdening a particular religious practice,"[117] *Hialeah* established the opposite rule: a law that is not neutral and of general applicability "must be justified by a compelling governmental interest and must be narrowly tailored to advance that interest."[118]

Neutrality will be absent when "the object of a law is to infringe upon or restrict practices because of their religious motivation."[119] When a law is facially neutral, it is necessary to look at "the effect of a law in its real operation"[120] to determine its object. At the same time, citing two polygamy cases, the Supreme Court noted that an adverse impact on a religious practice is not necessarily evidence that the religion has been targeted because "a social harm may have been a legitimate concern of government for reasons quite apart from discrimination."[121] In evaluating the ordinances in light of the stated public objectives of avoiding health risks, emotional injury to children, protecting animals from cruel and unnecessary killing, and confining animal slaughter to areas zoned for it, the Court found them to produce a "religious gerrymander."[122] "[F]ew if any killings of animals are prohibited other than Santeria sacrifice . . . . although . . . killings that are no more necessary or humane in almost all other circumstances are unpunished."[123] In addition, more religious conduct was prohibited than was necessary to advance the stated government objectives[124] as more narrowly tailored regulations addressing conditions, treatment, and methods of slaughter would have directly addressed the city's objectives. In finding the ordinances not to be neutral, Justice Kennedy and Justice Stevens also found relevant historical evidence surrounding the enactment of the ordinances showing animosity towards Santeria, including the events that triggered the ordinances and statements made by the city council.[125]

In addition, a law burdening religion must be generally applicable; it "cannot in a selective manner impose burdens only on conduct motivated by religious belief."[126] It cannot "target or single out" religious conduct.[127] To determine whether the animal sacrifice ordinances were generally applicable, the Supreme Court looked to see whether they were underinclusive relative to their stated objectives.[128] The Court found these ordinances underinclusive with regard to all four of the objectives, failing to regulate nonreligious killings of animals to address these concerns.[129] Thus, it concluded that they were "a prohibition that society is prepared to impose upon [Santeria worshippers] but not upon itself."[130] Once a law is found to be not neutral or not of general application, strict scrutiny is called for: "a law restrictive of religious practice must advance 'interests of the highest order' and must be narrowly tailored in pursuit of those interests."[131] The Court stated that both the overinclusiveness and underinclusiveness of the ordinances showed that it was not narrowly tailored. In addition, the underinclusiveness of the ordinances revealed that the interests sought to be advanced were not of the highest order or compelling, as a compelling interest would be more rigorously advanced.[132]

Utah's Bigamy Statute

Utah's Bigamy statute reads as follows: "A person is guilty of bigamy when, knowing that he has a husband or wife or knowing the other person has a husband of wife, the person purports to marry another person or cohabits with another person."[133] To follow the analysis below, it will be helpful to list and distinguish the various marital forms covered by the statute:

1. Fraudulent bigamy, additional "legal" marriage by a legally married person with a person who is unaware both of the first legal spouse and the void status of their own marriage, is covered under the "purports to marry" language.
2. Legal polygamy, attempted multiple legal marriages without any fraud to the marriage partners, is covered under the "purports to marry" language.
3. Polygamous marriages, ceremonial marriages to multiple spouses without seeking legal recognition of more than one marriage, is covered under the "purports to marry" language.
4. Polygamous cohabitation, multiple marital relationships, is covered under the "cohabits" language.

In State v. Green, the Utah Supreme Court addressed the meaning of "cohabitation."[134] Green was a Fundamentalist Mormon polygamist who did not attempt to legally marry more than one wife at a time; he would divorce the wife he was legally married to before getting a license and entering into a legal marriage with another wife.[135] Some wives he never legally married but instead married in an unlicensed religious ceremony.[136] The State alleged that Green had cohabited with four women while legally married to a fifth and thus sought to bring his conduct under the cohabitation prong of the bigamy statute.[137] The Green court found that Green had clearly engaged in bigamous cohabitation because his conduct "produced precisely the situation that bigamy statutes aim to prevent—all the indicia of marriage repeated more than once."[138] The "indicia" relied upon in Green to show cohabitation did not include the religious marriage ceremonies.[139]

In State v. Holm, the Utah Supreme Court was called upon to interpret the meaning of "purports to marry" in the bigamy statute. Holm was, like Green, a member of the Fundamentalist Church of Jesus Christ of Latter-day Saints.[140] After legally marrying Suzie Stubbs, he entered into a religious marriage with Wendy Holm.[141] Later, at the age of thirty-two, he entered into a religious marriage with sixteen-year old Ruth Stubbs, the sister of Suzie.[142] By shortly after her eighteenth birthday, Ruth had borne two children.[143] Holm was arrested and charged with both bigamy and unlawful sexual conduct with a sixteen- or seventeen-year-old.[144] The jury special verdict form showed that Holm was found "guilty of bigamy both because he 'purported to marry Ruth Stubbs' and because he had 'cohabited with Ruth Stubbs.'"[145]

Free Exercise Challenges to the Utah Bigamy Statute Before Brown

In both *Green* and *Holm,* the Utah Supreme Court had considered a free exercise challenge to the Utah bigamy law in the context of prosecutions of Mormon fundamentalist polygamists. Applying the *Hialeah* analysis, the court concluded that the statute was operationally neutral and generally applicable.[146] The Utah Supreme Court justified its determination that the bigamy statute was operationally neutral by noting that the bigamy statute "contains no exemptions that would restrict the practical application of the statute only to [religious] polygamists. In fact, the last reported decision of a prosecution under the current bigamy statute in our state courts involved a man who committed bigamy for non-religious reasons."[147] In the case referred to, *State v. Geer,*[148] the defendant was charged with "purport[ing] to marry another person" while "knowing [that] he . . . has a wife."[149] The case involved typical fraudulent bigamy (marital form 1), in which a man purported to legally marry a woman who was unaware that he was already legally married to another woman.[150] There was no evidence of any religious motivation in the case of Geer's multiple marriages; indeed, Geer unsuccessfully attempted to challenge his conviction on the ground that the State of Utah "selectively prosecutes only those bigamists who practice bigamy for other than religious reasons."[151]

By mentioning *Geer* as proof that Utah's bigamy statute operated to punish nonreligious bigamy, we can see that the *Green* court's operational neutrality analysis considered the bigamy statute as a whole. Rather than limiting its analysis strictly to the cohabitation prong Green was prosecuted under, it looked at the operational impact of both prongs and saw that while the cohabitation prong reached a religious polygamist in *Green,* the purport to marry prong in another case had reached a nonreligious polygamist.

Brown's Hialeah *Analysis of the Utah Bigamy Statute*

The *Brown* court found that the bigamy statute was "neither operationally neutral nor generally applicable."[152] I will offer three criticisms of this result. First, I will argue that the *Brown* court treated a single statute as if it were two separate statutes, which allowed it to improperly find that part of the bigamy statute was not operationally neutral. Second, I will argue that even as divided by the *Brown* court, all parts of the statute are operationally neutral. The third argument is one I have already made in large part above, that even if the statute were not operationally neutral, it would survive strict scrutiny.

Divide and Conquer

The first step in the *Brown* court's analysis was to reorganize the three targets of the statute as interpreted by the Utah Supreme Court in *Green* and *Holm* into what it saw as only two distinct targets. The first target, which fell within the purports to marry language, covers ineffective attempts to enter into multiple legal marriages, which the court called "actual bigamy"[153] (marital form 1 above) and "actual polygamy"[154] (marital form 2 above). An example of actual bigamy would be the *Geer* case, in which no religious motivation was behind the multiple marriages.[155] An example of actual polygamy would be the *Reynolds* case, in which the multiple licensed marriages were religiously motivated.[156] The second target of the statute according to the *Brown* court, which fell under both the purports to marry and cohabitation language, was what the *Brown* court called "religious cohabitation."[157] The *Brown* court defined "religious cohabitation" variously throughout the opinion as "to practice polygamy through private 'spiritual' marriages not licensed or otherwise sanctioned by the state"[158] and "choosing 'to enter into a relationship that [they know] would not be legally recognized as marriage, [they use] religious terminology to describe the relationship . . . [including] marriage and husband and wife [which] happens to coincide with the terminology used by the state to describe the legal status of married persons.'"[159] Examples of religious cohabitation would be *Green* (marital form 4 above) and *Holm* (marital form 3 above).

The second step in the *Brown* court's analysis was to evaluate these two broader targets separately for purposes of the operational neutrality analysis,[160] rather than evaluate the statute as a whole as the court in *Green* and *Holm* had done. The *Brown* court found the "actual bigamy" and "actual polygamy" target of the statute to be operationally neutral because the presence or absence of religious motivation was not determinative of the offense.[161] At the same time, removing "actual bigamy," the non-religiously motivated multiple legal marriages found in *Geer*, left religious cohabitation as, in the view of the *Brown* court,[162] the only remaining target of the statute.

If, on the other hand, religious cohabitation is understood as a target along with nonreligious bigamy, then what the *Brown* court was willing to see as the operational neutrality of the "actual bigamy" and "actual polygamy" target would have extended over all the targets of the statute. Indeed, one might ask why the *Brown* court was justified in lumping together actual bigamy and actual polygamy in one operational neutrality analysis of the purports to marry language, while removing cases of religious cohabitation also covered by the purports to marry language. Why not separate out actual bigamy from a combined target of actual polygamy and religious cohabitation, all of which the *Brown* court saw as religiously motivated? The reason is fairly obvious: either the *Brown* court would have to find that *Reynolds* controlled and the statute did not violate the Free Exercise Clause, or it would have to strike down *Reynolds*.[163] The latter would have allowed for the possibility of legal recognition of religiously motivated polygamous marriages in Utah.

Furthermore, there is no justification given by the *Brown* court for its refusal to undertake the operational neutrality analysis of the bigamy statute as a whole, in which all the possible targets of both the purports to marry and cohabitation language would be evaluated together, as had the courts in *Green* and *Holm*. When this is done, actual prosecutions of both religious and non-religiously motivated conduct can be shown.

Hialeah itself can offer no justification for the approach taken in *Brown*. In *Hialeah*, the Supreme Court was faced with four separate ordinances[164] that it first evaluated individually,[165] finding that three of them operated to create a "religious gerrymander."[166] It was necessary to look at both the exemptions and prohibitions within each ordinance to evaluate its neutrality. The lack of operational neutrality for each of these three was revealed by exemption within each ordinance that left Santeria animal sacrifice the sole possible target of each.[167] This does not justify the *Brown* court's approach of splitting up a single statute into three targets and then evaluating two together and one separately for operational neutrality. In addition, the fourth ordinance, on its own, appeared to apply to nonreligious conduct,[168] but the Court determined that "the four substantive ordinances may be treated as a group for neutrality purposes" because the neutral one was enacted on the same day and in response to the same event, the opening of a Santeria Church, as the other three.[169] If anything, the eventual treatment by the Court of the four ordinances as if they were one suggests that a single statute should at least be seen as a totality. Indeed, actual bigamy, actual polygamy, and religious cohabitation (marital forms 1, 2, 3, and 4 above) have been a combined target of single statutes since the 1887 Edmunds Act.[170]

Cohabitation is Cohabitation

To find that the statute was not operationally neutral in its targeting of religious cohabitation, the *Brown* court needed to show that while religious cohabitation is prohibited by the statute, "secular"[171] cohabitation is not so prohibited. It did this by identifying secular cohabitation with adulterous cohabitation. Adulterous cohabitation consists of persons "outside the community of those who practice polygamy for religious reasons"[172] who live together when at least one of them is legally married to a third party. It is cohabitation by virtue of the fact that they "live together 'as if' they are married in the sense that they share a household and a sexually intimate relationship."[173] The court noted that while adulterous cohabitation also falls within the separate crime of adultery,[174] it has not been prosecuted as a crime under that statute since 1928 and has never been prosecuted as polygamous cohabitation under the bigamy statute.[175] Of course, the latter is because both federal and Utah state courts had consistently interpreted the word cohabitation in a polygamy statute as a reference to something other than mere adulterous cohabitation.[176] The exclusion of adulterous cohabitation from the Utah bigamy statute led the *Brown* court to conclude that, in the language of *Hialeah*, "few if any [cohabitations] are prohibited other than [religious cohabitations]."[177] Thus, the *Brown* court concluded that the bigamy statute was not operationally neutral because it targeted only religious cohabitation and not non-religiously motivated or secular cohabitation, such as adultery.

The problem with this conclusion is that the real distinction consistently made by courts construing this word as used in a criminal polygamy law has been between marital cohabitation, which was the target of the polygamy laws, and mere sexual cohabitation, which was the target of adultery and fornication laws.[178] Under the Utah bigamy statute, the "indicia" of marital cohabitation are likely to be the same elements required by Utah's "common law" marriage statute.[179] Although in a bigamy or polygamy situation, one of the common law marriage elements—legal capacity to enter into a marriage—will never be present; all the remaining elements—the capacity to contract; the existence of a consensual contract; cohabitation; the assumption of marital duties, rights, and obligations; and a uniform reputation as married or as husband and wife[180] —can be present. The fact that cohabitation itself is just one of several essential factors that must be shown to find "marriage"[181] suggests that the word cohabitation in the common law marriage statute is meant narrowly[182] as "sexual cohabitation," meaning "common residency[,] . . . sharing of a common abode that both parties consider their principal domicile for more than a temporary or brief period of time" and "sexual conduct[, which] means participation in a relatively permanent sexual relationship akin to that generally existing between husband and wife."[183]

In contrast, when the court in *Green* found that cohabitation under the bigamy statute had occurred, it carefully mentioned facts that covered all of the five relevant elements of common law marriage. Common residency was established by the fact that Green and the women "shared a group of mobile homes."[184] Permanent sexual relationship was shown by the fact that "Green spent nights with each woman on a rotating schedule."[185] A consensual contract was found by the fact that both the women and their children adopted the Green surname.[186] Assumption of marital duties, rights, and obligations was also shown to be present: "Together, Green and the women undertook spousal and parental obligations."[187] Facts mentioned in *Green* showing uniform reputation as married or as husband and wife included Green "refer[ring] to each of these woman as a wife . . . . [and] [t]he woman likewise considered themselves Green's wives,"[188] and the fact that "[b]etween 1988 and 2001, Green appeared on various television shows with the women, consistently referring to the women as his wives, and the women likewise acknowledged spousal relationships."[189] Thus, the *Green* decision can be understood to define cohabitation in the bigamy statute as marital cohabitation, which includes sexual cohabitation but requires considerable additional proof.

None of the indicia mentioned by the *Green* court included either the religious ceremonies Green and his wives had participated in or the religious motivation for their unlicensed marriages. The *Brown* court found these omissions to be misleading because "the most important factor of such plural cohabitations in Utah" is "their religious nature."[190] However, the question is not whether the religious nature of polygamous cohabitations in Utah is important to the participants, but rather whether this is important to the State. I would argue that the crucial feature of these cohabitations is that they are marital rather than merely sexual in nature. Once it is understood that the target of the statute is marital cohabitation, the question under *Hialeah* becomes whether the statute targets only religious marital cohabitation or whether it also targets secular marital cohabitation, thereby showing that the religious or secular quality of the marital cohabitation is irrelevant.

The Utah common law marriage statute described above sets out the features of a secular marital cohabitation. For example, the *Holm* court cited the Utah case *Whyte v. Blair*[191] to demonstrate how "cohabitation alone"[192] (meaning marital cohabitation without a marriage ceremony rather than sexual cohabitation alone) can produce a "marital relationship"[193] that could be viewed as marriage under the common law statute. Whyte had sought to have a court recognize the relationship he had with a woman he was living with as a common law marriage so that he could be considered a "family member" under her insurance policy.[194] The facts showed an unlicensed, unsolemnized[195] relationship that did not seem to involve religious cohabitation. Such "marital relationships" or "marriages" can come to exist without a religious or secular solemnization ceremony, as may have been the case in *Whyte* itself. However, in the absence of such a ceremony, *Whyte* emphasized the importance of establishing the element of consent to marry in other ways,[196] providing a non-exhaustive list of what other evidence might show consent. This ranged from a written agreement or evidence showing an oral agreement to enter into a marital relationship to

> maintenance of joint banking and credit accounts; purchase and joint ownership of property; the use of the man's surname by the woman and/or the children of the union; the filing of joint tax returns; speaking of each other in the presence of third parties as being married; and declaring the relationship in documents executed by them while living together, such as deeds, wills, and other formal instruments.[197]

The emphasis on showing consent to marry reflects the statute's requirement that the marriage "arise out of a contract."[198] Evidence of such a contract is necessary to establish that the parties intended to create a relationship binding on the parties even after they no longer desire it to exist and to show that they intended to enjoy the benefits and take on the obligations that civil law provides for marriage. An unlicensed religious solemnization would satisfy the requirement for consent to marry under the common law marriage statute because, whatever its religious significance, the language of such ceremonies is also the language of contract. But this is hardly the only way to make such a contract. Creation of an express civil contract without the involvement of religion or other conduct that evidences the creation of such a contract, as described above, will suffice. Thus, in *Green*, it was possible to show the existence of marital relationships without reference to the religious ceremonies that had in fact occurred. Indeed, in *Green*, one of these marital relationships was judicially declared to be a legally recognized common law marriage,[199] thus making the other marital relationships unlawful cohabitation under the bigamy statute.

We can see that both religious marital relationships and nonreligious marital relationships can be found to be common law marriages under the Utah common law marriage statute. However, it must also be the case that secular cohabitation while legally married to another would produce a conviction under the cohabitation language of the Utah bigamy statute. Although no such actual prosecution or conviction can be shown in Utah, there is no reason to believe that the law would not apply to a proper case. Suppose a polygamist who had legally married both his first and second wives in his country of origin were to immigrate to the United States with his second wife and settle in Utah. Let us assume that this polygamous marriage was not based on any religious mandate, but rather was simply a culturally accepted marital practice.[200] Concealing his first marriage from immigration authorities, he presented his second wife as his legal wife and engaged in conduct that would satisfy the common law marriage statute, except for the fact that he would not have capacity to be married to the second wife because Utah would legally recognize the first marriage as prior. If Utah officials were to learn about the existence of the first wife, they could prosecute this polygamist under the cohabitation prong of the bigamy statute. The cohabitation prong of the Utah statute is therefore operationally neutral because the cohabitation that is sufficient to "show all the indicia of marriage" is not limited to cohabitation undertaken subsequent to a religious marriage ceremony. The fact that most known polygamists in Utah are Mormon Fundamentalists, and the State has not had an opportunity to prosecute a non-religiously motivated polygamist under the cohabitation language, is simply an accident of Utah's history and current population. As Utah becomes more diverse,[201] this may change, but it need not do so for the bigamy statute to be understood as operationally neutral.

Purports to Marry

The *Brown* court also found that the purports to marry language in the Utah bigamy statute, insofar as it referred to unlicensed, solemnized marriages rather than licensed, solemnized marriages, also targeted only religious marriage.[202] In particular, the *Brown* court found this to be established by the discussion in *Holm* of the importance of the religious solemnization ceremony to the determination that Holm had purported to marry an additional wife.[203]

When the *Holm* court subsequently held "that Holm's behavior is within the ambit of our bigamy statute's 'purports to marry' prong,"[204] from this the *Brown* court concluded that "it is the intention of the individuals to be religiously married . . . that, for the *Holm* majority, constituted a key consideration in whether the Statute had been violated."[205]

However, before the *Holm* court concluded that the purport to marry language had been violated, it indicated that "Holm and Stubbs [had both] formed a marital bond and commenced a marital relationship."[206] The *Holm* court described the religious ceremony as "the steps . . . by which two individuals commit themselves to undertake a marital relationship."[207] Indeed, from the perspective of the state, what is important about such religious ceremonies is simply that they also create a civil marital contract. It is for this reason that religious solemnizations are permitted, with a license, to act as the solemnization for legally recognized civil marriages. It is not the religious character of religious solemnization that has legal significance or effect. If it were, laws allowing religious solemnization to substitute for secular solemnization would themselves violate the Establishment Clause. Thus, it was precisely *not* the religious nature of the religious solemnization ceremony in *Holm* that created the marital bond.

Furthermore, there is no reason why polygamous marriages could not arise out of purporting to marry through unlicensed secular solemnization ceremonies. It just happens to be the case that unlicensed solemnization ceremonies are most often religious in nature. This is because, as we understand the marital bond, it must be binding upon the parties who enter into it. This requires the involvement of a power greater than the parties themselves. The only two possibilities for such a power are the state[208] and God. In the absence of a license, the state officers who are empowered to conduct secular solemnization ceremonies are not likely to be willing to do so. Thus, there may have been no opportunity for the State of Utah to prosecute a polygamy case involving a second secularly solemnized but unlicensed marriage. However, one could imagine the possibility of a corrupt state official who might choose for monetary or other reasons to pretend to legally marry a couple in the absence of a license. In contrast, there are religious leaders who are actually willing to conduct a religious solemnization ceremony without a license.[209] Prior to the legal recognition of same-sex marriage, many same-sex couples participated in religious solemnization ceremonies. Widows and widowers on social security have sometimes avoided the reduction in benefits a legal marriage would produce by participating in a religious solemnization ceremony without getting a marriage license.[210] Thus, as a practical matter, religious solemnization ceremonies are the usual route taken by those who seek to create a bond that justifies them in entering into an actual, real-world marital relationship in the absence of being able to or wanting to obtain a license. However, just because virtually all cases of unlicensed solemnization involve religious solemnization does not mean that the bigamy statute is operationally non-neutral. The prohibition on purporting to marry someone while legally married to another would apply to an unlicensed marriage solemnized by secular officials. Indeed, Utah has a law that makes it a crime to knowingly solemnize a marriage prohibited by law, with or without a license.[211] It applies to both the secular officials and the religious leaders who are authorized by law to solemnize marriages, but practically speaking will rarely if ever be violated by secular officials. It is not discrimination by the state if only the religious choose to violate a law that both religious and nonreligious people can violate.

Finally, the requirement that, in addition to this moment of binding commitment, the parties must actually establish by their conduct a marital relationship in order to purport to marry,[212] shows again that it is not the religious implications of even a religious ceremony that are legally significant. For example, imagine that two people engage in a religious ceremony that from the perspective of their religion resulted in what the religion called a marriage, but it was only to be acted on after the death of both. Then, imagine that the two people then immediately go their separate ways and engage in no conduct (including consummation) during their lifetime that is typical of married couples. In such a case, we could say that something of only religious significance had occurred and a merely religious marriage had been created, which the law cannot seek to regulate. What the law can regulate is the nonreligious aspect of marriage, in which the conduct of the parties toward each other and toward those outside of the marriage is affected. As the Supreme Court said in *R e yn old s*, marriage may be "a sacred obligation," but it is also a "civil contract" out of which "spring social relations and social obligations and duties, with which government is necessarily required to deal."[213] It was for this reason that the *Holm* court considered the subsequent cohabitation (in the narrow sense) of Holm and Stubbs—they lived in a house together and "'regularly' engaged in sexual intercourse"[214]—in addition to the ceremony to establish that they purported to marry. This ensured that that their religious marriage ceremony was meant to be followed by the actual creation of a relationship and life together that would be identical to a legal marriage. Thus, *Holm* establishes that in order for someone to violate the bigamy statute by purporting to marry another, it is necessary to insure that the religious ceremony is meant to have an impact in the secular world. It is this intention rather than the religious intention that the statute seeks to reach. This is consistent with what the Court in *Reynolds* described as the "rightful purposes of civil government for its officers to interfere when principles break out into overt acts."[215]

Thus, the application of the purports to marry language to unlicensed religiously solemnized marriages is not operationally non-neutral for three reasons. First, it is the civil contract created by saying "I do" in a religious marriage ceremony that is viewed as creating the crucial marital bond. Second, unlicensed secular solemnizations that created a marital bond would be equally problematic under the statute. Third, it is the intention to engage in marital conduct in the real world that is the true target of the purport to marry language. The presence or absence of religious meaning to either the ceremony or the subsequent marital conduct is of no significance to the statute.

Selective and Minimal Prosecution

The *Brown* court made one additional argument for the bigamy statute's operational non-neutrality, based on "the State's explicit 'policy of selective prosecution.'"[216] As applied to religiously motivated polygamy, the Utah bigamy statute prohibits all such marriages and marital cohabitations. The State of Utah simultaneously reserves the right to prosecute any conduct that falls within the statute but has for the most part chosen to only prosecute religiously motivated polygamy if a marriage with a girl under eighteen years of age has occurred.[217] *Hollm* was an example of this kind of prosecution.[218] *Green* might also be seen as an example of this, as Green had originally married one of his wives as a thirteen-year-old, even though all his wives were of age for the period he was charged with bigamy.[219] On the other hand, the *Brown* court viewed Green's prosecution as motivated by his open discussion of his polygamy in the media.[220] The threatened prosecution of Brown illustrated both possibilities. Brown made his family the subject of a nationwide reality television show, thus motivating a prosecutor to consider charging him. However, none of Brown's wives were underage at the time of marriage and the prosecutor dropped the investigation of Brown while the constitutional challenge was pending. In conjunction with dropping the case, the prosecutor swore that he would not prosecute bigamy unless it occurred "in the conjunction with another crime or a person under the age of [eighteen] was a party."[221] It was not clear whether this decision was motivated by the policy of limited prosecution or whether it was an attempt to moot the constitutional challenge. But the prosecutor also said that another prosecutor who did not adhere to the under-eighteen policy could seek charges against Brown under the statute.[222] Finally, the *Brown* court suggested that reserving the right to prosecute bigamy alone really allowed the state to address other crimes associated with polygamy, such as child abuse and domestic violence, which are hard to obtain evidence of in the isolated and closed polygamous communities without having evidence of those crimes.[223] The result, the *Brown* court argued was "apparently limitless prosecutorial discretion by individual State officials . . . to decide whether and when (and against whom) to enforce the cohabitation prong of the Statute."[224]

The *Brown* court concluded that this limitless prosecutorial discretion regarding religious cohabitation under the bigamy statute is "fatal to any claim to general applicability"[225] under *Hialeah*. However, we have already seen that the bigamy statute is generally applicable to both the religious and non-religious. Furthermore, the more limited enforcement of the law against specifically religious polygamists shows the opposite of religious targeting. If anything, the state, through this policy, eases the burden of the criminal law on religiously motivated conduct. Indeed, in *Geer*, the nonreligious defendant charged with attempted multiple legal marriages claimed that the state selectively prosecuted only nonreligious bigamists.[226] The nature of the selective prosecution in this case simply fails to show that the government is "in a selective manner impos[ing] burdens only on conduct motivated by religious belief."[227] Thus, the strict scrutiny the *Brown* court applied to the Utah bigamy statute is unjustified.

The state may also have limited its prosecution out of a concern that the criminalization of polygamy might be found unconstitutional. Since *Lawrence*, it has not been clear that the moral objections that may have once been thought to justify criminalizing polygamy would suffice. This would explain why the state only enforces the law when other "associated" crimes are present and then relies on crimes associated with polygamy to justify the criminalization of polygamy alone. However, if, as I argue here should be the case, Utah's criminalization of polygamy in all its forms can be confirmed to be constitutional, the state may be empowered to step up its prosecutorial efforts.

There is also another important reason why the state has minimally enforced the law. Because polygamy in Utah involves childbearing so importantly, prosecuting fathers and mothers for entering into polygamous marriages means taking parents away from their children. Utah closely observed the extreme negatives of prosecution that came from Arizona's 1953 raid of the polygamous town of Short Creek, on the border between Utah and Arizona, resulting in putting 236 children into state custody.[228] There are innocent victims of polygamy who can be greatly harmed by prosecution. This individual suffering is immediate and is therefore easily recognized by prosecutors in a way that the foundational harms of polygamy are not. Thus, the exercise of prosecutorial discretion with regard polygamists may reflect an attempt to weigh the harm of prosecution to the children of polygamy against the harm to the children of polygamy itself. This also explains the state's particular willingness to prosecute polygamy when harm to the children is already clearly present.

In light of all these factors, it is not surprising that prosecutors are ambivalent at best about actually enforcing the bigamy statute against polygamists. The failure of the state to both fully recognize what the primary compelling state and national interest is in criminalizing polygamy and prioritize prosecution as a way to advance that interest does not mean either that these interests do not exist or that statutory criminalization of polygamy itself does not serve an important deterrent purpose.[229] It was ultimately sufficient to convince the Mormon Church to repudiate polygamy as a religious practice, and it has been sufficient to largely restrain any natural tendencies we may have towards polygamy or at least reshape them into what we hope are less socially harmful practices, such as divorce and remarriage.[230]

CRIMINALIZATION OF POLYGAMY CAN SURVIVE STRICT SCRUTINY

I have thus far presented an account of the harms of polygamy that should be sufficient to establish a compelling state interest in criminalizing polygamy. I have also argued that strict scrutiny of the Utah bigamy statute is actually justified. However, should strict scrutiny be justified, there are two remaining arguments that have not yet been considered.

Would the Utah Bigamy Statute Be Viewed as Narrowly Tailored?

The Brown court argued that, in its application to unlicensed religious marriages and religious cohabitation, the statute is not narrowly tailored to advance even a compelling state interest.[231] The Brown court essentially claimed that the statute is both over-inclusive and under-inclusive in relation to the ends it seeks to advance. It is over-inclusive because "in the absence of any claim of legal marriage, neither participation in a religious ceremony nor cohabitation can plausibly be said to threaten marriage as a social or legal institution."[232] It is under-inclusive because the state fails to prosecute adulterous cohabitation either under the bigamy statute or the adultery statute, and there is "no rational basis to distinguish between [adulterous cohabitation and religious cohabitation], not least with regard to the State interest in protecting the institution of marriage."[233] The Brown court's distinctions make no more sense here than they did previously in the context of its operational non-neutrality analysis.[234] The marital cohabitation targeted by the bigamy statute, including both religious and nonreligious cohabitation, is importantly different from adulterous cohabitation. Not only do such marital relationships implicate the same interests the state seeks to address and regulate in the context of licensed monogamous marriage, such as the protection of children born to the relationship, financial dependency, and joint property, but polygamous cohabitation has broader social impacts that adultery does not have, whether it is on the marriage prospects of others, the status of women and children, or the resources available for social and individual advancement. It is the real-world impact of polygamous marital cohabitation in these arenas that the state is compellingly interested in,[235] and there is little difference in its interest, whether the relationship in question has been legally recognized or not.[236] In criminalizing all multiple marital relationships, whether or not they claim legal status or are motivated by religion, the State addresses all the conduct that creates such social problems. Thus, the statute is not over-inclusive in criminalizing polygamous cohabitation.

The argument that the statute is under-inclusive because it fails to target adulterous cohabitation assumes that the same harms of polygamy arise out of adulterous cohabitation as well: "Both scenarios . . . involve minors as the children born to women involved in such relationships, involve public conduct, and involve economic implications to [women] and children."[237] Because the Brown court refused to acknowledge the possibility of nonreligious marital cohabitation, it lumped all nonreligious cohabitation under the label "adulterous" cohabitation. As result, for the Brown court, there is a type of adulterous cohabitation that is marital in nature and will produce all the same consequences and be of interest to the state in the same way. However, as discussed above,[238] this type of cohabitation will be captured under the cohabitation prong of the bigamy statute. The non-marital adulterous cohabitation that is not prohibited by the bigamy statute is a different kind of relationship all together. With the advent of easily attainable divorce, adulterous cohabitation is not the only way to establish a new marital relationship. Today, one can get divorced and remarried. Access to contraceptives also means that adultery does not have to involve child bearing as a result of its sexual component. Thus, choosing to stay married yet engage in non-marital adulterous cohabitation means that the relationship is more likely to just be about sex and companionship. Individuals who intend to include child bearing as part of their adulterous cohabitation are much more likely to enter into a marital relationship, which would then subject them to the bigamy law should they already be legally married to someone else. Thus, because the bigamy law reaches all multiple relationships that are marital in nature, it is not under-inclusive.

If the bigamy law is neither over- nor under-inclusive in its attempt to deter the harmful effects of multiple simultaneous marital relationships, then it is narrowly tailored to advance its ends. Indeed, if one accepts the harms to women, men, children, and society itself that polygamy inevitably brings, it is hard to imagine how a law criminalizing all forms of polygamy is not the only way to avoid these harms.

Religious Polygamy Has Its Own Unique Harms

I have argued that, contrary to the holding of Brown, the Utah bigamy statute should not be subject to strict or heightened scrutiny despite its impact on religious practice. Merely appreciating the harms of all polygamy in contrast to the benefits of monogamy, whether the polygamy arises out of multiple legally recognized marriages or multiple marital relationships created by religious ceremonies, secular ceremonies, or contractual consent, allows us to see both that it would make little sense for Utah to target only religiously motivated polygamy and even less sense to read the Utah bigamy statute as if it does so. Yet, I would also like to consider the possible strict scrutiny of the statute as it was interpreted by the Brown court, as non-neutral and targeting only religiously motivated polygamy. This requires finding a special harm arising out of religiously motivated polygamy that is not present in cultural polygamy.

It is a peculiar feature of the application of the polygamy law to Mormon Fundamentalist polygamy that the very feature that is most protected, the relationship of the practice to religious belief, may be what makes this particular form of polygamy particularly pernicious. In *Reference*, the Attorney General of British Columbia pointed out that there was something paradoxical about the claim of religious liberty in that case:

> This case may be unique in the section 2(a) jurisprudence in that, because polygamy's harms are most obvious where there is the presence of an external, supposedly binding authority sanctioning it, the reli-

> giosity of the practice itself exacerbates the harm. The evidence that has emerged from expert and lay witnesses alike indicates that, the greater the religious fervor with which polygamy is intertwined, the more harmful it can expect to be. This is not so with any other case asserting a religious right to do something prohibited.[239]

To elaborate on the Attorney General's point, the greatest deprivation of individual rights arising from the practice of polygamy in the United States today is almost exclusively a feature of certain Mormon Fundamentalist polygamous communities.

Religion plays a crucial rule in the way this practice of polygamy is shaped. These communities fully embrace polygamy as a mandatory religious practice for both men and woman necessary to achieve eternal salvation.[240] They also accept the authority of a divinely chosen religious leader, a "Prophet," over all facets of life, including control over marriage partners.[241] These religious beliefs form the scaffolding of isolated communities in which religious authorities have near total control of the familial, educational, social, economic, and governmental environment and use this control to organize community life to ensure that all within it conform to these religious beliefs.[242] While religious power is buttressed by legal power, economic power, social power, and physical power, these real power structures are in turn always justified by the religious beliefs. It is this unique combination of religion and power that turns a belief in the religious value of polygamy into an actual practice of polygamy that can be extremely coercive.[243]

The coercive power of a community devoted to polygamy is further enhanced when those required to enter into the practice are least able to withstand such coercion. As discussed above, polygamy inevitably leads to younger ages of marriage for women.[244] Some of the communities that practice religious polygamy target young teenage girls for entry into polygamous marriages.[245] There are religious as well as practical explanations for why young women are targeted by religious polygamy. Religious doctrine postulates both a religious imperative and a religious payoff for maximizing reproduction by male adherents.[246] Not only does this make participation in polygamy of all female members of the community essential, but it also makes bringing them into polygamous marriage at the earliest possible reproductive age most effective for achieving these religious goals.

Young teenage girls are also more easily pressured into such marriages than they might be at age eighteen or older. They are still under the control of their parents, and their age-related pliability is enhanced by familial, social, and religious indoctrination that makes polygamous marriage the only possible future they can both value and imagine. These two factors make young teenage girls the perfect polygamous wives.

Finally, ensuring that these young women do not have the opportunity to grow to adulthood and leave the community to marry, perhaps monogamously, allows polygamy to be a self-sustaining practice over time. Male polygamists cannot maximize their reproduction without a large pool of women to marry. So long as the community continues to funnel all its female children into polygamous reproduction, there is a possibility that the community can sustain its polygamous practices over multiple generations without having to expand the pool of potential wives through new recruits. So it is possible to see how religious belief can and has shaped a particularly coercive practice of underage polygamy.

However, this justification is complicated by the fact that some religiously polygamous communities, such as the Apostolic United Brethren (AUP), have backed away from both underage and arranged marriages,[247] perhaps due to a concern about prosecution or as a result of evolving attitudes and beliefs about the autonomy of women, or some combination of the two. Furthermore, many of these AUP community members are relatively integrated into mainstream civil society, living in non-polygamous towns and cities and having their children attend public school. This presents the possibility of a gentler form of religious polygamy that may not be coercive. Yet, it is not clear whether this gentler practice of religious polygamy is sustainable. As many as fifty percent of children may leave this sect as adults, producing a shrinking pool of potential polygamous wives. [248] At some point in time, the religious need of male members of the community to create expansive polygamous families could trump these progressive steps and require restructuring of both community life and the age of polygamous marriage to ensure capture of female children within the community as polygamous wives. Thus, as long as polygamy is a religious imperative, it may well force adherents to take steps to minimize the autonomy of women so as to maximize their entry into polygamous marriages. Thus, coercion and religious polygamy may well be particularly inextricable. Furthermore, the extra coercion provided by religion may be a key feature in the continued existence of polygamous communities.

The question which then arises is to what extent does free exercise jurisprudence allow consideration of the way in which religious belief can be combined with autonomy-denying and -destroying practices to render individuals incapable of asserting or exercising their rights to avoid participation in the religious practice? Certainly, many who criticize *Yoder v. Wisconsin*[249] today focus on the rights of adolescents to an education that will make it possible for them to freely choose as adults whether to embrace the Amish lifestyle or reject it.[250] The issue of children's rights is even more starkly drawn in the context of religious polygamy. Here, the exchange is not just an education for the romanticized agrarian life of the Amish[251] but an exchange of education and freedom to choose monogamous marriage, a marriage partner and self-determination in matters of child-bearing for the very difficult life of a polygamous wife with a long period of childbearing, primary financial responsibility for a large family with little earning potential, and largely single parenting. Indeed, Yoder itself has contributed to the problem by allowing Mormon fundamentalist families to withdraw both boys and girls from school by age thirteen or fourteen, thus making it particularly difficult to provide these children with practical options to life within the community, let alone the psychological and intellectual tools to decide for themselves about polygamy. Reconsideration of Yoder in the context of religious polygamy will not be necessary so long as all polygamy is seen as socially harmful and laws criminalizing polygamy are understood as neutral and generally applicable, even when the practical reality in a particular state may be that polygamy is primarily chosen by those whose religion mandates it. However, should this practical reality be taken as confining the target of polygamy laws to religious polygamy, as Brown asserted, it may not be possible for the Court to avoid confronting Yoder.

CONCLUSION

American jurisprudence has long struggled to articulate the harms of polygamy, even as it has, until *Brown*, insisted that these harms were sufficient to overcome the burden on religious practice created by criminalizing polygamy. The apparent failure of the state interests thus far thought to be implicated by polygamy to survive the strict scrutiny applied in *Brown* gave some urgency to remedying this deficit. *Reference* provides this understanding of the considerable inherent harms of polygamy, backed by the best empirical data ever available on the social and individual impacts of polygamy. The "cruel arithmetic" of polygamy cannot help but produce deep repercussions on individuals, communities, and society in general. In light of this, it is difficult to credit *Brown*'s claim that only animus against a minority religious practice can explain the criminalization of unlicensed polygamous marriages and marital relationships. It is an accident of history that one religion chose to embrace as a fundamental practice a marital form antithetical to and destructive of the very social fabric that allowed the religion to emerge. The prohibition against polygamy is not about religion, but about women and men and children and the kind of society they can live in. Once this is recognized, it is impossible to see the Utah bigamy statute as anything but a neutral and generally applicable law that happens to be operating in a state with a great disproportion of religious polygamists. Consequently, the strict scrutiny applied in *Brown* is not justified. At the same time, it is hard to imagine that the interests at stake in the choice between monogamy and polygamy are not sufficient to survive strict scrutiny, even if it were to be justified.

NOTES

1. This Article addresses only the issue of criminalizing the practice of polygamy, which would have to be resolved in favor of decriminalization before the issue of legal recognition could be raised.

2. 98 U.S. 145 (1879).

3. See Church of the Lukumi Babalu Aye, Inc. v. City of Hialeah, 508 U.S. 520, 535 (1993); Emp't Div. v. Smith, 494 U.S. 872, 879 (1990).

4. 98 U.S. at 165–66 ("[A]ccording as monogamous or polygamous marriages are allowed, do we find the principles on which the government of the people . . . rests . . . .[P]olygamy leads to the patriarchal principle, and which, when applied to large communities, fetters the people in stationary despotism, while that principle cannot long exist in connection with monogamy.").

5. *Id.* at 164.

6. Lawrence v. Texas, 539 U.S. 558, 578–79 (2003).

7. E.g., United States v. Windsor, 133 S. Ct. 2675, 2695 (2013) (requiring the federal government to recognize same-sex marriages in certain states); Bostic v. Schaefer, 760 F.3d 352, 384 (4th Cir. 2014) (holding Virginia's ban on same-sex marriages unconstitutional); Kitchen v. Herbert, 755 F.3d 1193, 1229–30 (10th Cir. 2014) (holding Utah's ban on same-sex marriages unconstitutional).

8. Reference re: Section 293 of the Criminal Code of Canada, 2011 BCSC 1588, paras. 15–16 (Can.) [hereinafter *Reference*].

9. *See* Constitutional Question Act, R.S.B.C. 1996, c. 68, s. 1 (Can.) (allowing the government to refer constitutional questions to the courts).

10. U.S. CONST. art. III, §§ 1–2; *see also* Osborn v. Bank of the U.S., 22 U.S. (9 Wheat.) 738, 819 (1824) ("[W]hen the subject is submitted to it by a party who asserts his rights in the form prescribed by law . . . . [i]t then becomes a case . . . .").

11. *Reference*, 2011 BCSC 1588, at 2.

12. *Id.* para. 28

13. *Id.* para. 32.

14. *Id.* paras. 1271–1273

15. *Id.* para. 5 ("[T]his case is essentially about harm; more specifically, Parliament's reasoned apprehension of harm arising out of the practice of polygamy."); *id.* paras. 1279–1282 (setting out the positions of the parties regarding the pressing and substantial quality of the alleged harms).

16. *Id.* paras. 1331–1333.

17. *Id.* para. 1359.

18. Brown v. Buhman, 947 F. Supp. 2d 1170, 1190 (D. Utah 2013), vacated and remanded, Brown v. Buhman, 2016 WL 2848510 (10th Cir)(finding case moot).

19. *Id.* at 1178–80.

20. *Id.* at 1176–77.

21. UTAH CODE ANN. § 76-7-101 (West 2004). Utah does not distinguish between bigamy and polygamy in its criminal code.

22. *Brown*, 947 F. Supp. 2d at 1221–23.

23. *Id.* at 1234.

24. Brown v. Buhman, 2016 WL 2848510 at 12–19.

25. *Reference*, 2011 BCSC 1588, para. 18 (Can.).

26. *Id.* para. 21. Interested Person status corresponds more closely to what would be termed an amicus in a United States court.

27. *Id.* paras. 21–22.

28. 760 F.2d 1065 (10th Cir. 1985) (holding that a police officer's termination of employment due to his practice of polygamy did not violate his right to free exercise of religion).
29. 99 P.3d 820 (Utah 2004).
30. 137 P.3d 726 (Utah 2006).
31. 947 F.Supp. 2d at 1190.
32. *Id.* at 1189 ("*Reynolds* is not, or should no longer be considered, good law . . . .").
33. 508 U.S. 520 (1993) (finding a law to be operationally non-neutral and not of general applicability because the prohibition of animal slaughter contained so many exemptions that in the end it only targeted a particular religion's practice of animal sacrifice).
34. *Brown*, 947 F. Supp. 2d at 1222–25.
35. *Id.* at 1217–22.
36. *Reference*, 2011 BCSC 1588, para. 1331 (Can.).
37. *Id.* para. 1332.
38. *Id.* para. 885.
39. *Id.* para. 883.
40. *Id.* para. 576.
41. *Id.* para. 1343.
42. *Id.* paras. 487–491.
43. Dr. Joseph Henrich is "an Associate Professor in the Psychology and Economics Departments at the University of British Columbia. He also holds a prestigious Tier 1 Canada Research Chair in Culture, Cognition and Evolution," and he "was qualified as an expert in psychology, particularly evolutionary psychology, in economics and in anthropology, as well as in the interdisciplinary field of culture, cognition and co-evolution." *Id.* para. 495.
44. *Id.* para. 496.
45. Dr. Grossbard is a Professor of Economics at San Diego State University. *Id.* para. 588.
46. *Id.* paras. 589–590.
47. "Dr. Rose McDermott is a Professor of Political Science at Brown University. She also holds an M.A. in Experimental Social Psychology from Stanford University." *Id.* para. 580.
48. *Id.* paras. 609–612 (describing the work of Dr. Rose McDermott); *see also* Rose McDermott & Jonathan Cowden, *Polygyny and Violence Against Women*, 64 EMORY L.J. 1767 (2015).
49. *Reference*, 2011 BCSC 1588, paras. 613–615 (describing Dr. McDermott's Woman-Stats Project Database and another database).
50. *Id.* para. 624.
51. *Id.* para. 492.
52. *Id.* para. 1045.
53. *Id.*
54. *Id.* para. 772.
55. *See id.*
56. *Id.* para. 1044; *see also id.* para. 792 (finding that positive witness accounts could not withstand "the overwhelming weight of the evidence that polygyny has harmful consequences for both the individuals involved and the societies of which they are a part").
57. *Id.* para. 1333.
58. *Id.* para. 505.
59. *Id.*
60. *Id.* paras. 500, 555.
61. *Id.* para. 505 (omissions in original).
62. *Id.* para. 586.
63. *Id.* para. 779.
64. *Id.* para. 499; *see also id.* paras. 523–533, 621.

65. *Id.* para. 621.
66. *Id.* para. 784.
67. *Id.* para. 782.
68. *Id.* paras. 621, 784.
69. *Id.* paras. 622, 789.
70. *Id.* para. 533.
71. *Id.* para. 779.
72. *Id.* para. 532.
73. *Id.* para. 782.
74. *Id.* para. 621.
75. *Id.* paras. 532–533.
76. *Id.* paras. 584, 621.
77. *Id.* para. 621.
78. *Id.* para. 622.
79. *Id.* para. 584.
80. *Id.* para. 782.
81. *Id.*
82. *Id.*; *see also id.* paras. 603, 607–608, 696, 699–700, 780.
83. *Id.* para. 779.
84. *Id.* para. 783; *see also id.* para. 603.
85. *Id.* para. 621.
86. *Id.* para. 785.
87. *Id.* para. 586.
88. *Id.* paras. 586, 789.
89. *Id.* para. 505.
90. *Id.* paras. 499, 507–516, 587, 787.
91. *Id.* paras. 534, 536.
92. *Id.* para. 536.
93. *Id.* para. 621.
94. *Id.* para. 790.
95. *Id.* para. 787.
96. *Id.*
97. *Id.* para. 789.
98. *Id.* para. 787.
99. *See supra* note 146 and accompanying text.
100. *Reference*, 2011 BCSC 1588, para. 787.
101. *Id.* para. 621.
102. *Id.* para. 535.
103. *Cf. Potter*, 585 F. Supp. 1139–40 (arguing that should polygamy be decriminalized, and perhaps even legally recognized, it would be difficult to contain).
104. *Reference*, 2011 BCSC 1588, paras. 556, 558, 560, 567–568, 570, 573, 1317.
105. *Id.* para. 575.
106. *Id.* paras. 500–501, 575, 1304.
107. *Id.* paras. 555, 621, 649.
108. *Id.* para. 884.
109. *Compare id.* paras. 1142–1145 (summarizing arguments that the Canadian statute was overbroad because it prohibits polygamous relationships between consenting adults, penalizes coerced spouses the same as coercing spouses, penalizes beneficial polygamous relationships, and fails to address the actual abusive harms, which are in any event already addressed by other criminal statutes), *with* Brown v. Buhman, 947 F. Supp. 2d 1170, 1219–21 (D. Utah 2013) (finding Utah statute not narrowly tailored because there was no evidence of a causal relationship between polygamy and sexual abuse and financial neglect of children and other criminal statutes are sufficient to address these abuses).
110. *Brown*, 947. F. Supp. 2d at 1178 & n.5.

111. *Id.* at 1776. The investigation was closed after the constitutional challenge was filed, and the State then sought to dismiss the case for mootness, thus avoiding the constitutional review of the statute. However, while the current prosecutor assured the court that he would not prosecute the Browns unless he were to find that they also committed a collateral crime, such as child or spousal abuse, he could not assure the court that a future prosecutor would not seek to charge the Browns for their polygamy. *Id.* at 1179.

112. *Id.* at 1176-77.

113. 947 F. Supp. 2d at 1217.

114. 508 U.S. 520, 525–26 (1993).

115. *Id.* at 525.

116. 494 U.S. 872 (1990) (holding that a law prohibiting the use of peyote did not unconstitutionally infringe upon the free exercise rights of Native Americans who use peyote in religious rituals).

117. See *Hialeah*, 508 U.S. at 531 (citing *Smith*, 494 U.S. 872).

118. *Id.* at 531–32.

119. *Id.* at 533.

120. *Id.* at 535.

121. *Id.* The Court cited *Davis v. Beason*, 133 U.S. 333 (1890), where the Court previously held that mere membership in the Mormon Church, which at the time was still performing polygamous marriages, was a legitimate basis for denying an applicant the right to vote, and *Reynolds v. United States*, 98 U.S. 145 (1879). *Hialeah*, 508 U.S. at 535.

122. *Hialeah*, 508 U.S. at 535 (quoting Walz v. Tax Comm'n of the City of New York, 397 U.S. 664, 696 (1970) (Harlan, J., concurring)) (internal quotation marks omitted).

123. *Id.* at 536.

124. *Id.* at 538.

125. *Id.* at 540–41 (plurality opinion).

126. *Id.* at 543 (majority opinion).

127. Cohen v. Cowles Media Co., 501 U.S. 663, 670 (1991) (finding promissory estoppel was a law of general applicability that could be used to force a newspaper to pay damages for breaking a confidentiality promise without offending the First Amendment). *Cohen* was cited by *Hialeah* as an example of the principle of general applicability. 508 U.S. at 543.

128. *Hialeah*, 508 U.S. at 543.

129. *Id.* at 543–46.

130. *Id.* at 545 (alteration in original) (quoting Florida Star v. B.J.F., 491 U.S. 524, 542 (1989) (Scalia, J., concurring in part and concurring in judgment)) (internal quotation mark omitted).

131. *Id.* at 546 (quoting Wisconsin v. Yoder, 406 U.S. 205, 215 (1972)).

132. *Id.* at 546–47.

133. UTAH CODE ANN. § 76-7-101(1) (West 2004).

134. 99 P.3d 820, 832 (Utah 2004).

135. Id. at 822.

136. Id.

137. Id. at 823.

138. Id. at 831–32 ("[Green] referred to each of these women as a wife, regardless of whether a licensed marriage existed. The women likewise considered themselves Green's wives and adopted his surname. Green spent nights with each woman on a rotating schedule and succeeded in impregnating these four women eighteen times . . . . The children born of these associations also use the Green surname. Together, Green and the women undertook spousal and parental obligations. . . . [T]hey shared a group of mobile homes, 'Green Haven,' that possessed common areas for the entire family's use.").

139. Green's prosecution for cohabitation rather than for purporting to marry by either invalid licensed marriages or unlicensed ceremonial marriages was dictated by

the facts in his case. He had sequentially legally married and then divorced three of the five wives named in the indictment. 99 P.3d at 822 n.4. Of the two nonlegal religious marriage ceremonies that could have come under the purport to marry language, at least one took place outside of Utah, State v. Green, 108 P.3d 710, 713 (Utah 2005), and both were outside the four year statute of limitations for felonies, see UTAH CODE ANN. § 76-1-302 (LexisNexis 1999), by the time of the 2000indictment. See Green, 99 P.3d at 822 n.4, 823; see also State v. Ishaque, 711 A.2d 416, 418 (N.J. Super. Ct. Law Div. 1997) ("[C]ourts have consistently ruled that they are without jurisdiction to prosecute a defendant for a bigamous marriage solemnized in another state.").

140. *Holm*, 137 P.3d at 730.

141. Id.

142. Id.

143. . Id.

144. Id. at 731.

145. Id. at 731–32.

146. *Holm*, 137 P.3d 742 (following *Green*'s free exercise analysis); *Green*, 99 P.3d 827–28.

147. *Green*, 99 P.3d at 827.

148. 765 P.2d 1 (Utah Ct. App. 1988).

149. UTAH CODE ANN. § 76-7-101(1) (West 2004).

150. *Geer*, 765 P.2d at 2.

151. *Id.* at 3.

152. *Brown*, 947 F. Supp. 2d at 1217.

153. *Id.* at 1209.

154. *Id.* at 1190

155. *Geer*, 765 P.2d at 3

156. *Reynolds*, 98 U.S.at, 161.

157. *Brown*, 947 F. Supp. 2d at 1198.

158. *Id.* at 1181.

159. *Id.* at 1197 (first two alterations in original) (quoting *Holm*, 137 P.3d at 773 (Durham, C.J., concurring in part and dissenting in part)) (some internal quotation marks omitted).

160. *Id.* at 1203–05.

161. *Id.* at 1209.

162. This is not the case, however, as I argue below.

163. The court made it more than clear that it thought that *Reynolds* should in fact be struck down, but backed away from doing so. *Brown*, 947 F. Supp. 2d at 1188–89, 1204 n.49.

164. *Hialeah*, 508 U.S. at 526–28 (1993) (discussing Ordinance 87-40, incorporating Florida's animal cruelty laws; Ordinance 87-52, defining sacrifice as unnecessary killing of an animal in a ritual not primarily for food consumption; Ordinance 87-71, making it unlawful to sacrifice animals in City of Hialeah; and Ordinance 87-72, defining slaughter and prohibiting it outside areas not zoned for this purpose).

165. *Id.* at 535–40.

166. *Id.* at 535 (quoting Walz v. Tax Comm'n of the City of New York, 397 U.S. 664, 696 (1970) (Harlan, J., concurring)) (internal quotation marks omitted).

167. *Id.* at 537 ("A pattern of exemptions parallels the pattern of narrow prohibitions.").

168. *Id.* at 539–40.

169. *Id.* at 540.

170. Edmunds Anti-Polygamy Act of 1882, ch. 47, § 3, 22 Stat. 30, 31 (repealed 1910) (broading the coverage of criminal polygamy to include simultaneous marriages and cohabitation so as to capture attempts to evade the prohibition of polygamy by engaging in simultaneous marriages or not obtaining marriage licenses for multiple wives married in religious ceremonies).

171. *See Hialeah*, 508 U.S. at 542 ("[T]he texts of the ordinances were gerrymandered with care to proscribe religious killings of animals but to exclude almost all secular killings . . . .").
172. *Brown*, 947 F. Supp. 2d at 1210 (quoting *Holm*, 137 P.3d at 772 (Durham, C.J., concurring in part and dissenting in part)).
173. *Id.* (quoting *Holm*, 137 P.3d at 771–72 (Durham, C.J., concurring in part and dissenting in part)).
174. UTAH CODE ANN. § 76-7-103(1) (West 2004) ("A married person commits adultery when he voluntarily has sexual intercourse with a person other than his spouse.").
175. *Brown*, 947 F. Supp. 2d at 1210.
176. *Brown*, 947 F. Supp. 2d at 1210 (quoting *Holm*, 137 P.3d at 772 (Durham, C.J., concurring in part and dissenting in part)).
177. *Brown*, 947 F. Supp. 2d at 1210 (alterations in original) (quoting *Hialeah*, 508 U.S. at 536) (internal quotation marks omitted).
178. *See* Cannon v. United States, 6 S.Ct 278, 287 (1885) (holding that polygamous cohabitation could be proven by evidence that the defendant lived with multiple women he held out as his wives, even without proof of a shared bed or sexual intercourse).
179. UTAH CODE ANN. § 30-1-4.5 (West 2014) (addressing validity of marriage not solemnized)
180. *Id.*
181. Whyte v. Blair, 885 P.2d 791, 795 (Utah 1994) (holding that evidence of reputation, cohabitation, and assumptions of marital obligations were insufficient without evidence of consent, which could be shown by a written agreement; witness evidence of an oral agreement; joint banking or joint credit accounts; joint ownership of property; use of a man's name by a woman, children, or both of the relationship; filing joint tax returns; stating they are married in formal documents, such as deeds and wills; and telling third parties they are married).
182. *See* Haddow v. Haddow, 707 P.2d 669, 671–72 (Utah 1985) (noting that "the term 'cohabitation' does not lend itself to a universal definition that is applicable in all settings" and that "[t]o some extent, the meaning of the term depends upon the context in which it is used," and interpreting a divorce decree requiring payment of half the equity in the marital home if the ex-wife "cohabit[ed]" to require "common residency and sexual contact").
183. *Id.* at 672; *see also* Richards v. Brown, 274 P.3d 911, 913–14 (Utah 2012) (describing the trial court's finding that cohabitation ceased *no later* than when one party moved out of the shared home, implying that it could have occurred four years earlier when, after six years together, the parties ceased sexual relations).
184. *Green*, 99 P.3d at 832.
185. *Id.* at 831.
186. *Id.* at 831–32.
187. *Id.* at 832.
188. *Id.* at 831.
189. *Id.* at 823.
190. *Brown*, 947 F. Supp. 2d at 1211.
191. 885 P.2d 791 (Utah 1994).
192. *Holm*, 137 P.3d at 735.
193. *Id.* (quoting *Whyte*, 885 P.2d at 793).
194. *Whyte*, 885 P.2d at 792.
195. *Id.*
196. *Id.* at 795.
197. *Id.*
198. UTAH CODE ANN. § 30-1-4.5(1) (West 2014).

199. *Green*, 99 P.3d at 833–34(finding the State's use of the common law or "unsolemnized marriage statute" to establish Green's legal marriage to one woman while cohabiting with four others as appropriate).

200. *See* Penelope E. Andrews, "Big Love"? *The Recognition of Customary Marriages in South Africa*, 64 WASH. & LEE L. REV. 1483, 1493–95 (2007) (describing South Africa's Recognition of Customary Marriages Act, which recognizes polygamous marriages performed according to indigenous law).

201. It is estimated that there are currently "at least 15,000 African refugees in Utah." Elaine Jarvik, *Africans Pull Together in Utah, 8,000 Miles from Homeland*, DESERET NEWS (Aug. 8, 2010, 8:18 PM MDT), http://www.deseretnews.com/article/700054903/Africans-pull-together-in-Utah-8000-miles-from-homeland.htm.

202. *Brown*, 947 F. Supp. 2d at1226–34 (holding that the only constitutional application of the purports to marry language is to criminalize multiple attempted legal marriages).

203. *Holm*, 137 P.3d at737.

204. *Id.*

205. *Brown*, 947 F. Supp. 2d at 1212.

206. *Holm*, 137 P.3d at 737.

207. *Id.*

208. In marital cohabitation, the bond is created by "consent" to what amounts to a marital contract, which the state will enforce if the parties have the capacity to marry through the common law marriage statute. *See supra* notes 302–05 and accompanying text.

209. *See Holm*, 137 P.2d at 736 (describing Warren Jeffs, an official of the FLDS Church, who conducted the ceremony and strangely included in the vows that each was to become the "lawful and wedded" spouse of the other).

210. I know of one such case from my own personal knowledge.

211. UTAH CODE ANN. § 30-1-15(2) (West 2014).

212. *Holm*, 137 P.2d at 737.

213. *Reynolds*, 98 U.S. at 165.

214. *Holm*, 137 P.3d at 731.

215. *Reynolds*, 98 U.S. at 163.

216. *Brown*, 947 F. Supp. 2d at1216(quoting *Holm*, 137 P.3d at 775 (Durham, C.J., concurring in part and dissenting in part)).

217. *Id.* at 1215–16. There is no question that Utah has some ambivalence about its bigamy law as it applies to polygamy. In 1953, Arizona attempted to enforce its previous bigamy law by a mass arrest of polygamists in the community of Short Creek. The men and women were arrested, and children were taken into state custody. The result was a public relations nightmare for the state and weakened the appetite of the state to confront religious polygamists using its criminal law. *See* Neil J. Young, *Short Creek's Long Legacy*, SLATE (Apr. 16, 2008, 1:15 P.M.), http://www.slate.com/articles/life/faithbased/2008/04/short_creeks_long_legacy.html (describing the public backlash to the raid).

Changing sexual mores and attitudes toward the role of the criminal law regarding premarital sex, divorce, and adultery also weakened moral condemnations of polygamy, and the Supreme Court's decision in *Lawrence v. Texas* holding criminalization of homosexuality unconstitutional undermined moral justifications for the criminalization of polygamy.

218. *Holm*, 137 P.3d at 730.

219. *Green*, 108 P.3d at 713.

220. *Brown*, 947 F. Supp. 2d at 1216.

221. *Id.* at 1179.

222. *Id.*

223. *Id.* at 1216.

224. *Id.* at 1217.

225. *Id.* at 1216.

226. State v. Geer, 765 P.2d 1, 3 (Utah Ct. App. 1988).

227. *Hialeah*, 508 U.S. at 543.

228. *See* JANET BENNION, POLYGAMY IN PRIMETIME: MEDIA, GENDER, AND POLITICS IN MORMON FUNDAMENTALISM 27 (2012); *see also* Young, *supra* note

229. *Accord Reference*, 2011 BCSC 1588, paras. 1337–1338 (Can.) (emphasizing the deterrent effect of the law on those who take the rule of law seriously and rejecting arguments against the law based on the "miniscule number of prosecutions over the provision's 120 year history").

230. Divorce is certainly recognized as harmful to children and women, but it does not have the broader harmful social effects of polygamy described above.

231. Id. at 1218.

232. Id. (quoting *Holm*, 137 P.3d at 772 (Durham, C.J., concurring in part and dissenting in part)) (internal quotation mark omitted).

233. Id. at 1224.

234. See supra Part II.A.3.b.

235. *Holm*, 137 P.3d at 743 ("[D]ecisions made by individuals as to how to structure even the most personal of relationships are capable of dramatically affecting public life.").

236. Id. ("[T]he formation of relationships that are marital in nature is of great interest to this State, no matter what the participants in or the observers of that relationship venture to name the union.").

237. *Brown*, 947 F. Supp. 2d at 1223–24 (alteration in original) (internal quotation marks omitted).

238. See supra Part II.A.3.b.

239. *Reference*, 2011 BCSC 1588, para. 1081.

240. See Maura Strassberg, The Crime of Polygamy, 12 TEMP. POL. & CIV. RTS. L. REV. 353, 382 (2003) (noting that, according to Mormon fundamentalist religious doctrine, women who refuse to enter into polygamy are damned to hell); see also *Reference*, 2011 BCSC 1588, para. 318 (observing that "plural marriage is essential to personal and family salvation" for members of the FLDS fundamentalist sect).

241. Fundamentalist Church of Jesus Christ of Latter-Day Saints, SPLC, http://www.splcenter.org/getinformed/ intelligence-files/groups/fundamentalist-church-of-jesus-christ-of-latter-day-saints (last visited May 17, 2015) (describing the repressive rule of Prophet Warren Jeffs).

242. BONNIE L. PETERS, FAMILY SUPPORT CTR., THE PRIMER: A GUIDEBOOK FOR LAW ENFORCEMENT AND HUMAN SERVICES AGENCIES WHO OFFER ASSISTANCE TO FUNDAMENTALIST MORMON FAMILIES 18 (2011), available at http://www.familysupportcenter.org/Primer.pdf ("It has been alleged that the FLDS church controls the police force, city council, city government, and elected officials."); id. at 19 (noting that a church trust "owns most of the land, housing and businesses in the community").

243. Accord Michah Gottlieb, *Are We All Protestants Now?*, JEWISH REV. BOOKS, Summer 2012, at 15, 17 (2012) (book review) (describing similar coercion in the context of ultra-Orthodox Jewish communities as a result of "their poor command of English and lack of secular education" and noting the paradox "that while the ultra-Orthodox justify their separatism by appealing to religious freedom, they use that freedom to restrict the freedom of their individual members").

244. See supra Part I.B.2.

245. *Reference*, 2011 BCSC 1588, paras. 330, 649, 653 (Can.).

246. See Strassberg, *Distinctions of Form or Substance: Monogamy, Polygamy and Same-Sex Marriage, 75 N.C. L. Rev. 1501*, 1579 (1997).

247. PETERS, supra note 366, at 11–12.

248. *Id.* at 13. Contact with the non-polygamous world does, however, create the possibility of bringing new women into the community and polygamous marriage. For example, Kody Brown's first, third, and fourth wives came from within the Apos-

tolic United Brethren polygamous families, while his second wife was not raised in a polygamous family. BENNION, supra note 335, at 183.

249. 406 U.S. 205 (1972)(holding that Wisconsin's mandatory school attendance laws violated the free exercise rights of the Amish).

250. See MARCI HAMILTON, GOD VS. THE GAVEL 64 (rev. 2ND ed. 2014) (criticizing Yoder for making Amish children "martyr[s] to their parents' faith"); JEFFREY SHULMAN, THE CONSTITUTIONAL PARENT 200 (2014) ("[I]s not schooling beyond the eighth grade a prerequisite for the information and self-confidence required for independent judgment?").

251. HAMILTON, GOD VS. THE GAVEL 5–6 (describing Yoder as "a love letter to the Amish," whom the Court saw as upstanding citizens and parents, and noting how more recently the Amish have been shown to have serious issues with alcoholism, violence, incest, and practices of shunning that punish rape victims).

REFERENCES

Andrews, Penelope E. *"Big Love"? The Recognition of Customary Marriages in South Africa*, 64 Wash. & Lee L. Rev. 1483(2007).

Bennion, Janet. POLYGAMY IN PRIMETIME: MEDIA, GENDER, AND POLITICS IN MORMON FUNDAMENTALISM (2012).

Bostic v. Schaefer, 760 F.3d 352 (4th Cir. 2014).

Brown v. Buhman, 947 F. Supp. 2d 1170, 1190 (D. Utah 2013), vacated and remanded, Brown v. Buhman, 2016 WL 2848510 (10th Cir.).

Cannon v. United States, 6 S. Ct 278 (1885).

Church of the Lukumi Babalu Aye, Inc. v. City of Hialeah, 508 U.S. 520 (1993).

Constitutional Question Act, R.S.B.C. 1996, c. 68, s. 1 (Can.).

Davis v. Beason, 133 U.S. 333 (1890).

Edmunds Anti-Polygamy Act of 1882, ch. 47, § 3, 22 Stat. 30, 31 (repealed 1910).

Employment Division v. Smith, 494 U.S. 872, (1990).

Fundamentalist Church of Jesus Christ of Latter-Day Saints, SPLC, http://www.splcenter.org/getinformed/intelligence-files/groups/fundamentalist-church-of-jesus-christ-of-latter-day-saints (last visited May 17, 2015).

Gottlieb, Michah. *Are We All Protestants Now?*, Jewish Rev. Books, Summer 2012, at 15, 17 (2012).

Haddow v. Haddow, 707 P.2d 669 (Utah 1985).

Jarvik, Elaine. *Africans Pull Together in Utah, 8,000 Miles from Homeland*, Deseret News (Aug. 8, 2010, 8:18 PM MDT), http://www.deseretnews.com/article/700054903/Africans-pull-together-in-Utah-8000-miles-from- homeland.htm.

Kitchen v. Herbert, 755 F.3d 1193 (10th Cir. 2014).

Lawrence v. Texas, 539 U.S. 558, 578–79 (2003).

Hamilton, Marci. GOD VS. THE GAVEL 64 (rev. 2ND ed. 2014).

McDermott, Rose and Jonathan Cowden. *Polygyny and Violence Against Women*, 64 Emory L.J. 1767 (2015).

Osborn v. Bank of the U.S., 22 U.S. (9 Wheat.) 738 (1824).

Peters, Bonnie L. FAMILY SUPPORT CTR., THE PRIMER: A GUIDEBOOK FOR LAW ENFORCEMENT AND HUMAN SERVICES AGENCIES WHO OFFER ASSISTANCE TO FUNDAMENTALIST MORMON FAMILIES 18 (2011), available at http://www.familysupportcenter.org/Primer.pdf.

Potter v. Murray City, 760 F.2d 1065 (10th Cir. 1985).

Reference re: Section 293 of the Criminal Code of Canada, 2011 BCSC 1588 (Can.).

Reynolds v. United States, 98 U.S. 145 (1879).

Richards v. Brown, 274 P.3d 911 (Utah 2012).

Shulman, Jeffrey. THE CONSTITUTIONAL PARENT (2014).

State v. Geer, 765 P.2d 1 (Utah Ct. App. 1988).

State v. Green, 99 P.3d 820 (Utah 2004).

State v. Holm, 137 P.3d 726 (Utah 2006).

State v. Ishaque, 711 A.2d 416, 418 (N.J. Super. Ct. Law Div. 1997).

Strassberg, Maura. *Distinctions of Form or Substance: Monogamy, Polygamy and Same-Sex Marriage, 75 N.C. L. Rev. 1501* (1997).

Strassberg, Maura. The Crime of Polygamy, 12 Temp. Pol. & Civ. Rts. L. Rev. 353 (2003).

United States Constitution, art. III, §§ 1–2.

United States v. Windsor, 133 S. Ct. 2675 (2013).

UTAH CODE ANN. § 30-1-4.5 (West 2014).

UTAH CODE ANN. § 30-1-15(2) (West 2014).

UTAH CODE ANN. § 76-7-101(1) (West 2004).

UTAH CODE ANN. § 76-7-103(1) (West 2004).

UTAH CODE ANN. § 76-1-302 (LexisNexis 1999).

Whyte v. Blair, 885 P.2d 791(Utah 1994).

Yoder v. Wisconsin, 406 U.S. 205 (1972).

Young, Neil J. *Short Creek's Long Legacy*, Slate (Apr. 16, 2008, 1:15 P.M.), http://www.slate.com/articles/life/faithbased/2008/04/short_creeks_long_legacy.html.

TEN

The Paradox of Big Love in the Liberal State: Treating Adults like Children and Children like Adults

Olivia Newman

This chapter is about how the liberal state should respond to the unequal treatment of FLDS women and girls who voluntarily practice polygyny.[1] The number of Americans who practice polygyny is relatively small. Because polygyny occupies a legal gray zone, it is difficult to get accurate numbers, but it is estimated that there are 36,000 fundamentalist Mormons who engage in the practice, between 50,000 and 100,000 Muslims, and about 14,000 non-Mormon Christians.[2] While polygyny is uncommon, it has captured the attention and imagination of the broader American public, thanks to a successful HBO drama, *Big Love,* about a polygynous family in the suburbs of Salt Lake City, as well as the ultimately unsuccessful raid on a Fundamentalist Jesus Christ of Latter-Day Saints (FLDS) Yearning for Zion Ranch (YFZ) in Eldorado, Texas in 2008. *Big Love* portrays plural marriage as a complex tradition that can be practiced in ways that are more and less acceptable to liberal sensibilities. The main characters—a husband and his three wives—vary in their levels of religious commitment, independence, and autonomy, but each chose their lifestyle for reasons that are not patently unreasonable. The show urges its audience not to judge these people too harshly—they are different, to be sure, but not *so very different* from ordinary Americans. They wear the same clothes, they send their children to the same schools, and they worry about the same things.[3]

The picture that emerged in Texas is quite different. In April of 2008, Texas officials raided the YFZ Ranch after receiving an anonymous tip alleging sexual misconduct with underage girls. When all was said and done, over 460 children had been forcibly removed from their home due to allegations of sexual abuse and the marriage of underage girls to much older men. Many families were separated for months while social workers and investigators struggled to piece together the branches of very complicated family trees at YFZ Ranch, where many residents share the last names of Jeffs or Jessop. In the end, all but one child was returned to their families.[4] Twelve girls between the ages of 12 and 15 were returned to the ranch in spite of their marriages to older men. Seven of these girls already had children of their own. Several men were convicted of sexual assault of a child. Warren Jeffs was convicted of sexual assault of a child and as an accomplice to rape for his role in arranging marriages between underage girls and older men.[5]

Public opinion of the raid ranged from curiosity and disdain regarding the FLDS lifestyle to concerns regarding the nature of the raid, which was widely seen as unnecessarily forceful and which the Texas Supreme Court found to be unjustified.[6] But these two pictures of polygyny remain, and each tells part of a very interesting story. It is true, as *Big Love* suggests, that roughly half of polygynous fundamentalist Mormons are "independent fundamentalists," unaffiliated with any group and assimilated, more or less, into mainstream culture.[7] The other half, however, belong to various groups, like the FLDS, that remain relatively isolated and whose practices raise concerns regarding the treatment of women and girls.[8]

What is the liberal state to do, then, when groups engage in practices that seem to threaten the wellbeing of some of their members? Of course, this question is difficult to address on even the most practical level, as the raid on YFZ Ranch reveals. How can the state prove abuse when there are no forthcoming witnesses? When are the costs of raids too high, particularly regarding the disruption to families and the wellbeing of children? These are important questions. But I want to step back from these practical matters to pose a more fundamental normative question: How should the liberal state respond to the unequal treatment of women and girls when many women themselves endorse these practices?

This chapter explores this tension, asking how the concept of "consent" can clarify the discussion. Focusing on consent will immediately draw our attention to the critical differences between consenting adults and children who are too young to offer consent or fend off family and community efforts to groom them for potentially oppressive future relationships. Ultimately, I argue that polygamy (including but not limited to polygyny) should have the same legal status as monogamous marriages. While plural marriage raises difficult questions about the treatment of women, at least in some circumstances, these concerns do not diminish the individual right to live as one wishes, even when that includes (arguably) subjecting oneself to oppression. But this permissive approach can only be justified, I insist, if the state does considerably more to ensure that young people have a robust understanding of their own rights, including the right of exit from their communities. I conclude with thoughts on the kinds of practical demands this may place on the liberal state.

BETWEEN A ROCK AND A HARD PLACE: LIBERALISM AND POLYGYNY

Liberal theory has a Goldilocks problem: it is at times accused of being steadfastly indifferent to serious injustices in the private sphere (a claim many feminists make),[9] while at other times it is accused of prying too deeply into private affairs in order to enforce a divisive and sectarian notion of justice (a claim many religious true believers make).[10] Liberal theory is very rarely "just right." This tension can be understood as the clash between toleration and autonomy, as it is sometimes described,[11] or between multiculturalism and liberalism:[12] should the liberal state tolerate practices which diminish some individuals' autonomy or equality? This characterization highlights the ways in which cultural or religious groups may engage in practices which infringe upon their own members' rights, often (but not always!) with the seeming consent of those affected. Such practices include genital cutting; veiling; and traditional, patriarchal gender roles; as well as plural marriage. These practices are typically gendered, putting women and girls at a greater disadvantage. Susan Moller Okin posits that this state of affairs comes about due to the special role that women often play in the reproduction of culture.[13]

Plural marriage proves to be a particularly challenging test case for liberal theory, since John Stuart Mill grappled with what he called the "Mormonite Doctrine" in his 1859 *On Liberty*. Like many others then and now, Mill disdained Mormon plural marriage as an inequitable social arrangement. At the same time, he recognized the centrality of allowing individuals to live as they choose, even if that includes entering a polygamous marriage. I quote Mill at length, because his comments are still so instructive to these questions:

> No one has a deeper disapprobation than I have of this Mormon institution [plural marriage]; both for other reasons, and because, far from being in any way countenanced by the principle of liberty, it is a direct infraction of that principle, being a mere riveting of the chains of one-half of the community, and an emancipation of the other from reciprocity of obligation towards them. Still, it must be remembered that this relation is as much voluntary on the part of the women concerned in it, and who may be deemed the sufferers by it, as is the case with any other form of the marriage institution; and however surprising this fact may appear, it has its explanation in the common ideas and customs of

> the world, which teaching women to think marriage the one thing needful, make it intelligible that many a woman should prefer being one of several wives, to not being a wife at all. . . . A recent writer, in some respects of considerable merit, proposes (to use his own words) not a crusade, but a *civilizade,* against this polygamous community, to put an end to what seems to him a retrograde step in civilization. It also appears so to me, but I am not aware that any community has a right to force another to be civilized. . . . Let them send missionaries, if they please, to preach against it; and let them, by any fair means (of which silencing the teachers is not one,) oppose the progress of similar doctrines among their own people.[14]

Mill struggles here to balance the liberty to practice polygyny with his commitment to women's equality, which he presumes polygyny diminishes. He notes, though, that the women in question seem to endorse it, which obviously complicates any efforts to eradicate it. After all, their consent could negate what would otherwise be a morally impermissible practice. If all women were obviously coerced into polygyny, then a liberal state would quickly step in to end the practice. But as Mill recognizes elsewhere in *On Liberty* and in *The Subjection of Women,* our preferences are often distorted by received wisdom and the "despotism of culture." Perhaps these women have been misled by their communities.

Mill chooses to err—reluctantly, perhaps—on the side of tolerance and forbearance for polygamy, with two conditions. The first is that women must have a robust right of exit, which he describes as "perfect freedom of departure to those who are dissatisfied with their ways."[15] The second, which is only implicit, is that arguments *against* polygamy be allowed to circulate in the general marketplace of ideas. The availability of arguments against polygamy, Mill seems to assume, will increase the prejudices against polygamy.[16] It is also worth noting that Mill's own distaste for polygamy does not prevent him from recognizing that it arises from the same Victorian cultural values (namely that marriage is the only thing "needful for women") as monogamy.

Contemporary polygyny raises the same concerns regarding gender equality, in principle and in practice. It is certainly true that adults may legitimately consent to many practices that subject them to the power and authority of other individuals—in education or employment, for example. But polygyny is embedded in an institutionalized and clearly articulated form of patriarchy that extends over many domains of life. Of course, this patriarchy is unproblematic from the perspective of many polygynous families. The pro-polygamy group *Plural Voices* explains that patriarchy can, "provide strong leadership with democratic family support and respect for the traditional roles of each member," and only becomes concerning "when the husband sees himself as God, but doesn't exercise the attributes of Godliness," in which case, "there may be tyranny, but it only continues if the wives support it. Otherwise, he finds himself outnumbered and eventually (if he doesn't change) alone."[17] Anne Wilde, a founder of *Plural Voices*, insists that the chances of overbearing, abusive husbands are no greater in polygynous marriages than they are in monogamous ones.[18]

From a properly feminist liberal perspective, however, patriarchy represents a distribution of power that, however benevolently it is exercised, is inherently unequal and hence problematic. One of the most troubling features of patriarchy involves the way that it seems to reproduce itself by inculcating its values in the next generation.[19] Hence, children who grow up in a patriarchal family may come to prefer this lifestyle for themselves as adults. This concern is widely shared across academic fields. Feminist theorists of relational autonomy worry that social context can hinder the development of genuine preferences and autonomous choice.[20] Philosophers like Martha Nussbaum have carefully documented the ways in which women's autonomy may be compromised by their social milieus and lack of education.[21] And for many liberals, a limited education for children may lead to a diminished capacity for autonomy as adults.[22] The central issue, then, concerns the preferences of women in polygynous arrangements: are we to take them at face value—as the preferences of adults who may live their lives any way they see fit—or should we view them with skepticism—as preferences that may have formed in insular and oppressive circumstances? Can we do the latter without relying on paternalistic claims of "false consciousness"?

Nussbaum captures this dilemma nicely when she asks how much weight we should give to women's preferences and desires when evaluating the legitimacy of political and social arrangements. She concludes that we ought to avoid "trusting desire too much," since desires can be distorted in all sorts of ways, while also recognizing the importance of trusting desires "a little bit," since what people actually want must count for something.[23]

So this is the rub. Polygyny, particularly as it is practiced in some communities, raises red flags regarding the treatment of women and girls. These communities go out of their way to shield children from ideas or practices that may challenge their future commitment to plural marriage. At the same time, many women come to genuinely embrace polygyny, and for a wide range of personal reasons that cannot be reduced to fear or indoctrination. The liberal state must decide whether it will err on the side of tolerance regarding these practices, or whether it will instead err on the side of women's rights and freedoms. Neither option is perfect, but both find justification in liberal political thought.

Plural marriage is not the only practice that poses a serious challenge for contemporary liberal thought. Female genital cutting is another familiar example of a practice which occupies a gray area between oppression and consent. Many women and girls promote genital cutting for themselves and for their daughters on a number of grounds, including hygiene, standards of beauty and purity, appeals to the value of tradition, and cultural continuity.[24] There is a stark difference between symbolic cutting and infibulation, whereby the labia are removed and the vagina is stitched shut. There is, additionally, an unquestionable moral difference between an adult or adolescent who seeks genital cutting to fulfill her own standards for beauty or sexuality, and a prepubescent child who is cut against her will.[25] While forced or underage cutting and infibulation seem beyond the pale, the proper response to more modest forms of cutting for teens and adults is not nearly as obvious. A young woman may voluntarily consent to cutting, but we might still worry about her autonomy if she had been raised to believe that her natural body is ugly, or that she will not find a suitable husband if she remains in her natural state. Hence genital cutting is neither so awful that it is self-evidently unacceptable under all circumstances, but neither is it so unequivocally benign that we can turn our backs on it entirely. Contrast this with a practice like human sacrifice, which is beyond a shadow of a doubt unacceptable under all circumstances (a principle William Galston captures with the quip, "No free exercise for Aztecs").[26]

For a much more recent example, consider the German case of the cannibal who found a willing victim through an online want ad. While online chat records suggest that his victim genuinely gave his consent, the cannibal was convicted of murder.[27] No one really believes that such "consent" is genuine or worthy of our respect. Mill captures this sentiment in his famous metaphor of the faulty bridge: if we know that a bridge is faulty, we may warn someone of it, but we cannot forcibly stop him from crossing, as only "he can judge the sufficiency of the motive which may prompt him to incur the risk." But Mill presumes that such risk is undertaken for some greater cause, giving no credence to the possibility that one might "desire to fall in the river."[28] Preferences for self-harm have no independent value for Mill; the German cannibalism case indicates, I think, that most of us share that intuition.

For any egregious infringement of rights that we can imagine, then, we can probably find someone, with full rational capacities, who would willingly consent to it, at least under some circumstances. The question is whether that consent is or could be genuine, and whether it genuineness (or lack thereof) should matter. Philosophers often approach these problems from the perspective of the hypothetical "happy slave." If a slave is happy, is her slavery still morally objectionable? When the question is framed in broadly utilitarian terms, many people continue to seek other grounds for criticizing her slavery, even if she has no complaints. Perhaps her dignity is diminished, her rights are violated, or her autonomy is compromised, even in the face of her ostensible or perhaps real happiness. Slavery can and has been critiqued from each of these perspectives without recourse to the subjective experience of happiness, which is, as we know, hard to define, adaptable, fickle, and easily manipulated.

Indeed, we often lower our expectations to accord with reality. Jon Elster calls this "adaptive preference formation," which he likens this to the fox who, when he realizes that he cannot reach the grapes, rationalizes that they must be sour, anyway.[29] Adaptive preference formation alerts us to the possibility that oppressive circumstances may shape our desires so that we actually endorse our own oppression—which is a thoroughgoing injustice. On the other hand, as Nussbaum notes, some adaptation is natural and even good; what is the point of hopelessly lamenting for the impossible?[30]

Like Elster, Richard Arneson is skeptical of actual preferences, instructing us to ask what an individual's rational preferences *would be*, under the right circumstances.[31] But this kind of approach fails to treat individuals as persons, as their own ends, instead imputing to them a perspective which they may vehemently and perhaps with good reason, reject.[32] We are stuck, then, between relying exclusively on preferences, which might lead us to accept oppression, or instead relying on perfectly rational, hypothetical preferences, which ignores the actual desires of individuals. There appears to be no third way.

Onora O'Neill reframes this question in Kantian, constructivist terms, suggesting that we ask whether given arrangements could win the *possible consent of actual agents*.[33] This approach has the advantage of entailing an inquiry into the circumstances of the actual people involved, rather than imagining a hypothetical or abstract choice situation. But it does not depend upon their actual consent. Rather, it asks whether there was a genuine possibility for refusal or renegotiation. If there was, then as far as O'Neill is concerned, we can accept the consent as genuine and definitive. As she elaborates, "No plurality can choose to live by principles that aim to destroy, undercut or erode the agency (of whatever determinate shape) of some of its members. . . . Victims cannot share the principles on which others destroy or limit their very capacities to act."[34] This requirement implies that individuals cannot possibly endorse arrangements that undermine their future agency. Coercion, violence and deceit are prohibited for the same reasons.

Obviously, every decision opens some doors and shuts others. The standard for agency cannot be that future choices must be unlimited in every logically possible way. Rather, maintaining one's future agency demands that one not endorse arrangements that permanently diminish or eliminate one's ability to make free decisions in the future. Selling oneself into slavery is an obvious example of a decision which compromises future agency. Nussbaum describes this process as "permanently signing away capacities," particularly those which concern health and bodily integrity, since decisions in this realm cannot be undone. But other decisions appear to give up capacities, as well, such as marriage contracts which permanently consigned all decision-making powers to the husband, which are still a live possibility in some parts of the world.[35] For

Nussbaum, genital cutting may cross this line as well, since at least some forms of cutting will permanently diminish the capacity for sexual enjoyment.[36] Of course not all people value sexual enjoyment, but Nussbaum insists that the capacity must be protected so that future choices are not foreclosed.

In her view, polygamy exemplifies a borderline case. As she points out (and I will elaborate in the final part of the chapter), polygamy is not necessarily problematic, particularly when the right to take on additional spouses is extended to men *and* women. But polygamy as it is practiced is linked to a history of sex discrimination, among Muslims, Mormons, and other practitioners. Because she recognizes that it could be equitable, even if it is often not so as currently practiced, Nussbaum concludes that polygamy should be legal, provided that women are guaranteed legal equality and a true right of exit from their community.[37]

As I see it, this is a step in the right direction. At the same time, further steps must be taken to ensure that children will grow up able to truly take advantage of these rights, as I later discuss. Because children eventually become adults, political theorists cannot overlook the extent to which upbringing may make us less worried about whether consent is genuine. Following O'Neill's advice, I inquire into whether polygyny can win the *possible consent of actual agents*. The actual agents I have in mind are women and girls who are raised in fundamentalist polygynous Mormon families. The possible consent I am interested in could be obtained without any violence, coercion or deceit, could truly be refused or renegotiated, and would not forfeit future agency.

POSSIBLE CONSENT OF ACTUAL AGENTS? FUNDAMENTALIST MORMON POLYGYNY

In order to determine whether fundamentalist Mormon polygyny satisfies O'Neill's above criteria, we must attend to the circumstances, past and present, surrounding actual women and girls who consent to plural marriage. What matters here is whether consent could be won in the "right" ways—not whether it is garnered in these ways on every singular occasion. For instance, the institution of monogamous marriage is not seriously threatened by singular cases of coercion or deceit. But if we could not find any real women (or men) who would ever enter this institution freely, or if monogamous marriage were obligatory and could not be refused, then we would have a problem. Of course, some feminists would counter that *enough* monogamous marriages violate these criteria, or anther similar set of criteria, that we must reject marriage altogether. But I don't believe that monogamous marriage has crossed this threshold. Still, polygamy could not be vindicated if the possibilities for free consent were very slight, and rarely if ever actually realized. So "possible" cannot mean that it is barely within the bounds of possibility; it must have some real heft to it.

Before I assess the ways in which women enter polygynous marriages, I will provide a brief overview of the history of polygyny among Mormons. Joseph Smith established the Church of Jesus Christ of Latter-Day Saints (usually referred to as either the Mormon or LDS church) in 1830. Shortly thereafter, Smith received a revelation instructing him to establish the principle of plural marriage, sometimes referred to simply as "The Principle," as a means for men to increase their procreative power and hence reach higher levels of heaven after death. Because polygamy offended Victorian ideas regarding marriage and propriety, Mormons were forced further and further westward, until they settled in the Utah Territory.[38]

In 1852, polygamy became official church doctrine. At its height, it is estimated that 20% of Mormon families were polygynous.[39] In 1890, church leaders were compelled to end the church's official endorsement of polygamy as a condition for Utah's gaining statehood. At that time, LDS President and prophet Wilford Woodroof reported receiving a revelation, instructing Mormons to end plural marriage on the grounds that Mormons must always follow the law of the land.[40] Nevertheless, the church continued to secretly sanction plural marriage until 1904, when it was finally and fully disavowed. Shortly thereafter, the LDS church began excommunicating members engaged in plural marriage.

Not surprisingly, some LDS regarded the church's new position as a betrayal of Mormon principles. These groups splintered off into what are now called "fundamentalist Mormon" groups, which continue to practice plural marriage.[41] As I noted in my introduction, about half of today's fundamentalist Mormons live in more or less insular communities in Utah, Arizona and Texas, as well as Mexico and British Columbia, organized around various prophets. The practice of polygyny varies dramatically across these communities. In some, the prophet arranges all marriages and even "reassigns" wives and children in order to punish men who fall out of favor with church leadership. The FLDS community led by Warren Jeffs is probably the most aggressive in its practice of arranged and underage marriage (although since the 2008 raid, they claim to have ended all "spiritual marriages" for girls under the age of 16).[42] In other communities, and among independent fundamentalists, men and women select their own spouses. And while some husbands unilaterally select subsequent wives, in other families the existing wives have a great deal of say.

It may surprise the reader to learn that the reasons women offer today for entering into polygynous marriage are very similar to the kinds of reasons offered by the early Mormons. It might also surprise him or her to discover how much independence early Mormon women enjoyed in the Utah territory. These women were committed to demonstrating that they entered plural marriage freely—in contrast to the widespread perception "back East" that Mormon women were the degraded puppets of their lustful husbands. In 1886, over two thousand Mormon women gathered in Salt Lake City to address growing anti-polygamist sentiment across the country. Plural wife and medical doctor Ellis Shipp addressed the crowd: "We practice plural marriage . . . not . . . because we are compelled to, but because we are convinced that it is a divine revelation, and we find in this principle satisfaction, contentment, and more happiness than we could obtain in any other relationship."[43]

Shipp is a noteworthy figure because she illustrates the high levels of education and professional advancement enjoyed by many Mormon women at the time. The Church leadership encouraged women to "enlarge their activities," and evidence reveals that many more Mormon women worked outside the home and farm than was common among other pioneer families.[44] Additionally, women in the Utah Territory enjoyed suffrage long before women elsewhere (although they lost the vote as a result of federal legislation in 1887).[45]

In 1872, Mormon women established the journal, *The Woman's Exponent*, on the ground that it is better to represent one's own beliefs, rather than being misrepresented by others. In these pages, women offer a variety of religious, moral, practical and personal reasons for engaging in polygyny. Like other women at this time, Mormon women were committed to Victorian ideals and argued that plural marriage helped to promote these ideals. Consider the following argument made by Lucinda Lee Dalton:

> Since undeniably there are vastly more good women than good men on the earth, who would dare decide that it would not be better for all potent custom to allow two or more of these good women, to marry one good man, than to condemn them, whether they would or not, either to live single or to wed a man a thousand fathoms beneath them?[46]

This reasoning may strike modern readers as unusual, but similar arguments are made today. As the pro-polygamy group *Principle Voices* explains, plural marriage gives "a woman more options to be sealed to a "righteous man."[47] This kind of argument has also been advanced among contemporary black Muslims in inner cities with an abundance of single mothers.[48] Moreover, as the writers for *The Woman's Exponent* explained, men who take additional wives are less likely to abandon women who can't bear children, or to be tempted by prostitution or adultery.[49] For these women, polygyny wasn't the antithesis of Victorian morality—it was its realization.

Early Mormon women also experienced a great deal of independence, as each wife frequently had her own home. As one writer explained in 1894 in *The Woman's Exponent:*

> Whatever other qualities [plural marriage] may engender, it develops strength in character. Women are left to depend more upon their own judgment and to take more full charge of their own home and affairs. It brings out latent and dormant powers. A wife becomes literally the head of her household.[50]

Although Mormon theology only recognizes male leadership, these wives enjoyed a great deal of *de facto* independence, and were often listed by the US Census as "head of household."[51] Wilde makes a similar point regarding women's independence today, explaining that sister wives are able to divide and share household labor in such a way as to support the educational and professional objectives they may each have.[52] For her and for many other contemporary fundamentalists, plural marriage is not just a matter of "strongly held religious belief"; it also offers women a sense of community and cooperation, and it gives women an opportunity to pursue work outside the home without challenging the gendered division of labor. Robyn of the reality show *Sister Wives* describes her household as having "a lot more blessings," including the love and support she receives from the other wives in her family. In a group interview, the husband and four wives agree that plural marriage has allowed them to be better parents for their children, providing a broader network of support. As Meri puts it, plural marriage is "definitely tops for our kids."[53]

Polygynous wives also find in plural marriage the opportunity for self-knowledge and growth. In 1881, Romania Bunnell Pratt Penrose wrote in personal correspondence that, "though [plural marriage] be a fiery furnace for some period of our life, it will prove the one thing needful to cleanse and purify our inmost soul of selfishness, jealousy, and other mundane attributes."[54] Maggie, who lives at the YFZ Ranch today, has a similar view:

> If I didn't live with other women, I would never know about myself. I would never discover the weaknesses in my human flesh. The bottom line of our way of life is self-improvement, and what better way to improve yourself than to live with other women and learn to overcome your bad feelings and jealousy and just live to bless?[55]

Of course, this could easily be interpreted as a rationalization for an otherwise untenable situation. Nevertheless, women then and now regard this "martyr's crown" with approval.[56] This is clearly an asymmetrical concept of sacrifice, which emphasizes the ways in which *women* can grow through hardship. This reasoning does not seem to be as actively applied to men's situations (although sacrifice and hardship are important to Mormon theology generally). While this may be troubling from a feminist perspective, the women who subscribe to this view welcome it, and their feelings cannot be summarily dismissed.

Still, it seems that at least some women are not freely consenting to plural marriage. At one extreme, we see girls as young as twelve being married to older men. Consider Anna Eliza Berry, who was married to her stepfather in 1879 at the age of 14. She writes, "I remember of knelling on the alter and a man talking. Mr. H.C. said yes and after they said to me to say yes I wispered yes not noing what I was saying [sic]." Anna didn't realize she had just been married until the journey home, when her stepfather called her his "little wife."[57] Elisa Wall, who escaped the FLDS community in 2004, was married at the age of 14, against her will, to her 19 year-old first cousin. Elisa knew enough to worry that a union between first cousins might not produce healthy offspring. Beyond that, she reports that she did not know even the basics of anatomy or sex, and was confused and frightened by her husband's attempts at intimacy.[58]

Anna and Elisa offer us portraits of women who saw themselves as victims of an unjust system. But it is likely that some of the women who endorse polygyny had experiences resembling theirs. They may have felt they had little choice in their marriage, or they may have been married at an unsuitably young age, and yet they might still cherish their marriages. Is this post hoc consent genuine or manufactured? Can coercion ever be excused after the fact? It would seem that two factors might play into this: first, whether a given community tries to prohibit coercive and underage marriages; and second, whether women have a real possibility of "exiting" or escaping their marriages and/or communities in the present. I consider both in the final section of this chapter.

Although leaving any marriage can be difficult, the question is whether it is exceedingly more difficult to leave a plural marriage. One challenge that faces wives who wish to leave a plural marriage is legal; only the first wife in a polygamous marriage is married in the eyes of the law. Consequently, subsequent wives have few legal rights against their husband if they choose to leave. As I later explain, I believe that this difficulty is best addressed not by eliminating plural marriage, but rather by legalizing it, so that subsequent wives can enjoy all of the rights available to first wives, including a fair share of the marital property and spousal support.

The right of exit poses a more difficult challenge, particularly when it involves leaving an insular community like the FLDS.[59] Some observers are skeptical of the claim that the barriers are excessively high. For instance, according to Jeffrey Spinner-Halev, leaving insular communities, while difficult, is not an insurmountable proposition when the greater society is liberal. The following passage refers to territorially concentrated tribes, but these comments are equally applicable to fundamentalist Mormon enclaves:

> If women were refused education and subjected to humiliation, many would undoubtedly flee. While leaving an oppressive state is often hard, leaving a tribe is comparatively easy: no escape routes need to be plotted, no visas are needed, no plane tickets must be purchased, there

> are no oceans to traverse or mountains to cross. When a small group is surrounded by a much larger one, it is hard not to see how the outsiders live.[60]

As Okin notes, Spinner-Halev underestimates the trauma associated with leaving behind an entire way of life, which often includes severing ties with loved ones. Moreover, in the case of many fundamentalist communities, knowledge of the outside world is surprisingly limited. Women and children might only leave the community for visits to the doctor or dentist. It may *feel* impossible to leave. Individuals may believe they have nowhere to go, no way to support themselves, and no ideas about what the outside world is like. Additionally, many women who reject practices within their communities don't want to leave—they want to reform their communities' practices to make them more equitable.[61] Hence we cannot interpret "staying" as either a tacit endorsement of a community's practices or as implied consent. When a woman remains in a plural marriage only because she feels powerless over her own life, cannot imagine any alternatives, or cannot bear the thought of leaving her family, she is not offering genuine consent.

Spinner-Halev is not unaware of these difficulties, but regards them as unfortunate but unavoidable. He notes that liberal societies tend to liberalize illiberal groups within one or two generations, admitting that a generation of women may have to be "sacrificed" before this happens.[62] It is telling that Spinner-Halev refers primarily to "women," and only rarely to "girls" and "children." But the unfortunate sacrifice Spinner-Halev exhorts us to acquiesce to largely impacts children and their futures. Indeed, even in the context of education, he considers the ramifications for women (rather than girls) being "taught subordination at schools and at home."[63] This oversight indicates an unwillingness to consider the unique position of girls and children. Children cannot exercise the right of exit.[64]

Chandran Kukathas makes the same error when he insists that liberal states must tolerate the practices of minority groups, even when they refuse to educate their children, enforce arranged marriages, or deny medical care to minors.[65] Kukathas justifies this broad toleration by focusing on the right of exit and the implicit consent of practitioners who do not leave. But, again, children cannot exercise a right of exit. Indeed, many problematic practices are designed to render children suited for life only within their group and, by extension, completely unprepared for life outside their group. The forced illiteracy of girls, arranged marriages and genital cutting, for example, have been defended on the ground that they make it nearly impossible for girls and women to seriously consider leaving.[66] The right of exit is meaningless for children and it is likely to be seriously compromised for adults who have been raised from a young age to accept oppressive notions of desert and propriety.[67] Liberals who lean toward permissiveness and toleration fail to recognize the distinct vulnerability, malleability and dependence of children, projecting onto them an unrealistic ability to refuse to consent and act accordingly.

In practice, sorting these issues out may be incredibly difficult. Take the case of Carolyn Jessop, who escaped with her eight children from Colorado City, AZ, in 2003. She left, she tells us, because she was worried that the prophet would soon marry away her 14 year-old daughter, Betty. Jessop was unwilling to accept for her daughter a lifestyle she had endured for many years. As she explains, "When I left, it was like landing on another planet. I didn't even understand that there were basic human rights that I actually possessed as a woman." For Jessop, leaving FLDS was a major turning point in her life. But Betty didn't feel the same way, and returned to FLDS (then at the YFZ Ranch), upon turning 18. Jessop insists that her daughter is "brainwashed," but Betty says, "Other people might feel trapped in or confined, but I don't feel trapped at all." Even after four years on "the outside," Betty nevertheless preferred to return to the lifestyle and community she had known her whole life. It would seem, then, that some women prefer not just polygyny, but the particular FLDS brand of polygyny, even after they have experienced other ways of life.[68] So while some women only stay for a lack of information about (and competency for engaging in) other ways of life, others make the choice quite intentionally.

These problems are not as acute for independent fundamentalist Mormons, who are much less restricted, better educated, and better prepared to engage the outside world, even when they are not already fully assimilated. True, among this population, there is the possibility of entering plural marriage for the "wrong reasons." As the pro-polygamy group *Principle Voices* warns, "Confusion and misery can result when plural marriage is entered into for the sake of parental approval, God's approval, tradition, acceptance in community or family . . . without understanding the spiritual commitment required, or without one's own commitment."[69] Accordingly, individuals must be moved to enter into plural marriage—they cannot do for "superficial" reasons like winning acceptance in one's community. Nevertheless, these kinds of personal reasons are perfectly acceptable from the standpoint of the liberal state.

The possibility of genuine consent becomes even murkier when we consider personal revelation. Many women enter plural marriage on the basis of personal testimony, revelation, or a visitation. For instance, in 1880, one reluctant wife reported waking to a visitation, which told her that she must allow her husband to take a second wife: "If you don't," it warned her, "when you pass out of this life you'll just be cancelled out."[70] Helen Mar Whitney, another early Mormon, explains, "Had it not been for the powerful testimony from the Lord, which gave me knowledge for myself that this principle is of celestial birth, I do not believe that I could have submitted to it for a moment."[71] These women were only able to endure what they considered to be a grave hardship on the basis of these revelatory experiences. It is impossible to know the origins of these women's revelations. It is certainly conceivable that these revelations are elaborate rationalizations that these women developed to persuade themselves to do something that they felt strongly disinclined to do. But it would be the height of liberal arrogance to dismiss these experiences totally, as if they could not possibly be taken at face value. Moreover, women who have these kinds of experiences often appear to have a genuine change of heart. As such, revelation is one possible ingredient in the recipe for genuine consent.

This survey of early and contemporary fundamentalist Mormon women indicates that many women consent to plural marriage without coercion, deception or violence; that they could have refused to do so (remember that even in the early years of Mormonism only 20% of families were polygynous); and that they do not entirely undermine their future agency by entering a plural marriage. These women may, for instance, have equal voice in the selection of future wives, and they are likely to be quite independent, particularly if each wife runs her own household. Some early Mormon women found plural marriage to be an expression of and condition for their agency. This sentiment is echoed today.

At the same time, some girls and women *are* coerced or deceived, as Anna Eliza Berry, Elisa Wall, and Carolyn Jessop remind us. Jessop's harrowing story of escape demonstrates how difficult it can be to refuse, exit or dissent. And possibilities for renegotiation seem scant, particularly if we take that to mean, for instance, the possibility of negotiating a polyandrous marriage (in which a woman takes several husbands). Obviously in the context of fundamentalist Mormon doctrine this point is nonnegotiable—the only acceptable plural marriage is between one man and two or more wives.

This inquiry means that polygyny, as it is actually practiced by fundamentalist Mormons, can meet O'Neill's criteria: it can be shown to win the *possible consent of actual agents*. But just barely. We have encountered some women whose experiences reveal that Mormon polygyny is sometimes a threat to agency: that it can be coercive, and that it can victimize women. For these reasons, it is beyond dispute that the right of exit must be strengthened. Furthermore, more must be done to protect girls and young women from particularly manipulative practices which are meant to cultivate a slavish acceptance of polygyny. This is where Nussbaum arrives as well. She recognizes that, "polygamy . . . [is] typically seen as inextricable from a history of sex discrimination," and yet, she continues, "Mormon polygamy should have been permitted so long as the legal equality of women, and their freedom to leave the community should they wish to, were securely established and protected."[72] I agree, although I would go a bit farther than Nussbaum, who suggests that the

Mormons, Muslims and Hindus might receive an exemption to the law forbidding polygamy, on religious grounds. I see no reason to privilege religiously grounded polygamy over other kinds. The liberal state should legalize all forms of polygamy, while at the same time taking steps to mitigate the dangerous effects of a history of sexism and discrimination through a regulatory scheme. This is the topic for the final part of this chapter.

POLYGAMY AND THE LIBERAL STATE

In the case of polygamy in modern-day America, the state is in the unusual position of going both too far and not far enough.[73] What I mean is that the state goes *too far* in restricting the practice of polygamy among adults, while at the same time it *doesn't go far enough* in preventing children from being subjected to coercive or deceptive grooming, so that they will grow up to endorse polygamy. In short, the current law treats adults like children (by criminalizing polygamy) while at the same time treating children like adults (by using children's so-called right of exit to justify a relatively "hands off" approach in insular communities).

Historically, the criminalization of polygamy has proceeded on religious grounds: because polygamy offended the sensibilities of mainstream Christians, many states enacted laws against it. States have devised different kinds of felony and misdemeanor laws to get at plural marriage, from outright bans on polygamy to laws against bigamy (the act of fraudulently representing oneself as eligible to marry when in fact one is already married), and adultery. Of course, it goes without saying that laws that are justified on entirely religious grounds are unacceptable in a liberal state. Today, arguments regarding the legality and moral permissibility of polygamy tend to focus on concerns regarding the equality and autonomy of women.[74] These concerns are important, but autonomy poses a paradox, as we cannot "force someone to be free," as Rousseau would have said. Moreover, as Andrew March points out, the liberal state tolerates many practices that result in gender inequality. If polygamy cannot be shown to be inherently worse than all of these practices, then it is not clear why we ought to proceed with an outright ban.[75] After all, less draconian alternatives are available.

The current legal status of polygamy is complicated. While it is not possible to legally marry more than one person, one could violate bigamy laws by obtaining subsequent marriage licenses in different states. This occurrence is rare, however. The bigger issue is that plural *common-law* marriage violates Utah's anti-bigamy statute. But Utah, like other Western states with large polygynous populations, does not actively prosecute members of polygynous families, focusing instead on cases of sexual abuse and forced or underage marriage.[76]

Until 2003, polygamy could also be prosecuted under anti-adultery statutes, but the Supreme Court decision of *Lawrence v. Texas* casts doubt on the constitutionality of such statutes. In this decision, the Court overturned an anti-sodomy statute in Texas, on the ground that it violated the due process rights of consenting adults.[77] The same reasoning could easily apply to any consensual sexual relations among adults, including polygyny. But there is limited case law on this topic, and so the legal status of polygamy remains uncertain and thus risky from the perspective of those who engage in the practice.[78] For this reason, in 2010, the Brown family (the stars of the reality show *Sister Wives*) challenged Utah's bigamy statute in federal court, claiming that it violates their First and Fourteenth Amendment rights (the Utah County Attorney's Office had opened an investigation of the Browns on suspicion of bigamy after the airing of the show). The district court ruled that parts of Utah's anti-bigamy statute were unconstitutional and the Utah County Attorney's Office dropped its investigation of the Browns, adopting a policy of prosecutorial discretion whereby they would only investigate bigamy in cases involving violence, coercion, or underage marriage.[79]

Shortly thereafter County Attorney Buhman appealed the district court's decision, claiming that the case was moot after the Utah County Attorney's Office decided not to prosecute bigamy cases. In April of 2016 a three-judge Circuit Court ruled that the Brown family didn't have standing to file their original suit, since they no longer face a credible threat of prosecution under Utah's new prosecutorial guidelines. This decision has prevented the court from deciding the case on its merits, that is, whether entering polygamous marriage is a constitutionally protected right.[80]

Plural marriage advocates like the Browns understandably seek an unequivocal decriminalization of polygamy. Yet decriminalization, which would prevent prosecution on the grounds of polygamy, bigamy or adultery, doesn't go far enough. Many injustices can only be addressed if the state legalizes polygamy by issuing more than one marriage license to the same family. Under decriminalization (or prosecutorial discretion), no one faces the threat of criminal culpability, but only first wives enjoy any of the protections typically afforded to legal spouses—such as property rights, alimony, and the ability to make life and death decisions. This state of affairs leaves subsequent wives in an incredibly vulnerable position. Furthermore, without legally issued polygamous marriage licenses, sister-wives (or co-husbands, in a polyandrous or polyamorous arrangement) have no legally recognized relationship to each other. Even though they are "married" to one another, they cannot divorce each other—all subsequent relationships depend upon the will of the polygynous husband (or polyandrous wife).

As long as marriage vows aren't exchanged *multilaterally*, polygamy seems to be intrinsically unequal and vulnerable to coercion. Thom

Brooks takes this to be a reason why polygamy should be completely prohibited.[81] As I see it, though, this response is misguided. First, consent for polygamy is not only possible but not uncommon. Second, the history of Mormon polygyny shows that anti-polygamy laws are ineffective. If anything, the practice is gaining public acceptance via exposure through *Big Love*, *Sister Wives*, and the like, and increasingly, fundamentalist Mormons are no longer seen as the "other."[82] Others have argued that the liberal state should "get out of the marriage business" altogether. Accordingly, the state should only authorize civil unions, leaving "marriage" to religious and private authorities.[83] Now that gay marriage is recognized as constitutionally protected,[84] it makes even more sense to seek the same legal guarantees for polygamous families.

The state has an additional reason to legalize polygamy, and this is because legalization would bring greater transparency to the practice. As we have seen, some women enter plural marriages under dubious circumstances. Moreover, some communities, like the FLDS at YFZ Ranch, break a variety of other laws, including forced marriage, underage marriage, and statutory rape. Were the state to offer marriage licenses to all members of plural marriages, it would be able to obtain at least some assurance that subsequent wives are willing participants in their marriage. Obviously, such willingness can be "manufactured," but signing a marriage license in front of a civil official signals a basic awareness that one is entering a legal institution that comes with legal protections, including the right to dissolve such a union at the pleasure of any of the participants. It might also dissuade underage marriage, when such unions, if consensual, could be sanctioned by the state in just a few years.

Issuing marriage licenses to polygamous families ensures an important "point of contact" between the state and particularly insular polygynous communities. Some families may still decline a legal marriage even if it is available to them, but the hope is that awareness will spread through insular communities as more and more marriages are obtained from the state. One could imagine public service announcements and even posters in county clerk offices along the same lines as workplace employment law posters, which would explain laws surrounding marriage, divorce, and statutory and marital rape. With these sources of information in place, the liberal state ought to recognize the freedom of consenting adults to enter any kind of marriage that they wish.

That does not mean that the state has to be indifferent to situations that may put that consent into doubt or treat children like adults. The issue of children, who may be compelled to marry while they are minors, or who may be so aggressively indoctrinated as children that they reluctantly submit to plural marriage as adults, warrants its own treatment. Those who favor legalization must figure out how the liberal state can insulate children from the most troubling forms of indoctrination while still recognizing the general right of parents to raise their children as they see fit. Ian Shapiro's model of parallel fiduciaries may offer some guidance. Accordingly, the state acts as the primary custodian of children's *basic* interests in nutrition, security, health, and education (either providing for them directly or immediately stepping in when parents fail to do so), while making parents primary custodians of children's *best* interests, which Shapiro defines as children's interest in living a good life. Obviously, best interests can be subjective, and vary greatly from one family to the next. Still, as Shapiro notes, "Parents are also more likely than anyone else to care about their children unconditionally, to want what is good for them, and to try to continually translate that desire into efficacious action."[85]

Parents are acting in their capacity as primary custodians of their children's best interests, as they interpret them, when they teach their children the value of plural marriage, doctrinally or simply by raising them in a loving, polygynous family. The state's failsafe role as secondary custodian is only activated when parents' actions cross over to coercion and deception. It is worth noting that children are vulnerable and naïve; coercion in the case of a child is different than it would be for an adult and may look like a milder form of intimidation or parental discretion. But it can have the same chilling effect if its result is children or young adults whose decisions are based primarily on ignorance of alternatives or fear of violence or withheld love.

Like Shapiro's fiduciary model, Joel Feinberg suggests that children have rights-in-trust that must be protected until they are old enough to exercise them, most notably the right to "an open future."[86] Broadly interpreted, this requires children not be predisposed to any particular way of life. Of course, it is not possible to meet this ideal standard, and Shelley Burtt notes that parents rightly shape (or at least try to) the dispositions which will guide their children's future choices as adults.[87] A more realistic reading of Feinberg, and one that is more consistent with my aim here, is that the right to an open future requires that children's future agency not be seriously undermined. Freedom from violence, coercion, and deception, along with arrangements which can be accepted or denied, seems sufficient for this purpose.

I have already explained why legalizing polygamy may try to achieve this objective by disincentivizing purely 'spiritual' marriages which are not recognized by the law. But more may need to be done to empower women and girls to recognize and confront their own victimization in the most insular communities. For instance, during a visit to the YFZ Ranch, Oprah Winfrey asked a group of teenage girls if they knew that it was illegal for underage girls to have sex with older men. They did not.[88] Whatever else is covered in sex education curricula, there must be a basic awareness of children's rights, and the training necessary to identify and report sexual exploitation and abuse.

These goals are undoubtedly already being met, to varying degrees, in many public schools. In the public school system in Salt Lake City, for instance, it is likely that independent fundamentalist children already receive an adequate or nearly adequate education regarding such matters. But other fundamentalist communities have long exercised control over their local school districts, and it is likely that these "public" schools do not offer an education that is adequate in terms of sex education, and, in all likelihood, in many other subjects, as well. In 2005, the state of Arizona effectively took over the public school in Colorado City, after it was discovered that the school district had bankrupted itself after years of redirecting public funding into FLDS organizations, including a second, privately run FLDS school on public school property.[89] While it is commendable that the state of Arizona finally responded to this crisis, the state was motivated largely by the financial distress of the district, and not by the low quality of education being provided. States need to devote more resources to monitoring public schools in areas where there is good reason to believe that some educational standards are being deliberately circumvented. This reform might include, among other things, classroom observations, principal interviews, third party evaluation of curricula, and auditing. Such expenses could have been easily justified in the case of the Colorado City Unified School District, which ran up a debt of over two million dollars, thanks to a lack of oversight.

Undeniably, the state faces a much more difficult problem when it comes to private schools and homeschooling, which often fall far short of state and national standards. Take Tammy, a second grade teacher at the YFZ school. When asked by Winfrey whether she teaches that, "man never landed on the moon," Tammy responded, "It's not taught that it never happened but we don't teach that it did."[90] It is not difficult to imagine similar circumventions regarding, for instance, women's right to vote, or the rights of children to be safe from sexual abuse or abandonment.[91] Even if these schools don't explicitly teach students that these rights "don't exist," they do almost as much damage when they don't "teach that they do." This kind of curricula is essential, and private educators and homeschoolers should be held accountable for covering this material.[92] The practical and political obstacles are significant, however.[93] As an alternative, the state could mandate some kind of sex and civic education to be provided by external educators or social workers, as it did in the case of some of the children who were removed from the YFZ Ranch in 2008. Not only were children taught about identifying sexual abuse before they were returned to the ranch, but many parents attended court-mandated classed on the "appropriate discipline and the psychosexual development of children."[94]

A gentler paternalism might offer nudges, like tax breaks or other financial incentives, to schools or homeschooling families that send their children to public classes in certain subjects. "Hybrid" private-public schooling is a growing trend and offers promising possibilities.[95] Moreover, recalcitrant states could do more to catch up with states that heavily regulate homeschooling, by mandating, for instance, that homeschooling parents attend workshops on civics, legal rights, and sex abuse.[96] More could also be done to support the outside groups, like Holding Out Help, which assist those who escape insular polygynous communities.[97]

Some may find my approach too heavy-handed, allowing the state to intrude too far into the private lives of families. But some families provide their children with an education that intentionally diminishes their capacity to genuinely accept or reject plural marriage. When girls and boys don't understand their basic rights they are vulnerable to all kinds of injustices, including the likelihood that they may develop a preference for systematic oppression—as oppressors and as the oppressed. When children are kept in the dark regarding modern science and other subjects, they are ill-prepared to ever leave their community, and may find it inconceivable to even consider leaving, no matter how unpleasant they find their circumstances. Indeed, many insular communities provide an exceedingly one-sided picture of the outside world. For instance, Amish teenagers are more than familiar with drinking, drugs, and underage sex (which they often witness or experience firsthand during their *rumspringa*), but they have few opportunities to travel, attend college classes, or visit a museum. This imbalance has been credited with the high retention rates among the Amish, who sometimes find the outside world to be nothing more than a den of inequity.[98] Children have a right to an adequate education in the subjects that society has widely deemed to be important, including history, civics, and science. The more heavy-handed the state is with children and the provision of their education, the more comfortable it can be adopting a hands-off policy amongst adults. This is in everyone's best interests.

CONCLUSION

Over the last several decades, the rights of children have attracted significant attention among political theorists. This literature covers a wide range of issues, including the purposes of education in liberal states, the proper demarcation of state and parental authority over children, and the particular rights owed to children.[99] Few would deny the importance of these issues. However, this literature is often regarded as an interesting but non-essential subfield of liberal thought. As such, children's issues are approached with liberal principles that are already fixed in regard to adults and seem to require only a minor adjustment to account for the special needs and capacities of children.

It seems to me, though, as the case of polygyny shows, that children and their distinct needs and capacities must figure centrally in the development of liberal thought—not just as an extension of but as a crucial foundation for the credibility of liberal theory. The liberal state owes something fundamentally different to adults and children: it must treat adults as competent choosers, tolerating their choices even when they seem to lead to their own oppression. But the liberal state has a very different duty when it comes to children: to do everything in its power to ensure that children do not grow up to accept the oppression of themselves or others. This mandate falls short of the kind of autonomy that some perfectionist liberals promote, but it is still substantial. It requires a purposive public education, coupled with effective policy, laws, and enforcement designed to encourage private schools and homeschools to expose their students to basic information about their rights and the outside world.

A state that neglects its duties towards either adults or children is not properly liberal—it does not satisfy the principles of liberty and toleration, on the one hand, and the principle of consent, on the other. We need not choose between these important ideals. We should, instead, recognize that they each serve important purposes in the context of different ages. Only by acting upon the distinctive needs of adults and children can a liberal state treat them each as they ought to be treated. Only when the state is hands-on with the development of children while at the same time remaining hands-off regarding the decisions of adults does it truly deserve to be called *liberal*.

NOTES

1. While it is typically employed to describe *polygynous* marriages, *polygamy* is actually a more general term for any marriage in which a man or a woman has multiple spouses (a marriage with one woman and more than one husband is *polyandrous*). In this paper I am particularly interested in *polygyny*, or, as it is called by fundamentalist Mormons, *plural marriage*. While some of my comments will apply to the practice of polygyny generally, I will use as my primary reference and case study the practice of plural marriage amongst fundamentalist Mormons. As I will later discuss, fundamentalist Mormons consider themselves the "true" followers of Mormon doctrine, in contrast to the mainstream Mormon Church (the Church of Jesus Christ of Latter-day Saints), which has not practiced or endorsed polygyny since 1904.

2. Jason Matthew Smith, "Polygamy Primer: A guide to the history, major players, practitioners, and detractors surrounding Utah's peculiar predilection," *Salt Lake: The Magazine for Utah* (April 2009); Barbara Bradley Hagerty, "Some Muslims in U.S. Quietly Engage in Polygamy," *All Things Considered*, NPR (May 27, 2008); *Tapestry Against Polygamy*, "Frequently Asked Questions."

3. Following the popularity of "Big Love," cable channel TLC launched a reality show, "Sister Wives," which follows a fundamentalist Mormon family with one husband, four wives, and (as of today) twenty-two children. Like the fictitious family in "Big Love," the Brown family is a relatively integrated, mainstream, middleclass family.

4. One girl who was married to FDLS leader and prophet Warren Jeffs at the age of 12 now lives with a distant relative. "Alleged underage polygamist bride to leave foster care," *The Arizona Republic*, (5/7/2009).

5. Residents of YFZ Ranch continue to insist upon Jeffs's innocence. Dan Frosch, "Texas Report Says 12 Girls at Sect Ranch Were Married," *The New York Times* (12/23/08).

6. Ralph Blumenthal, "Texas Loses Court Ruling Over Taking of Children," *The New York Times* (5/30/08). See also Shannon K. Dunn, "The Yearning for Zion Raid and its Impact on Texas Child Welfare Cases: How a Botched Rescue Effort Exposed a Need to Refocus Efforts on Effective Service Plans," *St. Mary's Law Journal* Vol. 41 (2010), 405–443.

7. The Brown family in the reality show Sister Wives belongs to an independent group known as the Apostolic United Brethren.

8. Smith, *Polygamy Primer*, 4.

9. Susan Moller Okin, "Is Multiculturalism Bad for Women?" In *Is Multiculturalism Bad for Women?* Joshua Cohen, Matthew Howard and Martha Nussbaum, eds., (Princeton: Princeton University Press, 1999), 7–24.

10. Paul Weithman, ed., *Religion and Contemporary Liberalism* (Notre Dame, IN: University of Ntre Dame Press, 1997).

11. Steven V. Mazie, "Consenting Adults? Amish *Rumspringa* and the Quandary of Exit in Liberalism," *Perspectives on Politics*, Vol. 3, No. 4 (Dec. 2005), 745–759.

12. Okin, "Is Multiculturalism Bad for Women?"

13. Ibid.

14. John Stuart Mill, "On Liberty," *On Liberty and Other Essays*, John Gray, ed. (Oxford: Oxford University Press, 1991), 102–103.

15. Ibid, 103.

16. Baum suggests that Mill predicates his forbearance on the fact that the Mormons in the Utah Territory were rather "unconnected" from the rest of the country, and not on a general principle of nonintervention. This does not seem to me to be determinant for Mill, but rather a factor that further confounds an already complex tangle of principles and commitments. Bruce Baum, "Feminism, Liberalism and Cultural Pluralism: J.S. Mill on Mormon Polygyny," *The Journal of Political Philosophy* Vol. 5, No. 3 (1997), 230–253.

17. Linda Kelsch, "Possible Strengths and Needs in PolyFamilies," *Harmonious Harem Hows* (2004).

18. Anne Wilde, interview by Neal Conan, "Trial Brings Focus on Polygamy in America," *Talk of the Nation*, NPR (9/12/07).

19. To my knowledge we don't have data regarding the number of children raised in polygynous families who choose this lifestyle for themselves as adults.

20. Catriona Mackenzie and Natalie Stoljar, eds., *Relational Autonomy: Feminist Perspectives on Autonomy, Agency, and the Social Self* (New York: Oxford University Press, 2000).

21. Martha Nussbaum, *Women and Human Development: The Capabilities Approach* (Cambridge, MA: Cambridge University Press, 2000).

22. Eamonn Callon, "Autonomy, Child-rearing, and Good Lives," In *The Moral and Political Status of Children,"* David Archard and Colin M. Macleod, eds., (Oxford: Oxford University Press, 2002), 118–142; Stephen Macedo, "Liberal Civic Education and Religious Fundamentalism: The Case of God v. John Rawls?" *Ethics* 105 (April 1995) 468–496; William Galston, "Parents, Government and Children: Authority over Education in the Liberal Democratic State," In *Child, Family, and State, Nomos XLIV*, Stephen Macedo and Iris Marion Young, eds. (New York: New York University Press, 2003) 211–233.

23. Nussbaum, *Women and Human Development*, 156.

24. Richard, Shweder, "What about "Female Genital Mutilation"? And Why Understanding Culture Matters in the First Place," *Daedalus* 129, No. 4 (Fall 2000), 209–232.

25. Martha C. Nussbaum, *Sex and Social Justice* (New York: Oxford University Press, 1999) 118–129.

26. William A. Galston, *Liberal Pluralism: The Implications of Value Pluralism for Political Theory and Practice* (Cambridge University Press, 2002).

27. Bernd-Jürgen Brandes, Armin Meiwes, and Jina Moore, "Readings: 'My Dinner With Antrophagus,'" *Harper's Magazine* (January 2008).
28. Mill, "On Liberty," 107.
29. Jon Elster, "Sour Grapes – Utilitarianism and the Genesis of Wants," In *The Inner Citadel: Essays on Individual Autonomy*, John Christman, ed., (New York: Oxford University Press, 1989), 170–188.
30. Nussbaum, *Women and Human Development*, 137.
31. Richard Arneson, "Autonomy and Preference Formation," In *In Harm's Way: Essays in Honor of Joel Feinberg*, Jules L. Coleman and Allen Buchanan, eds. (Cambridge: Cambridge University Press, 1994), 43–75.
32. Onora O'Neill, *Constructions of Reason: Explorations of Kant's Practical Philosophy* (Cambridge: Cambridge University Press, 1989), 112.
33. Ibid, 215.
34. Ibid, 213.
35. Nussbaum, *Women and Human Development*, 93–95.
36. Nussbaum, *Sex and Social Justice*, 127.
37. Nussbaum, *Women and Human Development*, 229.
38. Kahlile Mehr, "Women's Response to Plural Marriage," *Dialogue: A Journal of Mormon Thought* Vol. 18, no. 3 (Fall 1985), 84–97.
39. Joan Iversen, "Feminist Implications of Mormon Polygyny," *Feminist Studies* Vol. 10, No. 3 (Fall 1984) 508.
40. Wilford Woodroof, "Official Declaration – 1," (10/6/1890), *The Church of Jesus Christ of Latter-Day Saints* website.
41. The LDS Church rejects the term "fundamentalist Mormon," insisting that no real Mormons practice polygyny. Nevertheless, I will use the term, because fundamentalist Mormons identify themselves thusly, and because they clearly rely upon Mormon doctrine.
42. "The Oprah Winfrey Show Exclusive: Oprah Goes Inside the Yearning for Zion Ranch," *The Oprah Winfrey Show*, (3/30/09).
43. Ellis Shipp, "Mormon Women's Protest: An Appeal for Freedom, Justice, and Equality," *Deseret News*, Salt Lake City, 1886, quoted in Mehr, 85.
44. Joan Iversen, "Feminist Implications," 510.
45. Ibid, 506.
46. Lucinda Lee Dalton, "Autobiography," The Bancroft Library, University of California, Berkeley, cited in Julie Dunfey, "Living the Principle" of Plural Marriage: Mormon Women, Utopia, and Female Sexuality in the Nineteenth Century," *Feminist Studies* 10, No. 3 (Fall 1984), 529.
47. *Plural Voices*, "Why Women Choose Polygamy."
48. Barbara Bradley Hagerty, "Philly's Black Muslims Increasingly Turn to Polygamy," *All Things Considered*, NPR (May 28, 2008).
49. Dunfey, "Living the Principle."
50. Iversen, "Feminist Implications," 513.
51. Ibid, 511.
52. Anne Wilde, interviewed by Neal Conan.
53. TLC website, *Sister Wives*: "What is the best part about plural marriage?" http://www.tlc.com/tv-shows/sister-wives/videos/polygamy-plural-marriage-what-is-the-best-part-about-plural-marriage/.
54. Romania B. Pratt Penrose, "Memoir of Romania B. Pratt, M.D.," 1881, Church Archives, quoted in Mehr, 86.
55. "Oprah Goes Inside the Yearning for Zion Ranch."
56. Dunfey, "Living the Principle," 534.
57. Anna Eliza Berry Day, "Reminiscences, 1899–1907," *Church Archives*, quoted in Mehr, 93.
58. "Forced to Marry at Fourteen: Lisa Ling's Special Report on Polygamy Continues," *The Oprah Winfrey Show*, (5/14/08).

59. While this discussion focuses on fundamentalist Mormons, it is important to note that women in Muslim polygamous families may also face enormous obstacles if they wish to leave their husbands, particularly if they are immigrants. Such women may not speak English, may have no outside support system, and may avoid any recourse to authorities if they are not in the country legally.

60. Jeff Spinner-Halev, "Feminism, Multiculturalism, Oppression, and the State," *Ethics* 112 (October 2001), 106.

61. Susan Moller Okin, "Mistresses of Their Own Destiny": Group Rights, Gender, and Realistic Rights of Exit, *Ethics* 112 (January 2002), 205–230.

62. Spinner-Halev,"Feminism, Multiculturalism, Oppression, and the State," 90. We should be skeptical of Spinner-Halev's confidence: FLDS traces its origins to 1912, when the LDS repudiated plural marriage. It does not seem that the community has been "liberalized" by the larger society over the last century; if anything, they appear more steadfast in their commitments.

63. Ibid, 89.

64. Okin, "Mistresses of Their Own Destiny," 216.

65. Chandran Kukathas, "Cultural Toleration," In *Ethnicity and Group Rights*, Ian Shapiro and Will Kymlicka, eds., (New York: New York University Press, 2000), 87.

66. Okin, "Is Multiculturalism Bad for Women?" 14.

67. Joel Feinberg, "The Child's Right to an Open Future," in *Whose Child? Children's Rights, Parental Authority, and State Power*, William Aiken and Hugh LaFollette, eds. (Totowa, NJ: Rowan and Littlefield, 1980), 125–153.

68. "Polygamy in America: Lisa Ling Reports," *The Oprah Winfrey Show* (10/26/2007); "Oprah Goes Inside the YFZ Ranch."

69. Kelsch, "Possible Strengths and Needs in PolyFamilies."

70. Charles Durfee, interviewed by Dean May, *LDS Polygamy Project* (11/24/79), quoted in Mehr, 88.

71. Helen Mar Whitney, "Scenes and Incidents in Nauvoo," *The Woman's Exponent* 10 (Oct. 15, 1881), quoted in Mehr, 86.

72. Nussbaum, *Women and Human Development*, 229.

73. In the following discussion I will refer to polygamy, as there is no reason to legally distinguish between polygyny and polyandry. Indeed, some have argued that many of the troubling aspects of polygyny would be greatly reduced if women also had the right to take more than one spouse. Of course, in practice most polygamous families will continue practicing polygyny, as Brooks notes. Nevertheless, I presume that any legal changes in the status of polygamy ought to begin with ensuring the legal rights of men *and* women to take additional spouses. Thom Brooks, "The Problem with Polygamy," *Philosophical Topics* Vol 37, No. 2 (2009), 109–122.

74. Brooks, "The Problem with Polygamy," Okin, "Is Multiculturalism Bad for Women?"

75. Andrew March, "Is There a Right to Polygamy? Marriage, Equality and Subsidizing Families in Liberal Public Justification," *Journal of Moral Philosophy* Vol. 8, No. 2 (2011), 246–272.

76. *Brown v. Buhman* 947 F.Supp.2d 1170 (D. Utah 2013); *Brown v. Buhman* No. 14–4117 10th Cir. (2016).

77. *Lawrence v. Texas* (02–102) 539 U.S. 558 (2003).

78. Ken Driggs, interview by Neal Conan, "Trial Brings Focus on Polygamy in America," *Talk of the Nation*, NPR (9/12/07).

79. *Brown v. Buhman 2016.*

80. Jacob Gershman, "Appeals Court Dismisses Challenge to Utah's Polygamy Ban," *The Wall Street Journal* (4/11/16); Erin Alberty, "Police probe 'Sister Wives' stars for bigamy," *The Salt Lake Tribune* (9/28/2010).

81. Brooks, "The Problem with Polygamy."

82. Hunter Schwarz, "Support for polygamy is rising. But it's not the new gay marriage," *The Washington Post* (7/2/2015).

83. March, "Is There a Right to Polygamy?"

84. *Obergerfell v. Hodges* 576 U.S. (2015).

85. Ian Shapiro, *Democratic Justice* (New Haven, CT: Yale University Press, 1999) 97.

86. Feinberg, "The Child's Right to an 'Open Future.'"

87. Shelley Burtt, "The Proper Scope of Parental Authority: Why We Don't Owe Children an "Open Future"" In *Child, Family, and State, Nomos XLIV,* edited by Stephen Macedo, and Iris Marion Young (New York: New York University Press, 2003), 244–268.

88. "Oprah Goes Inside the Yearning for Zion Ranch."

89. Pat Kossan, "Colorado City school district faces bankruptcy," *The Arizona Republic* (8/12/05); Howard Fischer, "State officials prepare to seize control of Colorado City school district," Capitol Media Services (8/11/05); Tom Zoellner, "Schools: Local Control, But Little Local Money," *Salt Lake City Tribune* (6/28/98); John Dougherty, "Crash Course: Fundamentalist Mormons lose control of Colorado City's school district, as a criminal investigation continues," *Phoenix New Times* (12/8/05).

90. "Oprah Goes Inside the Yearning for Zion Ranch."

91. In addition to the threat of inadequate education, young boys in prophetic communities face the continual threat of expulsion. This expulsion is typically justified on the grounds of the boys' delinquency, but it is necessary if the older and more powerful men in the community are to have a sufficient stock of single young women from which to choose their wives.

92. James Dwyer, *Religious Schools vs. Children's Rights* (Ithaca, NY: Cornell University Press, 2001); Robert Kunzman, "Understanding Homeschooling: A Better Approach to Regulation," *Theory and Research in Education* 7, No. 3 (2009), 311–330.

93. David Sikkink, "The Sources of Alienation from Public Schools," *Social Forces* 78 No. 1 (Sept. 1999), 51–86.

94. Frosch, "Texas Report."

95. Jeff Spinner-Halev, *Surviving Diversity: Religion and Democratic Citizenship* (Baltimore, MD: The Johns Hopkins University Press, 2000); Milton Gaither, "Homeschooling in the USA: Past, Present and Future," *Theory and Research in Education* 7, No. 3 (2009), 331–346.

96. Laws and regulations surrounding homeschooling vary widely from state to state. Some states put virtually no requirements on homeschooling families; others require parents to be certified teachers. Robert Reich, "Testing the Boundaries of Parental Authority Over Education: The Case of Homeschooling," In *Moral and Political Education: Nomos XLIII*, edited by Stephen Macedo and Yael Tamir (New York: New York University Press, 2002), 275–313.

97. Joanna Walters, "Fleeing the FLDS: Followers are abandoning the notorious sect in droves," *Al Jazeera* (3/16/2015), http://america.aljazeera.com/multimedia/2015/3/fleeing-the-flds-sect.html.

98. Mazie, "Consenting Adults?"

99. Representative work includes: Amy Gutmann, *Democratic Education* (Princeton: Princeton University Press, 1999); Martha Fineman, "Taking Children's Interests Seriously," in *Child, Family, and State: Nomos XLIV*, Stephen Macedo and Iris Marion Young, eds. (New York: New York University Press, 2003); Feinberg, "The Child's Right to an Open Future," and Shapiro, *Democratic Justice*.

REFERENCES

"Alleged underage polygamist bride to leave foster care." *The Arizona Republic*. (AP). (5/7/2009) http://www.azcentral.com/news/articles/2009/05/07/20090507polygamist-fostercare.html.

"Forced to Marry at Fourteen: Lisa Ling's Special Report on Polygamy Continues," *The Oprah Winfrey Show*. (5/14/08) http://www.oprah.com/oprahshow/Forced-to-Marry-at-14-Lisa-Lings-Special-Report-on-Polygamy-Continues.

"Polygamy in America: Lisa Ling Reports." *The Oprah Winfrey Show* (10/26/2007) http://www.oprah.com/relationships/polygamy-in-america.

"The Oprah Winfrey Show Exclusive: Oprah Goes Inside the Yearning for Zion Ranch." *The Oprah Winfrey Show* (3/30/09) http://www.oprah.com/article/oprah-show/20090325-orig-polygamist-ranch.

Alberty, Erin. "Police probe 'Sister Wives' stars for bigamy." *The Salt Lake Tribune* (9/28/2010) http://archive.sltrib.com/story.php?ref=/sltrib/home/50366251-76/bigamy-brown-wives-tribune.html.csp.

Arneson, Richard. "Autonomy and Preference Formation." In *In Harm's Way: Essays in Honor of Joel Feinberg*, edited by Jules L. Coleman and Allen Buchanan, 43–75. Cambridge: Cambridge University Press, 1994.

Baum, Bruce. "Feminism, Liberalism and Cultural Pluralism: J.S. Mill on Mormon Polygyny." *The Journal of Political Philosophy* 5, No. 3 (1997): 230–253.

Berry Day, Anna Eliza. "Reminiscences, 1899–1907," *Church Archives*, quoted in Mehr, "Living the Principle," 93.

Blumenthal, Ralph. "Texas Loses Court Ruling Over Taking of Children." *The New York Times* (5/30/08) http://www.nytimes.com/2008/05/30/us/30raid.html.

Bradley Hagerty, Barbara. "Some Muslims in U.S. Quietly Engage in Polygamy." *All Things Considered*. NPR (5/27/2008) http://www.npr.org/templates/story/story.php?storyId=90857818.

Brandes, Bernd-Jürgen Armin Meiwes, and Jina Moore, "Readings: 'My Dinner With Antrophagus.'" *Harper's Magazine* (January 2008).

Brooks, Thom. "The Problem with Polygamy." *Philosophical Topics* 37, No. 2 (2009): 109–122.

Burtt, Shelley. "The Proper Scope of Parental Authority: Why We Don't Owe Children an "Open Future."" In *Child, Family, and State, Nomos XLIV*. Edited by Stephen Macedo, and Iris Marion Young, 244–268. New York: New York University Press, 2003.

Callon, Eamonn. "Autonomy, Child-rearing, and Good Lives." In *The Moral and Political Status of Children*," edited by David Archard and Colin M. Macleod, 118–142. Oxford: Oxford University Press, 2002.

Dougherty, John. "Crash Course: Fundamentalist Mormons lose control of Colorado City's school district, as a criminal investigation continues." *Phoenix New Times* (12/8/05) http://www.phoenixnewtimes.com/2005-12-08/news/crash-course/.

Driggs, Ken, interview by Neal Conan. "Trial Brings Focus on Polygamy in America." *Talk of the Nation*, NPR (9/12/07) http://www.npr.org/templates/story/story.php?storyId=14350293&ps=rs.

Dunfey, Julie. "'Living the Principle'" of Plural Marriage: Mormon Women, Utopia, and Female Sexuality in the Nineteenth Century," *Feminist Studies* 10, No. 3 (Fall 1984): 523–536.

Dunn, Shannon K. "The Yearning for Zion Raid and its Impact on Texas Child Welfare Cases: How a Botched Rescue Effort Exposed a Need to Refocus Efforts on Effective Service Plans." *St. Mary's Law Journal* 41 (2010): 405–443.

Durfee, Charles, interviewed by Dean May. *LDS Polygamy Project* (11/24/79) quoted in Mehr, "Living the Principle," 88.

Dwyer, James. *Religious Schools vs. Children's Rights*. Ithaca, NY: Cornell University Press, 2001.

Elster, Jon. "Sour Grapes—Utilitarianism and the Genesis of Wants." In *The Inner Citadel: Essays on Individual Autonomy*, edited by John Christman, 170–188. New York: Oxford University Press, 1989.

Feinberg, Joel. "The Child's Right to an Open Future." In *Whose Child? Children's Rights, Parental Authority, and State Power*, edited by William Aiken and Hugh LaFollette, 125–153. Totowa, NJ: Rowan and Littlefield, 1980.

Fineman, Martha. "Taking Children's Interests Seriously." In *Child, Family, and State: Nomos XLIV*, edited by Stephen Macedo and Iris Marion Young, 234–242. New York: New York University Press, 2003.

Fischer, Howard. "State officials prepare to seize control of Colorado City school district." *Capitol Media Services* (8/11/05) http://www.azstarnet.com/sn/hourlyupdate/88285.php.

Frosch, Dan. "Texas Report Says 12 Girls at Sect Ranch Were Married." *The New York Times* (12/23/08) http://www.nytimes.com/2008/12/24/us/24abuse.html.

Gaither, Milton. "Homeschooling in the USA: Past, Present and Future." *Theory and Research in Education* 7, No. 3 (2009): 331–346.

Galston, William. "Parents, Government and Children: Authority over Education in the Liberal Democratic State." In *Child, Family, and State, Nomos XLIV,* edited by Stephen Macedo and Iris Marion Young, 211–233. New York: New York University Press, 2003.

Galston, William. Liberal Pluralism: The Implications of Value Pluralism for Political Theory and Practice. Cambridge: Cambridge University Press, 2002.

Gershman, Jacob. "Appeals Court Dismisses Challenge to Utah's Polygamy Ban." *The Wall Street Journal* (4/11/16) http://blogs.wsj.com/law/2016/04/11/appeals-court-dismisses-challenge-to-utahs-polygamy-ban/.

Gutmann, Amy. *Democratic Education*. Princeton: Princeton University Press, 1999.

Iversen, Joan. "Feminist Implications of Mormon Polygyny." *Feminist Studies* 10, No. 3 (Fall 1984): 505–522.

Kelsch, Linda. "Possible Strengths and Needs in PolyFamilies." *Harmonious Harem Hows* (2004) http://haremhome.blogspot.com/2008/04/possible-strengths-and-needs-in.html.

Kossan, Pat. "Colorado City school district faces bankruptcy." *The Arizona Republic* (8/12/05) http://www.azcentral.com/arizonarepublic/local/articles/0812coloradocity12.html.

Kukathas, Chandran. "Cultural Toleration." In *Ethnicity and Group Rights*, edited by Ian Shapiro and Will Kymlicka, 69–104. New York: New York University Press, 2000.

Kunzman, Robert. "Understanding Homeschooling: A Better Approach to Regulation." *Theory and Research in Education* 7, No. 3 (2009): 311–330.

Lawrence v. Texas (02–102) 539 U.S. 558 (2003).

Lee Dalton, Lucinda. "Autobiography." The Bancroft Library, University of California, Berkeley, cited in Dunfey, "Living the Principle," 529.

Macedo, Stephen. "Liberal Civic Education and Religious Fundamentalism: The Case of God v. John Rawls?" *Ethics* 105 (April 1995): 468–496.

Mackenzie, Catriona and Natalie Stoljar, eds. *Relational Autonomy: Feminist Perspectives on Autonomy, Agency, and the Social Self.* New York: Oxford University Press, 2000.

March, Andrew. "Is There a Right to Polygamy? Marriage, Equality and Subsidizing Families in Liberal Public Justification." *Journal of Moral Philosophy* 8, No. 2 (2011): 246–272.

Mazie, Steven. "Consenting Adults? Amish *Rumspringa* and the Quandary of Exit in Liberalism." *Perspectives on Politics* 3, No. 4 (Dec. 2005): 745–759.

Mehr, Kahlile. "Women's Response to Plural Marriage." *Dialogue: A Journal of Mormon Thought* 18, No. 3 (Fall 1985): 84–97.

Nussbaum, Martha. *Sex and Social Justice*. New York: Oxford University Press, 1999.

Nussbaum, Martha. *Women and Human Development: The Capabilities Approach*. Cambridge, MA: Cambridge University Press, 2000.

O'Neill, Onora. Constructions of Reason: Explorations of Kant's Practical Philosophy. Cambridge: Cambridge University Press, 1989.

Obergefell v. Hodges 576 U.S. (2015).

Okin, Susan Moller. "'Mistresses of Their Own Destiny': Group Rights, Gender, and Realistic Rights of Exit." *Ethics* 112 (January 2002): 205–230.

Okin, Susan Moller. "Is Multiculturalism Bad for Women?" In *Is Multiculturalism Bad for Women?* Edited by Joshua Cohen, Matthew Howard and Martha Nussbaum, 7–24. Princeton, NJ: Princeton University Press, 1999.

Pratt Penrose, Romania. "Memoir of Romania B. Pratt, M.D.," 1881, Church Archives, quoted in Mehr, "Living the Principle," 86.
Principle Voices. "Why Women Choose Polygamy." (Accessed 8/4/2009). http://principlevoices.org/handouts/reasons-why-women-choose-polygamy.
Reich, Robert. "Testing the Boundaries of Parental Authority Over Education: The Case of Homeschooling." In *Moral and Political Education: Nomos XLIII*, edited by Stephen Macedo and Yael Tamir, 275–313. New York: New York University Press, 2002.
Schwarz, Hunter. "Support for polygamy is rising. But it's not the new gay marriage." *The Washington Post* (7/2/2015) https://www.washingtonpost.com/news/the-fix/wp/2015/07/02/support-for-polygamy-is-rising-but-its-not-the-new-gay-marriage/.
Shapiro, Ian. *Democratic Justice*. New Haven, CT: Yale University Press, 1999.
Shipp, Ellis. "Mormon Women's Protest: An Appeal for Freedom, Justice, and Equality." *Deseret News*. Salt Lake City, 1886, quoted in Mehr, "Women's Response to Plural Marriage," 85.
Shweder, Richard. "What about "Female Genital Mutilation"? And Why Understanding Culture Matters in the First Place." *Daedalus* 129, No. 4 (Fall 2000): 209–232.
Sikkink, David. "The Sources of Alienation from Public Schools." *Social Forces* 78 No. 1 (Sept. 1999): 51–86.
Smith, Jason Matthew. "Polygamy Primer: A guide to the history, major players, practitioners, and detractors surrounding Utah's peculiar predilection." *Salt Lake: The Magazine for Utah* (4/2009).
Spinner-Halev, Jeff. "Feminism, Multiculturalism, Oppression, and the State." *Ethics* 112 (October 2001): 84–113.
Spinner, Halev, Jeff. *Surviving Diversity: Religion and Democratic Citizenship*. Baltimore, MD: The Johns Hopkins University Press, 2000.
Stephen Macedo and Iris Marion Young, 211–233. New York: New York University Press, 2003.
Tapestry Against Polygamy. "Frequently Asked Questions." (Accessed on 8/4/09) http://www.polygamy.org/faq.shtml.
TLC website, *Sister Wives*. "What is the best part about plural marriage?" (Accessed 5/4/2016) http://www.tlc.com/tv-shows/sister-wives/videos/polygamy-plural-marriage-what-is-the-best-part-about-plural-marriage/.
Walters, Joanna. "Fleeing the FLDS: Followers are abandoning the notorious sect in droves." *Al Jazeera* (3/16/2015) http://america.aljazeera.com/multimedia/2015/3/fleeing-the-flds-sect.html.
Weithman, Paul, ed. Religion and Contemporary Liberalism. Notre Dame, IN: University of Notre Dame Press, 1997.
Whitney, Helen Mar. "Scenes and Incidents in Nauvoo." *The Woman's Exponent* 10 (10/15/1881), quoted in Mehr, "Living the Principle," 86.
Wilde, Anne, interview by Neal Conan. "Trial Brings Focus on Polygamy in America." *Talk of the Nation*. NPR (9/12/07) http://www.npr.org/templates/story/story.php?storyId=14350293&ps=rs.
Woodroof, Wilford. "Official Declaration—1." *The Church of Jesus Christ of Latter-Day Saints* (10/6/1890) http://scriptures.lds.org/od/1.
Zoellner, Tom. "Schools: Local Control, But Little Local Money." *The Salt Lake Tribune* (6/28/98).

Index

accommodationists: burden of proof and, 43, 44; conscience and, 47–48, 49; discrimination by, 56; FEC and, 41–42, 48–49; McConnell as, 41, 43–44, 44–45; non-religious beliefs and, 47, 48; objection to, 42; parochialism of, 47; religion defined by, 47; Scalia as anti, 44
adaptive preference formation: Arneson on, 211; Elster on, 211; Nussbaum on, 211
adultery: in bigamy statute, 189–190; in *Brown v. Buhman*, 181, 189; in *Lawrence v. Texas and*, 221
The Alex Joseph Family, 33
Allred, Owen, 34; marriage rules of, 34; monogamy and, 34; as prophet of AUB, 34
Amish: *rumspringa* of, 225; *Yoder v. Wisconsin*, 192–193
anti-perfectionism, 7; defining, 8, 9; good life and legislation in, 9; religion and, 16
Apostolic United Brethren (AUB): Allred as prophet of, 34; female autonomy in, 192; progressive traits of, 28–29
Arneson, Richard, 211
artificial person, 64
attributed knowledge, 72
AUB. *See* Apostolic United Brethren

Baker v. State: civil union and, 9–10, 20n16; Equal Protection Clause in, 9; marriage as status in, 9–10
Barker, Meg John, 153
Bedi, Sonu: on argument against marriage, 3; *Obergefell and the Liberal Case Against Civil Marriage* by, 3
Bennion, Janet, 3–4
Benson, Ezra Taft, 29
Berry, Anna Eliza, 216
bigamy statute, Utah: adulterous cohabitation in, 189–190; in *Brown v. Buhman*, 183; defining, 220; fraudulent bigamy in, 177, 178; harms in enforcing, 188; legal polygamy in, 177; as narrowly tailored, 189–190; operational non-neutrality in, 179–180, 186; plural common-law marriage in, 220; polygamous cohabitation, 177, 183–184; polygamous marriages, 177; purports to marry in, 177, 178, 184–185; religious cohabitation targeted by, 181, 182; religious polygamy and, 190; *State v. Geer*, 178, 179, 187; *State v. Holm*, 178, 179, 184–185, 186; strict scrutiny in, 188, 190; text of, 177. *See also State v. Green*
Big Love, 32, 205
Blackmore, Winston, 25
The Brady Williams Family, 30–31; decriminalized polygamy and, 30–31; family structure of, 30; on New Polygamy, 31; selfhood in, 30
Brake, Elizabeth, 12–13
Brooks, Thom, 221–222
Brown v. Buhman, 5–6, 25, 179, 194n18; adulterous cohabitation in, 181, 189; analysis in, 169, 170; bigamy statute in, 183; criminalizing polygamy in, 168; criticism of conclusion in, 181–182; finding in, 221; The Kody Brown Family filing, 168, 175, 221; narrowly tailored analysis in, 189, 196n109–196n110; operational non-neutrality in, 179–180, 186; religious cohabitation as target in, 181, 182;

Reynolds v. United States drawn upon in, 169; standing in, 221; strict scrutiny in, 175, 187, 190, 193–202; two targets in, 179; Waddoups decision in, 27–28
Burawoy, Michael, 160

children's rights, 230n91; Amish, 192–193, 225; coercion and, 223; indoctrination and, 222–223; liberal state duties for, 225–226; open future and, 223; parallel fiduciaries model and, 223; private and home schools for, 224–225, 230n96; public schools and, 224, 225; religious polygamy and, 192–193; in *Yoder v. Wisconsin*, 192–193. *See also* underage marriage
"Chinese Room" experiment: intentionality and, 71; NLP and, 70–71; responses to, 71; Searle and, 70–71
Chopra, Samir, 71–72
Church of Jesus Christ of Latter-Day Saints (LDS): fundamentalist Mormon groups and, 213, 228n41; polygyny in, 213; Shipp on polygyny in, 214; Smith establishing, 213; *The Woman's Exponent* of, 214, 214–215; women in, 214, 215; Woodroof as prophet of, 213
Church of the Lukumi Babalu Aye, Inc. v. City of Hialeah, 198n164; FEC analysis in, 175–176; finding in, 176; generally applicable analysis in, 176–177, 187; operational neutrality in, 180; religious gerrymander in, 176
civil marriage: abolishing, 110–112, 114–115; child-rearing in, 113–114, 116; civil union distinct from, 9, 10, 12, 54; Dane on religion and, 15; defining, 112–113; equality objection for, 115; generalizations of, 116–117; individualized treatment and, 116; legal status of, 52; liberal neutrality and, 7, 9, 19, 105, 110; public reason in, 104, 115; reasons for, 113–114; retaining, 112–114; rights and protections in, 114, 116; right to, 117–118; women disadvantaged by, 114. *See also* polygamy; same-sex marriage
civil union: *Baker v. State* and, 9–10; Dane on religion and, 15; marriage distinct from, 9, 10, 12, 54; public welfare and, 15; Vermont statute of, 10
coercion: children's rights and, 223; in polygamy, 221–222; public reason and, 109, 110; religious polygamy and, 191, 192; of robots, 73, 78n96; in underage marriage, 192, 216, 222
Cohen v. Cowles Media Co., 197n127
Common Benefits Clause, 10
common law marriage, Utah: consent in, 200n208; secular cohabitation and conviction in, 183; in *State v. Green*, 183; in *Whyte v. Blair*, 182
companionship model, 13–14; Metz on, 14
compersion, 37n20; defining, 31; in The Joe Darger Family, 31
compulsory monogamy, x
conscience: accommodationists and, 47–48, 49; in exemptions, 48, 49; expansive understanding of, 49; FEC on religion and, 47–48, 49, 51–52
consent: cannibalism and, 210, 228n27; in common law marriage, 200n208; for corporations, 66–67; defining, 68; female genital cutting and, 209–210, 212; future agency and, 211; genuineness of, 210; "happy slave" question in, 210; legal concepts of, 68; Mill on, 208, 210; in monogamous marriage, 68, 68–69, 76n53, 77n55, 212; Nussbaum on, 209, 211, 211–212; Okin on severing communal ties and, 217; O'Neill on, 211; personal revelation and, 218–219; polygyny and, 206, 212–218, 219; relational autonomy and social context in, 209; robots and, 67, 68, 69–70; in *Whyte v. Blair*, 183

consequentialism, 117
corporations: cases securing rights of, 65–66; consent issue for, 66–67; legal personality and, 64, 76n34; Vogel marriage to, 66–67, 76n39

Dalton, Lucinda Lee, 214
Dane, Perry, 15
Darger, Joe, 31–32
Dennett, Daniel, 71
difference-splitting: Jordan on, 109; in liberal neutrality, 106, 109–110; marriage example of, 109–110
discrimination, 45, 148; by accommodationists, 56; equal treatment and anti, 118; indirect, 44; of nontraditional families, 149; polyamory and, 148, 150, 155; religious exemptions as, 56; of robots, 66; same-sex marriage and, 119, 158; in sexual orientation and identity, 158. *See also* specific topics
Dusky v. United States, 73
dyadic relationship model, x

Ebels-Duggan, Kyla, 111
Edmunds Anti-Polygamy Act, 198n170
Elster, Jon, 211
Emens, Elizabeth, xn4; on compulsory monogamy, x; *Monogamy's Law: Compulsory Monogamy and Polyamorous Existence* by, xn4; on polygyny, 120
Employment Division v. Smith, 43, 44, 58n30, 176; criticism of, 44, 46; drug laws and, 45–46; legislative discretion in, 46; rational basis standard of review in, 46; Scalia opinion in, 46, 50; strict scrutiny abandoned in, 46
Equal Protection Clause, 59n70, 66; *Baker v. State* and, 9; in *Obergefell v. Hodges*, 66; same-sex marriage and, 53
equal treatment: anti-caste, 118–119; anti-discrimination law and, 118; liberal neutrality and, 107, 108–109; plural marriage enthusiasts and, 52, 55; polygamy and, 118
exemptions: balancing, 51; conscience in, 48, 49; defining, 57n3; discriminatory religious, 56; religious and non-religious inequality in, 51. *See also* accommodationists

family models, 148–149, 151–152; feminist research on, 152; male-breadwinner, ix; monolithic family in, 152; paradigms shifting for, ix, 163n9; traditional, ix; types of, ix
FEC. *See* Free Exercise Clause
Feinberg, Joel, 223
female genital cutting: consent and, 209–210, 212; Nussbaum on, 212
feminism and feminist theory: family model research in, 152; The Kody Brown Family and, 35; liberal theory and, 207; monogamous marriage in, 212; patriarchy and, 209; polyamory and, 152; polygamy and, 28, 34–35; radical feminism in, 123n16; of relational autonomy, 209
FLDS. *See* Fundamentalist Jesus Christ of Latter-Day Saints
Fourteenth Amendment. *See* Equal Protection Clause
Free Exercise Clause (FEC), 4, 43; accommodationist view and, 41–42, 48–49; in *Church of the Lukumi Babalu Aye, Inc. v. City of Hialeah*, 175–176; conscience and religion in, 47–48, 49, 51–52; historical meaning of, 48–49, 50; religion and, 42; religious polygamy and, 192; in *State v. Green*, 178; in *State v. Holm*, 178
friendship model of sex, 83, 84, 84–85, 98–100; basics of, 84; "break ups" in, 91, 94–95; cheating and, 99n7, 99n10, 99n11; depth and intimacy in, 90–91, 92, 93; elements of friendship in, 86–87; evaluating friendships for, 87; family relationships and, 100n17; growth patterns in, 93; as heuristic, 84; high and low demand in, 94; Kant and, 98; levels of friendship in, 92–93; monogamy and, 87–88, 90, 97–98;

multiplicity in, 87, 88, 91, 91–92; polyamory in, 97–98; relationship length in, 93–94; "right" number of lovers in, 89–90; Savage on, 90, 100n15; sex and intimacy in, 96–97; "special purpose" friends in, 95–96; waxing and waning in, 94; Wittgenstein and, 85
A Friendship Model of Sex, Polyamory, and Plural Marriage (Klein), 4
Fundamentalist Jesus Christ of Latter-Day Saints (FLDS), 205; Jessop escaping, 218; polygyny in, 213, 219; public school control by, 224; Spinner-Halev in, 216–217; Wall on underage marriage in, 216; women choosing, 218. *See also* Yearning for Zion Ranch

Gaus, Gerald, 107–108
George, Robert, 13
Goldfeder, Mark, 4
good life: anti-perfectionism and, 9; marriage in, 55–56; Rawls defining, 8–9; religious ceremonies in, 16
Goodridge v. Dep't of Public Health, 20n22; companionship model in, 14; same-sex marriage and status in, 11
Greenwich, Alex, 158
Gruch, Mark, 5
Guisado, Angelo, 66

Haddow v. Haddow, 199n181
Halley, Janet, 11
Heidegger, Martin, 100n18–100n19
Henrich, Joseph, 171, 195n43; on military aggression, 173–174; polygyny and unmarried men analysis by, 171–172
hypergamy, 34; defining, 37n25

incest, ix; individualized treatment and, 121; March on, 120–121; Muhammed and, 137–138
individualized treatment, 119, 121–125; incest and, 121; polygamy and, 119; public reason and, 120–121
intentional communities, 163n19; polyamory and, 151, 152–153
intentionality: "Chinese Room" and, 71; for robots, 71, 72; Searle on, 71; Zhu components of, 71
Iran, 138
Islam, 5; contemporary women in, 140; patriarchy in, 131–132; polygamy in, 57n6; pre-Islamic era in, 132; *Quran* banning infanticide in, 132–133; *Quran* on polygyny in, 134–135, 138; removal of polygyny in, 139; theology of, 133

Jeffs, Warren: arranged and underage marriage of, 31, 213; conviction of, 206; YFZ and, 25, 154, 206, 227n5
Jessop, Carolyn, 218, 219
Jesus, 135
Joe Darger Family, 31–32; compersion in, 31
Jordan, Jeff, 109

Kant, Immanuel, 98
Kennedy, Anthony, 7–8, 20n24; on dignity, 12; liberal neutrality and, 14; on loneliness, 12, 14, 18; on marital choice, 54; on marriage as status, 9, 11, 12; marriage privileged by, 12, 17; on polygamy, 17; procreation arguments rejected by, 13. *See also Obergefell v. Hodges*
Khadijah, 133
Klein, Diane, 4
Klesse, Christian, 156
Kody Brown Family, 32, 201n248–202n249; *Brown v. Buhman* filed by, 168, 175, 221; feminism and, 35; progressive values of, 32; on *Sister Wives*, 32
Kukathas, Chandran, 217–218

Lawrence v. Texas: anti-adultery statutes and, 221; Scalia dissent in, 25; sodomy laws in, 18, 221
LDS. *See* Church of Jesus Christ of Latter-Day Saints
legal personality: corporations and, 64, 76n34; expansion of, 65; robots gaining, 64, 65, 66

liberal neutrality, 9, 106; civil marriage and, 7, 9, 19, 105, 110; contested premises in, 106; defining, 8; difference-splitting in, 106, 109–110; equal treatment and, 107, 108–109; Kennedy and, 14; marriage status and, 12; Metz on, 11–12; moral superiority failing, 12–13; non-intervention in, 106; polygamy and, 119; principles of, 105–106; public reason and, 108; Sandel on same-sex marriage and, 110
liberal theory: feminism and, 207; polygamy in, 207
Lister, Andrew, 5
loneliness, 12, 14, 18
Loving v. Virginia, 66

Macedo, Stephen: on polygamy and patriarchy, 116–117; on public welfare and marriage, 15
Maghzi, Ameneh, 5
male-breadwinner family, ix
March, Andrew: on gender inequality, 220; on incest, 120–121; on public reason and polygamy, 120
Marchant, Gary, 74
Maynard v. Hill, 10–11
McCarty, Kristin, 5
McConnell, Michael, 41, 43–44; intermediate scrutiny supported by, 44–45; religion definition as narrow for, 47; religious freedom defended by, 48
McDermott, Rose, 171
Metz, Tamara: Brake argument and, 12–13; on "coming of age" ceremonies, 16; on companionship model, 14; on liberal neutrality, 11–12
Mill, John Stuart: on conditions for polygamy, 208; faulty bridge metaphor of, 210; *On Liberty* by, 207–208; on "Mormonite Doctrine", 207; on origins of polygamy, 208; on polygamy, 207–208; *The Subjection of Women* by, 208
"Monogamy's Law: Compulsory Monogamy and Polyamorous Existence" (Emens), xn4
Mormon church. *See* Church of Jesus Christ of Latter-Day Saints
Mormon women studies: The Alex Joseph Family, 33; The Brady Williams Family, 30–31; family profiles in, 33–34; Goodman and Heaton 1986 sample, 29; The Joe Darger Family, 31; The Kody Brown Family, 32, 35; methodology for AUB in, 29, 37n27; The Rod Williams Family, 29–30
Muhammed, 138; incest and, 137; Khadijah as wife of, 133; mission in *Quran*, 140–141; monogamy of, 136; polygyny and, 133–134, 136–137; Zaynab Bint Jahash and, 137–138

natural language processing (NLP), 70; "Chinese Room" experiment for, 70–71; statistical machine learning in, 70
The Need for a Sociological Perspective on Polyamory (McCarty), 5
neutrality. *See* liberal neutrality
NLP. *See* natural language processing
Nussbaum, Martha, 45; on adaptive preference formation, 211; on consent, 209, 211, 211–212; on female genital cutting, 212; on future agency, 211; on polygamy, 212, 219–220; on relational autonomy and social context, 209; on trusting desires, 209

Obergefell and the Liberal Case Against Civil Marriage (Bedi), 3
Obergefell v. Hodges, xn2, 7, 19, 20n34, 53; Bedi on, 3; Due Process Clause in, 66; Equal Protection Clause in, 66; impacts of, 36n11; loneliness in, 12, 14, 18; marital choice in, 54; marriage equality in, x, 66; marriage status in, 14; monogamy in, x; public reason principle in, 104; Roberts dissent in, 2, 16, 18, 54, 55, 116, 158. *See also* Kennedy, Anthony
Okin, Susan Moller, 207; on severing communal ties, 217

O'Neill, Onora, 211; on *possible consent of actual agents* and polygyny, 212, 219
On Liberty (Mill), 207–208

parallel fiduciaries model, 223
patriarchy: feminism and, 209; in Islam, 131–132; Macedo on polygamy and, 116–117; *Plural Voices* on, 208; polygyny and, 131, 139, 208; in pre-Islamic Arabia, 133–134
Penrose, Romania Bunnell Pratt, 215
plural marriage. *See* polygamy
plural marriage enthusiasts, 2, 4, 59n77; equal treatment and, 52, 55; marriage equality for, 52
Plural Voices: on patriarchy, 208; Wilde founding, 209
Polikoff, Nancy, 150
The Polyamorists Next Door: Inside Multiple-Partner Relationships and Families (Sheff), 148, 152
polyamory, 1; Barker on, 153; choice and, 157–158; complexity of, 154; defining, 150–151, 155, 162n1; demographics of, 159; discrimination toward, 148, 150, 155; feminism and, 152; in friendship model of sex, 97–98; history of, 151; intentional communities and, 151, 152–153; LGBT+ community and, 158–159; Polikoff on, 150; psychology studies of, 153; sexual orientation and, 155–156; Sheff on, 148, 152–153, 162n1; sociology and, 147–148, 153, 153–154, 159–162; statistics on, 148
polyandry, x; fundamentalist Mormonism and, 219; in pre-Islamic Arabia, 133
polygamy, 25, 229n73; associated crimes and, 187–188; AUB and, 28–29, 34; bigamy statute and, 177, 190; coercion in, 221–222; consequentialism and, 117; countries legalizing, 138, 143n56; criminalizing, 167–168, 220, 221; "cruel arithmetic" of, 171, 193; defining, 28, 129, 226n1; Edmunds Anti-Polygamy Act, 198n170–199n171; equal treatment and, 118; feminism and, 28, 34–35; generalizations and, 119–120; history of, 26; individualized treatment and, 119; Iran, 138; in Islam, 57n6; Kennedy on, 17; laws governing, 17, 220, 221, 221–222; legalization arguments for, 30–31, 216, 221, 222, 223; liberal neutrality and, 119; liberal state and, 220; Macedo on patriarchy and, 116–117; "male compromise" theory of, 131; March on public reason and, 120; military defense and, 173–174; Mill on, 207–208; Muslim women and, 138–139, 229n59; Nussbaum on, 212, 219–220; *Principle Voices* on choice and, 218; progressive families and, 33–34, 34–35, 35–37; in *Progressive Polygamy in the Western United States*, 3–4; prosecution as harmful for, 188; in *Reference*, 170–171, 174; religious and secular, 52, 190–191, 192; in *Reynolds v. United States*, 167; right to, 117–118; Roberts on, 16, 54, 55, 158; sexual orientation in, 16, 17; sociology and, 154; television shows on, 27, 32, 205; Tunisia and, 138; Turkey and, 138; underage marriage and, 27, 191, 192–193, 222; U.S. statistics on, 26; women and, 28, 212–218. *See also* Allred, Owen; *Brown v. Buhman*; Mormon women studies; polygyny; religious polygamy
Polygamy in Islam: Origins, Challenges, and Responses (Maghzi and Gruch), 5
polygyny, 1, 5; American statics on, 205; banning, 135, 138; *Big Love* depicting, 32, 205; children in families of, 139, 173; consent and, 206, 212–218, 219; Dalton on, 214; defining, 129, 150; economic impacts from, 174; Emens on, 120; "female choice" theory in, 131; FLDS and, 213, 219; fundamentalist

Mormon groups and, 213; Henrich on, 171–172; historic economic structures in, 130; in Islam, 134–135, 138, 139; LDS church and, 213, 214; legalization arguments for, 216, 222; Muhammed and, 133–134, 136–137; Okin on severing communal ties in, 217; origins of, 130–131; patriarchy and, 131, 139, 208; personal revelation in, 218–219; *possible consent of actual agents* in, 212, 219; *Principle Voices* on, 214; in *Quran*, 134–135, 138; relational autonomy and social context in, 209; right of exit in, 219; Shipp on, 214; social harms from, 173–174; *The Woman's Exponent on*, 214, 214–215; women harmed in, 172, 215–216, 218, 219; women independence and, 213–215, 219

pre-Islamic Arabia, 132; as matrilineal, 133; patriarchy in, 133–134; poetry in, 132; polyandry in, 133; in *Quran*, 132; women in, 132–133

Principle Voices, 214; on choice and polygamy, 218

procreation arguments: George on, 13; Kennedy rejecting, 13

"Progressive Polygamy in the Western United States" (Bennion), 3–4

public justification: exclusionary approach to, 8; in public reason, 103; qualified acceptability test and, 107, 112; Schweber on, 8; Solum on, 8

public reason, 123n9; civil marriage and, 104, 115; coercion model of, 109, 110; core of, 103; Ebels-Duggan model of, 111; Gaus on, 107–108; God and, 103; incest and, 121; individualized treatment and, 120–121; liberal neutrality and, 108; March on polygamy and, 120; in *Obergefell v. Hodges*, 104; public justification in, 103; Rawls on, 8, 103, 107, 108–109, 122n8–123n9; reasons-for-decisions model of, 110; Sandel on abolition of marriage for, 110–111

public welfare claim: civil union and, 15; Macedo on, 15; stigmatization in, 15

purporting to marry: in bigamy statute, 177, 178, 184–185; operational neutrality and, 186; religion in, 185–186; in *State v. Green*, 197n139; in *State v. Holm*, 184–185; in unlicensed solemnization ceremonies, 185

Quran: Christian bible parallel to, 135; infanticide banned in, 132–133; limit to wives in, 135–136; Mission of Muhammed in, 140–141; orphans in, 135–136; polygyny in, 134–135, 138; pre-Islamic era in, 132; Zaynab Bint Jahash and Muhammed in, 137–138

radical feminism, 123n16

Rauch, Jonathan, 17

Rawls, John, 7, 99n1, 122n6; difference principle of, 108; good life defined by, 8–9; on public reason, 8, 103, 107, 108–109, 122n8–123n9; on Supreme Court, 8

Razin, Yosef, 4

Reference Re: Section 293 of the Criminal Code of Canada (Reference), 167, 169–170; constitutionality in, 168–169; expert witnesses in, 171; McDermott analysis in, 171; monogamy and polygamy in, 170–171, 174; "pressing and substantial" justification in, 168; religious polygamy in, 190–191

The Religious Freedom Restoration Act, 44, 57n16

religious polygamy, 200n217; AUP and, 192; bigamy statute and, 190; children's rights and, 192–193; coercion and, 191, 192; community survival and, 192; FEC jurisprudence and, 192; real power structures in, 191; in *Reference*, 190–191; young teenage girls and, 191

Reynolds v. United States, 27, 179; decision in, 55; polygamy and, 167; racism in, 45; use in *Brown v. Buhman*, 169
Richards v. Brown, 199n183
Roberts, John: *Obergefell* dissent by, 2, 16, 18, 54, 55, 116, 158; on polygamy, 16, 54, 55, 158; on sodomy laws and marriage, 18
"Robotic Marriage and the Law" (Goldfeder and Razin), 4
robots, 4; attributed knowledge for, 72; care by, 67, 68; "Chinese Room" experiment for, 70–71; coercion and, 73, 78n96; consent of, 67, 68, 69–70; discrimination of, 66; expression of, 70; in film and television, 63, 67; instrumental reasoning of, 69–70; intentionality for, 71, 72; legal personality for, 64, 65, 66; love and, 67; Marchant on human marriage with, 74; marriage fraud tests for, 67–68; memory storage of, 69; mental capacity and legal competence of, 73–74; natural language processing of, 70; planning and decision-making for, 72–73; social, 63; Turing Test for, 70, 71
Rod Williams Family, 29–30; home of, 29–30; lesbian wife accepted by, 30
Rosenblum, Darren, 19

same-sex marriage, 52–53; in *Baker v. State*, 9–10; civil unions and, 9, 10, 12, 54; discrimination and, 119, 158; Due Process Clause protecting, 53, 66; Ebels-Duggan on, 111; equal protection analysis for, 53; in *Goodridge v. Dep't of Public Health*, 11; marriage equality movement for, 1; procreation argument in, 13; Roberts dissent in *Obergefell* on, 2, 16, 18, 54, 55, 116, 158; Sandel on liberal neutrality and, 110; Vermont granting, 10. *See also* Kennedy, Anthony; *Obergefell v. Hodges*
Sandel, Michael: on abolition of marriage, 110–111; on neutrality and same-sex marriage, 110
Savage, Dan, 90, 100n15
Scalia, Antonin: as anti-accommodationist, 44; *Employment Division v. Smith* opinion by, 46, 50; *Lawrence v. Texas* dissent by, 25; "religion blindness" approach by, 46
school systems: FLDS and, 224; paternalism in, 224–225; private and home, 224–225, 230n96; public, 224, 225; at YFZ, 224
Schweber, Howard, 8
Scrutinizing Polygamy: Utah's Brown v. Buhman and British Columbia's Reference Re: Section 293 (Strassberg), 5–6
Searle, John: "Chinese Room" experiment of, 70–71; on intentionality, 71
sexual orientation and identity: choice and, 156–157; discrimination in, 158; polyamory and, 155–156; polygamy and, 16, 17; social constructions of, 157; Sullivan on, 16, 17. *See also* same-sex marriage
Shapiro, Ian, 223
Sheff, Elisabeth, x, 155; *The Polyamorists Next Door: Inside Multiple-Partner Relationships and Families* by, 148, 152; on polyamory, 148, 152–153, 162n1
Sherbert v. Verner, 43, 46
Shipp, Ellis: education and career of, 214; on polygyny, 214
Singer, Joseph, 11
Sister Wives, 175; child support in, 215; The Kody Brown Family on, 32; premise of, 226n3
Smith, Joseph, 213
sociology: defining, 149; family concepts in, 151–152; lack of polyamory studies in, 153–154; methodology in, 149; objectivity in, 160–161; and polyamory, 147–148, 153, 153–154, 159–162; polygamy and, 154; public, 161, 161–162
Solum, Lawrence, 75n15; on public justification as exclusionary, 8

Spinner-Halev, Jeffrey, 216–217; children and, 217; skepticism of, 229n62
State v. Geer: bigamy statute in, 178, 179, 187; operational neutrality analysis in, 178
State v. Green: background of, 197n138–197n139; cohabitation in, 177, 182, 197n139; common law marriage in, 183; FEC challenge in, 178; findings in, 177; purporting to marry in, 197n139
State v. Holm, 178, 179; cohabitation in, 186; FEC challenge in, 178; purports to marry language in, 184–185
status, marriage as: in *Baker v. State*, 9–10; companionship model and, 13–14; *Goodridge v. Dep't of Public Health* on, 11; Kennedy on, 9, 11, 12; liberal neutrality and, 12; moral superiority in, 12–13; *in Obergefell v. Hodges*, 14; Singer decision emphasizing, 11; stigmatization from, 15; in Vermont, 10
Strassberg, Maura, 5–6
The Subjection of Women (Mill), 208
Sullivan, Andrew, 16–17, 17–18
Sunstein, Cass, 1
Supreme Court, U.S.: *Church of the Lukumi Babalu Aye, Inc. v. City of Hialeah*, 175–177, 180, 187, 198n157, 198n164; corporate rights secured by, 65–66; *Lawrence v. Texas*, 18, 25, 36n1, 221; *Loving v. Virginia*, 66; *Maynard v. Hill*, 10, 20n20; *Reynolds v. United States*, 27, 45, 55, 167, 169, 179. *See also Obergefell v. Hodges*

Thaler, Richard, 1
Thoreau, Henry David, 50
traditional family: definition of, ix; era of, ix
Tunisia, 138
Turing Test, 70–71, 71
Turkey, 138
Tweedy, Ann, 155–156

underage marriage: AUP and, 192; Berry and, 216; coercion in, 192, 216, 222; Jeffs and, 31, 213; legalizing polygamy and, 222; polygamy and, 27, 191, 192–193, 222; prosecution of, 220; Wall on FLDS and, 216; at YFZ, 206, 213, 222, 223
United Nations Declaration of Human Rights, xn3
United States v. Flowerday, 77n81
unmarried individuals, 18, 21n56; Henrich on polygyny and, 171–172; Kennedy on, 12, 14, 18; Kennedy on loneliness and, 12, 14, 18; queer theory and, 18–19; state stigmatizing, 15. *See also* status, marriage as

Vermont: *Baker v. State* in, 9–10, 20n16; Civil Union Statute of, 10; Common Benefits Clause in, 10; same-sex marriage in, 10
Vermont Civil Union Statute, 10
Vogel, Angela Marie, 66–67, 76n39

Waddoups, Clark, 27–28
Wall, Elisa, 216
West, Mae, 1
Whyte v. Blair, 199n181; common law marriage in, 182; consent to marry in, 183
Wilde, Anne, 209; on Mormon women independence, 215
Williams, Brady: on decriminalized polygamy, 30–31. *See also* The Brady Williams Family
Winfrey, Oprah, 223
Wittgenstein, Ludwig: "family resemblance" concept by, 85, 86; on friendship model of sex, 85; philosophy of language of, 85; on unclear boundaries, 86
The Woman's Exponent: on polygyny, 214, 214–215; women leading household in, 214–215
Woodroof, Wilford, 213

Yearning for Zion Ranch (YFZ): children removed from, 206, 226n4; convictions from, 206; Jeffs in, 25, 154, 206, 227n5; raiding of, 205,

205–206, 206; schools at, 224; Texas Supreme Court on raid of, 206; underage marriage at, 206, 213, 222, 223; women and self-knowledge in, 215

YFZ. *See* Yearning for Zion Ranch

Yoder v. Wisconsin, 192–193

Zhu, Jichen, 71

About the Contributors

Ronald C. Den Otter is an Associate Professor of Political Science at California Polytechnic State University San Luis Obispo. He earned his J.D. from the University of Pennsylvania Law School in 1992 and his Ph.D. from UCLA in 2003. His most recent book, *In Defense of Plural Marriage*, was published by Cambridge University Press in 2015.

Sonu Bedi is associate professor of Government at Dartmouth College. His publications include *Rejecting Rights* (Cambridge University Press: 2009), *Beyond Race, Sex, and Sexual Orientation: Legal Equality without Identity* (Cambridge University Press: 2013) and numerous peer-reviewed articles, book chapters and law review articles. His research interests are in the areas of contemporary political theory, constitutional law and theory, and race, law and identity. He holds a doctorate in political science from Yale and a law degree from Harvard Law School. He routinely teaches courses on constitutional law, civil liberties, legal theory, freedom of speech, and theories of justice.

Janet Bennion is a Professor of Anthropology from Lyndon State College in Vermont. She has written five books on the variability of polygyny among Mormon Fundamentalist groups including, *Women of Principle* (University of Oxford Press, 1998) and *Polygamy in Primetime* (Brandeis University Press, 2012). Her latest endeavor is collaborative and international, stemming from several international conference discussions about how to handle the poly world legally, compiled in the volume, *The Polygamy Question* (Utah State and Colorado Presses, 2015).

Dr. Mark Goldfeder is Senior Lecturer at Emory Law School and Senior Fellow at the Center for the Study of Law and Religion. He holds a J.D. from NYU Law School, and an LLM and doctorate from Emory University. His research interests include law and religion, family law, and expanding notions of personhood. His new book, *Legalizing Plural Marriage*, is scheduled to be in print in early 2016.

Mark Gruchy is a criminal defense attorney in St. John's, Newfoundland and Labrador, Canada. He was called to the Bar in 2007 and has litigated the entire gamut of criminal offenses, including murder. He graduated in 2002 from Memorial University of Newfoundland and Labrador with a

Bachelor of Arts in History and Sociology. He attended the University of New Brunswick starting in 2003 where he obtained his LL. B. Gruchy was a Lord Beaverbrook Scholar, the most prestigious student scholarship title at the University of New Brunswick. He also received individual awards in Contract Law and Jurisprudence and the Spirit of the Jessup Award in the Jessup International Law Moot Court competition. More recently, Gruchy has become a visible mental health advocate in Newfoundland and Labrador.

Diane Klein is a Professor of Law at the University of La Verne College of Law in Ontario, California. She studied philosophy at Harvard and U.C. Berkeley, and holds a J.D. from UCLA and an LL.M. in taxation from the University of San Francisco. She teaches property, wills and trusts, and antidiscrimination law, with an emphasis on sex and gender.

Olivia Newman is an assistant professor of political theory at Rider University. She earned her Ph.D. from The New School for Social Research. Her first book, *Liberalism in Practice: The Psychology and Pedagogy of Public Reason* (2015) was published by The MIT Press.

Andrew Lister is Associate Professor of Political Studies, Queen's University. He has taught previously at Concordia University (2001-2003), was a postdoctoral fellow at the Centre de recherche en éthique de l'Université de Montréal (2003-4), and has been a visitor at the Center for the Study of Social Justice at the University of Oxford (2010-11). Lister specializes in normative political theory, particularly on topics related to pluralism and toleration, democracy, and distributive justice. He is the author of *Public Reason and Political Community* (Bloomsbury, 2013), which explores rival communitarian and libertarian interpretations of the idea of public justification.

Ameneh Maghzi received her Bachelor of Laws (LLB) degree from the Shahid Ashrafi Esfahani University, Isfahan, Iran, and is the member of Bar Association of Iran. In 2013, she completed the Master of Arts in Political Science (MA) from Memorial University of Newfoundland, St. John's, Newfoundland, Canada. She was awarded the title of Fellow of the School of Graduate Studies in recognition of outstanding academic achievement and continued academic excellence throughout her graduate program. In 2014, she attended the Emory University School of Law and received a Master of Laws (LLM) degree. Her primary areas of interests are Law and Religion, Human Rights, Gender and Islam, Women and Politics, and Islamic Family Law.

Kristin McCarty is a Ph.D. student in the Sociology department at the University of California, Davis. She is interested in family and kinship, legal sociology, gender, and sexuality. Her current work examines the changing landscape of the American family by analyzing the kinship systems utilized by polyamorists.

Yosef Razin is a Ph.D. student in Robotics at the Georgia Institute of Technology. Razin holds a B.S.E. from Princeton University in Mechanical and Aerospace Engineering, where he concentrated on adaptive optics and bio-mimetic robotics. His current research interests include human-robot interaction, machine learning, and intent estimation.

Maura Strassberg is a Professor of Law at Drake University Law School. She is a graduate of Swarthmore College (B.A.), Boston University (M.A.), and Columbia University Law School (J.D.). She has published a number of articles addressing the legal challenges posed by polygamy and has also published articles in the area of legal ethics. maura.strassberg@drake.edu.